Differential Equations and Asymptotic Analysis: Recent Advances and Applications

Differential Equations and Asymptotic Analysis: Recent Advances and Applications

Editor

Behzad Djafari-Rouhani

Basel • Beijing • Wuhan • Barcelona • Belgrade • Novi Sad • Cluj • Manchester

Editor
Behzad Djafari-Rouhani
University of Texas at El Paso
El Paso
USA

Editorial Office
MDPI
St. Alban-Anlage 66
4052 Basel, Switzerland

This is a reprint of articles from the Special Issue published online in the open access journal *Axioms* (ISSN 2075-1680) (available at: https://www.mdpi.com/journal/axioms/special_issues/Differential_Equations_Asymptotic_Analysis).

For citation purposes, cite each article independently as indicated on the article page online and as indicated below:

Lastname, A.A.; Lastname, B.B. Article Title. *Journal Name* **Year**, *Volume Number*, Page Range.

ISBN 978-3-7258-0335-4 (Hbk)
ISBN 978-3-7258-0336-1 (PDF)
doi.org/10.3390/books978-3-7258-0336-1

© 2024 by the authors. Articles in this book are Open Access and distributed under the Creative Commons Attribution (CC BY) license. The book as a whole is distributed by MDPI under the terms and conditions of the Creative Commons Attribution-NonCommercial-NoDerivs (CC BY-NC-ND) license.

Contents

About the Editor vii

Preface ix

Seong-Hoon Cho
Fixed Point Theorems for Set-Valued Contractions in Metric Spaces
Reprinted from: *Axioms* **2024**, *13*, 86, doi:10.3390/axioms13020086 1

Amira Essam, Osama Moaaz, Moutaz Ramadan, Ghada AlNemer and Ibrahim M. Hanafy
On the Monotonic and Asymptotic Properties of Positive Solutions to Third-Order Neutral Differential Equations and Their Effect on Oscillation Criteria
Reprinted from: *Axioms* **2023**, *12*, 1086, doi:10.3390/axioms12121086 17

Jingying Gao, Qingmei Bai, Siriguleng He and Eerdun Buhe
New Two-Level Time-Mesh Difference Scheme for the Symmetric Regularized Long Wave Equation
Reprinted from: *Axioms* **2023**, *12*, 1057, doi:10.3390/axioms12111057 39

Yousef Alnafisah and Osama Moaaz
Investigation of the Oscillatory Properties of Solutions of Differential Equations Using Kneser-Type Criteria
Reprinted from: *Axioms* **2023**, *12*, 876, doi:10.3390/axioms12090876 58

Moldir Serik, Rena Eskar, Pengzhan Huang
Numerical Solution of Time-Fractional Schrödinger Equation by Using FDM
Reprinted from: *Axioms* **2023**, *12*, 816, doi:10.3390/axioms12090816 69

Yan Tang and Aviv Gibali
Resolvent-Free Method for Solving Monotone Inclusions
Reprinted from: *Axioms* **2023**, *12*, 557, doi:10.3390/axioms12060557 84

Behzad Djafari Rouhani and Mohsen Rahimi Piranfar
Recent Results on Expansive-Type Evolution and Difference Equations: A Survey
Reprinted from: *Axioms* **2023**, *12*, 373, doi:10.3390/axioms12040373 99

Mahmoud A. Ibrahim and Attila Dénes
A Mathematical Model for Zika Virus Infection and Microcephaly Risk Considering Sexual and Vertical Transmission
Reprinted from: *Axioms* **2023**, *12*, 263, doi:10.3390/axioms12030263 114

Olawale K. Oyewole and Simeon Reich
An Inertial Subgradient Extragradient Method for Approximating Solutions to Equilibrium Problems in Hadamard Manifolds
Reprinted from: *Axioms* **2023**, *12*, 256, doi:10.3390/axioms12030256 140

Atanas Z. Atanasov, Slavi G. Georgiev and Lubin G. Vulkov
Parameter Estimation Analysis in a Model of Honey Production
Reprinted from: *Axioms* **2023**, *12*, 214, doi:10.3390/axioms12020214 160

Alexander J. Zaslavski
Two Convergence Results for Inexact Infinite Products of Non-Expansive Mappings
Reprinted from: *Axioms* **2023**, *12*, 88, doi:10.3390/axioms12010088 172

Seong-Hoon Cho
Fixed-Point Theorems for $\mathcal{L}_\gamma$ Contractions in Branciari Distance Spaces
Reprinted from: *Axioms* **2022**, *11*, 479, doi:10.3390/axioms11090479 . . . . **181**

Yousef Alnafisah and Moustafa El-Shahed
Deterministic and Stochastic Prey–Predator Model for Three Predators anda Single Prey
Reprinted from: *Axioms* **2022**, *11*, 156, doi:10.3390/axioms11040156 . . . . **201**

About the Editor

Behzad Djafari-Rouhani

Behzad Djafari-Rouhani received his Ph.D. degree from Yale University in 1981 under the direction of the late Professor Shizuo Kakutani. He has more than 40 years of academic experience in many universities worldwide. He is currently a Professor of Mathematics at the University of Texas, El Paso, USA. His interest is in nonlinear functional analysis, specifically, nonlinear ergodic theory, nonlinear evolution and difference equations, fixed point theory, variational inequalities, optimization, and mathematical biology. He has published more than 70 research papers in peer-reviewed journals in his field.

Preface

Many real-world problems in science and engineering, including physical, biological, social phenomena, etc., can be mathematically formulated and rigorously solved by modeling them in linear and nonlinear differential and partial differential equations. This Special Issue titled "Differential Equations and Asymptotic Analysis: Recent Advances and Applications" consists of a collection of papers written by eminent mathematicians and experts in their fields, covering many different areas of nonlinear analysis, both theoretical and applied, related to differential equations, including fixed point theory, monotone operator theory, equilibrium problems and optimization, asymptotic analysis, mathematical biology, and numerical computations. We hope that this Special Issue will be of interest to many researchers, as well as graduate students working in these fields. Finally, I would like to dedicate this Special Issue to my late parents, my wife, Roshanak, and my two sons, Salar and Sina, without whose patience this Special Issue would not have come to light.

Behzad Djafari-Rouhani
Editor

Article

Fixed Point Theorems for Set-Valued Contractions in Metric Spaces

Seong-Hoon Cho

Department of Mathematics, Hanseo University, Seosan 356-706, Chungnam, Republic of Korea; shcho@hanseo.ac.kr; Tel.: +82-41-660-1316

Abstract: In this paper, the concepts of Wardowski-type set-valued contractions and Işik-type set-valued contractions are introduced and fixed point theorems for such contractions are established. A positive answer to the open Question is given. Examples to support main theorems and an application to integral inclusion are given.

Keywords: fixed point; contraction; generalized contraction; set-valued contraction; metric space

MSC: 47H10; 54H25

1. Introduction and Preliminaries

Wardowski [1] introduced the notion of F-contraction mappings and the generalized Banach contraction principle by proving that every F-contractions on complete metric spaces have only one fixed point, where $F : (0, \infty) \to (-\infty, \infty)$ is a function such that

(F1) F is strictly increasing;

(F2) for all sequence $\{s_n\} \subset (0, \infty)$,

$$\lim_{n \to \infty} s_n = 0 \iff \lim_{n \to \infty} F(s_n) = -\infty;$$

(F3) there exists a point $q \in (0, 1) : \lim_{t \to 0^+} t^q F(t) = 0$.

Among several results ([2–18]) generalizing Wardowski's result, Piri and Kumam [19] introduced the concept of Suzuki-type F-contractions and obtained related fixed point results in complete metric spaces, where $F : (0, \infty) \to (-\infty, \infty)$ is a strictly increasing function such that

(F4) $\inf F = -\infty$;

(F5) F is continuous on $(0, \infty)$.

Nazam [20] generalized Wardowski's result to four maps defined on b-metric spaces and proved the existence of a common fixed point by using conditions (F2), (F3) and

(F6) $\tau + F(rs_n) \leq F(s_n) \implies \tau + F(r^n s_n) \leq F(r^{n-1} s_{n-1})$ for each $r > 0, n \in \mathbb{N}$, where $\tau > 0$.

Younis et al. [18] generalized Nazam's result in b-metric spaces using only condition (F1). That is, they only used the strictly growth of $F : (0, \infty) \to (-\infty, \infty)$ and distinguished two cases: $s = 1$ and $s > 1$, where s is the coefficient of b-metric spaces. Younis et al. [21] introduced the notion of Suzuki–Geraghty-type generalized (F, ψ)-contractions and generalized the result of [14] in partial b-metric spaces along with Geraghty-type contraction with conditions (F1), (F4) and (F5), and they gave applications to graph the theory and solution of some integral equations. Younis and Singh [22] extended Wardowski's result to b-metric-like spaces and obtained the sufficient conditions for the existence of solutions of some class of Hammerstein integral equations and fractional differential equations.

Citation: Cho, S.-H. Fixed Point Theorems for Set-Valued Contractions in Metric Spaces. *Axioms* **2024**, *13*, 86. https://doi.org/10.3390/axioms13020086

Academic Editor: Behzad Djafari-Rouhani

Received: 27 December 2023
Revised: 21 January 2024
Accepted: 22 January 2024
Published: 27 January 2024

Copyright: © 2024 by the author. Licensee MDPI, Basel, Switzerland. This article is an open access article distributed under the terms and conditions of the Creative Commons Attribution (CC BY) license (https://creativecommons.org/licenses/by/4.0/).

On the other hand, Abbas et al. [23] and Abbas et al. [24] extended and generalized Wadorski's result to two self mappings on partially ordered metric space and fuzzy mappings on metric spaces, respectively, and proved the existence of a fixed point using conditions (F1), (F2) and (F3).

Note that for a function $F : (0, \infty) \to (-\infty, \infty)$, the following are equivalent:

(1) (F2) is satisfied;
(2) (F4) is satisfied;
(3) $\lim_{t \to 0^+} F(t) = -\infty$.

Hence, we have that

$$\lim_{n \to \infty} s_n = 0 \Rightarrow \lim_{n \to \infty} F(s_n) = -\infty$$

whenever (F4) holds.

Very recently, Fabiano et al. [25] gave a generalization of Wardowski's result [1] by reducing the condition on function $F : (0, \infty) \to (-\infty, \infty)$ and by using the right limit of function $F : (0, \infty) \to (-\infty, \infty)$. They proved the following Theorem 1.

Theorem 1 ([25])**.** *Let (E, ρ) be a complete metric space. Suppose that $T : E \to E$ is a map such that for all $x, y \in E$ with $\rho(Tx, Ty) > 0$,*

$$\tau + F(\rho(Tx, Ty)) \leq F(\rho(x, y))$$

where $\tau > 0$ and $F : (0, \infty) \to (-\infty, \infty)$ is a function. If (F1) is satisfied, then T possesses only one fixed point.

In [25], Fabiano et al. asked the following question:

Question ([25]). Can conditions for the function F be reduced to (F1) and (F2), and can the proof be made simpler in some results for multivalued mappings in the same way as it was presented in [25] for single-valued mappings?

In this paper, we give a positive answer to the above question by extending the above theorem to set-valued maps and obtain a fixed point result for Işik-type set-valued contractions. We give examples to interpret main results and an application to integral inclusion.

Let (E, ρ) be a metric space. We denote by $CL(E)$ the family of all nonempty closed subsets of E, and by $CB(E)$ the set of all nonempty closed and bounded subsets of E.

Let $H(\cdot, \cdot)$ be the generalized Pompeiu–Hausdorff distance [26] on $CL(E)$, i.e., for all $A, B \in CL(E)$,

$$H(A, B) = \begin{cases} \max\{\sup_{a \in A} \rho(a, B), \sup_{b \in B} \rho(b, A)\}, & \text{if the maximum exists,} \\ \infty, & \text{otherwise,} \end{cases}$$

where $\rho(a, B) = \inf\{\rho(a, b) : b \in B\}$ is the distance from the point a to the subset B.

Let $\delta(A, B) = \sup\{\rho(a, b) : a \in A, b \in B\}$. When $A = \{x\}$, we denote $\delta(A, B)$ by $\delta(x, B)$.

For $A, B \in CL(E)$, let $D(A, B) = \sup_{x \in A} d(x, B) = \sup_{x \in A} \inf_{y \in B} d(x, y)$.
Then, we have that for all $A, B \in CL(E)$

$$D(A, B) \leq H(A, B) \leq \delta(A, B).$$

Note that the following Lemma 1 can be obtained by applying the assumptions of Lemma 1 to Theorem 4.29 of [27]. In fact, let $F : (0, \infty) \to (-\infty, \infty)$ be monotonically increasing ($x < y$ implies $F(x) \leq F(y)$) and $\{p_n\}$ be a given sequence of $(0, \infty)$ such that

$$\lim_{n \to \infty} p_n = l, \text{ where } l > 0.$$

Then, it follows from Theorem 4.28 of [27] that we obtain the conclusion of Lemma 1. Here, we give another proof of Lemma 1.

Lemma 1. *Let $l > 0$, and let $\{t_n\}, \{s_n\} \subset (l, \infty)$ be non-increasing sequences such that*

$$t_n < s_n, \forall n = 1, 2, 3, \cdots \text{ and } \lim_{n \to \infty} t_n = \lim_{n \to \infty} s_n = l.$$

If $F : (0, \infty) \to (-\infty, \infty)$ is strictly increasing, then we have

$$\lim_{n \to \infty} F(t_n) = \lim_{n \to \infty} F(s_n) = F(l^+) \geq F(l).$$

where $F(l^+)$ denotes $\lim_{t \to l^+} F(t)$.

Proof. As F is strictly increasing, the function $F_* : (0, \infty) \to F((0, \infty))$ defined by $F_*(t) = F(t) \; \forall t \in (0, \infty)$, is bijective and continuous on $(0, \infty)$. We infer that

$$\lim_{t \to l^+} F_*(t) \geq F_*(l), \; \lim_{n \to \infty} F_*(t_n) = \lim_{t \to l^+} F_*(t) \text{ and } \lim_{n \to \infty} F_*(s_n) = \lim_{t \to l^+} F_*(t).$$

Since $\{t_n\}$ and $\{s_n\}$ are non-increasing, it follows from the strict increasingness of F that

$$F_*(t_{n+1}) \leq F_*(t_n) < F_*(s_n) \leq F_*(s_{n-1}).$$

Hence, we obtain that

$$\lim_{t \to l^+} F_*(t) = \lim_{n \to \infty} F_*(t_{n+1}) \leq \lim_{n \to \infty} F_*(t_n) \leq \lim_{n \to \infty} F_*(s_n) \leq \lim_{n \to \infty} F_*(s_{n-1}) \leq \lim_{t \to l^+} F_*(t),$$

which implies

$$\lim_{n \to \infty} F_*(t_n) = \lim_{n \to \infty} F_*(s_n) = F_*(l^+).$$

Since $F_*(t) = F(t) \; \forall t \in (0, \infty)$, we have the desired result. □

Lemma 2 ([28]). *Let (E, ρ) be a metric space. If $\{x_n\}$ is not a Cauchy sequence, then there exists $\epsilon > 0$ for which we can find subsequences $\{x_{m(k)}\}$ and $\{x_{n(k)}\}$ of $\{x_n\}$ such that $m(k)$ is the smallest index for which*

$$m(k) > n(k) > k, \; \rho(x_{m(k)}, x_{n(k)}) \geq \epsilon \text{ and } \rho(x_{m(k)-1}, x_{n(k)}) < \epsilon. \tag{1}$$

Further, if

$$\lim_{n \to \infty} \rho(x_n, x_{n+1}) = 0,$$

then we have that

$$\lim_{k \to \infty} \rho(x_{n(k)}, x_{m(k)}) = \lim_{k \to \infty} \rho(x_{n(k)+1}, x_{m(k)})$$
$$= \lim_{k \to \infty} \rho(x_{n(k)}, x_{m(k)+1}) = \lim_{k \to \infty} \rho(x_{n(k)+1}, x_{m(k)+1}) = \epsilon. \tag{2}$$

Lemma 3. *Let (E, ρ) be a metric space, and let $A, B \in CL(E)$. If $a \in A$ and $\rho(a, B) < c$, then there exists $b \in B$ such that $\rho(a, b) < c$.*

Proof. Let $\epsilon = c - \rho(a, B)$. It follows from the definition of infimum that there exists $b \in B$ such that $\rho(a, b) < \rho(a, B) + \epsilon$. Hence, $\rho(a, b) < c$. □

Lemma 4. *Let (E, ρ) be a metric space, and let $A, B \in CL(E)$ and $\phi : [0, \infty) \to [0, \infty)$ be a strictly increasing function. If $a \in A$ and $\rho(a, B) + \phi(\rho(a, B)) < c$, then there exists $b \in B$ such that $\rho(a, b) + \phi(\rho(a, b)) < c$.*

Proof. Since ϕ is strictly increasing,
$$\rho(a, B) < \phi^{-1}(c - \rho(a, B)).$$

By Lemma 3, there exists $b' \in B$ such that
$$\rho(a, b') < \phi^{-1}(c - \rho(a, B))$$

which yields
$$\rho(a, B) < c - \phi(\rho(a, b')).$$

Again, by applying Lemma 3, there exists $b'' \in B$ such that
$$\rho(a, b'') < c - \phi(\rho(a, b')).$$

Let $\min\{\rho(a, b'), \rho(a, b'')\} = \rho(a, b)$. Then, we have that
$$\rho(a, b) + \phi(\rho(a, b)) < c.$$

□

Lemma 5. *If (E, ρ) is a metric space, then $K(E) \subset CL(E)$, where $K(E)$ is the family of nonempty compact subsets of E.*

2. Fixed Point Results

Let (E, ρ) be a metric space, and let $F : (0, \infty) \to (-\infty, \infty)$ be a strictly increasing function. A set-valued map $T : E \to CL(E)$ is called a Wardowski-type contraction if the following condition holds:

There exists a constant $\tau > 0$ such that for all $x, y \in E$ with $H(Tx, Ty) > 0$,
$$\tau + F(H(Tx, Ty)) \leq F(m(x, y)), \tag{3}$$

where $m(x, y) = \max\{\rho(x, y), \rho(x, Tx), \rho(y, Ty), \frac{1}{2}[\rho(x, Ty) + \rho(y, Tx)]\}$.

We now prove our main result.

Theorem 2. *Let (E, ρ) be a complete metric space. If $T : E \to CL(E)$ is a Wardowski-type set-valued contraction, then T possesses a fixed point.*

Proof. Let $x_0 \in E$ be a point, and let $x_1 \in Tx_0$.

If $x_1 \in Tx_1$, then the proof is completed.

Assume that $x_1 \notin Tx_1$. Then, $\rho(x_1, Tx_1) > 0$, because $Tx_1 \in CL(X)$. Hence, $H(Tx_0, Tx_1) \geq d(x_1, Tx_1) > 0$. From (3) we have that

$$\tau + F(H(Tx_0, Tx_1)) \leq F(m(x_0, x_1)). \tag{4}$$

We infer that

$$m(x_0, x_1) = \max\{\rho(x_0, x_1), \rho(x_0, Tx_0), \rho(x_1, Tx_1), \frac{1}{2}[\rho(x_0, Tx_1) + \rho(x_1, Tx_0)]\}$$
$$= \max\{\rho(x_0, x_1), \rho(x_1, Tx_1)\}, \text{ because that } \rho(x_0, Tx_0) \leq \rho(x_0, x_1) \text{ and}$$
$$\frac{1}{2}[\rho(x_0, Tx_1) + \rho(x_1, Tx_0)] \leq \frac{1}{2}[\rho(x_0, x_1) + \rho(x_1, Tx_1)].$$

If $m(x_0, x_1) = \rho(x_1, Tx_1)$, then from (4) we obtain that

$$F(\rho(x_1, Tx_1)) < \tau + F(H(Tx_0, Tx_1)) \leq F(\rho(x_1, Tx_1)),$$

which is a contradiction. Thus, $m(x_0, x_1) = \rho(x_0, x_1)$. It follows from (4) that

$$\frac{1}{2}\tau + F(\rho(x_1, Tx_1)) < \tau + F(H(Tx_0, Tx_1)) \leq F(\rho(x_0, x_1)). \tag{5}$$

Since (F1) is satisfied, we obtain that

$$\rho(x_1, Tx_1) < F^{-1}(\frac{1}{2}\tau + F(H(Tx_0, Tx_1))).$$

Applying Lemma 3, there exists $x_2 \in Tx_1$ such that

$$\rho(x_1, x_2) < F^{-1}(\frac{1}{2}\tau + F(H(Tx_0, Tx_1))),$$

which implies

$$F(\rho(x_1, x_2)) < \frac{1}{2}\tau + F(H(Tx_0, Tx_1)) \leq F(\rho(x_0, x_1)) - \frac{1}{2}\tau. \tag{6}$$

Again from (3) we have that

$$\frac{1}{2}\tau + F(\rho(x_2, Tx_2)) < \tau + F(H(Tx_1, Tx_2)) \leq F(\rho(x_1, x_2)) \tag{7}$$

which implies

$$\rho(x_2, Tx_2) < F^{-1}(\frac{1}{2}\tau + F(H(Tx_1, Tx_2))).$$

By Lemma 3, there exists $x_3 \in Tx_2$ such that

$$\rho(x_2, x_3) < F^{-1}(\frac{1}{2}\tau + F(H(Tx_1, Tx_2))).$$

Hence, we obtain that

$$F(\rho(x_2, x_3)) < \frac{1}{2}\tau + F(H(Tx_1, Tx_2)) \leq F(\rho(x_1, x_2)) - \frac{1}{2}\tau. \tag{8}$$

Inductively, we have that for all $n \in \mathbb{N}$,

$$x_n \in Tx_{n-1}$$

and

$$F(\rho(x_n, x_{n+1})) < \frac{1}{2}\tau + F(H(Tx_{n-1}, x_n)) \leq F(\rho(x_{n-1}, x_n)) - \frac{1}{2}\tau. \tag{9}$$

Because F is a strictly increasing function,

$$\rho(x_n, x_{n+1}) < \rho(x_{n-1}, x_n), \ \forall n \in \mathbb{N}.$$

Hence, there exists $r \geq 0$ such that

$$\lim_{n \to \infty} \rho(x_n, x_{n+1}) = r.$$

Assume that $r > 0$. By Lemma 1, we have that

$$\lim_{n \to \infty} F(\rho(x_n, x_{n+1})) = \lim_{n \to \infty} F(\rho(x_{n-1}, x_n)) = \lim_{t \to r^+} F(t) = F(r^+) \geq F(r). \tag{10}$$

Taking limit $n \to \infty$ in (9) and using (10), we obtain that

$$F(r^+) \leq F(r^+) - \frac{1}{2}\tau,$$

which is a contradiction, because $\tau > 0$. Thus, we obtain that

$$\lim_{n \to \infty} \rho(x_n, x_{n+1}) = 0. \tag{11}$$

Now, we show that $\{x_n\}$ is a Cauchy sequence. Assume that $\{x_n\}$ is not a Cauchy sequence. Then, there exists $\epsilon > 0$ for which we can find subsequences $\{x_{m(k)}\}$ and $\{x_{n(k)}\}$ of $\{x_n\}$ such that $m(k)$ is the smallest index for which (1) holds. That is, the following are satisfied:

$$m(k) > n(k) > k, \ \rho(x_{m(k)}, x_{n(k)}) \geq \epsilon \text{ and } \rho(x_{m(k)-1}, x_{n(k)}) < \epsilon.$$

It follows from (3) that

$$\begin{aligned}F(\rho(x_{n(k)+1}, Tx_{m(k)}) &< \tau + F(\rho(x_{n(k)+1}, Tx_{m(k)}) \\ &\leq \tau + F(H(Tx_{n(k)}, Tx_{m(k)}) \leq F(m(x_{n(k)}, x_{m(k)})).\end{aligned} \tag{12}$$

We infer that

$$\begin{aligned}\epsilon &\leq \rho(x_{n(k)}, x_{m(k)}) \leq m(x_{n(k)}, x_{m(k)}) \\ &= \max\{\rho(x_{n(k)}, x_{m(k)}), \rho(x_{n(k)}, Tx_{n(k)}), \rho(x_{m(k)}, Tx_{m(k)}), \\ &\quad \frac{1}{2}[\rho(x_{n(k)}, Tx_{m(k)}) + \rho(x_{m(k)}, Tx_{n(k)})]\} \\ &\leq \max\{\rho(x_{n(k)}, x_{m(k)}), \rho(x_{n(k)}, x_{n(k)+1}), \rho(x_{m(k)}, x_{m(k)+1}), \\ &\quad \frac{1}{2}[\rho(x_{n(k)}, x_{m(k)+1}) + \rho(x_{m(k)}, x_{n(k)+1})]\}\end{aligned} \tag{13}$$

Taking limit as $k \to \infty$ on both sides of (13) and using (2), we obtain that

$$\lim_{k \to \infty} m(x_{n(k)}, x_{m(k)}) = \epsilon. \tag{14}$$

Since F is strictly increasing, from (12) we have that

$$\rho(x_{n(k)+1}, Tx_{m(k)}) < F^{-1}(\tau + F(\rho(x_{n(k)+1}, Tx_{m(k)}))).$$

By applying Lemma 3, there exists $y_{m(k)} \in Tx_{m(k)}$ such that

$$\rho(x_{n(k)+1}, y_{m(k)}) < F^{-1}(\tau + F(\rho(x_{n(k)+1}, Tx_{m(k)}))).$$

Hence,

$$F(\rho(x_{n(k)+1}, y_{m(k)})) < \tau + F(\rho(x_{n(k)+1}, Tx_{m(k)})).$$

Thus, it follows from (12) that

$$\begin{aligned}&F(\rho(x_{n(k)+1}, y_{m(k)})) \\ &< \tau + F(\rho(x_{n(k)+1}, y_{m(k)})) < \tau + F(\rho(x_{n(k)+1}, Tx_{m(k)})) \\ &\leq \tau + F(H(Tx_{n(k)}, Tx_{m(k)})) \\ &\leq F(m(x_{n(k)}, x_{m(k)}))\end{aligned} \tag{15}$$

which leads to

$$\rho(x_{n(k)+1}, y_{m(k)}) < m(x_{n(k)}, x_{m(k)}), \ \forall k = 1, 2, 3, \cdots. \tag{16}$$

By taking $\limsup$ as $k \to \infty$ in (16) and using (14), we have that

$$\limsup_{k \to \infty} \rho(x_{n(k)+1}, y_{m(k)}) \leq \epsilon. \tag{17}$$

Since

$$\rho(x_{n(k)+1}, Tx_{m(k)}) \leq \rho(x_{n(k)+1}, y_{m(k)}),$$

$$\begin{aligned}\rho(x_{n(k)+1}, x_{m(k)}) &\leq \rho(x_{n(k)+1}, Tx_{m(k)}) + \rho(Tx_{m(k)}, x_{m(k)}) \\ &\leq \rho(x_{n(k)+1}, y_{m(k)}) + \rho(x_{m(k)+1}, x_{m(k)}).\end{aligned} \tag{18}$$

Taking $\liminf$ as $k \to \infty$ in (18) and using (2), we obtain that

$$\epsilon \leq \liminf_{k \to \infty} \rho(x_{n(k)+1}, y_{m(k)}). \tag{19}$$

It follows from (17) and (19) that

$$\lim_{k \to \infty} \rho(x_{n(k)+1}, y_{m(k)}) = \epsilon. \tag{20}$$

By applying Lemma 1 to (15) with (14), (16) and (20), we obtain that

$$F(\epsilon^+) \leq \tau + F(\epsilon^+) \leq F(\epsilon^+)$$

which leads to a contradiction. Hence, $\{x_n\}$ is a Cauchy sequence. From the completeness of E, there exists

$$x_* = \lim_{n \to \infty} x_n \in E.$$

It follows from (3) that

$$\begin{aligned}F(\rho(x_{n+1}, Tx_*)) &< \tau + F(\rho(x_{n+1}, Tx_*)) \\ &\leq \tau + F(H(Tx_n, Tx_*)) \leq F(m(x_n, x_*)),\end{aligned} \tag{21}$$

where $m(x_n, x_*) = \max\{\rho(x_n, x_*), \rho(x_n, x_{n+1}), \rho(x_*, Tx_*), \frac{1}{2}[\rho(x_*, x_{n+1}) + \rho(x_n, Tx_*)]\}$.
Since F is strictly increasing, from (21) we have that

$$\rho(x_{n+1}, Tx_*) < m(x_n, x_*), \tag{22}$$

and thus

$$\lim_{n \to \infty} \rho(x_{n+1}, Tx_*) = \lim_{n \to \infty} m(x_n, x_*) = \rho(x_*, Tx_*). \tag{23}$$

Assume that $\rho(x_*, Tx_*) > 0$. By Lemma 1, we have that

$$\begin{aligned}\lim_{n \to \infty} F(\rho(x_{n+1}, Tx_*)) &= \lim_{n \to \infty} F(m(x_n, x_*)) \\ &= \lim_{t \to \rho(x_*, Tx_*)^+} F(t) = F(\rho(x_*, Tx_*)^+).\end{aligned} \tag{24}$$

Applying (24) to (21), we obtain that

$$F(\rho(x_*, Tx_*)^+) \leq \tau + F(\rho(x_*, Tx_*)^+) \leq F(\rho(x_*, Tx_*)^+)$$

which leads to a contradiction. Hence, $\rho(x_*, Tx_*) = 0$, and $x_* \in Tx_*$. □

The following example interprets Theorem 2.

Example 1. Let $E = [0,1]$ and $\rho(x,y) = |x-y|$, $\forall x, y \in E$. Then (E, ρ) is a complete metric space. Define a set-valued map $T : E \to CL(E)$ by

$$Tx = \begin{cases} \{1\}, & (x = 0) \\ \{\frac{2}{5}, \frac{1}{2}\}, & (0 < x \leq 1). \end{cases}$$

Let $\tau = \ln \frac{2.1}{2}$ and $F(t) = \ln t$, $\forall t > 0$. We show that T is a Wardowski-type set-valued contraction. We now consider the following two cases.

First, let $x = 0$ and $0 < y \leq 1$.
Then, $H(Tx.Ty) = \frac{3}{5}$. We obtain that

$$\tau + F(H(Tx, Ty)) - F(\rho(x, Tx))$$
$$= \tau + F\left(\frac{3}{5}\right) - F(1)$$
$$= \ln \frac{2.1}{2} + \ln \frac{3}{5} - \ln 1$$
$$= \ln 6.3 - \ln 10 \approx -0.46 < 0.$$

Thus,

$$\tau + F(H(Tx, Ty)) < F(\rho(x, Tx)),$$

which implies

$$\tau + F(H(Tx, Ty)) < F(m(x, y)).$$

Second, let $0 \leq x < 1$ and $y = 1$.
Then $H(Tx, Ty) = \frac{4}{5}$. We infer that

$$\tau + F(H(Tx, Ty)) - F(\rho(y, Ty))$$
$$= \tau + F\left(\frac{4}{5}\right) - F(1)$$
$$= \ln \frac{2.1}{2} + \ln \frac{4}{5} - \ln 1$$
$$= \ln 8.4 - \ln 10 \approx -0.17 < 0.$$

Thus,

$$\tau + F(H(Tx, Ty)) < F(\rho(y, Ty))$$

which leads to

$$\tau + F(H(Tx, Ty)) < F(m(x, y)).$$

Hence, T is a Wardowski-type set-valued contraction. The assumptions of Theorem 2 are satisfied. By Theorem 2, T possesses two fixed points, $\frac{2}{5}$ and $\frac{1}{2}$.

Remark 1. Theorem 2 is a positive answer to Question 4.3 of [25].

Remark 2. Theorem 2 is an extention of Theorem 2.2 [13] to set-valued maps without conditions (F2) and (F3).

By Theorem 2, we have the following results.

Corollary 1. Let (E, ρ) be a complete metric space. Suppose that $T : E \to CL(E)$ is a set-valued map such that for all $x, y \in E$ with $H(Tx, Ty) > 0$,

$$\tau + F(H(Tx, Ty)) \leq F(l(x, y)) \qquad (25)$$

where $\tau > 0$ and $F : (0, \infty) \to (-\infty, \infty)$ is a function, and

$$l(x,y) = \max\{\rho(x,y), \frac{1}{2}[\rho(x,Tx) + \rho(y,Ty)], \frac{1}{2}[\rho(x,Ty) + \rho(y,Tx)]\}.$$

If (F1) is satisfied, then T possesses a fixed point.

Proof. Since $l(x,y) \leq m(x,y)$, $F(l(x,y)) \leq F(m(x,y))$. Thus, (25) implies (2). By Theorem 2, T possesses a fixed point. □

Corollary 2. Let (E, ρ) be a complete metric space. Suppose that $T : E \to CL(E)$ is a set-valued map such that for all $x, y \in E$ with $H(Tx, Ty) > 0$,

$$\tau + F(H(Tx, Ty)) \leq F(\rho(x, y)) \tag{26}$$

where $\tau > 0$ and $F : (0, \infty) \to (-\infty, \infty)$ is a function. If (F1) is satisfied, then T possesses a fixed point.

Proof. Since $\rho(x, y) \leq m(x, y)$ and (F1) holds, (26) implies (2). By Theorem 2, T possesses a fixed point. □

Corollary 3. Let (E, ρ) be a complete metric space. Suppose that $T : E \to CL(E)$ is a set-valued map such that for all $x, y \in E$ with $H(Tx, Ty) > 0$,

$$\begin{aligned}&\tau + F(H(Tx, Ty)) \\ &\leq F(a\rho(x,y) + b\rho(x,Tx) + c\rho(y,Ty) + e[\rho(x,Ty) + \rho(y,Tx)])\end{aligned} \tag{27}$$

where $\tau > 0$ and $F : (0, \infty) \to (-\infty, \infty)$ is a function, and $a, b, c, e \geq 0$ and $a + b + c + 2e = 1$. If (F1) is satisfied, then T possesses a fixed point.

Proof. It follows from (27) that

$$\begin{aligned}&\tau + F(H(Tx,Ty)) \\ &\leq F(a\rho(x,y) + b\rho(x,Tx) + c\rho(y,Ty) + e[\rho(x,Ty) + \rho(y,Tx)]) \\ &= F(a\rho(x,y) + b\rho(x,Tx) + c\rho(y,Ty)] + 2e\frac{1}{2}[\rho(x,Ty) + \rho(y,Tx)]) \\ &\leq F((a+b+c+2e)\max\{\rho(x,y),\rho(x,Tx),\rho(y,Ty),\frac{1}{2}[\rho(x,Ty)+\rho(y,Tx)]\}) \\ &= F(m(x,y)).\end{aligned}$$

By Theorem 2, T possesses a fixed point. □

Corollary 4. Let (E, ρ) be a complete metric space. Suppose that $T : E \to CL(E)$ is a set-valued map such that for all $x, y \in E$ with $H(Tx, Ty) > 0$,

$$\begin{aligned}&\tau + F(H(Tx, Ty)) \\ &\leq F(a\rho(x,y) + b[\rho(x,Tx) + \rho(y,Ty)] + c[\rho(x,Ty) + \rho(y,Tx)])\end{aligned} \tag{28}$$

where $\tau > 0$ and $F : (0, \infty) \to (-\infty, \infty)$ is a function, and $a, b, c \geq 0$ and $a + 2b + 2c = 1$. If (F1) is satisfied, then T possesses a fixed point.

Proof. It follows from (28) that

$$\tau + F(H(Tx, Ty))$$
$$\leq F(a\rho(x,y) + b[\rho(x, Tx) + \rho(y, Ty)] + c[\rho(x, Ty) + \rho(y, Tx)])$$
$$= F(a\rho(x,y) + 2b\frac{1}{2}[\rho(x, Tx) + \rho(y, Ty)] + 2c\frac{1}{2}[\rho(x, Ty) + \rho(y, Tx)])$$
$$\leq F((a + 2b + 2c)\max\{\rho(x,y), \frac{1}{2}[\rho(x, Tx) + \rho(y, Ty)], \frac{1}{2}[\rho(x, Ty) + \rho(y, Tx)]\})$$
$$= F(l(x,y)).$$

By Corollary 1, T possesses a fixed point. □

Corollary 5. *Let (E, ρ) be a complete metric space. Suppose that $T : E \to CL(E)$ is a set-valued map such that for all $x, y \in E$ with $H(Tx, Ty) > 0$,*

$$\tau + F(H(Tx, Ty)) \leq F(\frac{1}{2}[\rho(x, Tx) + \rho(y, Ty)]) \tag{29}$$

where $\tau > 0$ and $F : (0, \infty) \to (-\infty, \infty)$ is a function. If (F1) is satisfied, then T possesses a fixed point.

Proof. Since $\frac{1}{2}[\rho(x, Tx) + \rho(y, Ty)] \leq l(x,y)$ and (F1) holds, (29) implies (25). By Corollary 1, T possesses a fixed point. □

Corollary 6. *Let (E, ρ) be a complete metric space. Suppose that $T : E \to CL(E)$ is a set-valued map such that for all $x, y \in E$ with $H(Tx, Ty) > 0$,*

$$\tau + F(H(Tx, Ty)) \leq F(\frac{1}{2}[\rho(x, Ty) + \rho(y, Tx)]) \tag{30}$$

where $\tau > 0$ and $F : (0, \infty) \to (-\infty, \infty)$ is a function. If (F1) is satisfied, then T possesses a fixed point.

Proof. Since $\frac{1}{2}[\rho(x, Ty) + \rho(y, Tx)] \leq l(x,y)$ and (F1) holds, implies (25). By Corollary 1, T possesses a fixed point. □

Remark 3. *Corollary 4 is a generalization of the main theorem of [29]. Indeed, if $F(t) = \ln t, \forall t > 0$ and we take T to be the self-mapping of E, then Corollary 4 becomes the main theorem of [29].*

Nadler [30] extended Banach's fixed point theorem to set-valued maps. We are calling it Nadler's fixed point theorem. We now prove the following theorem, which is a generalization of Nadler's fixed point theorem.

Theorem 3. *Let (E, ρ) be a complete metric space. Suppose that $T : E \to CL(E)$ is an Işik-type set-valued contraction, i.e., for each $x, y \in E$ and each $u \in Tx$, there exists $v \in Ty$ such that*

$$\rho(u, v) \leq \phi(\rho(x, y)) - \phi(\rho(u, v)) \tag{31}$$

where $\phi : [0, \infty) \to [0, \infty)$ is a function such that

$$\lim_{t \to 0^+} \phi(t) = 0. \tag{32}$$

Then, T possesses a fixed point.

Proof. Let $x_0 \in E$, and let $x_1 \in Tx_0$. Then there exits $x_2 \in Tx_1$ such that

$$\rho(x_1, x_2) \leq \phi(\rho(x_0, x_1)) - \phi(\rho(x_1, x_2)).$$

Again, there exists $x_3 \in Tx_2$ such that
$$\rho(x_2, x_3) \leq \phi(\rho(x_1, x_2)) - \phi(\rho(x_2, x_3)).$$
Inductively, we have a sequence $\{x_n\} \subset E$ such that for all $n = 1, 2, 3, \cdots$,
$$x_n \in Tx_{n-1} \text{ and } \rho(x_n, x_{n+1}) \leq \phi(\rho(x_{n-1}, x_n)) - \phi(\rho(x_n, x_{n+1})). \tag{33}$$

It follows from (33) that $\{\phi(\rho(x_{n-1}, x_n))\}$ is a non-increasing sequence and bounded below by 0. Hence, there exists $r \geq 0$ such that
$$\lim_{n \to \infty} \phi(\rho(x_{n-1}, x_n)) = r.$$

We show that $\{x_n\}$ is a Cauchy sequence.
Let m, n be any positive integers such that $m > n$. Then we have that
$$\begin{aligned}&\rho(x_n, x_m)\\ &\leq \rho(x_n, x_{n+1}) + \rho(x_{n+1}, x_{n+2}) + \cdots + \rho(x_{m-1}, x_m)\\ &\leq \phi(\rho(x_{n-1}, x_n)) - \phi(\rho(x_{m-1}, x_m))\\ &\leq \phi(\rho(x_{n-1}, x_n)) - r.\end{aligned} \tag{34}$$

Letting $m, n \to \infty$ in (34), we obtain that
$$\lim_{n, m \to \infty} \rho(x_n, x_m) = 0.$$

Thus, $\{x_n\}$ is a Cauchy sequence. It follows from the completeness of E that
$$x_* = \lim_{n \to \infty} x_n \text{ exists.} \tag{35}$$

Now, we show that x_* is a fixed point for T.
It follows from (31) that for $x_n \in Tx_{n-1}$, there exists $v \in Tx_*$ such that
$$\rho(x_n, v) \leq \phi(\rho(x_{n-1}, x_*)) - \phi(\rho(x_n, v)) \leq \phi(\rho(x_{n-1}, x_*)). \tag{36}$$

Taking limit $n \to \infty$ in Equation (36) and using (32), we infer that
$$\lim_{n \to \infty} \rho(x_n, v) = 0$$
which implies
$$x_* = v \in Tx_*.$$

□

Example 2. Let $E = \{x_n : x_n = \sum_{k=1}^n, n \in \mathbb{N}\}$ and $\rho(x, y) = |x - y|, \forall x, y \in E$. Then (E, ρ) is a complete metric space.
Define a map $T : E \to CL(E)$ by
$$Tx = \begin{cases} \{x_1\}, & (x = x_1) \\ \{x_1, x_2, x_3, \cdots x_{n-1}\}, & (x = x_n). \end{cases}$$

Let $\phi(t) = \frac{1}{2}t, \forall t \geq 0$.
We show that condition (31) is satisfied.
Consider the following two cases.
First, let $x = x_1$ and $y = x_n, n = 2, 3, 4, \cdots$.

Then, for $u = x_1 \in Tx$, there exists $v = x_1 \in Ty$ such that

$$\rho(u,v) = 0 < \frac{1}{2}\rho(x_1, x_n) = \phi(\rho(x_1, x_n)) = \phi(\rho(x_1, x_n)) - \phi(\rho(u,v)).$$

Second, let $x = x_n$ and $y = x_m, m > n, n = 2, 3, 4, \cdots$.
For $u = x_k \in Tx$ ($k = 1, 2, 3, \cdots, n-1$), there exists $v = x_k \in Ty$ such that

$$\rho(u,v) = 0 < \frac{1}{2}\rho(x_n, x_m) = \phi(\rho(x_n, x_m)) = \phi(\rho(x_n, x_m)) - \phi(\rho(u,v)).$$

This show that T satisfies condition (31). Thus, all conditions of Theorem 3 hold. From Theorem 3, T possesses a fixed point, $x_* = x_1$.

Corollary 7. *Let (E, ρ) be a complete metric space. Suppose that $T : E \to CL(E)$ is a set-valued map such that for each $x, y \in E$,*

$$H(Tx, Ty) < \phi(\rho(x,y)) - \phi(H(Tx, Ty)),$$

where $\phi : [0, \infty) \to [0, \infty)$ is a strictly increasing function such that

$$\lim_{t \to 0^+} \phi(t) = 0.$$

Then, T possesses a fixed point.

Proof. Let $x, y \in E$ and let $u \in Tx$. As ϕ is strictly increasing,

$$\rho(u, Ty) + \phi(\rho(u, Ty)) < \phi(\rho(x,y)).$$

Applying Lemma 4, there exists $v \in Ty$ such that

$$\rho(u,v) + \phi(\rho(u,v)) < \phi(\rho(x,y)).$$

By Theorem 3, T possesses a fixed point. □

From Theorem 3 we have the following result.

Corollary 8 ([31])**.** *Let (E, ρ) be a complete metric space. Suppose that $f : E \to E$ is a map such that for each $x, y \in E$,*

$$\rho(fx, fy) \leq \phi(\rho(x,y)) - \phi(\rho(fx, fy))$$

where $\phi : [0, \infty) \to [0, \infty)$ is a function such that

$$\lim_{t \to 0^+} \phi(t) = 0.$$

Then, f possesses a fixed point.

3. Application

In this section, we give an application of our result to integral inclusion. Let $[a,b] \subset (-\infty, \infty)$ be a closed interval, and let $C([a,b], (-\infty, \infty))$ be the family of continuous mapping from $[a,b]$ into $(-\infty, \infty)$. Let $E = C([a,b], (-\infty, \infty))$ and $\rho(x,y) = \sup_{t \in [a,b]} |x(t) - y(t)|$ for all $x, y \in E$. Then, (E, ρ) is a complete metric space.

Consider the Fredholm type integral inclusion:

$$x(t) \in \int_a^b K(t, s, x(s))ds + f(t), t \in [a,b] \qquad (37)$$

where $f \in E$, $K : [a,b] \times [a,b] \times (-\infty,\infty) \to CB((-\infty,\infty))$, and $x \in E$ is the unknown function.

Suppose that the following conditions are satisfied:

(1st) For each $x \in E$, $K(\cdot,\cdot,x(s)) = K_x(\cdot,\cdot)$ is continuous;

(2nd) There exists a continuous function $Z : [a,b] \times [a,b] \to [0,\infty)$ such that for all $t,s \in [a,b]$ and all $u,v \in E$,

$$|k_u(t,s) - k_v(t,s)| \leq Z(t,s)\rho(u(s),v(s))$$

where $k_u(t,s) \in K_u(t,s)$, $k_v(t,s) \in K_v(t,s)$;

(3rd) There exists $\alpha > 1$ such that

$$\sup_{t \in [a,b]} \int_a^b Z(t,s)ds \leq \frac{1}{2+\alpha}.$$

We apply the following theorem, known as Michael's selection theorem, to the proof of Theorem 5.

Theorem 4 ([32]). *Let X be a paracompact space, and let B be a Banach space. Suppose that $F : X \to B$ is a lower semicontinuous set-valued map such that for all $x \in X$, $F(x)$ is a nonempty closed and convex subset of B. Then $F : X \to B$ admits a continuous single valued selection.*

Note that $(-\infty,\infty)$ with absolute value norm is a Banach space and closed intervals and singleton of real numbers are a convex subset of $(-\infty,\infty)$.

Theorem 5. *Let (E,ρ) be a complete metric space. If conditions (1st), (2nd) and (3rd) are satisfied, then the integral inclusion (37) has a solution.*

Proof. Define a set-valued map $T : E \to CB(E)$ by

$$Tx = \{y \in E : y(t) \in \int_a^b K(t,s,x(s))ds + f(t), t \in [a,b]\}.$$

Let $x \in E$ be given. For the set-valued map $K_x(t,s) : [a,b] \times [a,b] \to CB((-\infty,\infty))$, by applying Michael's selection theorem, there exists a continuous map $k_x(t,s) : [a,b] \times [a,b] \to (-\infty,\infty)$ such that

$$k_x(t,s) \in K_x(t,s), \forall t,s \in [a,b].$$

Thus,

$$\int_a^b k_x(t,s)ds + f(t) \in Tx,$$

and so $Tx \neq \emptyset$.

Since f and k_x are continuous, $Tx \in CB(E)$ for each $x \in E$.

Let $y_1 \in Tx_1$. Then,

$$y_1(t) \in \int_a^b K(t,s,x_1(s))ds + f(t), t \in [a,b].$$

Hence, there exists $k_{x_1}(t,s) \in K_{x_1}(t,s), \forall t,s \in [a,b]$ such that

$$y_1(t) = \int_a^b k_{x_1}(t,s)ds + f(t), \forall t,s \in [a,b].$$

It follows from (2nd) that there exists $z(t,s) \in K_{x_2}(t,s)$ such that

$$|k_{x_1}(t,s) - z(t,s)| \leq Z(t,s)\rho(x_1(s), x_2(s)), \forall t, s \in [a,b].$$

Let $U : [a,b] \times [a,b] \to CB((-\infty, \infty))$ be defined by

$$U(t,s) = K_{x_2}(t,s) \cap \{u \in (-\infty, \infty) : \rho(k_{x_1}(t,s), u) \leq \rho(x_1(s), x_2(s))\}.$$

From (1st) U is continuous. Hence, it follows that there exists a continuous map $k_{x_2} : [a,b] \times [a,b] \to (-\infty, \infty)$ such that

$$k_{x_2}(t,s) \in U(t,s), \forall t, s \in [a,b].$$

Let

$$y_2(t) = \int_a^b k_{x_2}(t,s)ds + f(t), \forall t, s \in [a,b].$$

Then,

$$y_2(t) \in \int_a^b K_{x_2}(t,s)ds + f(t) = \int_a^b K(t,s,x_2(s))ds + f(t), \forall t, s \in [a,b],$$

and so $y_2 \in Tx_2$.

Thus, we obtain that

$$\rho(y_1, y_2) = \left| \int_a^b k_{x_1}(t,s) - k_{x_2}(t,s)ds \right|$$

$$\leq \sup_{t \in [a,b]} \int_a^b |k_{x_1}(t,s) - k_{x_2}(t,s)|ds$$

$$\leq \sup_{t \in [a,b]} \int_a^b Z(t,s)ds\rho(x_1(s), x_2(s))$$

$$\leq \frac{1}{2+\alpha}\rho(x_1(s), x_2(s)).$$

Thus, we have that

$$(1 + \frac{1}{2}\alpha)\delta(Tx_1, Tx_2) \leq \frac{1}{2}\rho(x_1, x_2)$$

which implies

$$(1 + \frac{1}{2}\alpha)H(Tx_1, Tx_2) \leq \frac{1}{2}\rho(x_1, x_2).$$

Hence, we obtain that

$$H(Tx_1, Tx_2)) \leq \phi(\rho(x_1, x_2)) - \phi(\alpha H(Tx_1, Tx_2))$$

$$< \phi(\rho(x_1, x_2)) - \phi(H(Tx_1, Tx_2)) \text{ where } \phi(t) = \frac{1}{2}t, \forall t \geq 0.$$

By Corollary 7, T possesses a fixed point, and hence the integral inclusion (37) has a solution. □

4. Conclusions

Our results are generalizations and extensions of F-contractions and Işik contractions to set-valued maps on metric spaces. We give a positive answer to Question 4.3 of [25] and an application to integral inclusion.

Funding: This research received no external funding.

Data Availability Statement: Data are contained within the article.

Acknowledgments: The author express his gratitude to the referees for careful reading and giving variable comments.

Conflicts of Interest: The author declares that he has no competing interest.

References

1. Wardowski, D. Fixed point theory of a new type of contractive mappings in complete metric spacs. *Fixed Point Theory Appl.* **2012**, *2012*, 94. [CrossRef]
2. Ahmad, J.; Al-Rawashdeh, A.; Azam, A. Some new fixed point theorems for generalized F-contractions in complete metric spaces. *Fixed Point Theory Appl.* **2015**, *2015*, 80. [CrossRef]
3. Alfaqih,W.M.; Imdad, M.; Gubran, R. An observation on F-weak contractions and discontinuity at the fixed point with an applications. *J. Fixed Point Theory Appl.* **2020**, *22*, 66. [CrossRef]
4. Arshad, M.; Khan, S.; Ahmad, J. Fixed point results for F-contractions involving some new rational expressions. *JP J. Fixed Point Theory Appl.* **2016**, *11*, 79–97. [CrossRef]
5. Bedre, S.V. Remarks on F-weak contractions and discontinuity at the fixed point. *Adv. Theory Nonlinear Anal. Appl.* **2020**, *4*, 260–265. [CrossRef]
6. Cosentino, M.; Vetro, P. Fixed point results for F-contractive mappings of Hardy Rogers-Type. *Filomat* **2014**, *28*, 715–722. [CrossRef]
7. Dung, N.V.; Hang, V.L. A fixed point theorem for generalized F-contractions on complete metric spaces. *Vietnam J. Math.* **2015**, *43*, 743–753. [CrossRef]
8. Huang, H.; Mitrović, Z.D.; Zoto, K.; Radenović, S. On convex F-contraction in b-metric spaces. *Axioms* **2021**, *10*, 71. [CrossRef]
9. Hussain, A. Ćirić type α-ψ F-contraction involving fixed point on a closed ball. *Honam Math. J.* **2019**, *41*, 19–34.
10. Hussain, A.; Arshad, M. New type of multivalued F-Contraction involving fixed Point on Closed Ball. *J. Math. Comp. Sci.* **2017**, *10*, 246–254. [CrossRef]
11. Hussain, N.; Salimi, P. Suzuki-wardowski type fixed point theorems for α-GF-contractions. *Taiwan. J. Math.* **2014**, *18*, 1879–1895. [CrossRef]
12. Konwar, N.; Debnath, P. Fixed point results for a family of Interpolative F-contractions in b-metric spaces. *Axioms* **2022**, *11*, 621. [CrossRef]
13. Minak, G.; Halvaci, A.; Altun, I. Ćirić type generalized F-contractions on complete metric spaces and fixed point results. *Filomat* **2014**, *28*, 1143–1151. [CrossRef]
14. Piri, H.; Kumam, P. Fixed point theorems for generalized F-Suzuki-contraction mappings in complete b-metric spaces. *Fixed Point Theory Appl.* **2016**, *2016*, 90. [CrossRef]
15. Secelean, N.A. Iterated function systems consisting of F-contractions. *Fixed Point Theory Appl.* **2013**, *2013*, 277. [CrossRef]
16. Stephen, T.; Rohen, Y.; Singh, M.K.; Devi, K.S. Some rational F-contractions in b-metric spaces and fixed points. *Nonlinear Funct. Anal. Appl.* **2022**, *27*, 309–322.
17. Wardowski, D.; Dung, N.V. Fixed points f-weak contractions on complete metric spaces. *Demonstr. Math.* **2014**, *1*, 146–155 [CrossRef]
18. Younis, M.; Mirkov, N.; Savić, A.; Pantović, M.; Radenović, S. Some critical remarks on recent results concerning F-contractions in b-metric spaces. *Cubo* **2023**, *25*, 57–66. [CrossRef]
19. Piri, H.; Kumam, P. Some fixed point theorems concerning F-contraction in complete metric spaces. *Fixed Point Theory Appl.* **2014**, *2014*, 210. [CrossRef]
20. Nazam, M.; Arshad, M.; Postolache, M. Coincidence and common fixed point theorems for four mappings satisfying (α_s, F)-contraction. *Nonlinear Anal. Model. Control* **2018**, *23*, 664–690. [CrossRef]
21. Younis, M.; Singh, D.; Radenović, S.; Imdad, M. Convergence Theorems for generalized contractions and applications. *Filomat* **2020**, *34*, 945–964. [CrossRef]
22. Younis, M.; Singh, D. On the existence of the solution of Hammerstein integral equations and fractional differential equations. *J. Appl. Math. Comp.* **2022**, *68*, 1087–1105. [CrossRef]
23. Abbas, M.; Ali, B.; Rizzo, O.; Vetro, C. Fuzzy fixed points of generalized F_2-Geraghty type fuzzy mappings and complementary results. *Nonlinear Anal. Model. Control* **2016**, *21*, 274–292. [CrossRef]
24. Abbas, M.; Ali, B.; Romaguera, S. Fixed and periodic points of generalized contractions in metric spaces. *Fixed Point Theory Appl.* **2013**, *2013*, 243. [CrossRef]
25. Fabiano, N.; Kadelburg, Z.; Mirkov, N.; Čavić, V.Š.; Radenović, S. On F-contractions: A Survey. *Contemp. Math.* **2022**, *3*, 327–342. [CrossRef]
26. Berinde, V.; Păcurar, M. The role of the Pompeiu-Hausdorff metric in fixed point theory. *Creat. Math. Inform.* **2013**, *22*, 142–150. [CrossRef]
27. Rudin, W. *Principles of Mathematical Analysis*; McGraw-Hill Book Company: New York, NY, USA; San Francisco, CA, USA; Toronto, ON, Canada; London, UK, 1964.
28. Cho, S.H.; Bae, J.S. Fixed points of weak α-contraction type maps. *Fixed Point Theory Appl.* **2014**, *2014*, 175. [CrossRef]
29. Bogin, J. A generalization of a fixed point theorem of Goebel, Kirk and Shimi. *Canad. Math. Bull.* **1976**, *19*, 7–12. [CrossRef]

30. Nadler, C.B. Multi-valued contraction mappings. *Pac. J. Math.* **1969**, *30*, 475–488. [CrossRef]
31. Işik, H.; Mohammadi, B.; Haddadi, M.R.; Parvaneh, V. On a new generalization of Banach contraction principle with application. *Mathematics* **2019**, *7*, 862. [CrossRef]
32. Michael, E.A. Continuous selections, I. *Ann. Math.* **1956**, *63*, 361–382. [CrossRef]

Disclaimer/Publisher's Note: The statements, opinions and data contained in all publications are solely those of the individual author(s) and contributor(s) and not of MDPI and/or the editor(s). MDPI and/or the editor(s) disclaim responsibility for any injury to people or property resulting from any ideas, methods, instructions or products referred to in the content.

Article

On the Monotonic and Asymptotic Properties of Positive Solutions to Third-Order Neutral Differential Equations and Their Effect on Oscillation Criteria

Amira Essam [1], Osama Moaaz [2,3,*], Moutaz Ramadan [1], Ghada AlNemer [4] and Ibrahim M. Hanafy [1]

[1] Department of Mathematics and Computer Science, Faculty of Science, Port Said University, Port Said 42511, Egypt; amira.essam@sci.psu.edu.eg (A.E.); motaz_ramadan@sci.psu.edu.eg (M.R.); ihanafy@hotmail.com (I.M.H.)

[2] Department of Mathematics, College of Science, Qassim University, P.O. Box 6644, Buraydah 51452, Saudi Arabia

[3] Department of Mathematics, Faculty of Science, Mansoura University, Mansoura 35516, Egypt

[4] Department of Mathematical Science, College of Science, Princess Nourah bint Abdulrahman University, P.O. Box 105862, Riyadh 11564, Saudi Arabia; gnnemer@pnu.edu.sa

* Correspondence: o_moaaz@mans.edu.eg

Abstract: The monotonic properties of positive solutions to functional differential equations of the third order are examined in this paper. It is generally known that by optimizing the relationships between a solution and its corresponding function, as well as its derivatives, one can improve the oscillation criterion for neutral differential equations. Based on this, we obtain new relationships and inequalities and test their effect on the oscillation parameters of the studied equation. To obtain the oscillation parameters, we used Riccati techniques and comparison with lower-order equations. Finally, the progress achieved in oscillation theory for third-order equations was measured by comparing our results with previous relevant results.

Keywords: functional differential equations; third-order; monotonic properties of the positive solutions; canonical case

MSC: 34C10; 34K11

1. Introduction

Third-order differential equations are used in many models, such as the model for studying blood entry flows into a "stenosed artery", an artery partially or totally occluded due to the thickening of the arterial wall [1]. In addition, in nuclear reactor kinetics [2], by constructing phase space solutions to third-order systems of equations and considering the solutions to the equations as explicit functions of the independent variable, which enables computer-aided phase space analysis, to perform a comprehensive and expeditious study of the system behavior for any combination of parameter values of interest. Although third-order differential equations have appeared in many models of life, they have received less attention from researchers of first- and second-order differential equations. This lethargy is due to the fact that this type of equation has a greater number of positive solution classifications than equations of the first and second order, which further complicates its study. In addition, its characteristic equation must contain a solution or solutions belonging to the set of real numbers [3].

On the other hand, functional differential equations (FDEs) are one of the classes of differential equations in which oscillatory behavior is common. The study of FDEs has attracted the attention of many researchers recently, in terms of the qualitative behavior of the solutions as well as the numerical solutions of these equations, see [4–8]. This type of equation deals with the after-effects of life phenomena, which means the presence of deviating arguments that express the previous and current times of a phenomenon, and it is known that these arguments increase the possibility of the existence of oscillatory solutions. The retarded functional differential equation, or the delay differential equation (DDE) is one of the basic subclasses of functional differential equations. This type is based on past and current values of the time derivatives, which leads to more accurate and effective future predictions. The deviating arguments, in this case, are called delays or time lags, see [9,10]. When the highest order derivative appears with and without delay, it creates another subclass of functional differential equations known as neutral delay differential equations (NDDEs). This subclass has a wide scope for modeling, as we find many models of chemistry, electricity, mechanics, and economics represented by NDDEs; see [11–13], where the study of the asymptotic and monotonic properties, together with the oscillatory behavior, of solutions to the third-order neutral delay differential equations was used to model many life phenomena.

The study of the oscillatory behavior of differential equations has received great and continuous attention from researchers. Philos [14] and Santra et al. [15,16] were interested in first-order differential equations. While, the works in [17–22] were concerned with even- and odd-order differential equations, with their various classifications. By reviewing the previous literature, we can note that it included three basic steps in the conclusion of oscillation criteria, regardless of the quality. These essential points can be summed up by first classifying all positive solutions to the studied equation and then developing a new or updated method to obtain improved relations and inequalities linking the solution, its derivatives, and its corresponding function; lastly, excluding the positive solutions using these improved relations and the chosen technique.

Therefore, this paper aimed to study and improve the monotonic properties of positive solutions and then use them to develop new oscillation criteria for the half-linear third-order neutral delay differential equation

$$\left(r(s)\left(z''(s)\right)^{\alpha}\right)' + q(s)x^{\alpha}(\sigma(s)) = 0, \tag{1}$$

for all $s \geq s_0$, where $z(s)$ stands for the corresponding function

$$z(s) = x(s) + p(s)x(\tau(s)). \tag{2}$$

We assume the following assumptions hold:

(A_1) α is a quotient of two odd positive integers;
(A_2) $r(s) \in C^1([s_0, \infty), (0, \infty))$ and satisfies

$$R(a,b) = \int_a^b \frac{1}{r^{1/\alpha}(v)} dv,$$

with $R(s_0, \infty) = \infty$;
(A_3) $q(s) \in C([s_0, \infty), \mathbb{R}^+)$ and does not eventually vanish;
(A_4) $p(s) \in C([s_0, \infty), \mathbb{R}^+)$ and there exists a constant p_0 such that $p_0 \geq p$;
(A_5) $\tau(s), \sigma(s) \in C^1([s_0, \infty), \mathbb{R})$ symbolize the delayed functions, where $\tau(s) \leq s$, $\sigma(s) \leq s$, and $\lim_{s \to \infty} \tau(s) = \lim_{s \to \infty} \sigma(s) = \infty$.

Definition 1. *A solution to (1) is defined as a function $x \in C([s_0, \infty), \mathbb{R})$, which has the properties $z \in C^2([s_0, \infty), \mathbb{R})$ and $r(z'')^{\alpha} \in C^1([s_0, \infty), \mathbb{R})$ and satisfies (1) on $[s_0, \infty)$.*

Our interest is directed to the solutions of (1) that satisfy the condition

$$\sup\{|x(s)| : s \geq s_*\} > 0,$$

for all $s_* \geq s_0$.

Definition 2. *A nontrivial solution to (1) is said to be oscillatory if it has arbitrarily large zeros, and otherwise it is called non-oscillatory.*

Definition 3. *Equation (1) is said to be oscillatory if all its solutions are oscillatory. Otherwise, it is called non-oscillatory.*

Remark 1. *The term half-linear equation refers to the fact that the solution space of (1) has just one half of the properties that characterize linearity, namely homogeneity (but not additivity).*

Finding solutions to differential equations is a rich research topic that has attracted great interest from researchers in the past decades, and this remains so to this day. This is because it was and still is one of the most significant tools used to describe and deduce the ways in which quantities change in systems, as well as to shed light on how and why these changes occur. However, the problem occurs when nonlinear differential equations are used to describe systems, because most of these equations are difficult to solve in a closed form. Therefore, researchers resort to using the qualitative theory of differential equations, where a topological description of the local and global properties of the solutions to these equations is developed, regardless of finding their exact form. Oscillation theory is one of these subfields of qualitative theory and is concerned with analyzing the oscillatory and non-oscillatory behavior of solutions to differential equations. For more information about oscillation theory, please see the monographs in [23,24] and the papers in [25,26].

However, the stage of classifying differential equation solutions is the first and most important step, which precedes the study of the asymptotic and monotonic properties of positive solutions, which in turn paves the way for determining the behavior of the oscillatory equation. The positive solutions to Equation (1) can be classified into four possible classes. However, under the condition (A_2), these classifications are reduced to two, since the probabilities that the $z''(s)$ derivative of solutions are negative are rejected. In light of this, we can conclude that the positive solutions to Equation (1) follow one of the following classes:

C_1: $z > 0$, $z' > 0$, $z'' > 0$, and $z''' < 0$;
C_2: $z > 0$, $z' < 0$, $z'' > 0$, and $z''' < 0$.

Studying the properties of solutions to third-order differential equations has many different applications. In addition to scientific applications, this study often contains many open and complex analytical problems and issues. Due to these relative difficulties, the previous works related to Equation (1) are few and appeared over long periods of time. The first study of the oscillation of third-order differential equations was in 1961 by Hanah [27]. She considered the linear case of (1) with $r(s) \equiv 1$, $p(s) \equiv 0$, and $\alpha \equiv 1$, and established the following very famous sufficient criterion of oscillation:

$$\liminf_{s \to \infty} s^3 q(s) > \frac{2}{3\sqrt{3}}. \tag{3}$$

Following that, authors were interested in studying the oscillatory behavior and the properties of solutions to (1), but in the case of $p(s) \equiv 0$; that is, in the case that the highest derivative appears with only a delay argument. For more details, one can see the works of Grace et al. [28] and Candan and Dahiya [29]. Li et al. [30] and Dzurina et al. [31], studied the half-linear type for α states for a quotient of two odd positive integers. Meanwhile, Qaraad et al. [32] considered the mixed type, in which the equation contains both delayed and advanced functions. On the other hand, Bohner et al. [33] obtained oscillation results for damped third-order differential equations. Chatzarakis et al. were interested in the Emden–Flower and quasi-linear type in [34] and [35], respectively, while Grace et al. [36] investigated oscillation criteria for the superlinear type.

In 2010, Li et al. [37] extended the results given in [27] by considering the neutral delay type, where $p(s) \in C([s_0, \infty), \mathbb{R}^+)$, and relied on comparison theorem to confirm that the following differential equation

$$(x(s) - p(s)x(\tau(s)))''' + q(s)x(\sigma(s)) = 0,$$

is oscillatory or tends to zero if

$$\lim_{s \to \infty} \int_{s_0}^{s} \left(\sigma^2(v)q(v) - \frac{2}{3\sqrt{3}v} \right) dv = \infty.$$

In the same year, Baculikova and Dzurina [38], used another methodology based on the Riccati technique, where for $\ell \in (0,1)$ and s_ℓ that are large enough, then every solution of the half-linear NDDE (1) oscillates or tends to zero if

$$\liminf_{s \to \infty} \frac{s^\alpha}{r(s)} \int_s^\infty \ell^\alpha (1-p(v))^\alpha q(v) \left(\frac{\sigma(v)}{v} \right)^\alpha \left(\frac{\sigma(v) - v_\ell}{2} \right)^\alpha dv > \frac{\alpha^\alpha}{(\alpha+1)^{\alpha+1}}, \quad (4)$$

under the assumption that $r'(s) \geq 0$ and

$$\int_{s_0}^{\infty} \int_v^{\infty} \left[\frac{1}{r(u)} \int_u^{\infty} q(\mu) d\mu \right]^{1/\alpha} du\, dv = \infty$$

holds. Furthermore, they presented a simplified condition for (4), see Corollary 1 in [38], as follows:

$$\liminf_{s \to \infty} \frac{s^\alpha}{r(s)} \int_s^\infty q(v) \frac{\sigma^{2\alpha}(v)}{v^\alpha} dv > \frac{(2\alpha)^\alpha}{(\alpha+1)^{\alpha+1}(1-p_0)^\alpha}. \quad (5)$$

In 2011, Li and Thandapani [39], used the same technique, but by obtaining improved properties of the solutions, they were able to set the condition

$$\limsup_{s \to \infty} \int_{s_2}^{s} \left[\delta(v) \frac{q(v)}{2\alpha - 1} - \frac{1 + \frac{p_0^\alpha}{\tau_0}}{(\alpha+1)^{\alpha+1}} \left(\frac{(\delta'(v)_+)^{\alpha+1}}{(\delta(v)R(\sigma(v), s_1)\sigma'(v))^\alpha} \right) \right] dv = \infty, \quad s_2 \geq s, \quad (6)$$

where $\alpha \geq 1$, $\sigma'(s) > 0$, $\sigma(s) \leq \tau(s)$, $\delta(s) \in C^1([s_0, \infty), (0, \infty))$, and

$$\delta'(s)_+ = \max\{0, \delta'(s)\}.$$

This criterion is considered simpler and more effective and does not assume the previous conditions, to ensure that every solution of (1) is either oscillatory or converges to zero ($C_1 = \emptyset$). Later, Grace et al. [40], extended the previous condition under the same assumptions and $\alpha \geq 2$ to

$$\limsup_{s \to \infty} \int_{s_2}^{s} \left[\delta(v)q(v)(p_*(\sigma(v)))^\alpha \left(\frac{\tau^{-1}((\sigma(v)))}{v} \right)^{2\alpha} - \delta'_+(v) \left(\frac{8}{v^2} \right)^\alpha \right] dv = \infty, \quad (7)$$

where

$$p_*(s) = \frac{1}{p(\tau^{-1}(s))} \left(1 - \frac{1}{p(\tau^{-1}(\tau^{-1}(s)))} \cdot \frac{m(\tau^{-1}(\tau^{-1}(s)))}{m(\tau^{-1}(s))} \right)$$

and $m(s) = s^2$, $m(s) = s^3$, $m(s) = e^s$, or $m(s) = s^\alpha e^{es}$.

On the other hand, Dzurina et al. [41] proved that case C_2 does not happen if

$$\liminf_{s \to \infty} \int_{\tau^{-1}(\omega(s))}^{s} q^*(v) \left(\int_{\sigma(v)}^{\rho(v)} \int_u^{\rho(v)} \frac{1}{r(\mu)} d\mu\, du \right) dv > \frac{\tau_0 + p_0}{\tau_0 e},$$

where $q^*(s) = \min\{q(s), q(\tau(s))\}$ and $\omega \in ([s_0, \infty), \mathbb{R})$ is a positive function that satisfies $\tau(s) > \omega(s) > \sigma(s)$. Moaaz et al. [42,43] presented several interesting results on the oscillation of solutions to odd-order delay differential equations. Very recently, Moaaz et al. [44] developed new criteria for the nonexistence of class C_2 of (1), under the condition

$$\liminf_{s \to \infty} \int_{\tau^{-1}(\varpi(s))}^{s} q^*(\nu) \Psi_n^\alpha(\varpi(\nu), \sigma(\nu)) d\nu > \frac{\tau_0 + p_0^\alpha}{\delta \tau_0 e},$$

where $\varpi(s) \leq \tau(\varpi(s))$ and

$$\Psi_{n+1}^\alpha(h,k) = \int_h^k \int_u^k \frac{1}{r(\mu)} \exp\left[\frac{\delta \tau_0}{\tau_0 + p_0^\alpha} \int_{\tau^{-1}(\mu)}^k q^*(\nu) \Psi_n^\alpha(\varpi(\nu), \sigma(\nu)) d\nu \right] d\mu \, du.$$

In this paper, we will derive some new monotonic properties and use them as in application for

1. Improving the relationships between the solution and its derivatives;
2. Improving the relationships between the solution and its corresponding function;
3. Obtaining improved criteria that ensure that there are no positive solutions;
4. Obtaining oscillation criteria that improve on the criteria mentioned in the previous literature.

Comparing these criteria mentioned in earlier works with our results revealed that our results improved them and provided a broader and greater scope of applicability. The following is a focused summary of what makes the results of this paper distinctive:

1. The criteria require fewer assumptions about the coefficients and the auxiliary functions than their predecessors, which reduces the complexities when applying them;
2. The half-linear property (exponent α of the first and second derivatives) allows for a larger area when determining where the same results can be applied to the linear ($\alpha = 1$) and ordinary ($\tau(s) = \sigma(s) = 1$) type;
3. Our results consider two cases of the constant p_0; i.e., for $p_0 > 1$ and $p_0 < 1$.

The paper structure is divided into five basic sections. The first section is divided into two introductory parts. In the first part, we give introductions to the important points of the study, define the equation under our interest, and establish the major assumptions that have been applied to all of our results. It also contains a summary chronology of the most important previous works related to the studied equation, which we will use to compare our results later. In Sections 2 and 3, we study the monotonicity properties of the positive solutions to (1) and improve these properties, in addition to giving criteria to ensure that there are no positive solutions for both class C_1 and C_2. Section 4 relies on the previous criteria to derive theorems that ensure the oscillation of all solutions of (1). In the last section, a summary of the paper's content is given, in terms of the basic theorems and results, as well as an explanation of the most important points that distinguish our results.

Remark 2. *All functional inequalities are assumed to hold for all sufficiently large s in following sections.*

2. Improved Monotonic Properties

In this section, we study and improve the monotonic properties of positive solutions to (1), which we will rely on later to obtain our basic results. First, let us introduce some auxiliary lemmas to facilitate the study of the properties of later solutions.

Lemma 1 ([45]). *Assume that x is a positive real variable, and*

$$F(x) = b_1 x - b_2 x^{\frac{\alpha+1}{\alpha}},$$

where b_i are constants, $i = 1, 2$, $b_2 > 0$, and α defined as in (A_1). Then the following properties hold:

(P_1) *F has a maximum value at $x^* = \left(\frac{b_1 \alpha}{b_2(\alpha+1)}\right)^\alpha$;*

(P2) $F(x^*) = \max\limits_{x \in \mathbb{R}}(F) = \frac{\alpha^\alpha}{(\alpha+1)^{\alpha+1}} b_1^{\alpha+1} b_2^{-\alpha};$

(P3) $b_1 x - b_2 x^{\frac{\alpha+1}{\alpha}} \leq \frac{\alpha^\alpha}{(\alpha+1)^{\alpha+1}} b_1^{\alpha+1} b_2^{-\alpha}.$

The following lemma considers an improvement of the known relationship between variables x and z

$$x(s) \geq (1 - p(s))z(s), \tag{8}$$

introduced by Moaaz et al. [46]. Based on this lemma, we can obtain results that are superior to those obtained by employing (8).

Lemma 2. *Assume that x is a positive solution of (1). Then*

$$x(s) > \sum_{\ell=0}^{k} \left(\prod_{m=0}^{2\ell} p\left(\tau^{[m]}(s)\right) \right) \left[\frac{z\left(\tau^{[2\ell]}(s)\right)}{p\left(\tau^{[2\ell]}(s)\right)} - z\left(\tau^{[2\ell+1]}(s)\right) \right], \tag{9}$$

eventually holds for any nonnegative integer k.

2.1. Properties for Solutions to Class C_1

This subsection concerns studying the monotonic properties of the positive solutions of (1) that belong to Class C_1. To simplify the basic lemmas and main results, let us define the following notations for sufficiently large s, and j stands for any nonnegative integer, then $\tau^{[0]}(s) := s$,

$$\tau^{[j]}(s) = \tau\left(\tau^{[j-1]}(s)\right), \tag{10}$$

and

$$\tau^{[-j]}(s) = \tau^{-1}\left(\tau^{[-j+1]}(s)\right). \tag{11}$$

Moreover,

$$\eta(s) := \int_{s_0}^{s} R(s_0, \nu) d\nu, \tag{12}$$

and

$$\Phi_k(s) := \begin{cases} 1 & \text{for } p_0 = 0; \\ \sum_{\ell=0}^{k} \left(\prod_{m=0}^{2\ell} p\left(\tau^{[m]}(s)\right) \right) \left[\frac{1}{p\left(\tau^{[2\ell]}(s)\right)} - 1 \right] \frac{\eta\left(\tau^{[2\ell]}(s)\right)}{\eta(s)} & \text{for } p_0 < 1; \\ \sum_{\ell=1}^{k} \left(\prod_{m=1}^{2\ell-1} \frac{1}{p\left(\tau^{[-m]}(s)\right)} \right) \left[1 - \frac{1}{p\left(\tau^{[-2\ell]}(s)\right)} \right] \frac{\eta\left(\tau^{-2\ell}(s)\right)}{\eta\left(\tau^{[-2\ell+1]}(s)\right)} & \text{for } p_0 > \frac{\eta(s)}{\eta(\tau)}, \end{cases} \tag{13}$$

for any nonnegative integers ℓ, m, and k. Additionally, let's also define some notations that we will use for the improved lemmas in this section. So, let

$$\lambda_n(s) := R(s_0, s) + \int_{s_0}^{s} R(s_0, \nu) \rho_n(\nu) \eta(\sigma(\nu)) d\nu \tag{14}$$

where

$$\rho_n(s) = \frac{1}{\alpha} \eta^{\alpha-1}(\sigma(s)) \tilde{\Phi}_{k,n}^\alpha(\sigma(s)) q(s), \tag{15}$$

and $\tilde{\Phi}_{k,n}(s)$ is an improved coefficient, to be specified later. In addition, let

$$\tilde{\lambda}_n(s) = \int_{s_0}^{s} \lambda_n(\nu) d\nu, \tag{16}$$

$$\tilde{R}_n(s) := \exp\left[\int_{s_0}^{s} \frac{d\nu}{\lambda_n(\nu) r^{1/\alpha}(\nu)} \right], \tag{17}$$

and
$$\tilde{\eta}_{n+1}(s) := \int_{s_0}^{s} \tilde{R}_n(v)dv \qquad (18)$$

for any nonnegative integer n.

Lemma 3. *Assume that $x \in C_1$, then the following properties hold, for sufficiently large s,*

(P$_4$) $(z'(s)/R(s_0,s))' \leq 0$;
(P$_5$) $(z(s)/\eta(s))' \leq 0$.

Proof. Assume that $x \in C_{1''}$, then from the nature of $r(s)(z''(s))^\alpha$, which is an eventually positive non-increasing function, we obtain

$$z'(s) \geq \int_{s_0}^{s} \frac{r^{1/\alpha}(v)z''(v)}{r^{1/\alpha}(v)}dv \geq r^{1/\alpha}(s)z''(s)\int_{s_0}^{s}\frac{1}{r^{1/\alpha}(v)}dv = r^{1/\alpha}(s)z''(s)R(s_0,s). \qquad (19)$$

But
$$\left(\frac{z'(s)}{R(s_0,s)}\right)' = \frac{R(s_0,s)z''(s) - z'(s)r^{-1/\alpha}(s)}{R^2(s_0,s)}$$
$$= \frac{r^{-1/\alpha}(s)}{R^2(s_0,s)}\left[r^{1/\alpha}(s)z''(s)R(s_0,s) - z'(s)\right] \leq 0.$$

So, (P$_4$)-part holds.

Similarly, we prove (P$_5$)-part but through the increasing monotonicity of $z'(s)$, where

$$z(s) \geq \int_{s_0}^{s}\frac{z'(v)}{R(s_0,v)}R(s_0,v)dv \geq \frac{z'(s)}{R(s_0,s)}\int_{s_0}^{s}R(s_0,v)dv = \frac{z'(s)}{R(s_0,s)}\eta(s),$$

which shows that
$$\left(\frac{z(s)}{\eta(s)}\right)' = \frac{R(s_0,s)}{\eta^2(s)}\left[\frac{z'(s)}{R(s_0,s)}\eta(s) - z(s)\right]$$
$$\leq 0.$$

and this completes the proof. □

Lemma 4. *Assume that $x \in C_1$. Then, for sufficiently large s,*

(P$_6$) $x(s) > \Phi_k(s)z(s)$;
(P$_7$) $(r(s)(z''(s))^\alpha)' + q(s)(\Phi_k(\sigma(s))z(\sigma(s)))^\alpha \leq 0$.

Proof. Assume that $x \in C_1$. We can see from the definition of Φ_k in (13) that its value depends on the value of p_0, where p_0 has three possible cases.
In the first case, where $p_0 = 0$, the proof is obvious, so we omit it.
Case two: for $p_0 < 1$, it is obvious from (10) and (A$_5$) that

$$s \geq \tau^{[2\ell]}(s) \geq \tau^{[2\ell+1]}(s).$$

Since $z(s)$ is a positive increasing function, then

$$z\left(\tau^{[2\ell]}(s)\right) \geq z\left(\tau^{[2\ell+1]}(s)\right),$$

but from (P$_5$)-part of Lemma 3 we have that

$$z\left(\tau^{[2\ell]}(s)\right) \geq \frac{\eta\left(\tau^{[2\ell]}(s)\right)}{\eta(s)}z(s),$$

for ℓ any nonnegative integer. Substituting (9) into Lemma 2, yields

$$x(s) > \sum_{\ell=0}^{k}\left(\prod_{m=0}^{2\ell} p\left(\tau^{[m]}(s)\right)\right)\left[\frac{1}{p(\tau^{[2\ell]}(s))} - 1\right] z\left(\tau^{[2\ell]}(s)\right)$$

$$> \sum_{\ell=0}^{k}\left(\prod_{m=0}^{2\ell} p\left(\tau^{[m]}(s)\right)\right)\left[\frac{1}{p(\tau^{[2\ell]}(s))} - 1\right] \frac{\eta\left(\tau^{[2\ell]}(s)\right)}{\eta(s)} z(s),$$

which in turn with (1), verifies (P_7).

Now, for $p_0 > 1$ case. It is obvious from the definition of the corresponding function in (2) that

$$z\left(\tau^{-1}(s)\right) = x\left(\tau^{-1}(s)\right) + p\left(\tau^{-1}(s)\right) x(s)$$

$$= \left[\frac{z\left(\tau^{[-2]}(s)\right) - x\left(\tau^{[-2]}(s)\right)}{p(\tau^{[-2]}(s))}\right] + p\left(\tau^{-1}(s)\right) x(s)$$

$$= \prod_{m=2}^{2} \frac{z\left(\tau^{[-2]}(s)\right)}{p(\tau^{[-m]}(s))} - \prod_{m=2}^{3} \frac{\left[z\left(\tau^{[-3]}(s)\right) - x\left(\tau^{[-3]}(s)\right)\right]}{p(\tau^{[-m]}(s))} + p\left(\tau^{-1}(s)\right) x(s).$$

Substituting (9) into Lemma 2, we obtain

$$x(s) > \sum_{\ell=1}^{k}\left(\prod_{m=1}^{2\ell-1} \frac{1}{p(\tau^{[-m]}(s))}\right)\left[z\left(\tau^{[-2\ell+1]}(s)\right) - \frac{1}{p(\tau^{[-2\ell]}(s))} z\left(\tau^{[-2\ell]}(s)\right)\right]. \quad (20)$$

Now, again from (11) and (A_5), we have

$$\tau^{[-2\ell]}(s) \geq \tau^{[-2\ell+1]}(s) \geq s,$$

using the above inequality in the (P_5)-part of Lemma 3 and the monotonicity of $z(s)$ yields

$$\frac{\eta\left(\tau^{[-2\ell]}(s)\right)}{\eta\left(\tau^{[-2\ell+1]}(s)\right)} z\left(\tau^{[-2\ell+1]}(s)\right) \geq z\left(\tau^{[-2\ell]}(s)\right),$$

and

$$z\left(\tau^{[-2\ell+1]}(s)\right) \geq z(s).$$

As a result, inequality (20) turns into

$$x(s) > z(s) \sum_{\ell=1}^{k}\left(\prod_{m=1}^{2\ell-1} \frac{1}{p(\tau^{[-m]}(s))}\right)\left[1 - \frac{1}{p(\tau^{[-2\ell]}(s))} \frac{\eta\left(\tau^{[-2\ell]}(s)\right)}{\eta\left(\tau^{[-2\ell+1]}(s)\right)}\right],$$

which, when combined with (1), yields (P_7). And this completes the proof. □

Remark 3. *By choosing $k = 0$, then (P_6) reduces to obtain the well known classical relation (8) for $p_0 < 1$.*

Lemma 5. *Assume that $x \in C_1$ and $\alpha \geq 1$. Then,*

$$\left(r^{1/\alpha}(s) z''(s)\right)' + \rho(s) z(\sigma(s)) \leq 0, \quad (21)$$

where

$$\rho(s) = \frac{1}{\alpha} \eta^{\alpha-1}(\sigma(s)) \Phi_k^\alpha(\sigma(s)) q(s),$$

holds eventually.

Proof. Assume that $x \in C_1$. Since

$$\left(r(s)(z''(s))^\alpha\right)' = \left(\left(r^{1/\alpha}(s)(z''(s))\right)^\alpha\right)' \qquad (22)$$
$$= \alpha\left(r^{1/\alpha}(s)z''(s)\right)^{\alpha-1}\left(r^{1/\alpha}(s)z''(s)\right)'.$$

From the (P_4) and (P_5) parts of Lemma 3, we have

$$r^{1/\alpha}(s)z''(s) \leq \frac{z'(s)}{R(s_0,s)} \leq \frac{z(s)}{\eta(s)}$$

and so

$$r^{1/\alpha}(\sigma(s))z''(\sigma(s)) \leq \frac{z(\sigma(s))}{\eta(\sigma(s))}.$$

The monotonicity of $r^{1/\alpha}(s)z''(s)$ implies

$$r^{1/\alpha}(s)z''(s) \leq r^{1/\alpha}(\sigma(s))z''(\sigma(s)),$$

then

$$r^{1/\alpha}(s)z''(s) \leq r^{1/\alpha}(\sigma(s))z''(\sigma(s)) \leq \frac{z(\sigma(s))}{\eta(\sigma(s))}.$$

By taking power $\alpha - 1$ for both sided, we obtain

$$\left(r^{1/\alpha}(s)z''(s)\right)^{\alpha-1} \leq \left(\frac{1}{\eta(\sigma(s))}\right)^{\alpha-1} z^{\alpha-1}(\sigma(s)).$$

Substituting from the last inequality into (22)

$$\left(r(s)(z''(s))^\alpha\right)' \geq \alpha\left(\frac{1}{\eta(\sigma(s))}\right)^{\alpha-1} z^{\alpha-1}(\sigma(s))\left(r^{1/\alpha}(s)(z''(s))\right)',$$

and once again substituting from the last inequality into (1), we obtain

$$-q(s)x^\alpha(\sigma(s)) = \left(r(s)(z''(s))^\alpha\right)'$$
$$\geq \alpha\left(\frac{1}{\eta(\sigma(s))}\right)^{\alpha-1} z^{\alpha-1}(\sigma(s))\left(r^{1/\alpha}(s)(z''(s))\right)'.$$

But from (A_4) and (P_6), we obtain

$$-x^\alpha(\sigma(s)) \leq -\Phi_k^\alpha(\sigma(s))z^\alpha(\sigma(s)),$$

and the monotonicity of $z(s)$ implies that

$$-\Phi_k^\alpha(\sigma(s))q(s)z^\alpha(\sigma(s)) \geq -q(s)x^\alpha(\sigma(s))$$
$$\geq \alpha\left(\frac{1}{\eta(\sigma(s))}\right)^{\alpha-1} z^{\alpha-1}(\sigma(s))\left(r^{1/\alpha}(s)(z''(s))\right)'.$$

i.e.,

$$\left(r^{1/\alpha}(s)(z''(s))\right)' + \frac{1}{\alpha}\Phi_k^\alpha(\sigma(s))q(s)(\eta(\sigma(s)))^{\alpha-1}z(\sigma(s)) \leq 0.$$

which gives (21). And this completes the proof. □

Remark 4. *The functions $\rho(s)$, $\rho_0(s)$ defined in Lemma 5 and (15) are equivalent, i.e., $\rho(s) = \rho_0(s)$.*

In the following lemma, we use the definition of functional sequences given in (14), (17) and (18) to obtain improved monotonic properties of class C_1 solutions.

Lemma 6. *Assume that $x \in C_1$ and $\alpha \geq 1$. Then, the following improved properties hold for a sufficiently large s and n any positive integer:*

(P_8) $\left(z'(s)/\tilde{R}_{n-1}(s)\right)' \leq 0;$
(P_9) $\left(z(s)/\tilde{\eta}_n(s)\right)' \leq 0;$
(P_{10}) $\left(r(s)(z''(s))^\alpha\right)' + q(s)(\tilde{\Phi}_{k,n}(\sigma(s))z(\sigma(s)))^\alpha \leq 0,$
where

$$\tilde{\Phi}_{k,n}(s) := \begin{cases} 1 & \text{for } p_0 = 0; \\ \sum_{\ell=0}^{k}\left(\prod_{m=0}^{2\ell} p\left(\tau^{[m]}(s)\right)\right)\left[\frac{1}{p(\tau^{[2\ell]}(s))} - 1\right]\frac{\tilde{\eta}_n(\tau^{[2\ell]}(s))}{\tilde{\eta}_n(s)} & \text{for } p_0 < 1; \\ \sum_{\ell=1}^{k}\left(\prod_{m=1}^{2\ell-1}\frac{1}{p(\tau^{[-m]}(s))}\right)\left[1 - \frac{1}{p(\tau^{[-2\ell]}(s))}\frac{\tilde{\eta}_n(\tau^{-2\ell}(s))}{\tilde{\eta}_n(\tau^{[-2\ell+1]}(s))}\right] & \text{for } p_0 > \frac{\eta(s)}{\eta(\tau)}. \end{cases} \quad (23)$$

and $\tilde{\Phi}_{k,0}(s) = \Phi_k(s).$

Proof. Assume that $x \in C_1$. Define the function $G(s)$, where
$$G(s) = -z'(s) + R(s_0,s)r^{1/\alpha}(s)z''(s).$$

Then, it is obvious that

$$\begin{aligned} G'(s) &= -z''(s) + R(s_0,s)r^{1/\alpha}(s)z'''(s) + R(s_0,s)\left(r^{1/\alpha}(s)\right)'z''(s) + r^{-1/\alpha}(s)r^{1/\alpha}(s)z''(s) \\ &= R(s_0,s)r^{1/\alpha}(s)z'''(s) + R(s_0,s)\left(r^{1/\alpha}(s)\right)'z''(s) \\ &= R(s_0,s)\left(r^{1/\alpha}(s)z''(s)\right)'. \end{aligned}$$

From (21), we obtain
$$\left(r^{1/\alpha}(s)z''(s)\right)' \leq -\rho(s)z(\sigma(s)),$$

and so
$$G'(s) \leq -R(s_0,s)\rho(s)z(\sigma(s)).$$

Integrating the last inequality from s_0 to s, then
$$z'(s) \geq R(s_0,s)r^{1/\alpha}(s)z''(s) + \int_{s_0}^{s} R(s_0,v)\rho(v)z(\sigma(v))\,\mathrm{d}v. \quad (24)$$

Again, by integrating (19) from s_0 to s and using (12), we obtain
$$\begin{aligned} z(s) &\geq \int_{s_0}^{s} r^{1/\alpha}(v)z''(v)R(s_0,v)\,\mathrm{d}v \\ &\geq r^{1/\alpha}(s)z''(s)\int_{s_0}^{s} R(s_0,v)\,\mathrm{d}v \\ &= r^{1/\alpha}(s)z''(s)\eta(s). \end{aligned}$$

But the non-increasing monotonicity of $r^{1/\alpha}(s)z''(s)$ implies
$$z(\sigma(s)) \geq r^{1/\alpha}(s)z''(s)\eta(\sigma(s)). \quad (25)$$

Substituting from (25) into (24), we obtain

$$z'(s) \geq R(s_0,s)r^{1/\alpha}(s)z''(s) + \int_{s_0}^{s} R(s_0,v)\rho(v)r^{1/\alpha}(v)z''(v)\eta(\sigma(v))dv \qquad (26)$$

$$\geq R(s_0,s)r^{1/\alpha}(s)z''(s) + r^{1/\alpha}(s)z''(s)\int_{s_0}^{s} R(s_0,v)\rho(v)\eta(\sigma(v))dv$$

$$= r^{1/\alpha}(s)z''(s)\left[R(s_0,s) + \int_{s_0}^{s} R(s_0,v)\rho(v)\eta(\sigma(v))dv\right]$$

$$= \lambda_0(s)r^{1/\alpha}(s)z''(s).$$

Now, by multiplying the last inequality by $\tilde{R}_0^{-1}(s)$, then

$$\frac{\tilde{R}_0^{-1}(s)}{\lambda_0(s)r^{1/\alpha}(s)}z'(s) \geq \tilde{R}_0^{-1}(s)z''(s). \qquad (27)$$

From (17), it is clear that

$$\tilde{R}_0'(s) = \frac{\tilde{R}_0(s)}{\lambda_0(s)r^{1/\alpha}(s)}.$$

So,

$$\left(\frac{z'(s)}{\tilde{R}_0(s)}\right)' = \frac{\tilde{R}_0(s)z''(s) - \frac{\tilde{R}_0(s)}{\lambda_0(s)r^{1/\alpha}(s)}z'(s)}{\tilde{R}_0^2(s)}$$

$$= \frac{1}{\lambda_0(s)r^{1/\alpha}(s)\tilde{R}_0(s)}\left[\lambda_0(s)r^{1/\alpha}(s)z''(s) - z'(s)\right].$$

which, in view of (27), implies (P_8); i.e.,

$$\frac{z'(s)}{\tilde{R}_0(s)} \text{ is decreasing.}$$

The monotonicity of $z'(s)$ gives

$$z(s) \geq \int_{s_0}^{s} \frac{z'(v)}{\tilde{R}_0(v)}\tilde{R}_0(v)dv \geq \tilde{\eta}_1(s)\frac{z'(v)}{\tilde{R}_0(s)},$$

therefore,

$$\frac{z(s)}{\tilde{\eta}_1(s)} \text{ is also decreasing.}$$

Now, the (P_{10}) part is clearly proven using the last monotonicity and (23) into (9), which becomes

$$x(s) > \Phi_{k,1}(\sigma(s))z(s),$$

and as a result (1) implies (P_{10}) for $n = 1$, i.e.,

$$\left(r(s)(z''(s))^\alpha\right)' + q(s)(\Phi_{k,1}(\sigma(s))z(\sigma(s)))^\alpha \leq 0.$$

For $n = 2$, we obtain (P_{10}) by replacing (P_7) with the last inequality and concluding the proof using the same technique as before. For $n = 3, 4, \ldots$, we can similarly follow the same technique and complete the proof. □

2.2. Properties for Solutions of Class C_2

This subsection concerns the study of the monotonic properties of the positive solutions to (1) that belong to Class C_2. First, let us define auxiliary notations such as

$$\tilde{\eta}_0(h,k) := \int_h^k R(v,k)dv,$$

and

$$q^*(s) = \min\{q(s), q(\tau(s))\}.$$

Additionally, this section's proofs need to add another assumption to the basic ones (A_1)–(A_5) in the introduction section, in which

(A_6) $\tau(\sigma(s)) = \sigma(\tau(s))$ and $\tau'(s) \geq \tau_0 > 0$.

Lemma 7. *Assume that $x \in C_2$ and there exists ϖ a positive function $\varpi \in ([s_0, \infty), \mathbb{R})$ such that*
$$\tau(s) > \varpi(s) > \sigma(s).$$

Then, for $\tau^{-1}(h) \leq k$,

$$z(h) \geq \breve{\eta}_n(h,k) r^{1/\alpha}(k) z''(k), \quad n = 0, 1, \ldots, \tag{28}$$

where

$$\breve{\eta}_{n+1}(h,k) := \int_h^k \int_u^k \frac{1}{r^{1/\alpha}(\mu)} \exp \frac{1}{\alpha} \left[\frac{\tau_0}{\tau_0 + p_0} \int_{\tau^{-1}(\mu)}^k q^*(\nu) \breve{\eta}_n^\alpha(\sigma(\nu), \varpi(\nu)) d\nu \right] d\mu \, du. \tag{29}$$

Proof. Assume that $x \in C_2$. From the non-increasing monotonicity of $r^{1/\alpha}(s) z''(s)$, then

$$\begin{aligned}
-z'(h) &\geq \int_h^k \frac{r^{1/\alpha}(\nu) z''(\nu)}{r^{1/\alpha}(\nu)} d\nu \geq r^{1/\alpha}(k) z''(k) \int_h^k \frac{1}{r^{1/\alpha}(\nu)} d\nu \\
&= r^{1/\alpha}(k) z''(k) R(h,k),
\end{aligned}$$

where $h \leq k$. Integrating the last inequality again from h to k, we obtain

$$\begin{aligned}
z(h) &\geq r^{1/\alpha}(k) z''(k) \int_h^k R(\nu, k) d\nu \\
&= r^{1/\alpha}(k) z''(k) \breve{\eta}_0(h,k),
\end{aligned}$$

also for all $h \leq k$. Next, we employ the mathematical induction to prove the rest of the proof by assuming for every $n \in \mathbb{N}_0$ and sufficiently large s that

$$z(h) \geq \breve{\eta}_n(h,k) r^{1/\alpha}(k) z''(k). \tag{30}$$

In the following, we prove that (28) is valid for $n+1$. From (1) it is clear that

$$q(\tau(s)) x^\alpha(\sigma(\tau(s))) = -\frac{\left(r(\tau(s))(z''(\tau(s)))^\alpha\right)'}{\tau'(s)},$$

but (A_6) implies that

$$\begin{aligned}
p_0 q(\tau(s)) x^\alpha(\tau(\sigma(s))) &= p_0 q(\tau(s)) x^\alpha(\sigma(\tau(s))) \\
&= -\frac{p_0}{\tau'(s)} \left(r(\tau(s))(z''(\tau(s)))^\alpha\right)' \\
&\leq -\frac{p_0}{\tau_0} \left(r(\tau(s))(z''(\tau(s)))^\alpha\right)'.
\end{aligned}$$

By adding the above inequality to (1), we obtain

$$\begin{aligned}
q^*(s) z^\alpha(\sigma(s)) &\leq q(s) x^\alpha(\sigma(s)) + p_0 q(\tau(s)) x^\alpha(\tau(\sigma(s))) \tag{31} \\
&\leq -\left(r(s)(z''(s))^\alpha\right)' - \frac{p_0}{\tau_0} \left(r(\tau(s))(z''(\tau(s)))^\alpha\right)' \\
&= -\left(r(s)(z''(s))^\alpha + \frac{p_0}{\tau_0} r(\tau(s))(z''(\tau(s)))^\alpha\right)'.
\end{aligned}$$

Putting $h(s) = \sigma(s)$ and $k(s) = \varpi(s)$ in (30), yields

$$z^\alpha(\sigma(s)) \geq \breve{\eta}_n^\alpha(\sigma(s), \varpi(s)) r(\varpi(s)) (z''(\varpi(s)))^\alpha.$$

Substituting into (31), then

$$q^*(s)\breve{\eta}_n^\alpha(\sigma(s),\varpi(s))r(\varpi(s))(z''(\varpi(s)))^\alpha \leq -\left(r(s)(z''(s))^\alpha + \frac{p_0}{\tau_0}r(\tau(s))(z''(\tau(s)))^\alpha\right)'. \tag{32}$$

Now, let us define the auxiliary function

$$M(s) := r(s)(z''(s))^\alpha + \frac{p_0}{\tau_0}r(\tau(s))(z''(\tau(s)))^\alpha.$$

Using C_1 or C_2 and (A_5), we obtain

$$\left(\frac{\tau_0+p_0}{\tau_0}\right)r(s)(z''(s))^\alpha \leq M(s) \leq \left(\frac{\tau_0+p_0}{\tau_0}\right)r(\tau(s))(z''(\tau(s)))^\alpha, \tag{33}$$

and so

$$\left(\frac{\tau_0}{\tau_0+p_0}\right)M\left(\tau^{-1}(s)\right) \leq r(s)(z''(s))^\alpha.$$

Substituting into (32), we arrive at

$$\begin{aligned} M'(s) &\leq -q^*(s)\breve{\eta}_n^\alpha(\sigma(s),\varpi(s))r(\varpi(s))(z''(\varpi(s)))^\alpha \\ &\leq -\frac{\tau_0}{\tau_0+p_0}q^*(s)\breve{\eta}_n^\alpha(\sigma(s),\varpi(s))M\left(\tau^{-1}(\varpi(s))\right), \end{aligned} \tag{34}$$

which indicates that $M'(s) \leq 0$. So, we conclude that $M(s)$ is a non-increasing function. As a result, (34) becomes

$$M'(s) \leq -\frac{\tau_0}{\tau_0+p_0}q^*(s)\breve{\eta}_n^\alpha(\sigma(s),\varpi(s))M(s).$$

Integrating the last inequality again from h to k, we obtain

$$\ln\left(\frac{M(h)}{M(k)}\right) \geq \frac{\tau_0}{\tau_0+p_0}\int_h^k q^*(v)\breve{\eta}_n^\alpha(\sigma(v),\varpi(v))dv,$$

or

$$M(h) \geq M(k)\exp\left[\frac{\tau_0}{\tau_0+p_0}\int_h^k q^*(v)\breve{\eta}_n^\alpha(\sigma(v),\varpi(v))dv\right].$$

Using (33), we obtain

$$M\left(\tau^{-1}(h)\right) \geq \left(\frac{\tau_0+p_0}{\tau_0}\right)r(k)(z''(k))^\alpha \exp\left[\frac{\tau_0}{\tau_0+p_0}\int_{\tau^{-1}(h)}^k q^*(v)\breve{\eta}_n^\alpha(\sigma(v),\varpi(v))dv\right],$$

i.e.,

$$z''(h) \geq \frac{1}{r^{1/\alpha}(h)}r^{1/\alpha}(k)z''(k)\exp\frac{1}{\alpha}\left[\frac{\tau_0}{\tau_0+p_0}\int_{\tau^{-1}(h)}^k q^*(v)\breve{\eta}_n^\alpha(\sigma(v),\varpi(v))dv\right].$$

Integrating the last inequality from h to k, we have

$$-z'(h) \geq r^{1/\alpha}(k)z''(k)\int_h^k \frac{1}{r^{1/\alpha}(\mu)}\exp\frac{1}{\alpha}\left[\frac{\tau_0}{\tau_0+p_0}\int_{\tau^{-1}(\mu)}^k q^*(v)\breve{\eta}_n^\alpha(\sigma(v),\varpi(v))dv\right]d\mu,$$

once more, from h to k

$$\begin{aligned} z(h) &\geq r^{1/\alpha}(k)z''(k)\int_h^k\int_u^k \frac{1}{r^{1/\alpha}(\mu)}\exp\frac{1}{\alpha}\left[\frac{\tau_0}{\tau_0+p_0}\int_{\tau^{-1}(\mu)}^k q^*(v)\breve{\eta}_n^\alpha(\sigma(v),\varpi(v))dv\right]d\mu\,du \\ &= r^{1/\alpha}(k)z''(k)\breve{\eta}_{n+1}(h,k), \end{aligned}$$

for every $n+1, n \in \mathbb{N}_0$. And this completes the proof. □

3. Nonexistence of Positive Solution Theorems

In this section, we will use the comparison method, the Riccati technique, and the improved monotonic properties that we obtained in the previous section as an application to exclude the existence of any positive solutions to (1).

3.1. Nonexistence of Solutions in Class C_1

Theorem 1. *Assume that there exists a differentiable function $\delta(s) \in \mathbf{C}^1([s_0, \infty), (0, \infty))$ satisfies that*

$$\limsup_{s \to \infty} \int_{s_0}^{s} \left[\delta(\nu) \cdot q(\nu) \cdot \Phi_k^\alpha(\sigma(\nu)) \cdot \left(\frac{\eta(\sigma(\nu))}{\eta(\nu)} \right)^\alpha - \frac{(\delta'(\nu))^{\alpha+1}}{(\alpha+1)^{\alpha+1} \cdot (\delta(\nu) R(s_0, \nu))^\alpha} \right] d\nu = \infty. \tag{35}$$

Then, the class C_1 is empty.

Proof. Contrarily, assume that $x \in C_1$. Let us define the positive function

$$\omega := \delta \cdot \frac{r(z'')^\alpha}{z^\alpha}.$$

Differentiating the last equation implies

$$\begin{aligned}
\omega' &= \delta' \cdot r(z'')^\alpha \cdot z^{-\alpha} + \delta \cdot \left(r(z'')^\alpha \right)' \cdot z^{-\alpha} - \alpha \delta \cdot r(z'')^\alpha \cdot z^{-\alpha-1} z' \\
&= \frac{\delta'}{\delta} \omega + \delta \cdot \left(r(z'')^\alpha \right)' \cdot z^{-\alpha} - \alpha \delta \cdot \frac{r(z'')^\alpha}{z^{\alpha+1}} z'.
\end{aligned} \tag{36}$$

Substituting from (P_7) into (36), we obtain

$$\omega' \leq \frac{\delta'}{\delta} \omega - \frac{\delta \cdot q \cdot [\Phi_k(\sigma) z(\sigma)]^\alpha}{z^\alpha} - \alpha \delta \cdot \frac{r(z'')^\alpha}{z^{\alpha+1}} z',$$

and from (19)

$$\begin{aligned}
\omega' &\leq \frac{\delta'}{\delta} \omega - \frac{\delta \cdot q \cdot [\Phi_k(\sigma) z(\sigma)]^\alpha}{z^\alpha} - \alpha \delta \cdot R \cdot \left(\frac{r^{1/\alpha} z''}{z} \right)^{\alpha+1} \\
&= \frac{\delta'}{\delta} \omega - \delta \cdot q \cdot \Phi_k^\alpha(\sigma) \cdot \left(\frac{z(\sigma)}{z} \right)^\alpha - \alpha \delta \cdot R \cdot \left(\frac{r^{1/\alpha} z''}{z} \right)^{\alpha+1} \\
&= \frac{\delta'}{\delta} \omega - \delta \cdot q \cdot \Phi_k^\alpha(\sigma) \cdot \left(\frac{z(\sigma)}{z} \right)^\alpha - \alpha \delta^{-1/\alpha} \cdot R \cdot (\omega)^{1+1/\alpha}.
\end{aligned}$$

By using the monotonicity of $z(s)/\eta(s)$ given in (P_5)-part of Lemma 3, we have

$$\omega' \leq \frac{\delta'}{\delta} \omega - \delta \cdot q \cdot \Phi_k^\alpha(\sigma) \cdot \left(\frac{\eta(\sigma)}{\eta} \right)^\alpha - \alpha \delta^{-1/\alpha} \cdot R \cdot (\omega)^{1+1/\alpha}. \tag{37}$$

Now, for $\frac{\delta'}{\delta} \omega - \alpha \delta^{-1/\alpha} \cdot R \cdot (\omega)^{1+1/\alpha}$, by using (P_3) in Lemma 1 with $b_1 = \frac{\delta'}{\delta}$, $b_2 = \alpha \delta^{-1/\alpha} \cdot R$, and $x = \omega$, then

$$\begin{aligned}
\frac{\delta'}{\delta} \omega - \alpha \cdot \delta^{-1/\alpha} \cdot R \cdot \omega^{\frac{\alpha+1}{\alpha}} &\leq \frac{\alpha^\alpha}{(\alpha+1)^{\alpha+1}} \left(\frac{\delta'}{\delta} \right)^{\alpha+1} \left(\alpha \cdot \delta^{-1/\alpha} \cdot R \right)^{-\alpha} \\
&\leq \frac{(\delta')^{\alpha+1}}{(\alpha+1)^{\alpha+1} \cdot (\delta R)^\alpha}.
\end{aligned}$$

Substituting into (37), we have

$$\omega' \leq -\delta \cdot q \cdot \Phi_k^\alpha(\sigma) \cdot \left(\frac{\eta(\sigma)}{\eta} \right)^\alpha + \frac{(\delta')^{\alpha+1}}{(\alpha+1)^{\alpha+1} \cdot (\delta R)^\alpha}.$$

Integrating the last inequality from s_0 into s, yields

$$\omega(s_0) \geq \int_{s_0}^{s} \delta(\nu) \cdot q(\nu) \cdot \Phi_k^\alpha(\sigma(\nu)) \cdot \left(\frac{\eta(\sigma(\nu))}{\eta(\nu)}\right)^\alpha - \frac{(\delta'(\nu))^{\alpha+1}}{(\alpha+1)^{\alpha+1} \cdot (\delta(\nu)R(s_0,\nu))^\alpha} d\nu.$$

A contradicts (35). And this completes the proof. □

Example 1. *Consider the following half-linear NDDE:*

$$\left((z''(s))^\alpha\right)' + \frac{b_0}{s^{2\alpha+1}} y^\alpha(\mu s) = 0, \quad s > 0, \tag{38}$$

where the corresponding function $z(s)$ is defined as

$$z(s) = y(s) + a_0 y(\gamma s).$$

Moreover, we assume that α is a quotient of two odd positive integers, $a_0 \in [0, \infty)$, $b_0 \in (0, \infty)$, and $\gamma, \mu \in (0,1)$. Since $\tau(s) = \gamma s$, $\sigma(s) = \mu s$, and $R(0,s) = s$, then assumptions (A_1)–(A_5) are easily satisfied. With some calculations, we obtain from (10)–(13) that

$$\tau^{[i]}(s) := \gamma^i s, \quad \tau^{[-i]}(s) := \gamma^{-i} s, \quad \eta(s) := \frac{s^2}{2},$$

and

$$\Phi_k(s) := \begin{cases} 1 & \text{for } a_0 = 0; \\ (1-a_0)\sum_{i=0}^{k} a_0^{2i} \cdot \gamma^{4i} & \text{for } a_0 < 1; \\ \sum_{i=1}^{k} a_0^{-2i} \cdot \left[a_0 - \gamma^{-2}\right] & \text{for } a_0 > \frac{1}{\gamma^2}. \end{cases}$$

By taking $\delta(s) = s^{2\alpha}$, it follows from Theorem 1 that (38) does not possess a increasing positive solution ($C_1 = \varnothing$) if

$$b_0 > \left(\frac{2\alpha}{\alpha+1}\right)^{\alpha+1} \cdot \frac{1}{R_0^\alpha \cdot \mu^{2\alpha}}, \tag{39}$$

for $R_0 = \Phi_k(s)$.

Theorem 2. *Assume that $\alpha \geq 1$ and there exists a differentiable function $\delta(s) \in C^1([s_0, \infty), (0, \infty))$ satisfies that*

$$\limsup_{s \to \infty} \int_{s_0}^{s} \left[\delta(\nu) \cdot q(\nu) \cdot \tilde{\Phi}_{k,n}^\alpha(\sigma(\nu)) \cdot \left(\frac{\tilde{\eta}_n(\sigma(\nu))}{\tilde{\eta}_n(\nu)}\right)^\alpha - \frac{(\delta'(\nu))^{\alpha+1}}{(\alpha+1)^{\alpha+1} \cdot (\delta(\nu)R(s_0,\nu))^\alpha}\right] d\nu = \infty, \tag{40}$$

for any nonnegative integer n, k. Then, the class C_1 is empty.

Proof. Contrarily, assume that $x \in C_1$. By using (23) and replacing (P_4) and (P_5) with (P_8) and (P_9), the proof of this theorem becomes similar to the proof of Theorem 1, so we omit it. □

Remark 5. *Criterion (40) given in the previous theorem is considered an improvement on Criterion (35) in Theorem 1; i.e., it gives better results when applied.*

Example 2. *As in the last example, consider the half-linear NDDE (38), where $\alpha \geq 1$. To apply Theorem 2 in (38), we need to first calculate the iterative functions given in (14)–(18); so, let us define the following auxiliary sequences $\{R_i\}$ and $\{T_i\}$ for $i = 0, 1, \ldots$ and $T_0 = 1$, as*

$$R_i := \begin{cases} 1 & \text{for } a_0 = 0; \\ (1-a_0)\sum_{i=0}^{k} a_0^{2i} \cdot \gamma^{2(T_i+1)i} & \text{for } a_0 < 1; \\ \left(a_0 - \gamma^{-1-T_i}\right)\sum_{i=1}^{k} a_0^{-2i} & \text{for } a_0 > \frac{1}{\gamma^2} \end{cases} \tag{41}$$

and

$$T_{i+1} := \frac{1}{1 + \frac{\mu^{2\alpha} \cdot R_i^\alpha \cdot b_0}{\alpha \cdot 2^\alpha}}. \tag{42}$$

Using the previous notations and mathematical induction yields
$$R_i = \Phi_{k,i}(s).$$
Hence,
$$\rho_i(s) = \frac{\mu^{2(\alpha-1)} \cdot R_i^\alpha \cdot b_0}{\alpha \cdot 2^{\alpha-1}} \cdot \frac{1}{s^3},$$
$$\lambda_i(s) = \left(1 + \frac{\mu^{2\alpha} \cdot R_i^\alpha \cdot b_0}{\alpha \cdot 2^\alpha}\right) s = \frac{s}{T_{i+1}},$$
$$\tilde{R}_i(s) = s^{1/\left(1 + \frac{\mu^{2\alpha} \cdot R_i^\alpha \cdot b_0}{\alpha \cdot 2^\alpha}\right)} = s^{T_{i+1}},$$
and
$$\tilde{\eta}_i(s) = \frac{s^{T_i+1}}{T_i + 1}.$$

Now, Theorem 2 implies that (38) does not possess any increasing positive solutions ($C_1 = \emptyset$), if
$$b_0 \cdot R_i^\alpha \cdot \left(\mu^{T_i+1}\right)^\alpha > \left(\frac{2\alpha}{\alpha+1}\right)^{\alpha+1}. \tag{43}$$

Theorem 3. *Assume that $\alpha \geq 1$ and*
$$\liminf_{s \to \infty} \int_{\sigma(s)}^{s} q(\nu) \Phi_{k,n}^\alpha(\sigma(\nu)) \tilde{\lambda}_n^\alpha(\sigma(\nu)) d\nu > \frac{1}{e}, \tag{44}$$

for any nonnegative integer n, k and $\tilde{\lambda}_n(s)$ are defined as in (16). Then, the class C_1 is empty.

Proof. Contrarily, assume that $x \in C_1$. As in (26), we obtain
$$z'(s) \geq \lambda_n(s) r^{1/\alpha}(s) z''(s).$$

Integrating the above inequality from s_0 to s, then
$$\begin{aligned} z(s) &\geq r^{1/\alpha}(s) z''(s) \int_{s_0}^{s} \lambda_n(\nu) d\nu \\ &= r^{1/\alpha}(s) z''(s) \tilde{\lambda}_n(s). \end{aligned} \tag{45}$$

Combining (45) and the (P_{10}) part of lemma 6, we arrive at
$$\left(r(s)(z''(s))^\alpha\right)' \leq -q(s) r(\sigma(s)) \left(\Phi_{k,n}(\sigma(s)) z''(\sigma(s)) \tilde{\lambda}_n(\sigma(s))\right)^\alpha. \tag{46}$$

Now, let us define the positive function
$$U(s) := r(s)(z''(s))^\alpha.$$

Therefore, (46) becomes
$$U'(s) + q(s) \Phi_{k,n}^\alpha(\sigma(s)) \tilde{\lambda}_n^\alpha(\sigma(s)) U(\sigma(s)) \leq 0. \tag{47}$$

But Theorem 2.1.1 in [47] indicates that under (44) every solution of (47) oscillates. A contradiction, and this completes the proof. □

Example 3. *Recall the NDDE (38) for $\alpha \geq 1$. Exactly as in Example 2, where we used auxiliary sequences (41), (42), and mathematical induction to obtain that $R_i := \Phi_{k,i}(s)$ for $i = 0, 1, \ldots$. Consequently,*
$$\tilde{\lambda}_i(s) := \frac{s^2}{2T_{i+1}}.$$

Substituting this into (44) in Theorem 3 ensures that (38) does not possess any increasing positive solution ($C_1 = \varnothing$) if

$$\frac{b_0 \cdot R_i^\alpha \cdot \mu^{2\alpha}}{2^\alpha T_{i+1}^\alpha} \ln \frac{1}{\mu} > \frac{1}{e}. \tag{48}$$

Theorem 4. *Assume that $\alpha \geq 1$ and*

$$\liminf_{s \to \infty} \frac{s^\alpha}{r(s)} \int_s^\infty q(\nu) \frac{\sigma^{2\alpha}(\nu)}{\nu^\alpha} d\ell > \frac{(2\alpha)^\alpha}{(1+\alpha)^{\alpha+1} \bar{\Phi}_{k,n}^\alpha(s)}, \tag{49}$$

for any nonnegative integer n, k. Then, the class C_1 is empty.

Proof. Contrarily, assume that $x \in C_1$. From Corollary 1 in [38] and using (P_{10}) instead of the inequality

$$\left(r(s)(z''(s))^\alpha \right)' \leq -q(s)(1 - p(\sigma(s)))^\alpha z^\alpha(\sigma(s)).$$

The proof becomes similar to the proof of Theorem 1 in [38], so we can omit it. □

Example 4. *Again, consider the half-linear NDDE (38) where $\alpha \geq 1$. As in the previous examples, Theorem 4 implies that (38) does not possess any increasing positive solutions ($C_1 = \varnothing$) if*

$$b_0 > \frac{2^\alpha \alpha^{\alpha+1}}{(1+\alpha)^{\alpha+1} \mu^{2\alpha} R_i^\alpha}. \tag{50}$$

Remark 6. *Applying criteria (5)–(7) given in the works of Baculikova and Dzurina [38], Li and Thandapani [39], and Grace et al. [40] to (38), we obtain the following criteria:*

$$b_0 > \left(\frac{\alpha}{\alpha+1} \right)^{\alpha+1} \cdot \left(\frac{2}{(1-a_0)\mu^2} \right)^\alpha, \tag{51}$$

$$b_0 > (2\alpha - 1) \cdot \left(\frac{2\alpha}{\alpha+1} \right)^{\alpha+1} \cdot \frac{1 + \frac{a_0^\alpha}{\gamma}}{\mu^{2\alpha}}, \tag{52}$$

and

$$b_0 > \frac{\alpha \cdot 2^{3\alpha+1}}{(a_0 - \gamma^{-2})^\alpha} \left(\frac{a_0 \cdot \gamma}{\mu} \right)^{2\alpha}, \tag{53}$$

respectively. In the following table, we compare the effectiveness and novelty of our results for Theorems 3 and 4 with the criteria (51)–(53) in the previous works. In Table 1, we determined the lower bounds of the coefficient b_0 for different values of a_0, α, γ, and μ, as follows:

Table 1. Comparison of oscillation criteria using the lower bounds of the value of the coefficient b_0.

	α	γ	μ	a_0	(48)	(50)	(51)	(52)	(53)
(a)	1	0.1	0.5	0.4	5.1143	3.3332	3.3333	20	Fail
(b)	3	0.1	0.5	0.4	766.3601	749.9242	750.0043	2656.8000	Fail
(c)	1	0.6	0.3	5	52.6300	53.5450	Fail	103.7037	720
(d)	1	0.9	0.7	2.5	10.3430	4.1661	Fail	7.7097	130.6322

We can notice from the previous table that

1. Criterion (50) produced by applying Theorem 3 provides the best results for Cases a, b, and d;
2. Criterion (48) produced by applying Theorem 4 provides the best results for Case c;
3. Our results improved on the previous results in the literature, which demonstrates the importance of improving the relationships between a solution and its corresponding function and derivatives.

Figure 1 illustrates this comparison on a larger scale.

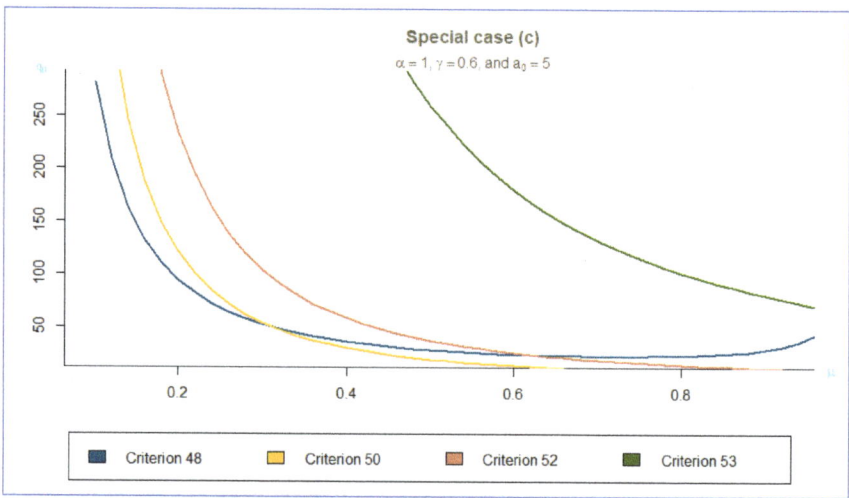

Figure 1. The lower bounds of the q_0-values for the Criteria (48), (50), (52), and (53).

3.2. Nonexistance of Solutions in Class C_2

Theorem 5. *Assume that there exists a positive function $\varpi \in ([s_0, \infty), \mathbb{R})$, such that*

$$\tau(s) > \varpi(s) > \sigma(s),$$

and $\varpi(s) \geq \tau^{-1}(\sigma(s))$. If

$$\liminf_{s \to \infty} \int_{\tau^{-1}(\varpi(s))}^{s} q^*(v) \breve{\eta}_n^\alpha(\sigma(v), \varpi(v)) \mathrm{d}v > \frac{\tau_0 + p_0}{e\tau_0}, \quad (54)$$

Then, the class C_2 is empty.

Proof. Assume that $x \in C_2$. From (32) in the proof of Lemma 7, we can define the positive auxiliary function

$$F(s) := r(s)(z''(s))^\alpha + \frac{p_0}{\tau_0} r(\tau(s))(z''(\tau(s)))^\alpha.$$

But from C_1 or C_2 and (32), we have

$$\begin{aligned} F'(s) &\leq -q^*(s)\breve{\eta}_n^\alpha(\sigma(s), \varpi(s))r(\varpi(s))(z''(\varpi(s)))^\alpha \\ &\leq \frac{-\tau_0}{\tau_0 + p_0} q^*(s)\breve{\eta}_n^\alpha(\sigma(s), \varpi(s))F\left(\tau^{-1}(\varpi(s))\right), \end{aligned}$$

then

$$F'(s) + \frac{\tau_0}{\tau_0 + p_0} q^*(s)\breve{\eta}_n^\alpha(\sigma(s), \varpi(s))F\left(\tau^{-1}(\varpi(s))\right) \leq 0. \quad (55)$$

This means that F is a positive solution to (55). Now, using (54) and Theorem 2.1.1 in [47], we arrive at a contradiction with (55). And this completes the proof. □

Example 5. *Again, recall the half-linear NDDE (38). For $0 < \mu < \frac{\gamma^2}{2-\gamma}$ and $\varpi(s) = \varrho s = \frac{\gamma+\mu}{2} s$, then it becomes clear that assumptions (A_6) and*

$$\gamma s > \frac{\gamma + \mu}{2} s > \mu s$$

are easily satisfied. In order to apply this example to Theorem 5, we first need to calculate the iterative function (29), which in turn requires defining some auxiliary sequences, just as we did previously in Example 2. So, let us define the sequence $\left\{\widetilde{R}_i\right\}$ and $\left\{\widetilde{T}_i\right\}$ for $i = 0, 1, \ldots$, as:

$$\widetilde{R}_{i+1} := \frac{\gamma^{\widetilde{T}_i}\varrho^{\widetilde{T}_i}}{\widetilde{T}_i - 1}\left[\mu\varrho^{1-\widetilde{T}_i} + \frac{\mu^{2-\widetilde{T}_i}}{\widetilde{T}_i - 2} - \frac{\widetilde{T}_i - 1}{\widetilde{T}_i - 2}\varrho^{2-\widetilde{T}_i}\right],$$

$$\widetilde{T}_i := \frac{\gamma b_0}{\gamma + a_0}\widetilde{R}_i^\alpha,$$

and

$$\widetilde{R}_0 := \breve{\eta}_0(\mu, \varrho) = \frac{(\varrho - \mu)^2}{2}.$$

Then, by using mathematical induction, we obtain

$$\breve{\eta}_i(h,k) := \frac{k^{\widetilde{T}_i}\gamma^{\widetilde{T}_i}}{\left(\widetilde{T}_i - 1\right)\left(\widetilde{T}_i - 2\right)}\left[\left(\widetilde{T}_i - 2\right)hk^{1-\widetilde{T}_i} + h^{2-\widetilde{T}_i} - \left(\widetilde{T}_i - 1\right)k^{2-\widetilde{T}_i}\right].$$

Substituting into (29) in Theorem 5 implies that (38) does not possess any decreasing positive solutions (C$_2$ = ∅), if

$$b_0 > \frac{\gamma + a_0}{e\gamma} \cdot \frac{1}{\widetilde{R}_i^\alpha \ln \frac{\gamma}{\varrho}}. \tag{56}$$

4. Oscillation Theorems

This section concerns giving oscillation theorems for (1) by combining criteria that ensure that the class C$_1$ and C$_2$ are both empty.

Theorem 6. *Assume that there exists a function $\delta(s) \in \mathbf{C}^1([s_0, \infty), (0, \infty))$ and $\omega \in ([s_0, \infty), \mathbb{R})$ such that $\tau(s) > \omega(s) > \sigma(s)$, $\omega(s) \geq \tau^{-1}(\sigma(s))$. If (35) and (54) hold, then every solution to (1) is oscillatory.*

Theorem 7. *Assume that for $\alpha \geq 1$ there exists a function $\delta(s) \in \mathbf{C}^1([s_0, \infty), (0, \infty))$, and $\omega \in ([s_0, \infty), \mathbb{R})$ such that $\tau(s) > \omega(s) > \sigma(s)$, $\omega(s) \geq \tau^{-1}(\sigma(s))$. If (40) and (54) hold, for any nonnegative integer n, k, then every solution to (1) is oscillatory.*

Theorem 8. *Assume that for $\alpha \geq 1$ there exists a function $\delta(s) \in \mathbf{C}^1([s_0, \infty), (0, \infty))$, and $\omega \in ([s_0, \infty), \mathbb{R})$ such that $\tau(s) > \omega(s) > \sigma(s)$, $\omega(s) \geq \tau^{-1}(\sigma(s))$. If (44) and (54) hold, for any nonnegative integer n, k, then every solution to (1) is oscillatory.*

Theorem 9. *Assume that for $\alpha \geq 1$ there exists a function $\delta(s) \in \mathbf{C}^1([s_0, \infty), (0, \infty))$, and $\omega \in ([s_0, \infty), \mathbb{R})$ such that $\tau(s) > \omega(s) > \sigma(s)$, $\omega(s) \geq \tau^{-1}(\sigma(s))$ If (49) and (54) hold, for any nonnegative integer n, k, then every solution to (1) is oscillatory.*

Example 6. *Recall the half-linear NDDE (38). Exactly as we applied in Examples 1 and 5, we can obtain that (35) in Theorem 1 reduces to (39) to ensure that there are no positive solutions in Class C$_1$, and (54) in Theorem 5 reduces to (56) to ensure that there are no positive solutions in Class C$_2$. By combining these two criteria (39) and (56), we determine that all solutions of (1) are oscillatory if*

$$b_0 > \max\left\{\left(\frac{2\alpha}{\alpha+1}\right)^{\alpha+1} \cdot \frac{1}{R_0^\alpha \cdot \mu^{2\alpha}}, \frac{\gamma + a_0}{e\gamma} \cdot \frac{1}{\widetilde{R}_i^\alpha \ln \frac{\gamma}{\varrho}}\right\}.$$

5. Conclusions

In this paper, we deduced and improved some monotonic properties of positive solutions to (1) and their corresponding functions for classes C$_1$ and C$_2$. After that, these relationships were used to set simple criteria with only one condition, to ensure that there are no positive solutions for either class, and then used them to ensure that all solutions to (1) oscillate. The results and criteria obtained in the previous sections were distinguished by several important points that confirm their originality and novelty. Our results were applied in Examples 1–6 and compared with previous works in Remarks 5 and 6. Through these comparisons, we noted that our results were an improvement on the oscillation criteria in many previous works. This requires fewer restrictions on coefficients and covers a larger area when applied. There were nine fundamental theorems provided, and their applicability and effectiveness were verified by testing the conditions they contained using more than one example.

Author Contributions: Conceptualization, A.E., O.M., M.R., G.A. and I.M.H.; methodology, A.E., O.M., M.R., G.A. and I.M.H.; investigation, A.E., O.M., M.R., G.A. and I.M.H.; writing—original draft preparation, A.E., M.R. and G.A.; writing—review and editing, O.M. and I.M.H. All authors have read and agreed to the published version of the manuscript.

Funding: This research was funded by Princess Nourah bint Abdulrahman University Researchers Supporting Project number (PNURSP2023R45), Princess Nourah bint Abdulrahman University, Riyadh, Saudi Arabia.

Data Availability Statement: Data are contained within the article.

Acknowledgments: Princess Nourah bint Abdulrahman University Researchers Supporting Project number (PNURSP2023R45), Princess Nourah bint Abdulrahman University, Riyadh, Saudi Arabia.

Conflicts of Interest: The authors declare no conflict of interest.

References

1. Jayaraman, G.; Padmanabhan, N.; Mehrotra, R. Entry flow into a circular tube of slowly varying cross-section. *Fluid Dyn. Res.* **1986**, *1*, 131. [CrossRef]
2. Vreeke, S.A.; Sandquist, G.M. Phase space analysis of reactor kinetics. *Nucl. Sci. Eng.* **1970**, *42*, 295–305. [CrossRef]
3. Gregus, M. *Third Order Linear Differential Equations*; Springer Science & Business Media: Berlin/Heidelberg, Germany, 2012; Volume 22.
4. Ali, K.K.; Mehanna, M.S.; Akbar, M.A. Approach to a (2 + 1)-dimensional time-dependent date-Jimbo-Kashiwara-Miwa equation in real physical phenomena. *Appl. Comput. Math.* **2022**, *21*, 193–206.
5. Iskandarov, S.; Komartsova, E. On the influence of integral perturbations on the boundedness of solutions of a fourth-order linear differential equation. *TWMS J. Pure Appl. Math.* **2022**, *13*, 3–9.
6. Shokri, A. The Symmetric P-Stable Hybrid Obrenchkoff Methods for the Numerical Solution of Second Order IVPs. *TWMS J. Pure Appl. Math.* **2012**, *5*, 28–35.
7. Juraev, D.A.; Shokri, A.; Marian, D. On an approximate solution of the cauchy problem for systems of equations of elliptic type of the first order. *Entropy* **2022**, *24*, 968. [CrossRef]
8. Rahmatan, H.; Shokri, A.; Ahmad, H.; Botmart, T. Subordination Method for the Estimation of Certain Subclass of Analytic Functions Defined by the-Derivative Operator. *J. Fun. Spaces* **2022**, *2022*, 5078060. [CrossRef]
9. Győri, I.; Ladas, G. *Oscillation Theory of Delay Differential Equations with Applications*; Clarendon Press: Oxford, UK, 1991.
10. Hale, J.K. Functional differential equations. In *Oxford Applied Mathematical Sciences*; Springer: New York, NY, USA, 1971; Volume 3.
11. Liu, M.; Dassios, I.; Tzounas, G.; Milano, F. Stability analysis of power systems with inclusion of realistic-modeling WAMS delays. *IEEE Trans. Power Syst.* **2018**, *34*, 627–636. [CrossRef]
12. Milano, F.; Dassios, I. Small-signal stability analysis for non-index 1 Hessenberg form systems of delay differential-algebraic equations. *IEEE Trans. Circuits Syst. I* **2016**, *63*, 1521–1530. [CrossRef]
13. Agarwal, R.P.; Berezansky, L.; Braverman, E.; Domoshnitsky, A. *Nonoscillation Theory of Functional Differential Equations with Applications*; Springer Science & Business Media: Berlin/Heidelberg, Germany, 2012.
14. Philos, C. On the existence of nonoscillatory solutions tending to zero at ∞ for differential equations with positive delays. *Arch. Math.* **1981**, *36*, 168–178. [CrossRef]
15. Santra, S.S.; Tripathy, A.K. On oscillatory first order nonlinear neutral differential equations with nonlinear impulses. *J. Appl. Math. Comput.* **2019**, *59*, 257–270. [CrossRef]
16. Santra, S.S.; Baleanu, D.; Khedher, K.M.; Moaaz, O. First-order impulsive differential systems: Sufficient and necessary conditions for oscillatory or asymptotic behavior. *Adv. Differ. Equ.* **2021**, *1*, 283. [CrossRef]

17. Tunç, E.; Ozdemir, O. Comparison theorems on the oscillation of even order nonlinear mixed neutral differential equations. *Math. Methods Appl. Sci.* **2023**, *46*, 631–640. [CrossRef]
18. Moaaz, O.; Elabbasy, E.M.; Muhib, A. Oscillation criteria for even-order neutral differential equations with distributed deviating arguments. *Adv. Differ. Equ.* **2019**, *2019*, 297. [CrossRef]
19. Agarwal, R.P.; Zhang, C.; Li, T. Some remarks on oscillation of second order neutral differential equations. *Appl. Math. Comput.* **2016**, *274*, 178–181. [CrossRef]
20. Li, T.; Rogovchenko, Y.V. On asymptotic behavior of solutions to higher-order sublinear emden–fowler delay differential equations. *Appl. Math. Lett.* **2017**, *67*, 53–59. [CrossRef]
21. Cesarano, C.; Moaaz, O.; Qaraad, B.; Alshehri, N.A.; Elagan, S.K.; Zakarya, M. New results for oscillation of solutions of odd-order neutral differential equations. *Symmetry* **2021**, *13*, 1095. [CrossRef]
22. Jadlovska, I.; Džurina, J.; Graef, J.R.; Grace, S.R. Sharp oscillation theorem for fourth-order linear delay differential equations. *J. Inequal. Appl.* **2022**, *2022*, 122. [CrossRef]
23. Agarwal, R.P.; Grace, S.R.; O'Regan, D. *Oscillation Theory for Second Order Linear, Half-Linear, Superlinear and Sublinear Dynamic Equations*; Kluwer Academic Publishers: Dordrecht, The Netherlands, 2002.
24. Agarwal, R.P.; Bohner, M.; Li, W.T. *Nonoscillation and Oscillation Theory for Functional Differential Equations*; CRC Press: Boca Raton, FL, USA, 2004; Volume 267.
25. Kneser, A. Untersuchungen über die reellen Nullstellen der Integrale linearer Differentialgleichungen. *Math. Ann.* **1893**, *42*, 409–435. [CrossRef]
26. Fite, W.B. Concerning the zeros of the solutions of certain differential equations. *Trans. Am. Math.* **1918**, *19*, 341–352. [CrossRef]
27. Hanan, M. Oscillation criteria for third-order linear differential equations. *Pac. J. Math.* **1961**, *11*, 919–944. [CrossRef]
28. Grace, S.R.; Agarwal, R.P.; Pavani, R.; Thandapani, E. On the oscillation of certain third order nonlinear functional differential equations. *Appl. Math. Comput.* **2008**, *202*, 102–112. [CrossRef]
29. Candan, T.; Dahiya, R.S. Oscillation of third order functional differential equations with delay. *Electron. J. Differ. Equ.* **2003**, *2003*, 79–88.
30. Li, T.; Zhang, C.; Xing, G. Oscillation of third-order neutral delay differential equations. *Abstr. Appl. Anal.* **2012**, *2012*, 569201. [CrossRef]
31. Dzurina, J.; Thandapani, E.; Tamilvanan, S. Oscillation of Solutions to Third Order Half-Linear Neutral Differential Equations. *Electron. J. Differ. Equ.* **2010**, *2012*, 1–9.
32. Qaraad, B.; Moaaz, O.; Baleanu, D.; Santra, S.S.; Ali, R.; Elabbasy, E.M. Third-order neutral differential equations of the mixed type: Oscillatory and asymptotic behavior. *Math. Biosci. Eng.* **2022**, *19*, 1649–1658. [CrossRef]
33. Bohner, M.; Grace, S.R.; Sağer, I.; Tunç, E. Oscillation of third-order nonlinear damped delay differential equations. *Appl. Math. Comput.* **2016**, *278*, 21–32. [CrossRef]
34. Chatzarakis, G.E.; Grace, S.R.; Jadlovska, I.; Li, T.; Tunç, E. Oscillation criteria for third-order Emden—Fowler differential equations with unbounded neutral coefficients. *Complexity* **2019**, *2019*, 5691758. [CrossRef]
35. Chatzarakis, G.E.; Dzurina, J.; Jadlovsk, I. Oscillatory and asymptotic properties of third-order quasilinear delay differential equations. *J. Inequal. Appl.* **2019**, *2019*, 23. [CrossRef]
36. Grace, S.R.; Jadlovska, I.; Tunç, E. Oscillatory and asymptotic behavior of third-order nonlinear differential equations with a superlinear neutral term. *Turk. J. Math.* **2020**, *44*, 1317–1329. [CrossRef]
37. Han, Z.; Li, T.; Sun, S.; Zhang, C. An oscillation criteria for third order neutral delay differential equations. *J. Appl. Anal.* **2010**, *16*. [CrossRef]
38. Baculikova, B.; Dzurina, J. Oscillation of third-order neutral differential equations. *Math. Comput. Model.* **2010**, *52*, 215–226. [CrossRef]
39. Thandapani, E.; Li, T. On the oscillation of third-order quasi-linear neutral functional differential equations. *Arch. Math.* **2011**, *47*, 181–199.
40. Graef, J.R.; Tunç, E.; Grace, S.R. Oscillatory and asymptotic behavior of a third-order nonlinear neutral differential equation. *Opusc. Math.* **2017**, *37*, 839–852. [CrossRef]
41. Dzurina, J.; Grace, S.R.; Jadlovska, I. On nonexistence of Kneser solutions of third-order neutral delay differential equations. *Appl. Math. Lett.* **2019**, *88*, 193–200. [CrossRef]
42. Moaaz, O.; Awrejcewicz, J.; Muhib, A. Establishing new criteria for oscillation of odd-order nonlinear differential equations. *Mathematics* **2020**, *8*, 937. [CrossRef]
43. Moaaz, O.; Dassios, I.; Muhsin, W.; Muhib, A. Oscillation theory for non-linear neutral delay differential equations of third order. *Appl. Sci.* **2020**, *10*, 4855. [CrossRef]
44. Moaaz, O.; Mahmoud, E.E.; Alharbi, W.R. Third-order neutral delay differential equations: New iterative criteria for oscillation. *J. Funct. Spaces* **2020**, *2020*, 6666061. [CrossRef]
45. Zhang, S.Y.; Wang, Q.R. Oscillation of second-order nonlinear neutral dynamic equations on time scales. *Appl. Math. Comput.* **2010**, *216*, 2837–2848. [CrossRef]

46. Moaaz, O.; Cesarano, C.; Almarri, B. An Improved Relationship between the Solution and Its Corresponding Function in Fourth-Order Neutral Differential Equations and Its Applications. *Mathematics* **2023**, *11*, 1708. [CrossRef]
47. Ladde, G.S.; Lakshmikantham, V.; Zhang, B.G. *Oscillation Theory of Differential Equations with Deviating Arguments*; M. Dekker: New York, NY, USA, 1987.

Disclaimer/Publisher's Note: The statements, opinions and data contained in all publications are solely those of the individual author(s) and contributor(s) and not of MDPI and/or the editor(s). MDPI and/or the editor(s) disclaim responsibility for any injury to people or property resulting from any ideas, methods, instructions or products referred to in the content.

Article

New Two-Level Time-Mesh Difference Scheme for the Symmetric Regularized Long Wave Equation

Jingying Gao *, Qingmei Bai, Siriguleng He and Eerdun Buhe

School of Mathematics Science, Hohhot Minzu College, Hohhot 010051, China; baiqingmei@email.imnc.edu.cn (Q.B.); t53000839@email.imnc.edu.cn (S.H.); eerdunbuhe@163.com (E.B.)
* Correspondence: minzugjy@email.imnc.edu.cn

Abstract: The paper introduces a new two-level time-mesh difference scheme for solving the symmetric regularized long wave equation. The scheme consists of three steps. A coarse time-mesh and a fine time-mesh are defined, and the equation is solved using an existing nonlinear scheme on the coarse time-mesh. Lagrange's linear interpolation formula is employed to obtain all preliminary solutions on the fine time-mesh. Based on the preliminary solutions, Taylor's formula is utilized to construct a linear system for the equation on the fine time-mesh. The convergence and stability of the scheme is analyzed, providing the convergence rates of $O(\tau_F^2 + \tau_C^4 + h^4)$ in the discrete L_∞-norm for $u(x,t)$ and in the discrete L_2-norm for $\rho(x,t)$. Numerical simulation results show that the proposed scheme achieves equivalent error levels and convergence rates to the nonlinear scheme, while also reducing CPU time by over half, which indicates that the new method is more efficient. Furthermore, compared to the earlier time two-mesh method developed by the authors, the proposed scheme significantly reduces the error between the numerical and exact solutions, which means that the proposed scheme is more accurate. Additionally, the effectiveness of the new scheme is discussed in terms of the corresponding conservation laws and long-time simulations.

Keywords: SRLW equation; finite difference; second-order; two-level time-mesh; convergence analysis

MSC: 65M06

1. Introduction

In this paper, the following initial boundary value problem of the symmetric regularized long wave (SRLW) Equation [1] is considered:

$$\begin{cases} u_t + \rho_x + uu_x - u_{xxt} = 0, & x_L \leq x \leq x_R,\ 0 < t \leq T, \\ \rho_t + u_x = 0, & x_L \leq x \leq x_R,\ 0 < t \leq T, \\ u(x_L, t) = u(x_R, t) = 0, & \rho(x_L, t) = \rho(x_R, t) = 0, & 0 < t \leq T, \\ u(x, 0) = u_0(x), & \rho(x, 0) = \rho_0(x), & x_L \leq x \leq x_R, \end{cases} \quad (1)$$

where $u(x,t)$ and $\rho(x,t)$ are the fluid velocity and the density, respectively.

The SRLW equation is a partial differential equation that takes into account the effects of dispersion and nonlinearity utilized to depict a range of physical phenomena such as nonlinear optics, fluid dynamics, and quantum mechanics. In nonlinear optics, it is employed to study the propagation of optical pulses in materials with nonlinear properties. In fluid dynamics, it is used to model the behavior of shallow water waves and to study wave interactions in coastal regions. In quantum mechanics, it is applied to describe the dynamics of Bose–Einstein condensates and other quantum systems. Currently, many researchers have employed various methods to obtain exact traveling and solitary wave solutions for the SRLW equation, such as the exp-function method [2], (G'/G)-expansion method [3], Lie symmetry approach [4], analytical method [5], sine–cosine method [6], etc.

Significant achievements have also been made in the research of numerical solutions for the SRLW equation. Guo [7] conducted a study on the existence, uniqueness, and regularity of numerical solutions for the periodic initial value problem of the generalized SRLW equation using the spectral method. Zheng et al. [8] proposed a Fourier pseudospectral method with a restraint operator for the SRLW equation that demonstrated stability and optimal error estimates. Shang et al. [9] analyzed a Chebyshev pseudospectral scheme for multi-dimensional generalized SRLW equations. Fang et al. [10] studied the presence of global attractors of the SRLW equation. Wang et al. [11] investigated a coupled two-level and nonlinear-implicit finite difference method for solving the SRLW equation, achieving second-order accuracy in both space and time. Bai et al. [12] studied a finite difference scheme with two layers for the SRLW equation, which is a conservative scheme and converges with an order of $O(\tau + h^2)$ in the L^∞ norm for u and in the L_2 norm for ρ. Xu et al. [13] solved a dissipative SRLW equation containing a damping term using a mixed finite element method. Yimnet et al. [14] introduced a novel finite difference method in which a new average difference technique with four levels is employed to solve the u independently from the ρ of the SRLW equation. In order to achieve better solving results, many researchers have constructed difference schemes with higher convergence orders. Nie [15] constructed a decoupled finite difference scheme with fourth-order accuracy for solving the SRLW equation. Hu et al. [16] introduced a novel conservative Crank–Nicolson finite difference scheme for the SRLW equation. This scheme achieves an accuracy of $O(\tau^2 + h^4)$ without refined mesh. Kerdboon et al. [17] proposed a three-point compact difference scheme for the SRLW equation. He et al. [18] presented a compact difference scheme with four time-levels for the SRLW equation. The scheme is constructed for the SRLW equation with a sole nonlinear velocity term and exhibits a high accuracy of $O(\tau^2 + h^4)$. However, most of the high convergence accuracy scheme deal with the points near the boundary via the use of ghost points or fictitious points. Li et al. [19] proposed a compact scheme for the SRLW equation that avoids the use of ghost points by utilizing inverse compact operators. He et al. [20] also proposed a novel conservative three-point linearized compact difference scheme to handle the challenges posed by discrete boundaries and nonlinear terms in solving SRLW equations.

The combination of the time two-mesh (TT-M) technique [21–27] with other numerical methods also can improve the efficiency of solving nonlinear partial differential equations. Liu et al. [21] investigated a finite element method with the TT-M technique, which was successfully applied to solve the fractional water wave model and other fractional models. Afterward, other authors [22–26] used the TT-M method to study the numerical solutions for the partial differential equations such as the Allen–Cahn model, Sobolev model and the nonlinear Schrödinger equation. Gao et al. [27] introduced a TT-M finite difference scheme for the SRLW equation, achieving first-order accuracy in time and second-order accuracy in space. However, the error in the numerical solutions of the scheme increases rapidly over a long time period, making it hard to simulate the long-time behavior of Equation (1).

To improve the efficiency and accuracy of numerical schemes for the SRLW equation, in this paper, we construct a second-order two-level time-mesh finite difference scheme based on the nonlinear scheme in [16]. As a result, the proposed scheme achieves a convergence rate of $O(\tau_F^2 + \tau_C^4 + h^4)$ in the discrete L_∞-norm for $u(x,t)$ and in the discrete L_2-norm for $\rho(x,t)$. The proposed scheme has several advantages: (i) Combined with the two level time-mesh technique, the scheme utilizes the nonlinear scheme on a coarse time-mesh and then constructs a linear difference system on a fine time-mesh, which more efficiently solves the SRLW equation than the nonlinear scheme in [16]; (ii) The new scheme obtains a high accuracy in solving the SRLW equation. The proposed scheme has a second-order convergence rate in time and a fourth-order convergence rate in space, which is higher than that of the scheme in [27]; (iii) The convergence and stability of the scheme have been verified through detailed proofs. Theoretical analysis of the scheme is more intricate compared to existing TT-M methods since a function with three variables is used in the process of the linear system construction.

The rest of this article is structured as follows: Section 2 introduces the notations and lemmas. Following that, Section 3 outlines the construction of the two-level time-mesh finite difference numerical scheme. In Section 4, we delve into the convergence and stability of the scheme. Next, Section 5 offers numerical results to test the theoretical findings, computational efficiency, and accuracy of the scheme. Finally, in Section 6, we conclude the paper.

2. Some Notations and Lemmas

For time and space intervals $(0, T]$ and $[x_L, x_R]$, let $t_n = n\tau, (n = 1, 2, \ldots, [T/\tau] = N)$ be the time-level and $x_j = x_L + jh, (j = 0, 1, 2, \ldots, \frac{x_R - x_L}{h} = J)$ be the space mesh point, where τ and h represent time and space step sizes.

Let $Z_h^0 = \{u^n = (u_j^n) \mid u_{-1}^n = u_0^n = u_J^n = u_{J+1}^n = 0, j = -1, 0, 1, \ldots, J, J+1\}$ be the space of mesh functions, where $j = -1$ and $J + 1$ are ghost points. The following notations will be used in this paper:

$$\left(u_j^n\right)_x = \frac{u_{j+1}^n - u_j^n}{h}, \quad \left(u_j^n\right)_{\bar{x}} = \frac{u_j^n - u_{j-1}^n}{h}, \quad \left(u_j^n\right)_{\hat{x}} = \frac{u_{j+1}^n - u_{j-1}^n}{2h},$$

$$\left(u_j^n\right)_{\tilde{x}} = \frac{u_{j+2}^n - u_{j-2}^n}{4h}, \quad \left(u_j^n\right)_t = \frac{u_j^{n+1} - u_j^n}{\tau}, \quad u_j^{n+\frac{1}{2}} = \frac{u_j^{n+1} + u_j^n}{2},$$

M is used to denote a general positive constant, which may have different values in different locations.

We define the discrete inner product and norms with respect to any pair of mesh functions $u^n, w^n \in Z_h^0$ as follows:

$$(u^n, w^n) = h \sum_{j=1}^{J-1} u_j^n w_j^n, \quad \|u^n\| = \sqrt{(u^n, u^n)}, \quad \|u^n\|_\infty = \max_{1 \leq j \leq J-1} |u_j^n|.$$

Lemma 1 (See [16]). *For a mesh function $u^n \in Z_h^0$, by Cauchy–Schwarz inequality, we have*

$$\|u_{\tilde{x}}^n\|^2 \leq \|u_{\hat{x}}^n\|^2 \leq \|u_x^n\|^2.$$

Lemma 2 (See [18]). *If $u^n, w^n \in Z_h^0$ are two mesh functions, we have*

$$(u_x^n, w^n) = -(u^n, w_{\bar{x}}^n) = -(u^n, w_x^n), \quad (u_{x\bar{x}}^n, w^n) = -(u_x^n, w_x^n), \quad (u_{\hat{x}}^n, w^n) = -(u^n, w_{\hat{x}}^n).$$

Furthermore,

$$(u_{x\bar{x}}^n, u^n) = -\|u_x^n\|^2, \quad \|u_{\hat{x}}^n\| \leq \|u_x^n\| = \|u_{\bar{x}}^n\|.$$

Lemma 3 (See [26]). *Assume that a sequence of non-negative real numbers $\{a_j\}_{j=0}^\infty$ satisfying*

$$a_{n+1} \leq \alpha + \beta \sum_{j=0}^n a_j \tau, \quad n \geq 0,$$

has the inequality $a_{n+1} \leq (\alpha + \tau \beta a_0) e^{\beta(n+1)\tau}$, where $\alpha \geq 0, \beta$ and τ are positive constants.

Lemma 4 (See [28]). *For a mesh function $u^n \in Z_h^0$, there exists constants C_1 and C_2, such that*

$$\|u^n\|_\infty \leq C_1 \|u^n\| + C_2 \|u_x^n\|.$$

3. Construction of Two-Level Time-Mesh Difference Scheme

This article is inspired by the approach presented in [16], which involves a nonlinear implementation and requires a significant amount of CPU time. To address the problem, this study constructed a numerical difference scheme by incorporating the two-level time-mesh technique for the SRLW equation.

Prior to introducing the proposed scheme, we define the coarse time-mesh and the fine time-mesh. First, the time interval $(0, T]$ is equally divided into P small time intervals. This divided time-mesh is called a coarse time-mesh. Secondly, each small time interval is further partitioned into $s(2 \leq s \in \mathbb{Z}^+)$ intervals. The mesh after this second segmentation is called a fine time-mesh. The coarse time-mesh has the time levels $t_{ks} = k\tau_C (k = 0, 1, \ldots, P)$ and $0 = t_0 < t_s < t_{2s} < \ldots < t_{Ps} = T$, and the fine time-mesh has the time levels $t_n = n\tau_F (n = 0, 1, 2, \ldots, Ps = N)$ and $0 = t_0 < t_1 < t_2 < \ldots < t_N = T$, where $\tau_C = s\tau_F$ and τ_F are the coarse and fine time step size, respectively. The combination of above two different time-meshes is referred to as a two-level time-mesh.

The two-level time-mesh difference scheme for the SRLW equation is presented as follows. Let $u_{C,j}^{ks} = u(x_j, t_{ks}), \rho_{C,j}^{ks} = \rho(x_j, t_{ks})$ be the numerical solutions on the coarse time-mesh, then we calculate the $u_{C,j}^{ks}$ and $\rho_{C,j}^{ks}$ by the following nonlinear scheme in [16],

$$(u_{C,j}^{ks})_t - \frac{4}{3}(u_{C,j}^{ks})_{x\hat{x}t} + \frac{1}{3}(u_{C,j}^{ks})_{\hat{x}\hat{x}t} + \frac{4}{3}(\rho_{C,j}^{ks+\frac{1}{2}})_{\hat{x}} - \frac{1}{3}(\rho_{C,j}^{ks+\frac{1}{2}})_{\check{x}}$$
$$+ \frac{4}{9}\{u_{C,j}^{ks+\frac{1}{2}}(u_{C,j}^{ks+\frac{1}{2}})_{\hat{x}} + [(u_{C,j}^{ks+\frac{1}{2}})^2]_{\hat{x}}\} - \frac{1}{9}\{u_{C,j}^{ks+\frac{1}{2}}(u_{C,j}^{ks+\frac{1}{2}})_{\check{x}} + [(u_{C,j}^{ks+\frac{1}{2}})^2]_{\check{x}}\} = 0, \qquad (2)$$

$$(\rho_{C,j}^{ks})_t + \frac{4}{3}(u_{C,j}^{ks+\frac{1}{2}})_{\hat{x}} - \frac{1}{3}(u_{C,j}^{ks+\frac{1}{2}})_{\check{x}} = 0, \qquad (3)$$

$$u_{C,0}^{ks} = u_{C,J}^{ks} = 0, \quad \rho_{C,0}^{ks} = \rho_{C,J}^{ks} = 0, \quad 1 \leq k \leq P,$$
$$u_{C,j}^0 = u_0(x_L + jh), \quad \rho_{C,j}^0 = \rho_0(x_L + jh), \quad 1 \leq j \leq J - 1,$$

where $u_{C,j}^{ks+\frac{1}{2}} = \frac{1}{2}(u_{C,j}^{(k+1)s} + u_{C,j}^{ks}), \rho_{C,j}^{ks+\frac{1}{2}} = \frac{1}{2}(\rho_{C,j}^{(k+1)s} + \rho_{C,j}^{ks})$.

Then, using the solutions u_C^{ks} and ρ_C^{ks} obtained at time levels t_{ks} from the initial step, we employ Lagrange's linear interpolation formula to calculate $u_C^{ks-l}, \rho_C^{ks-l}$ at time levels $t_{ks-l}(l = s-1, s-2, \ldots, 2, 1 \text{ and } k = 1, 2, \ldots, P)$ and have

$$u_C^{ks-l} = \frac{t_{ks-l} - t_{ks}}{t_{(k-1)s} - t_{ks}} u_C^{(k-1)s} + \frac{t_{ks-l} - t_{(k-1)s}}{t_{ks} - t_{(k-1)s}} u_C^{ks} = \frac{l}{s} u_C^{(k-1)s} + (1 - \frac{l}{s}) u_C^{ks}, \qquad (4)$$

$$\rho_C^{ks-l} = \frac{t_{ks-1} - t_{ks}}{t_{(k-1)s} - t_{ks}} \rho_C^{(k-1)s} + \frac{t_{ks-1} - t_{(k-1)s}}{t_{ks} - t_{(k-1)s}} \rho_C^{ks} = \frac{l}{s} \rho_C^{(k-1)s} + (1 - \frac{l}{s}) \rho_C^{ks}. \qquad (5)$$

By following the previous two steps, we obtain all the numerical solutions $u_{C,j}^n$ and ρ_C^n ($n = 1, 2, \ldots, Ps = N, j = 1, 2, \ldots, J - 1$) on the fine time-mesh. It is important to note that the numerical solutions $u_{C,j}^n$ and ρ_C^n are only preliminary solutions and not the ultimate numerical solutions we aim to achieve for the SRLW equation.

Remark 1. *The solutions ρ_C^n are not essential for the subsequent step but are used for convergence and stability analysis of the proposed scheme.*

Next, we design a linear system on the fine time-mesh to obtain the final numerical solutions for the SRLW equation. Let $u_{F,j}^n = u(x_j, t_n), \rho_{F,j}^n = \rho(x_j, t_n)$ be the numerical solutions on the fine time-mesh, then similar to Equations (2) and (3), we obtain

$$(u_{F,j}^n)_t - \frac{4}{3}(u_{F,j}^n)_{x\hat{x}t} + \frac{1}{3}(u_{F,j}^n)_{\hat{x}\hat{x}t} + \frac{4}{3}(\rho_{F,j}^{n+\frac{1}{2}})_{\hat{x}} - \frac{1}{3}(\rho_{F,j}^{n+\frac{1}{2}})_{\check{x}}$$
$$+ \frac{4}{9}\{u_{F,j}^{n+\frac{1}{2}}(u_{F,j}^{n+\frac{1}{2}})_{\hat{x}} + [(u_{F,j}^{n+\frac{1}{2}})^2]_{\hat{x}}\} - \frac{1}{9}\{u_{F,j}^{n+\frac{1}{2}}(u_{F,j}^{n+\frac{1}{2}})_{\check{x}} + [(u_{F,j}^{n+\frac{1}{2}})^2]_{\check{x}}\} = 0, \qquad (6)$$

$$(\rho_{F,j}^n)_t + \frac{4}{3}(u_{F,j}^{n+\frac{1}{2}})_{\hat{x}} - \frac{1}{3}(u_{F,j}^{n+\frac{1}{2}})_{\check{x}} = 0, \qquad (7)$$

However, as we know, Equation (6) is still a nonlinear scheme. In order to construct the linear system, we use Taylor's formula to linearize the nonlinear terms of Equation (6) as follows. Using the notations in Section 2, we have

$$
\begin{aligned}
&\frac{4}{9}\{u_{F,j}^{n+\frac{1}{2}}(u_{F,j}^{n+\frac{1}{2}})_{\hat{x}} + [(u_{F,j}^{n+\frac{1}{2}})^2]_{\hat{x}}\} - \frac{1}{9}\{u_{F,j}^{n+\frac{1}{2}}(u_{F,j}^{n+\frac{1}{2}})_{\check{x}} + [(u_{F,j}^{n+\frac{1}{2}})^2]_{\check{x}}\} \\
&= \frac{2}{9h}\{u_{F,j}^{n+\frac{1}{2}}(u_{F,j+1}^{n+\frac{1}{2}} - u_{F,j-1}^{n+\frac{1}{2}}) + (u_{F,j+1}^{n+\frac{1}{2}})^2 - (u_{F,j-1}^{n+\frac{1}{2}})^2\} \\
&\quad - \frac{1}{36h}\{u_{F,j}^{n+\frac{1}{2}}(u_{F,j+2}^{n+\frac{1}{2}} - u_{F,j-2}^{n+\frac{1}{2}}) + (u_{F,j+2}^{n+\frac{1}{2}})^2 - (u_{F,j-2}^{n+\frac{1}{2}})^2\} \\
&= \frac{2}{9h}f(u_{F,j-1}^{n+\frac{1}{2}}, u_{F,j}^{n+\frac{1}{2}}, u_{F,j+1}^{n+\frac{1}{2}}) - \frac{1}{36h}f(u_{F,j-2}^{n+\frac{1}{2}}, u_{F,j}^{n+\frac{1}{2}}, u_{F,j+2}^{n+\frac{1}{2}})
\end{aligned}
\tag{8}
$$

where $f(x,y,z) = (z-x)y + z^2 - x^2$. Then, the Taylor's formula expansion is used to linearize the first part of Equation (8) at point $(u_{C,j-1}^{n+\frac{1}{2}}, u_{C,j}^{n+\frac{1}{2}}, u_{C,j+1}^{n+\frac{1}{2}})$ and the second part of Equation (8) at point $(u_{C,j-2}^{n+\frac{1}{2}}, u_{C,j}^{n+\frac{1}{2}}, u_{C,j+2}^{n+\frac{1}{2}})$, respectively, to obtain

$$
\begin{aligned}
&f(u_{F,j-1}^{n+\frac{1}{2}}, u_{F,j}^{n+\frac{1}{2}}, u_{F,j+1}^{n+\frac{1}{2}}) \\
&\approx f(u_{C,j-1}^{n+\frac{1}{2}}, u_{C,j}^{n+\frac{1}{2}}, u_{C,j+1}^{n+\frac{1}{2}}) + f_x(u_{C,j-1}^{n+\frac{1}{2}}, u_{C,j}^{n+\frac{1}{2}}, u_{C,j+1}^{n+\frac{1}{2}})(u_{F,j-1}^{n+\frac{1}{2}} - u_{C,j-1}^{n+\frac{1}{2}}) \\
&\quad + f_y(u_{C,j-1}^{n+\frac{1}{2}}, u_{C,j}^{n+\frac{1}{2}}, u_{C,j+1}^{n+\frac{1}{2}})(u_{F,j}^{n+\frac{1}{2}} - u_{C,j}^{n+\frac{1}{2}}) + f_z(u_{C,j-1}^{n+\frac{1}{2}}, u_{C,j}^{n+\frac{1}{2}}, u_{C,j+1}^{n+\frac{1}{2}})(u_{F,j+1}^{n+\frac{1}{2}} - u_{C,j+1}^{n+\frac{1}{2}})
\end{aligned}
\tag{9}
$$

and

$$
\begin{aligned}
&f(u_{F,j-2}^{n+\frac{1}{2}}, u_{F,j}^{n+\frac{1}{2}}, u_{F,j+2}^{n+\frac{1}{2}}) \\
&\approx f(u_{C,j-2}^{n+\frac{1}{2}}, u_{C,j}^{n+\frac{1}{2}}, u_{C,j+2}^{n+\frac{1}{2}}) + f_x(u_{C,j-2}^{n+\frac{1}{2}}, u_{C,j}^{n+\frac{1}{2}}, u_{C,j+2}^{n+\frac{1}{2}})(u_{F,j-2}^{n+\frac{1}{2}} - u_{C,j-2}^{n+\frac{1}{2}}) \\
&\quad + f_y(u_{C,j-2}^{n+\frac{1}{2}}, u_{C,j}^{n+\frac{1}{2}}, u_{C,j+2}^{n+\frac{1}{2}})(u_{F,j}^{n+\frac{1}{2}} - u_{C,j}^{n+\frac{1}{2}}) + f_z(u_{C,j-2}^{n+\frac{1}{2}}, u_{C,j}^{n+\frac{1}{2}}, u_{C,j+2}^{n+\frac{1}{2}})(u_{F,j+2}^{n+\frac{1}{2}} - u_{C,j+2}^{n+\frac{1}{2}})
\end{aligned}
\tag{10}
$$

Substituting Equations (8)–(10) into Equation (6) and denoting $f_j = f(u_{C,j-1}^{n+\frac{1}{2}}, u_{C,j}^{n+\frac{1}{2}}, u_{C,j+1}^{n+\frac{1}{2}})$, $f_{x,j} = f_x(u_{C,j-1}^{n+\frac{1}{2}}, u_{C,j}^{n+\frac{1}{2}}, u_{C,j+1}^{n+\frac{1}{2}})$, $f_{y,j} = f_y(u_{C,j-1}^{n+\frac{1}{2}}, u_{C,j}^{n+\frac{1}{2}}, u_{C,j+1}^{n+\frac{1}{2}})$, $f_{z,j} = f_z(u_{C,j-1}^{n+\frac{1}{2}}, u_{C,j}^{n+\frac{1}{2}}, u_{C,j+1}^{n+\frac{1}{2}})$, $\tilde{f}_j = f(u_{C,j-2}^{n+\frac{1}{2}}, u_{C,j}^{n+\frac{1}{2}}, u_{C,j+2}^{n+\frac{1}{2}})$, $\tilde{f}_{x,j} = f_x(u_{C,j-2}^{n+\frac{1}{2}}, u_{C,j}^{n+\frac{1}{2}}, u_{C,j+2}^{n+\frac{1}{2}})$, $\tilde{f}_{y,j} = f_y(u_{C,j-2}^{n+\frac{1}{2}}, u_{C,j}^{n+\frac{1}{2}}, u_{C,j+2}^{n+\frac{1}{2}})$, $\tilde{f}_{z,j} = f_z(u_{C,j-2}^{n+\frac{1}{2}}, u_{C,j}^{n+\frac{1}{2}}, u_{C,j+2}^{n+\frac{1}{2}})$, we construct a novel linear difference scheme that achieves a second-order convergence rate in time and a fourth-order convergence rate in space on the fine time-mesh as follows:

$$
\begin{aligned}
&(u_{F,j}^n)_t - \frac{4}{3}(u_{F,j}^n)_{x\hat{x}t} + \frac{1}{3}(u_{F,j}^n)_{\hat{x}\check{x}t} + \frac{4}{3}(\rho_{F,j}^{n+\frac{1}{2}})_{\hat{x}} - \frac{1}{3}(\rho_{F,j}^{n+\frac{1}{2}})_{\check{x}} \\
&+ \frac{2}{9h}\{f_j + f_{x,j} \cdot (u_{F,j-1}^{n+\frac{1}{2}} - u_{C,j-1}^{n+\frac{1}{2}}) + f_{y,j} \cdot (u_{F,j}^{n+\frac{1}{2}} - u_{C,j}^{n+\frac{1}{2}}) \\
&+ f_{z,j} \cdot (u_{F,j+1}^{n+\frac{1}{2}} - u_{C,j+1}^{n+\frac{1}{2}})\} - \frac{1}{36h}\{\tilde{f}_j + \tilde{f}_{x,j} \cdot (u_{F,j-2}^{n+\frac{1}{2}} - u_{C,j-2}^{n+\frac{1}{2}}) \\
&+ \tilde{f}_{y,j} \cdot (u_{F,j}^{n+\frac{1}{2}} - u_{C,j}^{n+\frac{1}{2}}) + \tilde{f}_{z,j} \cdot (u_{F,j+2}^{n+\frac{1}{2}} - u_{C,j+2}^{n+\frac{1}{2}})\} = 0,
\end{aligned}
\tag{11}
$$

$$
(\rho_{F,j}^n)_t + \frac{4}{3}(u_{F,j}^{n+\frac{1}{2}})_{\hat{x}} - \frac{1}{3}(u_{F,j}^{n+\frac{1}{2}})_{\check{x}} = 0,
\tag{12}
$$

$$
u_{F,0}^n = u_{F,J}^n = 0, \quad \rho_{F,0}^n = \rho_{F,J}^n = 0, \quad 1 \leq n \leq N,
$$
$$
u_{F,j}^0 = u_0(x_L + jh), \quad \rho_{F,j}^0 = \rho_0(x_L + jh), \quad 1 \leq j \leq J-1,
$$

where
$$f_x(x,y,z) = -y - 2x, f_y(x,y,z) = z - x, f_z(x,y,z) = y + 2z$$
are the three partial derivatives of $f(x,y,z)$ with respect to x, y, z. The benefit of our method is that we avoid having to solve nonlinear equations at many time levels, and that instead, solve a much less expensive linear system.

Remark 2. *From Equation (11), one knows that the values u_F^n, u_C^n, u_C^{n+1} are utilized to obtain the u_F^{n+1}. However, similar to the Gauss–Seidel method applied to linear systems, our scheme has been modified by using u_F^n obtained from the previous time level instead of u_C^n in the calculation process to enhance the accuracy of the numerical solutions u_F^{n+1}.*

Remark 3. *The nonlinear system (2)–(3) is solved by Newton's method and when $|u_{F,j}^{n(k+1)} - u_{F,j}^{n(k)}| < 10^{-10}$, iteration stops, where k is the number of iterations. The linear system (11)–(12) is computed by a direct solver.*

4. The Convergence and Stability Analysis of the Scheme

In this section, we focus on conducting a convergence and stability analysis of scheme (2)–(5) on the coarse time-mesh and scheme (11)–(12) on the fine time-mesh. Let $v_j^n = u(x_j, t_n)$, $\varphi_j^n = \rho(x_j, t_n)$ be the exact solutions of problem (1), then the truncation errors of the difference scheme (2)–(3) are obtained as follows:

$$Er_{C,j}^{ks} = (v_j^{ks})_t - \frac{4}{3}(v_j^{ks})_{x\hat{x}t} + \frac{1}{3}(v_j^{ks})_{\hat{x}\hat{x}t} + \frac{4}{3}(\varphi_j^{ks+\frac{1}{2}})_{\hat{x}} - \frac{1}{3}(\varphi_j^{ks+\frac{1}{2}})_{\check{x}}$$
$$+ \frac{4}{9}\{v_j^{ks+\frac{1}{2}}(v_j^{ks+\frac{1}{2}})_{\hat{x}} + [(v_j^{ks+\frac{1}{2}})^2]_{\hat{x}}\} - \frac{1}{9}\{v_j^{ks+\frac{1}{2}}(v_j^{ks+\frac{1}{2}})_{\check{x}} + [(v_j^{ks+\frac{1}{2}})^2]_{\check{x}}\}, \tag{13}$$

$$Es_{C,j}^{ks} = (\varphi_j^{ks})_t + \frac{4}{3}(v_j^{ks+\frac{1}{2}})_{\hat{x}} - \frac{1}{3}(v_j^{ks+\frac{1}{2}})_{\check{x}}, \tag{14}$$

$$v_0^{ks} = v_J^{ks} = 0, \varphi_0^{ks} = \varphi_J^{ks} = 0, \quad 1 \leq k \leq P,$$
$$v_j^0 = v_0(x_L + jh), \varphi_j^0 = \varphi_0(x_L + jh), \quad 1 \leq j \leq J - 1.$$

By Taylor series expansion, we conclude

$$Er_{C,j}^{ks} = (u_t + \rho_x + uu_x - u_{xxt})_{(x_j, t_{ks})} + O(\tau_C^2 + h^4),$$

$$Es_{C,j}^{ks} = (\rho_t + u_x)_{(x_j, t_{ks})} + O(\tau_C^2 + h^4).$$

Theorem 1. *Suppose that $u_C^0 \in H_0^1[x_L, x_R], \rho_C^0 \in L_2[x_L, x_R]$, then the solutions of difference scheme (2)–(5) converge to the solutions of problem (1) with an order of $(\tau_C^2 + h^4)$ by the L_∞ norm for u_C^n and by the L_2 norm for ρ_C^n.*

Proof of Theorem 1. Denote $e_{C,j}^{ks} = v_j^{ks} - u_{C,j}^{ks}$, $\eta_{C,j}^{ks} = \varphi_j^{ks} - \rho_{C,j}^{ks}$, $1 \leq j \leq J-1, 1 \leq k \leq P$. Subtracting Equation (2) from Equation (13), we obtain

$$Er_{C,j}^{ks} = (e_{C,j}^{ks})_t - \frac{4}{3}(e_{C,j}^{ks})_{x\hat{x}t} + \frac{1}{3}(e_{C,j}^{ks})_{\hat{x}\hat{x}t} + \frac{4}{3}(\eta_{C,j}^{ks+\frac{1}{2}})_{\hat{x}} - \frac{1}{3}(\eta_{C,j}^{ks+\frac{1}{2}})_{\check{x}}$$
$$+ \frac{4}{9}\{v_j^{ks+\frac{1}{2}}(v_j^{ks+\frac{1}{2}})_{\hat{x}} + [(v_j^{ks+\frac{1}{2}})^2]_{\hat{x}}\} - \frac{4}{9}\{u_{C,j}^{ks+\frac{1}{2}}(u_{C,j}^{ks+\frac{1}{2}})_{\hat{x}} + [(u_{C,j}^{ks+\frac{1}{2}})^2]_{\hat{x}}\} \tag{15}$$
$$- \frac{1}{9}\{v_j^{ks+\frac{1}{2}}(v_j^{ks+\frac{1}{2}})_{\check{x}} + [(v_j^{ks+\frac{1}{2}})^2]_{\check{x}}\} + \frac{1}{9}\{u_{C,j}^{ks+\frac{1}{2}}(u_{C,j}^{ks+\frac{1}{2}})_{\check{x}} + [(u_{C,j}^{ks+\frac{1}{2}})^2]_{\check{x}}\}.$$

Subtracting Equation (3) from Equation (14), we obtain

$$Es_{C,j}^{ks} = (\eta_{C,j}^{ks})_t + \frac{4}{3}(e_{C,j}^{ks+\frac{1}{2}})_{\hat{x}} - \frac{1}{3}(e_{C,j}^{ks+\frac{1}{2}})_{\hat{x}}, \qquad (16)$$

$$e_{C,j}^0 = 0, \quad \eta_{C,j}^0 = 0,$$
$$u_0^{ks} = u_J^{ks} = 0, \quad \rho_0^{ks} = \rho_J^{ks} = 0.$$

The following validation of the theorem consists of two situations: (i) We first prove the situation of $n = ks(k = 1, 2, \ldots, P)$; please refer to the references [16,27] for the proof of this part. In the end, we obtain

$$\|e_C^n\| \leq O(\tau_C^2 + h^4), \quad \|e_{C,x}^n\| \leq O(\tau_C^2 + h^4), \quad \|\eta_C^n\| \leq O(\tau_C^2 + h^4). \qquad (17)$$

From Lemma 4, we have

$$\|e_C^n\|_\infty \leq O(\tau_C^2 + h^4); \qquad (18)$$

(ii) Next, we prove the situation of $n = ks - l(l = s - 1, s - 2, \ldots, 2, 1$ and $k = 1, 2, \ldots, P)$. We use Lagrange's interpolation formula and obtain

$$\begin{aligned} v^{ks-l} &= \frac{t_{ks-l} - t_{ks}}{t_{(k-1)s} - t_{ks}} v^{(k-1)s} + \frac{t_{ks-l} - t_{(k-1)s}}{t_{ks} - t_{(k-1)s}} v^{ks} \\ &= \frac{l}{s} v^{(k-1)s} + (1 - \frac{l}{s}) v^{ks} + \frac{v''(\theta_1)}{2}(t - t_{(k-1)s})(t - t_{ks}), \quad \theta_1 \in (t_{(k-1)s}, t_{ks}), \end{aligned} \qquad (19)$$

$$\begin{aligned} \varphi^{ks-l} &= \frac{t_{ks-l} - t_{ks}}{t_{(k-1)s} - t_{ks}} \varphi^{(k-1)s} + \frac{t_{ks-l} - t_{(k-1)s}}{t_{ks} - t_{(k-1)s}} \varphi^{ks} \\ &= \frac{l}{s} \varphi^{(k-1)s} + (1 - \frac{l}{s}) \varphi^{ks} + \frac{\varphi''(\theta_2)}{2}(t - t_{(k-1)s})(t - t_{ks}), \quad \theta_2 \in (t_{(k-1)s}, t_{ks}). \end{aligned} \qquad (20)$$

Subtracting Equation (4) from Equation (19), we obtain

$$\begin{aligned} v^{ks-l} - u_C^{ks-l} &= \frac{l}{s}(v^{(k-1)s} - u_C^{(k-1)s}) + (1 - \frac{l}{s})(v^{ks} - u_C^{ks}) \\ &+ \frac{v''(\theta_1)}{2}(t - t_{(k-1)s})(t - t_{ks}). \end{aligned}$$

Subtracting Equation (5) from Equation (20), we obtain

$$\begin{aligned} \varphi^{ks-l} - \rho_C^{ks-l} &= \frac{l}{s}(\varphi^{(k-1)s} - \rho_C^{(k-1)s}) + (1 - \frac{l}{s})(\varphi^{ks} - \rho_C^{ks}) \\ &+ \frac{\varphi''(\theta_2)}{2}(t - t_{(k-1)s})(t - t_{ks}). \end{aligned}$$

From the triangle inequality and the results (17) and (18), we conclude

$$\|e_C^{ks-l}\| \leq O(\tau_C^2 + h^4), \quad \|e_{C,x}^{ks-l}\| \leq O(\tau_C^2 + h^4), \quad \|\eta_C^{ks-l}\| \leq O(\tau_C^2 + h^4), \qquad (21)$$

and

$$\|e_C^{ks-l}\|_\infty \leq O(\tau_C^2 + h^4). \qquad (22)$$

We derive the result of Theorem 1 by combining the two above-mentioned cases. □

Theorem 2. *Suppose that* $u_C^0 \in H_0^1[x_L, x_R], \rho_C^0 \in L_2[x_L, x_R]$, *then the solutions of difference scheme (2)–(5) are stable by the L_∞ norm for u_C^n and by the L_2 norm for ρ_C^n.*

Proof of Theorem 2. The theorem can be proved in the same way as that used to prove Theorem 1. □

Next, we analyze the convergence and stability of linear system (11) and (12) on the fine time-mesh. For simplification, we further denote $f_{xx,j} = f_{xx}(\xi_{j-1}, \varepsilon_j, \delta_{j+1})$, $f_{yy,j} = f_{yy}(\xi_{j-1}, \varepsilon_j, \delta_{j+1})$, $f_{zz,j} = f_{zz}(\xi_{j-1}, \varepsilon_j, \delta_{j+1})$, $\tilde{f}_{xx,j} = f_{xx}(\tilde{\xi}_{j-2}, \tilde{\varepsilon}_j, \tilde{\delta}_{j+2})$, $\tilde{f}_{yy,j} = f_{yy}(\tilde{\xi}_{j-2}, \tilde{\varepsilon}_j, \tilde{\delta}_{j+2})$, $\tilde{f}_{zz,j} = f_{zz}(\tilde{\xi}_{j-2}, \tilde{\varepsilon}_j, \tilde{\delta}_{j+2})$, $f_{xy,j} = f_{xy}(\xi_{j-1}, \varepsilon_j, \delta_{j+1})$, $f_{xz,j} = f_{xz}(\xi_{j-1}, \varepsilon_j, \delta_{j+1})$, $f_{yz,j} = f_{yz}(\xi_{j-1}, \varepsilon_j, \delta_{j+1})$, $\tilde{f}_{xy,j} = f_{xy}(\tilde{\xi}_{j-2}, \tilde{\varepsilon}_j, \tilde{\delta}_{j+2})$, $\tilde{f}_{xz,j} = f_{xz}(\tilde{\xi}_{j-2}, \tilde{\varepsilon}_j, \tilde{\delta}_{j+2})$, $\tilde{f}_{yz,j} = f_{yz}(\tilde{\xi}_{j-2}, \tilde{\varepsilon}_j, \tilde{\delta}_{j+2})$, where $f_{xx}(x,y,z) = -2$, $f_{yy}(x,y,z) = 0$, $f_{zz}(x,y,z) = 2$, $f_{xy}(x,y,z) = -1$, $f_{xz}(x,y,z) = 0$, $f_{yz}(x,y,z) = 1$ are the second-order partial derivatives of $f(x,y,z)$, $\xi_{j-1} \in (v_{j-1}^n, u_{C,j-1}^n)$, $\varepsilon_j \in (v_j^n, u_{C,j}^n)$, $\delta_{j+1} \in (v_{j+1}^n, u_{C,j+1}^n)$, $\tilde{\xi}_{j-2} \in (v_{j-2}^n, u_{C,j-2}^n)$, $\tilde{\varepsilon}_j \in (v_j^n, u_{C,j}^n)$, $\tilde{\delta}_{j+2} \in (v_{j+2}^n, u_{C,j+2}^n)$, then the truncation errors of the scheme (11)–(12) are obtained as follows:

$$\begin{aligned}
Er_{F,j}^n = & (v_j^n)_t - \frac{4}{3}(v_j^n)_{x\hat{x}t} + \frac{1}{3}(v_j^n)_{\hat{x}\hat{x}t} + \frac{4}{3}(\varphi_j^{n+\frac{1}{2}})_{\hat{x}} - \frac{1}{3}(\varphi_j^{n+\frac{1}{2}})_{\hat{x}} \\
& + \frac{2}{9h}\{f_j + f_{x,j} \cdot (v_{j-1}^{n+\frac{1}{2}} - u_{C,j-1}^{n+\frac{1}{2}}) + f_{y,j} \cdot (v_j^{n+\frac{1}{2}} - u_{C,j}^{n+\frac{1}{2}}) + f_{z,j} \cdot (v_{j+1}^{n+\frac{1}{2}} - u_{C,j+1}^{n+\frac{1}{2}}) \\
& + \frac{1}{2}f_{xx,j} \cdot (v_{j-1}^{n+\frac{1}{2}} - u_{C,j-1}^{n+\frac{1}{2}})^2 + \frac{1}{2}f_{yy,j} \cdot (v_j^{n+\frac{1}{2}} - u_{C,j}^{n+\frac{1}{2}})^2 + \frac{1}{2}f_{zz,j} \cdot (v_{j+1}^{n+\frac{1}{2}} - u_{C,j+1}^{n+\frac{1}{2}})^2 \\
& + f_{xy,j} \cdot (v_{j-1}^{n+\frac{1}{2}} - u_{C,j-1}^{n+\frac{1}{2}})(v_j^{n+\frac{1}{2}} - u_{C,j}^{n+\frac{1}{2}}) + f_{xz,j} \cdot (v_{j-1}^{n+\frac{1}{2}} - u_{C,j-1}^{n+\frac{1}{2}})(v_{j+1}^{n+\frac{1}{2}} - u_{C,j+1}^{n+\frac{1}{2}}) \\
& + f_{yz,j} \cdot (v_j^{n+\frac{1}{2}} - u_{C,j}^{n+\frac{1}{2}})(v_{j+1}^{n+\frac{1}{2}} - u_{C,j+1}^{n+\frac{1}{2}})\} \\
& - \frac{1}{36h}\{\tilde{f}_j + \tilde{f}_{x,j} \cdot (v_{j-2}^{n+\frac{1}{2}} - u_{C,j-2}^{n+\frac{1}{2}}) + \tilde{f}_{y,j} \cdot (v_j^{n+\frac{1}{2}} - u_{C,j}^{n+\frac{1}{2}}) + \tilde{f}_{z,j} \cdot (v_{j+2}^{n+\frac{1}{2}} - u_{C,j+2}^{n+\frac{1}{2}}) \\
& + \frac{1}{2}\tilde{f}_{xx,j} \cdot (v_{j-2}^{n+\frac{1}{2}} - u_{C,j-2}^{n+\frac{1}{2}})^2 + \frac{1}{2}\tilde{f}_{yy,j} \cdot (v_j^{n+\frac{1}{2}} - u_{C,j}^{n+\frac{1}{2}})^2 + \frac{1}{2}\tilde{f}_{zz,j} \cdot (v_{j+2}^{n+\frac{1}{2}} - u_{C,j+2}^{n+\frac{1}{2}})^2 \\
& + \tilde{f}_{xy,j} \cdot (v_{j-2}^{n+\frac{1}{2}} - u_{C,j-2}^{n+\frac{1}{2}})(v_j^{n+\frac{1}{2}} - u_{C,j}^{n+\frac{1}{2}}) + \tilde{f}_{xz,j} \cdot (v_{j-2}^{n+\frac{1}{2}} - u_{C,j-2}^{n+\frac{1}{2}})(v_{j+2}^{n+\frac{1}{2}} - u_{C,j+2}^{n+\frac{1}{2}}) \\
& + \tilde{f}_{yz,j} \cdot (v_j^{n+\frac{1}{2}} - u_{C,j}^{n+\frac{1}{2}})(v_{j+2}^{n+\frac{1}{2}} - u_{C,j+2}^{n+\frac{1}{2}})\},
\end{aligned} \tag{23}$$

$$Es_{F,j}^n = (\varphi_j^n)_t + \frac{4}{3}(v_j^{n+\frac{1}{2}})_{\hat{x}} - \frac{1}{3}(v_j^{n+\frac{1}{2}})_{\hat{x}}, \tag{24}$$

$$v_0^n = v_J^n = 0, \quad \varphi_0^n = \varphi_J^n = 0, \quad 1 \leq n \leq N,$$
$$v_j^0 = v_0(x_L + jh), \quad \varphi_j^0 = \varphi_0(x_L + jh), \quad 1 \leq j \leq J - 1.$$

Theorem 3. *Suppose that $u_F^0 \in H_0^1[x_L, x_R], \rho_F^0 \in L_2[x_L, x_R]$, then the solutions of difference scheme (11)–(12) converge to the solutions of problem (1) with an order of $(\tau_F^2 + \tau_C^4 + h^4)$ by the L_∞ norm for u_F^n and by the L_2 norm for ρ_F^n.*

Proof of Theorem 3. Denote $e_{F,j}^n = v_j^n - u_{F,j}^n$, $\eta_{F,j}^n = \varphi_j^n - \rho_{F,j}^n$, $1 \leq j \leq J - 1, 1 \leq n \leq N$. Subtracting Equation (11) from Equation (23), we obtain

$$\begin{aligned}
Er_{F,j}^n = & (e_{F,j}^n)_t - \frac{4}{3}(e_{F,j}^n)_{x\hat{x}t} + \frac{1}{3}(e_{F,j}^n)_{\hat{x}\hat{x}t} + \frac{4}{3}(\eta_{F,j}^{n+\frac{1}{2}})_{\hat{x}} - \frac{1}{3}(\eta_{F,j}^{n+\frac{1}{2}})_{\hat{x}} \\
& + \frac{2}{9h}\{f_{x,j} \cdot e_{F,j-1}^{n+\frac{1}{2}} + f_{y,j} \cdot e_{F,j}^{n+\frac{1}{2}} + f_{z,j} \cdot e_{F,j+1}^{n+\frac{1}{2}} + Q_1\} \\
& - \frac{1}{36h}\{\tilde{f}_{x,j} \cdot e_{F,j-2}^{n+\frac{1}{2}} + \tilde{f}_{y,j} \cdot e_{F,j}^{n+\frac{1}{2}} + \tilde{f}_{z,j} \cdot e_{F,j+2}^{n+\frac{1}{2}} + Q_2\},
\end{aligned} \tag{25}$$

where

$$Q_1 = -(e_{C,j-1}^{n+\frac{1}{2}})^2 + (e_{C,j+1}^{n+\frac{1}{2}})^2 - (e_{C,j-1}^{n+\frac{1}{2}})(e_{C,j}^{n+\frac{1}{2}}) + (e_{C,j}^{n+\frac{1}{2}})(e_{C,j+1}^{n+\frac{1}{2}}),$$

$$Q_2 = -(e_{C,j-2}^{n+\frac{1}{2}})^2 + (e_{C,j+2}^{n+\frac{1}{2}})^2 - (e_{C,j-2}^{n+\frac{1}{2}})(e_{C,j}^{n+\frac{1}{2}}) + (e_{C,j}^{n+\frac{1}{2}})(e_{C,j+2}^{n+\frac{1}{2}}).$$

Subtracting Equation (12) from Equation (24), we have

$$Es_{F,j}^n = (\eta_{F,j}^n)_t + \frac{4}{3}(e_{F,j}^{n+\frac{1}{2}})_{\hat{x}} - \frac{1}{3}(e_{F,j}^{n+\frac{1}{2}})_{\check{x}}. \tag{26}$$

Taking the inner product $(\cdot, \cdot)$ on both sides of Equation (25) with $2e_F^{n+\frac{1}{2}}$, we have

$$(Er_F^n, 2e_F^{n+\frac{1}{2}}) = (e_{F,t}^n, 2e_F^{n+\frac{1}{2}}) - \frac{4}{3}(e_{F,x\hat{x}t}^n, 2e_F^{n+\frac{1}{2}}) + \frac{1}{3}(e_{F,\hat{x}xt}^n, 2e_F^{n+\frac{1}{2}}) + \frac{8}{3}(\eta_{F,\hat{x}}^{n+\frac{1}{2}}, e_F^{n+\frac{1}{2}})$$
$$- \frac{2}{3}(\eta_{F,\check{x}}^{n+\frac{1}{2}}, e_F^{n+\frac{1}{2}}) + \frac{4}{9}\sum_{j=1}^{J-1}(f_{x,j} \cdot e_{F,j-1}^{n+\frac{1}{2}} + f_{y,j} \cdot e_{F,j}^{n+\frac{1}{2}} + f_{z,j} \cdot e_{F,j+1}^{n+\frac{1}{2}} + Q_1)e_{F,j}^{n+\frac{1}{2}} \tag{27}$$
$$- \frac{1}{18}\sum_{j=1}^{J-1}(\tilde{f}_{x,j} \cdot e_{F,j-2}^{n+\frac{1}{2}} + \tilde{f}_{y,j} \cdot e_{F,j}^{n+\frac{1}{2}} + \tilde{f}_{z,j} \cdot e_{F,j+2}^{n+\frac{1}{2}} + Q_2)e_{F,j}^{n+\frac{1}{2}}.$$

Notice that

$$(e_{F,t}^n, 2e_F^{n+\frac{1}{2}}) = \frac{1}{\tau_F}(\|e_F^{n+1}\|^2 - \|e_F^n\|^2), \tag{28}$$

$$(e_{F,x\hat{x}t}^n, 2e_F^{n+\frac{1}{2}}) = -\frac{1}{\tau_F}(\|e_{F,x}^{n+1}\|^2 - \|e_{F,x}^n\|^2), \tag{29}$$

$$(e_{F,\hat{x}xt}^n, 2e_F^{n+\frac{1}{2}}) = -\frac{1}{\tau_F}(\|e_{F,\hat{x}}^{n+1}\|^2 - \|e_{F,\hat{x}}^n\|^2), \tag{30}$$

$$(\eta_{F,\hat{x}}^{n+\frac{1}{2}}, e_F^{n+\frac{1}{2}}) = -(\eta_F^{n+\frac{1}{2}}, e_{F,\hat{x}}^{n+\frac{1}{2}}), \tag{31}$$

$$(\eta_{F,\check{x}}^{n+\frac{1}{2}}, e_F^{n+\frac{1}{2}}) = -(\eta_F^{n+\frac{1}{2}}, e_{F,\check{x}}^{n+\frac{1}{2}}), \tag{32}$$

$$(Er_F^n, 2e_F^{n+\frac{1}{2}}) \leq \|Er_F^n\|^2 + \|e_F^{n+1}\|^2 + \|e_F^n\|^2. \tag{33}$$

Furthermore, from Lemmas 1 and 2, Lemma 4.2 in [16], and the Cauchy–Schwarz inequality, we have

$$\sum_{j=1}^{J-1}(f_{x,j} \cdot e_{F,j-1}^{n+\frac{1}{2}} + f_{y,j} \cdot e_{F,j}^{n+\frac{1}{2}} + f_{z,j} \cdot e_{F,j+1}^{n+\frac{1}{2}})e_{F,j}^{n+\frac{1}{2}}$$
$$= h\sum_{j=1}^{J-1}[-f_{x,j} \cdot (e_{F,j}^{n+\frac{1}{2}})_{\hat{x}} + \frac{3}{h}f_{y,j} \cdot e_{F,j}^{n+\frac{1}{2}} + f_{z,j} \cdot (e_{F,j}^{n+\frac{1}{2}})_x]e_{F,j}^{n+\frac{1}{2}} \tag{34}$$
$$= -(f_x \cdot e_{F,\hat{x}}^{n+\frac{1}{2}}, e_F^{n+\frac{1}{2}}) + \frac{3}{h}(f_y \cdot e_F^{n+\frac{1}{2}}, e_F^{n+\frac{1}{2}}) + (f_z \cdot e_{F,x}^{n+\frac{1}{2}}, e_F^{n+\frac{1}{2}})$$
$$\leq M(\|e_{F,x}^{n+\frac{1}{2}}\|^2 + \|e_F^{n+\frac{1}{2}}\|^2),$$

$$\sum_{j=1}^{J-1}Q_1 e_{F,j}^{n+\frac{1}{2}} = 2h\sum_{j=1}^{J-1}(e_{C,j}^{n+\frac{1}{2}})_{\hat{x}}^2 e_{F,j}^{n+\frac{1}{2}} + 2h\sum_{j=1}^{J-1}(e_{C,j}^{n+\frac{1}{2}})_{\hat{x}} e_{C,j}^{n+\frac{1}{2}} e_{F,j}^{n+\frac{1}{2}}$$
$$= 2((e_C^{n+\frac{1}{2}})_{\hat{x}}^2, e_F^{n+\frac{1}{2}}) + 2(e_{C,\hat{x}}^{n+\frac{1}{2}} e_C^{n+\frac{1}{2}}, e_F^{n+\frac{1}{2}}) \tag{35}$$
$$\leq M(\|e_C^{n+\frac{1}{2}}\|_\infty^2 \|e_C^{n+\frac{1}{2}}\|^2 + \|e_C^{n+\frac{1}{2}}\|_\infty^2 \|e_{C,x}^{n+\frac{1}{2}}\|^2 + \|e_{F,x}^{n+\frac{1}{2}}\|^2 + \|e_F^{n+\frac{1}{2}}\|^2),$$

$$\sum_{j=1}^{J-1}(\tilde{f}_{x,j}\cdot e_{F,j-2}^{n+\frac{1}{2}}+\tilde{f}_{y,j}\cdot e_{F,j}^{n+\frac{1}{2}}+\tilde{f}_{z,j}\cdot e_{F,j+2}^{n+\frac{1}{2}})e_{F,j}^{n+\frac{1}{2}}$$

$$=h\sum_{j=1}^{J-1}[-\tilde{f}_{x,j}\cdot (e_{F,j-1}^{n+\frac{1}{2}})_{\bar{x}}+\tilde{f}_{z,j}\cdot (e_{F,j+1}^{n+\frac{1}{2}})_{x}]e_{F,j}^{n+\frac{1}{2}}$$

$$+\sum_{j=1}^{J-1}(\tilde{f}_{x,j}\cdot e_{F,j-1}^{n+\frac{1}{2}}+\tilde{f}_{y,j}\cdot e_{F,j}^{n+\frac{1}{2}}+\tilde{f}_{z,j}\cdot e_{F,j+1}^{n+\frac{1}{2}})e_{F,j}^{n+\frac{1}{2}}$$

$$=h^2\sum_{j=1}^{J+1}\tilde{f}_{x,j}\cdot (e_{F,j}^{n+\frac{1}{2}})_{\bar{x}\bar{x}}e_{F,j}^{n+\frac{1}{2}}-h\sum_{j=1}^{J-1}\tilde{f}_{x,j}\cdot (e_{F,j}^{n+\frac{1}{2}})_{\bar{x}}e_{F,j}^{n+\frac{1}{2}}+h^2\sum_{j=1}^{J-1}\tilde{f}_{z,j}\cdot (e_{F,j}^{n+\frac{1}{2}})_{xx}e_{F,j}^{n+\frac{1}{2}} \quad (36)$$

$$+h\sum_{j=1}^{J-1}\tilde{f}_{z,j}\cdot (e_{F,j}^{n+\frac{1}{2}})_{x}e_{F,j}^{n+\frac{1}{2}}-(\tilde{f}_{x}\cdot e_{F,\bar{x}}^{n+\frac{1}{2}},e_{F}^{n+\frac{1}{2}})+\frac{3}{h}(\tilde{f}_{y}\cdot e_{F}^{n+\frac{1}{2}},e_{F}^{n+\frac{1}{2}})+(\tilde{f}_{z}\cdot e_{F,x}^{n+\frac{1}{2}},e_{F}^{n+\frac{1}{2}})$$

$$=h(\tilde{f}_{x}\cdot e_{F,\frac{1}{2}}^{n+\frac{1}{2}}e_{F}^{n+\frac{1}{2}})+h(\tilde{f}_{z}\cdot e_{F,xx}^{n+\frac{1}{2}},e_{F}^{n+\frac{1}{2}})-2(\tilde{f}_{x}\cdot e_{F,\bar{x}}^{n+\frac{1}{2}},e_{F}^{n+\frac{1}{2}})$$

$$+\frac{3}{h}(\tilde{f}_{y}\cdot e_{F}^{n+\frac{1}{2}},e_{F}^{n+\frac{1}{2}})+2(\tilde{f}_{z}\cdot e_{F,x}^{n+\frac{1}{2}},e_{F}^{n+\frac{1}{2}})$$

$$\leq M(\|e_{F,x}^{n+\frac{1}{2}}\|^2+\|e_{F}^{n+\frac{1}{2}}\|^2),$$

$$\sum_{j=1}^{J-1}Q_2 e_{F,j}^{n+\frac{1}{2}}=4h\sum_{j=1}^{J-1}(e_{C,j}^{n+\frac{1}{2}})_{\bar{x}}^2 e_{F,j}^{n+\frac{1}{2}}+4h\sum_{j=1}^{J-1}(e_{C,j}^{n+\frac{1}{2}})_{\bar{x}} e_{C,j}^{n+\frac{1}{2}} e_{F,j}^{n+\frac{1}{2}}$$

$$=4((e_{C}^{n+\frac{1}{2}})_{\bar{x}}^2,e_{F}^{n+\frac{1}{2}})+4(e_{C,\bar{x}}^{n+\frac{1}{2}} e_{C}^{n+\frac{1}{2}},e_{F}^{n+\frac{1}{2}}) \quad (37)$$

$$\leq M(\|e_{C}^{n+\frac{1}{2}}\|_{\infty}^2 \|e_{C}^{n+\frac{1}{2}}\|^2+\|e_{C}^{n+\frac{1}{2}}\|_{\infty}^2 \|e_{C,x}^{n+\frac{1}{2}}\|^2+\|e_{F,x}^{n+\frac{1}{2}}\|^2+\|e_{F}^{n+\frac{1}{2}}\|^2).$$

Substituting Equations (28)–(37) into Equation (27), then

$$\|e_F^{n+1}\|^2+\frac{4}{3}\|e_{F,x}^{n+1}\|^2-\frac{1}{3}\|e_{F,\bar{x}}^{n+1}\|^2-\frac{8\tau_F}{3}(\eta_F^{n+\frac{1}{2}},e_{F,\bar{x}}^{n+\frac{1}{2}})+\frac{2\tau_F}{3}(\eta_F^{n+\frac{1}{2}},e_{F,\bar{x}}^{n+\frac{1}{2}})$$

$$\leq \|e_F^n\|^2+\frac{4}{3}\|e_{F,x}^n\|^2-\frac{1}{3}\|e_{F,\bar{x}}^n\|^2+M\tau_F(\|e_F^{n+1}\|^2+\|e_F^n\|^2+\|e_{F,x}^{n+1}\|^2+\|e_{F,x}^n\|^2) \quad (38)$$

$$+M\tau_F(\|e_C^{n+\frac{1}{2}}\|_{\infty}^2\|e_C^{n+\frac{1}{2}}\|^2+\|e_C^{n+\frac{1}{2}}\|_{\infty}^2\|e_{C,x}^{n+\frac{1}{2}}\|^2)+\tau_F\|Er_F^n\|^2.$$

Taking the inner product $(\cdot,\cdot)$ on both sides of Equation (26) with $2\eta_F^{n+\frac{1}{2}}$, we obtain

$$(Es_{F,j}^n,2\eta_F^{n+\frac{1}{2}})=(\eta_{F,t}^n,2\eta_F^{n+\frac{1}{2}})+\frac{8}{3}(e_{F,\bar{x}}^{n+\frac{1}{2}},\eta_F^{n+\frac{1}{2}})-\frac{2}{3}(e_{F,\bar{x}}^{n+\frac{1}{2}},\eta_F^{n+\frac{1}{2}}). \quad (39)$$

We also have

$$(\eta_{F,t}^n,2\eta_F^{n+\frac{1}{2}})=\frac{1}{\tau_F}(\|\eta_F^{n+1}\|^2-\|\eta_F^n\|^2), \quad (40)$$

$$(Es_{F,j}^n,2\eta_F^{n+\frac{1}{2}})\leq \|Es_F^n\|^2+\|\eta_F^{n+1}\|^2+\|\eta_F^n\|^2. \quad (41)$$

Substituting Equations (40) and (41) into Equation (39), then

$$\|\eta_F^{n+1}\|^2+\frac{8\tau_F}{3}(e_{F,\bar{x}}^{n+\frac{1}{2}},\eta_F^{n+\frac{1}{2}})-\frac{2\tau_F}{3}(e_{F,\bar{x}}^{n+\frac{1}{2}},\eta_F^{n+\frac{1}{2}})$$

$$\leq \|\eta_F^n\|^2+M\tau_F(\|\eta_F^{n+1}\|^2+\|\eta_F^n\|^2)+\tau_F\|Es_F^n\|^2. \quad (42)$$

Adding Equations (38) and (42), we have

$$\|e_F^{n+1}\|^2 + \frac{4}{3}\|e_{F,x}^{n+1}\|^2 - \frac{1}{3}\|e_{F,\hat{x}}^{n+1}\|^2 + \|\eta_F^{n+1}\|^2$$
$$\leq \|e_F^n\|^2 + \frac{4}{3}\|e_{F,x}^n\|^2 - \frac{1}{3}\|e_{F,\hat{x}}^n\|^2 + \|\eta_F^n\|^2 \qquad (43)$$
$$+ M\tau_F(\|e_F^{n+1}\|^2 + \|e_F^n\|^2 + \|e_{F,x}^{n+1}\|^2 + \|e_{F,x}^n\|^2 + \|\eta_F^{n+1}\|^2 + \|\eta_F^n\|^2)$$
$$+ M\tau_F(\|e_C^{n+\frac{1}{2}}\|_\infty^2\|e_C^{n+\frac{1}{2}}\|^2 + \|e_C^{n+\frac{1}{2}}\|_\infty^2\|e_{C,x}^{n+\frac{1}{2}}\|^2) + \tau_F\|Er_F^n\|^2 + \tau_F\|Es_F^n\|^2.$$

Let $B_F^n = \|e_F^n\|^2 + \frac{4}{3}\|e_{F,x}^n\|^2 - \frac{1}{3}\|e_{F,\hat{x}}^n\|^2 + \|\eta_F^n\|^2$, then

$$B_F^{n+1} - B_F^n \leq M\tau_F(B_F^{n+1} + B_F^n) + M\tau_F(\|e_C^{n+\frac{1}{2}}\|_\infty^2\|e_C^{n+\frac{1}{2}}\|^2 + \|e_C^{n+\frac{1}{2}}\|_\infty^2\|e_{C,x}^{n+\frac{1}{2}}\|^2)$$
$$+ \tau_F\|Er_F^n\|^2 + \tau_F\|Es_F^n\|^2.$$

By using the result of the Theorem 1, we obtain

$$(1 - M\tau_F)(B_F^{n+1} - B_F^n) \leq 2M\tau_F B_F^n + M\tau_F(\tau_F^4 + \tau_C^8 + h^8).$$

Choosing τ_F to be sufficiently small such that $(1 - M\tau_F) > \lambda > 0$, then

$$B_F^{n+1} - B_F^n \leq M\tau_F(\tau_F^4 + \tau_C^8 + h^8) + M\tau_F B_F^n. \qquad (44)$$

Summing the inequalities in Equation (44) from 0 to $N-1$, we obtain

$$B_F^N \leq B_F^0 + M(\tau_F^4 + \tau_C^8 + h^8) + M\tau_F \sum_{n=0}^{N-1} B_F^n.$$

From Lemma 3, we have

$$B_F^N \leq [B_F^0 + M(\tau_F^4 + \tau_C^8 + h^8)]e^{MN\tau_F}. \qquad (45)$$

Using the initial and boundary conditions, we get following results from Equation (45)

$$\|e_F^n\| \leq O(\tau_F^2 + \tau_C^4 + h^4), \|e_{F,x}^n\| \leq O(\tau_F^2 + \tau_C^4 + h^4), \|\eta_F^n\| < O(\tau_F^2 + \tau_C^4 + h^4).$$

Using Lemma 4, this leads to

$$\|e_F^n\|_\infty \leq O(\tau_F^2 + \tau_C^4 + h^4).$$

This completes the proof of the Theorem. □

Theorem 4. *Suppose that $u_F^0 \in H_0^1[x_L, x_R], \rho_F^0 \in L_2[x_L, x_R]$, then the solutions of difference scheme (11)–(12) are stable by the L_∞ norm for u_F^n and by the L_2 norm for ρ_F^n.*

Proof of Theorem 4. The way used to prove Theorem 3 can also be applied to demonstrate the validity of this theorem. □

5. Numerical Simulation Results

In this section, we conducted several numerical simulations of the proposed scheme for solving the SRLW equation. On the one hand, we present the computational efficiency and numerical accuracy of the proposed scheme and compare the obtained results with the nonlinear scheme in [16] and the TT-M difference scheme in [27], respectively. On the other hand, we focus on the conservation laws and the long-time behavior simulation of the proposed scheme. All simulations are implemented on a personal computer running Windows 10 with an Intel(R) i7-10710U 1.61 GHz CPU and 16 GB of memory using Matlab R2019b.

For all experiments, we selected the following domains and parameters: $-50 \leq x \leq 50$, $0 < t \leq 10$, and $s = 4, m = 1.5$. The SRLW equation possesses the following solitary wave solution

$$u(x,t) = \frac{3(m^2-1)}{m}\text{sech}^2(\sqrt{\frac{m^2-1}{4v^2}}(x-mt)),$$

$$\rho(x,t) = \frac{3(m^2-1)}{m^2}\text{sech}^2(\sqrt{\frac{m^2-1}{4m^2}}(x-mt)),$$

and

$$u_0(x) = \frac{5}{2}\text{sech}^2\frac{\sqrt{5}}{6}x, \quad \rho_0(x) = \frac{5}{3}\text{sech}^2\frac{\sqrt{5}}{6}x.$$

The error and convergence rate of the numerical solutions with respect to the exact velocity v and density φ are defined as follows:

$$e(h,\tau) = \|v^n - u^n\|_\infty, \quad \eta(h,\tau) = \|\varphi^n - \rho^n\|,$$
$$uRate_x = \log_2\left(\frac{e(2h,4\tau)}{e(h,\tau)}\right), \quad \rho Rate_x = \log_2\left(\frac{\eta(2h,4\tau)}{\eta(h,\tau)}\right),$$
$$uRate_t = \log_2\left(\frac{e(2h,2\tau)}{e(h,\tau)}\right), \quad \rho Rate_t = \log_2\left(\frac{\eta(2h,2\tau)}{\eta(h,\tau)}\right).$$

First, we verify that the proposed scheme can achieve second-order convergence in time and fourth-order convergence in space. To do so, we obtain the errors between the numerical and exact solution at $t = 10$ with various time and space steps. The convergence rates and CPU times determined by both the nonlinear scheme in [16] and the proposed scheme are summarized in Tables 1 and 2. From the results presented the tables, we can see that: (i) the errors provided by the proposed scheme are nearly identical to those obtained from the nonlinear scheme; (ii) Both schemes exhibit approximately second-order convergence in time when $h = \tau_F$ and fourth-order convergence in space when $\tau_F = h^2$. These results verify the analysis results stated in Theorem 3; however, (iii) The proposed scheme is significantly more cost-effective than the nonlinear scheme. In other words, the CPU time required by the proposed scheme is approximately half that needed by the nonlinear scheme. The results in Tables 1 and 2 clearly demonstrate that a significant improvement has been achieved by proposed scheme compared to the nonlinear scheme in [16].

Table 1. The errors and convergence rates with $\tau_F = h^2$.

Nonlinear Scheme [16]					
(h, τ_F)	$e(h, \tau_F)$	$uRate_x$	$\eta(h, \tau_F)$	$\rho Rate_x$	CPU(s)
$\left(\frac{1}{2}, \frac{1}{4}\right)$	6.0793×10^{-2}	—	8.4371×10^{-2}	—	1.83
$\left(\frac{1}{4}, \frac{1}{16}\right)$	3.9382×10^{-3}	3.9482	5.4315×10^{-3}	3.9573	17.30
$\left(\frac{1}{8}, \frac{1}{64}\right)$	2.4688×10^{-4}	3.9956	3.4032×10^{-4}	3.9963	283.50
$\left(\frac{1}{16}, \frac{1}{256}\right)$	1.5452×10^{-5}	3.9979	2.1277×10^{-5}	3.9995	5664.93
Proposed Scheme					
(h, τ_F)	$e(h, \tau_F)$	$uRate_x$	$\eta(h, \tau_F)$	$\rho Rate_x$	CPU(s)
$\left(\frac{1}{2}, \frac{1}{4}\right)$	7.5147×10^{-2}	—	1.0501×10^{-1}	—	1.00
$\left(\frac{1}{4}, \frac{1}{16}\right)$	3.9370×10^{-3}	4.2545	5.5879×10^{-3}	4.2320	9.57
$\left(\frac{1}{8}, \frac{1}{64}\right)$	2.4687×10^{-4}	3.9952	3.4096×10^{-4}	4.0346	142.86
$\left(\frac{1}{16}, \frac{1}{256}\right)$	1.5452×10^{-5}	3.9978	2.1279×10^{-5}	4.0021	2956.44

Table 2. The errors and convergence rates with $h = \tau_F$.

Nonlinear Scheme [16]

(h, τ_F)	$e(h, \tau_F)$	$uRate_t$	$\eta(h, \tau_F)$	$\rho Rate_t$	CPU(s)
$\left(\frac{1}{4}, \frac{1}{4}\right)$	5.5120×10^{-2}	—	7.6668×10^{-2}	—	6.47
$\left(\frac{1}{8}, \frac{1}{8}\right)$	1.3991×10^{-2}	1.9780	1.9390×10^{-2}	1.9833	62.37
$\left(\frac{1}{16}, \frac{1}{16}\right)$	3.5125×10^{-3}	1.9939	4.8616×10^{-3}	1.9958	459.76
$\left(\frac{1}{32}, \frac{1}{32}\right)$	8.7882×10^{-4}	1.9988	1.2162×10^{-3}	1.9990	5357.84

Proposed Scheme

(h, τ_F)	$e(h, \tau_F)$	$uRate_t$	$\eta(h, \tau_F)$	$\rho Rate_t$	CPU(s)
$\left(\frac{1}{4}, \frac{1}{4}\right)$	7.2702×10^{-2}	—	9.8577×10^{-2}	—	3.06
$\left(\frac{1}{8}, \frac{1}{8}\right)$	1.4349×10^{-2}	2.3410	2.1666×10^{-2}	2.1858	23.59
$\left(\frac{1}{16}, \frac{1}{16}\right)$	3.5100×10^{-3}	2.0314	5.0243×10^{-3}	2.1084	206.61
$\left(\frac{1}{32}, \frac{1}{32}\right)$	8.7874×10^{-4}	1.9979	1.2267×10^{-3}	2.0341	2472.98

The three-dimensional plots of the numerical solutions of $u(x,t)$ and $\rho(x,t)$ for problem (1) using the proposed scheme by taking $h = 1/8$ and $\tau_F = 1/64$ are presented in Figure 1. These visualizations provide insights into the evolution of wave propagation over the time interval $[0,10]$. Additionally, Figure 2 shows the exact and numerical solutions of $u(x,t)$ and $\rho(x,t)$ with $h = 1/8$ and $\tau_F = 1/64$ at $t = 10$ obtained from the proposed scheme. A comparison clearly illustrates a remarkable agreement between our numerical solutions and the exact solution. Moreover, Figure 3 displays the computational times (CPU times) required by the nonlinear scheme in [16] and the proposed scheme for different choices of $\tau_F = h^2$ and $h = \tau_F$. Notably, our proposed scheme demonstrates a large reduction in computation time. In conclusion, in contrast to the nonlinear method presented in [16], the proposed scheme not only preserves nearly the same accuracy and convergence rate as the nonlinear scheme but also substantially decreases the CPU time needed to obtain numerical solutions.

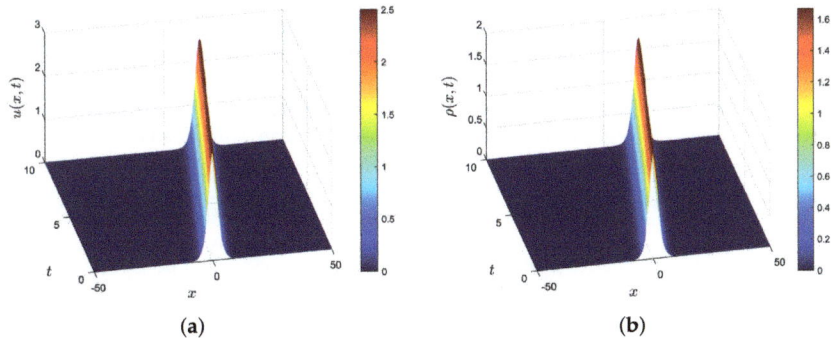

Figure 1. Three-dimensional plots of $u(x,t)$ (**a**) and $\rho(x,t)$ (**b**) with $h = 1/8$, $\tau_F = 1/64$.

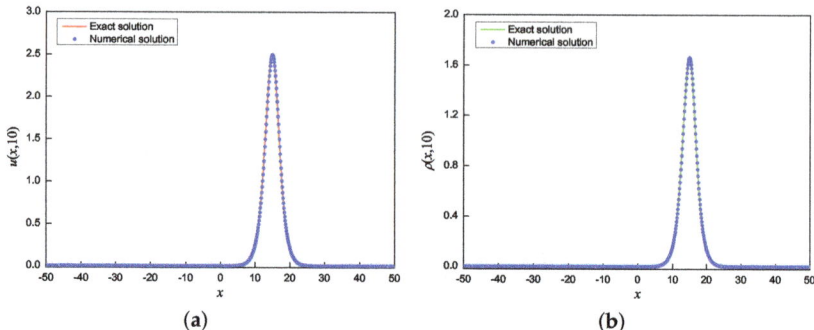

Figure 2. Exact and numerical solution of $u(x,t)$ (**a**) and $\rho(x,t)$ (**b**) at $t = 10$ with $h = 1/8, \tau_F = 1/64$.

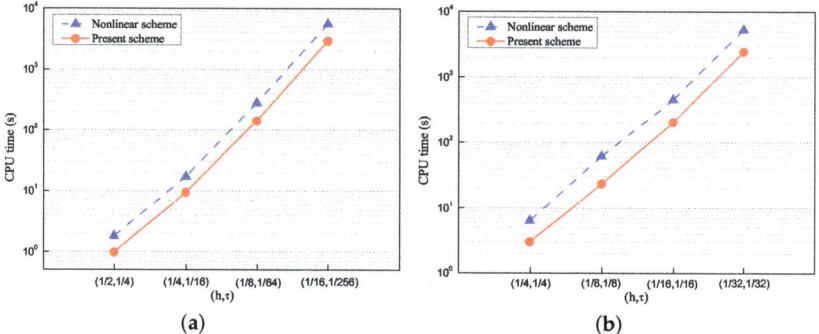

Figure 3. Comparison of CPU times with $\tau_F = h^2$ (**a**) and $h = \tau_F$ (**b**).

Next, we compare the accuracy of two schemes for the SRLW equation: the previous TT-M scheme in [27] and the proposed scheme. The former scheme exhibits first-order convergence in time and second-order convergence in space. Under the same temporal and spatial domain conditions as in this article, we use the previous TT-M scheme to calculate the errors of $u(x,t)$ and $\rho(x,t)$ as well as the CPU time for different time and space steps. The resulting data are presented in Table 3. By comparing the errors and CPU times presented in Tables 1–3, it is evident that the proposed scheme exhibits significantly lower CPU time requirements compared to that of the previous TT-M scheme under similar error value. This indicates that the computational efficiency of the proposed scheme is higher than that of the previous TT-M scheme. Figures 4 and 5 illustrate the error comparison between the two methods with $h = 1/8, \tau_F = 1/64$ and $h = 1/16, \tau_F = 1/16$, respectively. The results show that the errors in numerical solutions of $u(x,t)$ and $\rho(x,t)$ obtained from the proposed scheme are considerably smaller than the errors provided by the previous TT-M scheme, which implies that our proposed method has superior accuracy than the previous TT-M scheme for solving the SRLW equation.

Furthermore, based on Tables 1–3, we present the errors of $u(x,t)$ and $\rho(x,t)$ versus the CPU time using the three numerical schemes (i.e., nonlinear scheme, previous TT-M scheme and proposed scheme) in Figure 6. Figure 6 plots the errors versus the CPU time under $\tau_F = h^2$ and $h = \tau_F$, respectively. From the figure, one can see that the cost of the previous TT-M scheme is the most expensive; the cost of the proposed scheme is the cheapest; and the cost of the nonlinear scheme is more expensive than that provided by the proposed scheme.

Table 3. The errors and CPU times of the previous TT-M scheme with various time and space steps.

Previous TT-M Scheme [27]			
(h, τ_F)	$e(h, \tau_F)$	$\eta(h, \tau_F)$	CPU(s)
$\left(\frac{1}{2}, \frac{1}{4}\right)$	7.7523×10^{-1}	7.6225×10^{-1}	0.18
$\left(\frac{1}{4}, \frac{1}{16}\right)$	1.7627×10^{-1}	1.7062×10^{-1}	1.90
$\left(\frac{1}{8}, \frac{1}{64}\right)$	4.2888×10^{-2}	4.1560×10^{-2}	26.32
$\left(\frac{1}{16}, \frac{1}{256}\right)$	1.0658×10^{-2}	1.0324×10^{-2}	366.92
$\left(\frac{1}{4}, \frac{1}{4}\right)$	8.9609×10^{-1}	8.2590×10^{-1}	1.01
$\left(\frac{1}{8}, \frac{1}{8}\right)$	4.1952×10^{-1}	3.9001×10^{-1}	5.40
$\left(\frac{1}{16}, \frac{1}{16}\right)$	2.0123×10^{-1}	1.8915×10^{-1}	31.49
$\left(\frac{1}{32}, \frac{1}{32}\right)$	9.8428×10^{-2}	9.3111×10^{-2}	240.06

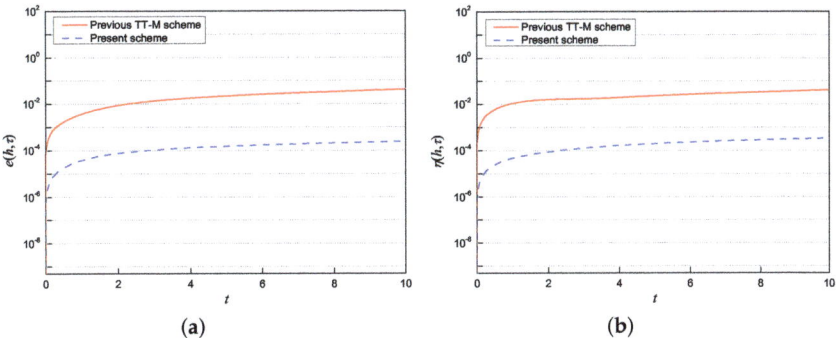

Figure 4. Comparison of $e(h, \tau_F)$ (**a**) and $\eta(h, \tau_F)$ (**b**) with $h = 1/8, \tau_F = 1/64$.

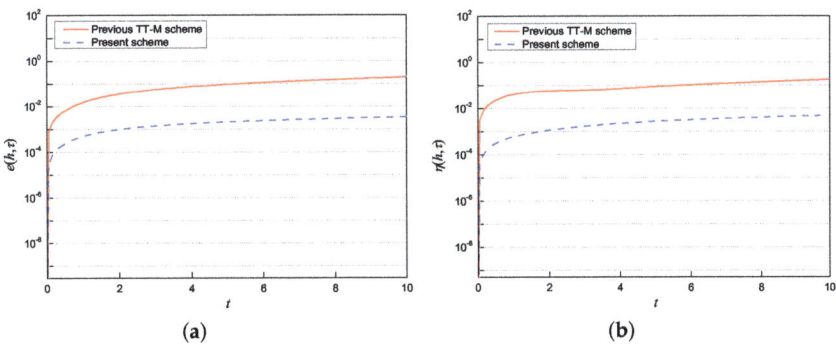

Figure 5. Comparison of $e(h, \tau_F)$ (**a**) and $\eta(h, \tau_F)$ (**b**) with $h = 1/16, \tau_F = 1/16$.

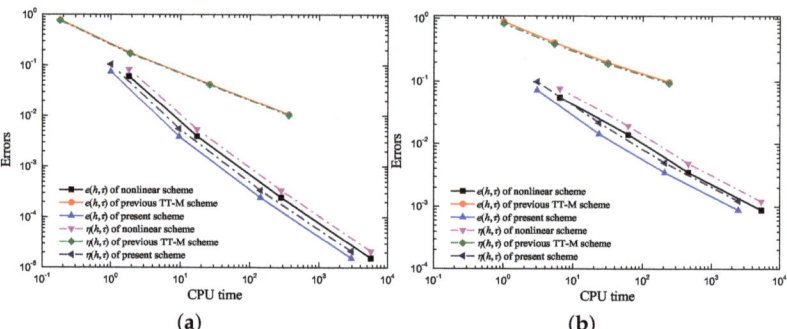

Figure 6. The numerical error versus the CPU time using the three different numerical schemes with $\tau_F = h^2$ (**a**) and $h = \tau_F$ (**b**).

Next, we consider the three conservation laws of the SRLW Equation (1), namely:

$$Q_1(t) = \int_{-\infty}^{\infty} u(x,t)dx, \quad Q_2(t) = \int_{-\infty}^{\infty} \rho(x,t)dx, \quad E(t) = \|u\|^2 + \|u_x\|^2 + \|\rho\|^2.$$

Subsequently, by utilizing discretized formulations, we are able to evaluate three approximate conservative quantities as follows:

$$Q_1 = h \sum_{j=1}^{J-1} u_j^n, \quad Q_2 = h \sum_{j=1}^{J-1} \rho_j^n, \quad E = h \sum_{j=1}^{J-1} (u_j^n)^2 + \frac{1}{h} \sum_{j=1}^{J-1} (u_{j+1}^n - u_j^n)^2 + h \sum_{j=1}^{J-1} (\rho_j^n)^2,$$

where $n = 0, 1, 2, \ldots, N$.

The values of these three quantities under different time and spatial steps are recorded in Tables 4–6. Tables 4 and 5 demonstrate that the discrete masses Q_1 and Q_2 remain well-preserved at various times, regardless of the time and space steps. From the results presented in Table 6, for the case where the grid spacing is $h = 1/2$ and the time step is $\tau_F = 1/4$, it can be observed that the discrete energy E undergoes a slight change over time. However, as the spatial and temporal step sizes become smaller, the tables show that our proposed scheme preserves the two discrete masses well and almost maintains discrete energy when the time and space steps are made smaller.

Table 4. Discrete mass Q_1 under different mesh steps h and τ_F at various times.

Present Scheme				
	$\left(\frac{1}{2}, \frac{1}{4}\right)$	$\left(\frac{1}{4}, \frac{1}{16}\right)$	$\left(\frac{1}{8}, \frac{1}{64}\right)$	$\left(\frac{1}{16}, \frac{1}{256}\right)$
$t = 0$	13.4164078649	13.4164078649	13.4164078649	13.4164078649
$t = 2$	13.4164078649	13.4164078649	13.4164078649	13.4164078649
$t = 4$	13.4164078649	13.4164078649	13.4164078649	13.4164078649
$t = 6$	13.4164078649	13.4164078649	13.4164078649	13.4164078649
$t = 8$	13.4164078649	13.4164078649	13.4164078649	13.4164078649
$t = 10$	13.4164078648	13.4164078648	13.4164078648	13.4164078648

Table 5. Discrete mass Q_2 under different mesh steps h and τ_F at various times.

Present Scheme				
	$\left(\frac{1}{2}, \frac{1}{4}\right)$	$\left(\frac{1}{4}, \frac{1}{16}\right)$	$\left(\frac{1}{8}, \frac{1}{64}\right)$	$\left(\frac{1}{16}, \frac{1}{256}\right)$
$t = 0$	8.9442719099	8.9442719099	8.9442719099	8.9442719099
$t = 2$	8.9442719099	8.9442719099	8.9442719099	8.9442719099
$t = 4$	8.9442719099	8.9442719099	8.9442719099	8.9442719099
$t = 6$	8.9442719099	8.9442719099	8.9442719099	8.9442719099
$t = 8$	8.9442719099	8.9442719099	8.9442719099	8.9442719099
$t = 10$	8.9442719099	8.9442719099	8.9442719099	8.9442719099

Table 6. Discrete energy E under different mesh steps h and τ_F at various times.

Present Scheme				
	$\left(\frac{1}{2}, \frac{1}{4}\right)$	$\left(\frac{1}{4}, \frac{1}{16}\right)$	$\left(\frac{1}{8}, \frac{1}{64}\right)$	$\left(\frac{1}{16}, \frac{1}{256}\right)$
$t = 0$	34.7628720201	34.7781529556	34.7819964190	34.7829587447
$t = 2$	34.7647712611	34.7781634038	34.7819965109	34.7829587460
$t = 4$	34.7537001446	34.7780876049	34.7819962655	34.7829587461
$t = 6$	34.7185711285	34.7778355542	34.7819952701	34.7829587428
$t = 8$	34.6591320134	34.7773916731	34.7819934746	34.7829587360
$t = 10$	34.5775373861	34.7767645581	34.7819909256	34.7829587262

Finally, we present the long-time behavior of the $u(x,t)$ and $\rho(x,t)$ using the proposed scheme with the parameter $x_L = -40, x_R = 160, T = 80, h = 1/8, \tau_F = 1/64$. The waveforms of $u(x,t)$ and $\rho(x,t)$ at $t = 0, 40,$ and 80 obtained from the present scheme are illustrated in Figure 7. From the figure, it is evident that the waveforms at three different time instances are nearly identical. This observation strongly indicates the high accuracy of our proposed scheme. The long-time errors in $u(x,t)$ and $\rho(x,t)$ over the time interval $[0, 80]$ are presented in Figure 8. Although the errors of the proposed scheme increase over time, the rate of growth is relatively slow, which also indicates the high effectiveness of the proposed scheme.

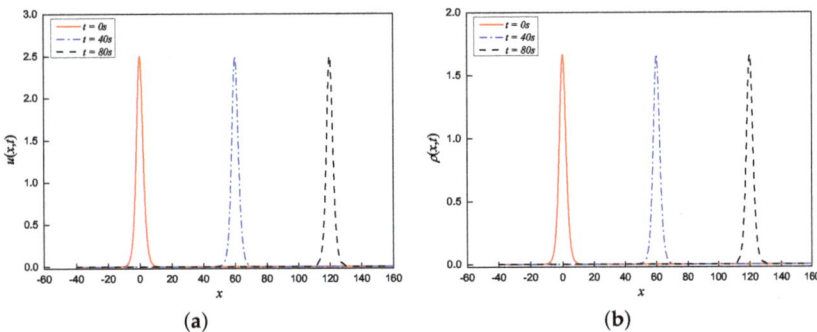

Figure 7. Long-time behavior of $u(x,t)$ (**a**) and $\rho(x,t)$ (**b**) under mesh steps with $h = 1/8, \tau_F = 1/64$.

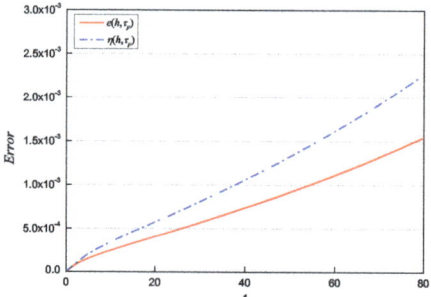

Figure 8. Errors in long-time behavior of $u(x,t)$ and $\rho(x,t)$ with $h = 1/8, \tau_F = 1/64$.

6. Conclusions

In this paper, based on a two-level time-mesh technique, a novel finite difference scheme with a second-order convergence rate in time and a fourth-order convergence rate in space is developed for effectively solving the SRLW Equation (Equation (1)). The proposed scheme is nonlinear on the coarse time-mesh and linear on the fine time-mesh to make it easier to implement. The proposed scheme offers several advantages over existing methods, including improved efficiency and accuracy. We performed a convergence and stability analysis of the proposed scheme; compared to the nonlinear scheme in [16], the proposed scheme not only maintains the same errors and convergence rates as the nonlinear scheme but can also save in computational time, which makes the proposed scheme a valuable tool for practical applications. Moreover, a comparison of the errors obtained using the previous TT-M difference scheme in [27] and the proposed scheme is presented. The results indicate that our proposed scheme exhibits significantly smaller errors than the previous TT-M scheme. The higher accuracy of our scheme ensures stable and reliable solutions throughout the simulation. We also plotted the errors against the CPU time for three methods and found that our proposed scheme is the cheapest of the three schemes in the comparison in terms of CPU time. Finally, the discrete conservation laws were investigated and the long-time simulations that demonstrate the waveform's preservation were conducted to illustrate the effectiveness of the proposed scheme. Overall, the proposed numerical scheme for the SRLW equation is more accurate and efficient than other earlier schemes in the literature. The new difference scheme presents an important advancement in numerical methods for solving the SRLW equation. However, as shown in Figure 8, one of the shortcomings of our scheme is that the error will become large over a very long simulation time. This will be addressed and enhanced through the use of alternative methods in our future work.

Author Contributions: Conceptualization, J.G.; methodology, J.G.; software, J.G. and S.H.; validation, S.H., Q.B., and E.B.; formal analysis, J.G. and S.H.; writing—original draft preparation, J.G.; writing—review and editing, J.G. and S.H.; funding acquisition, S.H., Q.B., and E.B. All authors have read and agreed to the published version of the manuscript.

Funding: Basic Scientific Research Funds of Subordinate Universities of Inner Mongolia (No. ZSLJ202213).

Data Availability Statement: All data were computed using our method.

Acknowledgments: We are grateful to the anonymous reviewers for their valuable suggestions and comments.

Conflicts of Interest: The authors declare that the research was conducted in the absence of any commercial or financial relationships that could be construed as a potential conflict of interest.

References

1. Seyler, C.E.; Fenstermacher, D.L. A symmetric regularized-long-wave equation. *Phys. Fluids* **1984**, *27*, 4–7. [CrossRef]
2. Xu, F. Application of Exp-function method to symmetric regularized long wave (SRLW) equation. *Phys. Lett. A* **2008**, *372*, 252–257. [CrossRef]
3. Abazari, R. Application of (G'/G)-expansion method to travelling wave solutions of three nonlinear evolution equation. *Comput. Fluids* **2010**, *39*, 1957–1963. [CrossRef]
4. Hussain, A.; Jhangeer, A.; Abbas, N.; Khan, I.; Nisar, K.S. Solitary wave patterns and conservation laws of fourth-order nonlinear symmetric regularized long-wave equation arising in plasma. *Ain Shams Eng. J.* **2021**, *12*, 3919–3930. [CrossRef]
5. Manafian, J.; Zamanpour, I. Exact travelling wave solutions of the symmetric regularized long wave (SRLW) using analytical methods. *Stat. Optim. Inf. Comput.* **2014**, *2014*, 47–55.
6. Bekir, A. New solitons and periodic wave solutions for some nonlinear physical models by using the sine–cosine method. *Phys. Scr.* **2008**, *77*, 045008. [CrossRef]
7. Guo, B. The spectral method for symmetric regularized wave equations. *J. Comput. Math.* **1987**, *5*, 297–306.
8. Zheng, J.; Zhang, R.; Guo, B. The Fourier pseudo-spectral method for the SRLW equation. *Appl. Math. Mech.* **1989**, *10*, 801–810.
9. Shang, Y.; Guo, B. Analysis of chebyshev pseudospectral method for multi-dimentional generalized SRLW equations. *Appl. Math. Mech.* **2003**, *24*, 1035–1048.
10. Fang, S.; Guo, B.; Qiu, H. The existence of global attractors for a system of multi-dimensional symmetric regularized wave equations. *Commun. Nonlinear Sci. Numer. Simul.* **2009**, *14*, 61–68.
11. Wang, T.C.; Zhang, L.M.; Chen, F.Q. Conservative schemes for the symmetric regularized long wave equations. *Appl. Math. Comput.* **2007**, *190*, 1063–1080. [CrossRef]
12. Bai, Y.; Zhang L.M. A conservative finite difference scheme for symmetric regularized long wave equations. *Acta Math. Appl. Sin.* **2007**, *30*, 248–255.
13. Xu, Y.C.; Hu, B.; Xie, X.P.; Hu, J.S. Mixed finite element analysis for dissipative SRLW equations with damping term. *Phys. Fluids* **2012**, *218*, 4788–4797. [CrossRef]
14. Yimnet, S.; Wongsaijai, B.; Rojsiraphisal, T.; Poochinapan, K. Numerical implementation for solving the symmetric regularized long wave equation. *Appl. Math. Comput.* **2016**, *273*, 809–825. [CrossRef]
15. Nie, T. A decoupled and conservative difference scheme with fourth-order accuracy for the symmetric regularized long wave equations. *Appl. Math. Comput.* **2013**, *219*, 9461–9468. [CrossRef]
16. Hu, J.; Zheng, K.; Zheng, M. Numerical simulation and convergence analysis of a high-order conservative difference scheme for SRLW equation. *Appl. Math. Model.* **2014**, *38*, 5573–5581. [CrossRef]
17. Kerdboon, J.; Yimnet, S.; Wongsaijai, B.; Mouktonglang, T.; Poochinapan, K. Convergence analysis of the higher-order global mass-preserving numerical method for the symmetric regularized longwave equation. *Int. J. Comput. Math.* **2021**, *98*, 27. [CrossRef]
18. He, Y.Y.; Wang, X.F.; Cheng, H.; Deng, Y.Q. Numerical analysis of a high-order accurate compact finite difference scheme for the SRLW equation. *Appl. Math. Comput.* **2022**, *418*, 126837. [CrossRef]
19. Li, S.G. Numerical study of a conservative weighted compact difference scheme for the symmetric regularized long wave equations. *Numer. Methods Partial. Differ. Equ.* **2018**, *35*, 60–83. [CrossRef]
20. He, Y.Y.; Wang, X.F.; Zhong, R.H. New linearized fourth-order conservative compact difference scheme for the SRLW equations. *Adv. Comput. Math.* **2022**, *48*, 27. [CrossRef]
21. Liu, Y.; Yu, Z.D.; Li, H.; Liu, F.W.; Wang, J.F. Time two-mesh algorithm combined with finite element method for time fractional water wave model. *Int. J. Heat Mass Transf.* **2018**, *120*, 1132–1145. [CrossRef]
22. Yin, B.L.; Liu, Y.; Li, H.; He, S. Fast algorithm based on TT-M FE system for space fractional Allen-Cahn equations with smooth and non-smooth solutions. *J. Comput. Phys.* **2019**, *379*, 351–372. [CrossRef]
23. Qiu, W.L.; Xu, D.; Guo, J.; Zhou, J. A time two-grid algorithm based on finite difference method for the two-dimensional nonlinear time-fractional mobile/immobile transport model. *Numer. Algorithms* **2020**, *85*, 39–58. [CrossRef]
24. Xu, D.; Guo, J.; Qiu, W.L. Time two-grid algorithm based on finite difference method for two-dimensional nonlinear fractional evolution equations. *Appl. Numer. Math.* **2019**, *152*, 169–184. [CrossRef]
25. Niu, Y.X.; Liu, Y.; Li, H.; Liu, F.W. Fast high-order compact difference scheme for the nonlinear distributed-order fractional Sobolev model appearing in porous media. *Math. Comput. Simul.* **2023**, *203*, 387–407. [CrossRef]
26. He, S.; Liu, Y.; Li, H. A time two-mesh compact difference method for the one-dimensional nonlinear schrödinger equation. *Entropy* **2022**, *24*, 806. [CrossRef] [PubMed]
27. Gao, J.Y.; He, S.; Bai, Q.M.; Liu, J. A Time Two-Mesh Finite Difference Numerical Scheme for the Symmetric Regularized Long Wave Equation. *Fractal Fract.* **2023**, *7*, 487. [CrossRef]
28. Zhou, Y.L. *Application of Discrete Functional Analysis to the Finite Difference Method*; International Academic Publishers: Beijing, China, 1990.

Disclaimer/Publisher's Note: The statements, opinions and data contained in all publications are solely those of the individual author(s) and contributor(s) and not of MDPI and/or the editor(s). MDPI and/or the editor(s) disclaim responsibility for any injury to people or property resulting from any ideas, methods, instructions or products referred to in the content.

Article

Investigation of the Oscillatory Properties of Solutions of Differential Equations Using Kneser-Type Criteria

Yousef Alnafisah [1] and Osama Moaaz [1,2,*]

[1] Department of Mathematics, College of Science, Qassim University, Buraydah 51452, Saudi Arabia; nfiesh@qu.edu.sa
[2] Department of Mathematics, Faculty of Science, Mansoura University, Mansoura 35516, Egypt
* Correspondence: o_moaaz@mans.edu.eg

Abstract: This study investigates the oscillatory properties of a fourth-order delay functional differential equation. This study's methodology is built around two key tenets. First, we propose optimized relationships between the solution and its derivatives by making use of some improved monotonic features. By using a comparison technique to connect the oscillation of the studied equation with some second-order equations, the second aspect takes advantage of the significant progress made in the study of the oscillation of second-order equations. Numerous applications of functional differential equations of the neutral type served as the inspiration for the study of a subclass of these equations.

Keywords: delay differential equations; oscillatory behavior; Kneser-type criteria; comparison theorems

MSC: 34C10; 34K11

1. Introduction

In this study, we consider the functional differential equation with p-Laplacian-like operators

$$\frac{d}{dt}\left[a_0(t)\phi\left(\frac{d^3}{dt^3}x(t)\right)\right] + a_1(t)\phi\left(\frac{d^3}{dt^3}x(t)\right) + a_2(t)\phi(x(g(t))) = 0, \quad (1)$$

where $t \in \mathbb{I} := [t_0, \infty)$, $\phi(u) = |u|^{p-2}u$, and the following assumptions are satisfied:

(A1) $p > 1$ is a constant;
(A2) $a_0 \in \mathbf{C}^1(\mathbb{I}, \mathbb{R}^+)$, $a_i \in \mathbf{C}(\mathbb{I}, [0, \infty))$ for $i = 1, 2$, $a_0'(t) \geq 0$, and $a_2(t) > 0$;
(A3) $g \in \mathbf{C}(\mathbb{I}, \mathbb{R})$, $g(t) \leq t$, $g'(t) \geq 0$, and $\lim_{t \to \infty} g(t) = \infty$;
(A4) $\lim_{t \to \infty} \mathcal{A}_0(t) = \infty$, where

$$\mathcal{A}_0(t) := \int_{t_1}^{t} \left(\frac{\widehat{a}(\mathfrak{z})}{a_0(\mathfrak{z})}\right)^{\frac{1}{p-1}} d\mathfrak{z},$$

and

$$\widehat{a}(t) := \exp\left[-\int_{t_1}^{t} \frac{a_1(\mathfrak{z})}{a_0(\mathfrak{z})} d\mathfrak{z}\right].$$

Functional differential equations (FDEs) are used in the natural sciences, engineering technology, and automatic control, as stated by Hale [1–5]. According to [6], the p-Laplace FDE has a wide variety of applications in continuum mechanics.

The great development witnessed by various sciences has been accompanied by many nonlinear mathematical models. However, it is difficult to find solutions to these models using traditional methods. Therefore, researchers resort to obtaining approximate solutions through numerical methods, or studying the properties of the solutions of these equations.

Citation: Alnafisah, Y.; Moaaz, O. Investigation of the Oscillatory Properties of Solutions of Differential Equations Using Kneser-Type Criteria. *Axioms* **2023**, *12*, 876. https://doi.org/10.3390/axioms12090876

Academic Editor: Behzad Djafari-Rouhani

Received: 8 August 2023
Revised: 7 September 2023
Accepted: 11 September 2023
Published: 13 September 2023

Copyright: © 2023 by the authors. Licensee MDPI, Basel, Switzerland. This article is an open access article distributed under the terms and conditions of the Creative Commons Attribution (CC BY) license (https://creativecommons.org/licenses/by/4.0/).

Many biological, chemical, and physical phenomena have mathematical models that use differential equations of the fourth-order delay. Examples of these applications include soil settlement and elastic issues. The oscillatory traction of a muscle, which takes place when the muscle is subjected to an inertial force, is one model that can be modeled using a fourth-order oscillatory equation with delay.

The qualitative study of differential equations contributes significantly to understanding and analyzing phenomena and problems without obtaining solutions. Qualitative studies have been developed in many theoretical and numerical ways. The qualitative studies include the study of stability, control, oscillation, bifurcation, periodicity, boundedness, and others.

One type of differential equation in which oscillatory behavior is frequent is the class of FDEs. It is known that deviating arguments that express the phenomenon's prior and present times are present in equations of this type when they deal with the aftereffects of life phenomena, which increase the likelihood that oscillatory solutions will exist (see [7]). One of the fundamental subclasses of FDEs is the delayed functional differential equation, also known as the delay differential equation. This type is based on the past and present values of the temporal derivatives, which results in forecasts for the future that are more precise and successful.

Oscillation theory, as one of the branches of qualitative theory, is interested in investigating the asymptotic and oscillatory properties of the solutions of FDEs. Studies in oscillation theory began by relating the oscillatory behavior of the linear differential equation to complex solutions of the characteristic equation, see [8,9]. Then, many methods and techniques have been developed that investigate the oscillatory behavior of different FDEs, which include delay, advanced, neutral, and mixed, as well as in canonical and noncanonical cases, see [10,11].

Here, we mention the basic definitions and some elementary previous results that we use to prove our results.

Definition 1. *A function $x \in \mathbf{C}^{(n-1)}([t_*, \infty), \mathbb{R})$, $t_* \in \mathbb{I}$, is said to be a solution of (1) if $a_0 \cdot \phi\left(x^{(n-1)}\right) \in \mathbf{C}^1([t_*, \infty), \mathbb{R})$, x satisfies (1), and $\sup\{|x(t)| : t \geq t_1\} > 0$ for $t_1 \geq t_*$.*

Definition 2. *Such a solution x is called nonoscillatory if x is positive or negative, eventually; otherwise, x is called oscillatory.*

Definition 3. *FDE (1) is called oscillatory if every solution to it is oscillatory.*

Next, we review some of the previous results that contributed to the development of the oscillation theory for equations of the middle term and for equations of the fourth order.

In 1979, Onose [12] studied the oscillation of the FDEs

$$\frac{d^2}{dt^2}\left[a_0(t)\frac{d^2}{dt^2}x(t)\right] + w(t, x(g(t))) = 0$$

and

$$\frac{d^2}{dt^2}\left[a_0(t)\frac{d^2}{dt^2}x(t)\right] + w(t, x(g(t))) = r(t),$$

under the condition

$$\int_{t_0}^{\infty} a_0^{-1}(\mathfrak{z})d\mathfrak{z} = \infty.$$

In [13], Grace et al. presented some oscillation conditions for the FDE

$$\frac{d^3}{dt^3}\left[a_0(t)\frac{d}{dt}x(t)\right] + a_2(t)w(x(g(t))) = 0.$$

Wu [14] and Kamo and Usami [15] addressed the oscillatory properties of the equation

$$\frac{d^2}{dt^2}\left[a_0(t)\left|\frac{d^2}{dt^2}x(t)\right|^{\alpha-1}\frac{d^2}{dt^2}x(t)\right]+a_2(t)|x(t)|^{\beta-1}x(t)=0,$$

where $\alpha,\beta\in\mathbb{R}^+$.

For even-order equations, Zhang et al. [16,17] and Baculikova et al. [18] studied the FDE

$$\frac{d}{dt}\left[a_0(t)\left(\frac{d^{n-1}}{dt^{n-1}}x(t)\right)^{\alpha}\right]+q(t)f(x(g(t)))=0, \qquad (2)$$

where $\alpha>0$ is a quotient of odd integers. In [16,17], under the condition

$$\int_{t_0}^{\infty}a_0^{-1/\alpha}(\mathfrak{z})d\mathfrak{z}<\infty, \qquad (3)$$

Zhang et al. used the Riccati approach, and provided some oscillation criteria for Equation (2) when $f(x)=x^{\beta}$, $\beta\leq\alpha$, whereas Baculikova et al. [18] used the comparison technique to test the oscillation of FDE (1), and considered the two cases (3) and

$$\int_{t_0}^{\infty}a_0^{-1/\alpha}(\mathfrak{z})d\mathfrak{z}=\infty.$$

For equations with a middle term, Grace [19] inspected the oscillatory behavior of the FDE

$$\frac{d}{dt}\left[a_0(t)\frac{d}{dt}x(t)\right]+a_1(t)x(h(t))+a_2(t)w(x(g(t)))=0. \qquad (4)$$

In [20], Saker et al. obtained Kamenev-type criteria for FDE (4), and improved results in [19]. Tunc and Kaymaz [21] studied the neutral FDE

$$\frac{d^2}{dt^2}z(t)+a_1(t)\frac{d}{dt}z(t)+a_2(t)x(g(t))=0,$$

under the condition

$$\int_{t_0}^{\infty}\exp\left(-\int_{t_0}^{t}a_1(\mathfrak{z})d\mathfrak{z}\right)dt=\infty,$$

where $z(t)=x(t)+a_3(t)x(h(t))$, and $h(t)\leq t$. Graef et al. [22] studied the oscillation of the mixed neutral FDE

$$\frac{d}{dt}\left[a_0(t)\frac{d}{dt}z(t)\right]+a_1(t)\frac{d}{dt}z(t)+a_2(t)x(g(t))=0, \qquad (5)$$

under the condition

$$\int_{t_0}^{\infty}a_0^{-1}(\mathfrak{z})\exp\left(-\int_{t_0}^{\mathfrak{z}}\frac{a_1(s)}{a_0(t)}ds\right)d\mathfrak{z}=\infty, \qquad (6)$$

where

$$z(t)=x(t)+c_0(t)x(h_0(t))+c_1(t)x(h_1(t)), h_0(t)<t, \text{ and } h_1(t)>t.$$

Jadlovská and Džurina [23] derived Kneser-type criteria to test the oscillation of the FDE

$$\frac{d}{dt}\left[a_0(t)\phi\left(\frac{d}{dt}x(t)\right)\right]+a_2(t)\phi(x(g(t)))=0. \qquad (7)$$

Theorem 1 ([23], Theorem 2). *Assume that $p\geq 2$ and*

$$\alpha:=\liminf_{t\to\infty}\frac{\eta(t)}{\eta(g(t))}<\infty.$$

FDE (7) is oscillatory if

$$\liminf_{t\to\infty} \left[a_0^{1/(p-1)}(t) \eta^{p-1}(g(t)) \eta(t) a_2(t) \right] > \delta,$$

where

$$\delta = (p-1) \max \left\{ \frac{\ell(1-\ell)^{p-1}}{\alpha^{(p-1)\ell}} : \ell \in (0,1) \right\}$$

and

$$\eta(t) := \int_{t_0}^{t} a_0^{-1/(p-1)}(\jmath) \mathrm{d}\jmath.$$

Using the comparison method with second-order equations, Elabbasy et al. [24] studied the oscillation of FDE (1) when $\phi(u) = u$.

Theorem 2 ([24], Theorem 2). *If the differential equations*

$$\frac{\mathrm{d}}{\mathrm{d}t}\left(a_0(t) \frac{\mathrm{d}}{\mathrm{d}t} w(t) \right) + \frac{\kappa}{2} a_2(t) g^2(t) w(t) = 0$$

and

$$\frac{\mathrm{d}^2}{\mathrm{d}t^2} w(t) + w(t) \int_t^\infty \left[\frac{1}{a_0(s)} \int_s^\infty a_2(u) \frac{g^2(u)}{u^2} \mathrm{d}u \right] \mathrm{d}s = 0$$

are oscillatory, where $\kappa \in (0,1)$, then FDE (1) is oscillatory.

2. Main Results

Assume first that x is an eventually positive solution of FDE (1), i.e., $x(t) > 0$ for $t \geq t_1 \in \mathbb{I}$. According to Lemma 4 in [25], we have, eventually,

$$x'(t) > 0, \ x'''(t) > 0, \text{ and } x^{(4)}(t) \leq 0,$$

under the condition (A4). Therefore, we can classify the solutions of FDE (1) into the following two cases:

[C1] $x^{(i)}(t) \geq 0$ for $i = 0, 1, 2, 3$, and $x^{(4)} \leq 0$;
[C2] $x^{(i)}(t) \geq 0$ for $i = 0, 1, 3$, $x''(t) < 0$, and $x^{(4)} \leq 0$.

For convenience, we define

$$\mathcal{A}_i(t) := \int_{t_1}^{t} \mathcal{A}_{i-1}(\jmath) \mathrm{d}\jmath, \text{ for } i = 1, 2.$$

2.1. Monotonic Properties of Solutions in [C1]

In the following, we deduce some monotonic properties of the solutions in [C1] and their derivative.

Lemma 1. *Assume that x satisfies [C1], eventually. Then,*

$$\frac{\mathrm{d}}{\mathrm{d}t}\left[\frac{x^{(i)}(t)}{\mathcal{A}_{2-i}(t)} \right] \leq 0, \tag{8}$$

for $i = 0, 1, 2$.

Proof. Assume that x satisfies [C1] for $t \geq t_1 \in \mathbb{I}$. From FDE (1), we have

$$\frac{\mathrm{d}}{\mathrm{d}t}\left[\frac{a_0(t)}{\widehat{a}(t)} \phi(x'''(t)) \right] \leq 0.$$

Thus,

$$x''(t) \geq \int_{t_1}^{t} \left(\frac{\widehat{a}(\mathfrak{z})}{a_0(\mathfrak{z})}\right)^{\frac{1}{p-1}} \left[\frac{a_0(\mathfrak{z})}{\widehat{a}(\mathfrak{z})}\phi(x'''(\mathfrak{z}))\right]^{\frac{1}{p-1}} d\mathfrak{z}$$

$$\geq \left[\frac{a_0(t)}{\widehat{a}(t)}\phi(x'''(t))\right]^{\frac{1}{p-1}} \mathcal{A}_0(t)$$

$$= \left(\frac{a_0(t)}{\widehat{a}(t)}\right)^{\frac{1}{p-1}} \mathcal{A}_0(t) x'''(t).$$

This leads to

$$\frac{d}{dt}\left[\frac{x''(t)}{\mathcal{A}_0(t)}\right] = \frac{1}{\mathcal{A}_0^2(t)}\left[\mathcal{A}_0(t)x'''(t) - \left(\frac{\widehat{a}(t)}{a_0(t)}\right)^{\frac{1}{p-1}} x''(t)\right]$$

$$\leq 0.$$

Next, using this fact, we obtain

$$x'(t) \geq \int_{t_1}^{t} \frac{x''(\mathfrak{z})}{\mathcal{A}_0(\mathfrak{z})} \mathcal{A}_0(\mathfrak{z}) d\mathfrak{z} \geq \frac{x''(t)}{\mathcal{A}_0(t)} \mathcal{A}_1(t),$$

which in turn gives

$$\frac{d}{dt}\left[\frac{x'(t)}{\mathcal{A}_1(t)}\right] \leq 0.$$

Similarly, we obtain

$$\frac{d}{dt}\left[\frac{x(t)}{\mathcal{A}_2(t)}\right] \leq 0.$$

The proof is complete. □

Lemma 2. *Assume that x satisfies [C1], eventually. Then,*

$$\mathcal{A}_0(t)x(t) \geq \mathcal{A}_2(t)x''(t)$$

and

$$x(t) \geq \mathcal{A}_2(t)\left(\frac{a_0(t)}{\widehat{a}(t)}\right)^{\frac{1}{p-1}} x'''(t).$$

Proof. Assume that x satisfies [C1] for $t \geq t_1 \in \mathbb{I}$. From Lemma 1, we have that (8) holds. Thus,

$$x(t) \geq \frac{\mathcal{A}_2(t)}{\mathcal{A}_1(t)}x'(t) \geq \frac{\mathcal{A}_2(t)}{\mathcal{A}_1(t)}\frac{\mathcal{A}_1(t)}{\mathcal{A}_0(t)}x''(t)$$

$$= \frac{\mathcal{A}_2(t)}{\mathcal{A}_0(t)}x''(t)$$

$$\geq \frac{\mathcal{A}_2(t)}{\mathcal{A}_0(t)}\left(\frac{a_0(t)}{\widehat{a}(t)}\right)^{\frac{1}{p-1}} \mathcal{A}_0(t)x'''(t)$$

$$= \mathcal{A}_2(t)\left(\frac{a_0(t)}{\widehat{a}(t)}\right)^{\frac{1}{p-1}} x'''(t).$$

The proof is complete. □

2.2. Comparison Theorem

The comparison technique is usually used to benefit from the development of oscillation criteria for solutions to first- and second-order equations. This is acheived by linking the oscillation of higher-order equations to one or more equations of the first or second order. This technique relies primarily on the relationships between the solution and the derivatives of the second and third orders, so improving these relationships is reflected in turn in improving the results derived from the use of the comparison technique. In the following theorem, we use a comparison approach to relate the oscillation of FDE (1) with a pair of equations of the second order.

Theorem 3. Assume that $p \geq 2$. FDE (1) is oscillatory if the second-order FDEs

$$\frac{d}{dt}\left[\left(\frac{a_0(t)}{\widehat{a}(t)}\right)^{\frac{1}{p-1}} w'(t)\right] + \frac{1}{p-1} \frac{a_2(t)}{\widehat{a}(t)} \frac{\mathcal{A}_2^{p-1}(g(t))}{\mathcal{A}_0(g(t))} w(g(t)) = 0 \tag{9}$$

and

$$x''(t) + x(g(t)) \int_t^\infty \left[\frac{\widehat{a}(\tau)}{a_0(\tau)} \int_\tau^\infty \frac{a_2(\mathfrak{z})}{\widehat{a}(\mathfrak{z})} d\mathfrak{z}\right]^{\frac{1}{p-1}} d\tau = 0 \tag{10}$$

are oscillatory.

Proof. Based on the converse hypothesis, we assume that FDE (1) has a nonoscillatory solution, which in turn inevitably leads to the existence of an eventually positive solution to this equation. Therefore, there is a $t_1 \in \mathbb{I}$ such that x satisfies [C1] or [C2] for $t \geq t_1$.

Suppose first that x satisfies [C1]. Then, we have

$$\frac{d}{dt}\left[\left(\frac{a_0(t)}{\widehat{a}(t)}\right)^{\frac{1}{p-1}} x'''(t)\right]$$

$$= \frac{d}{dt}\left[\left(\frac{a_0(t)}{\widehat{a}(t)} \phi(x'''(t))\right)^{\frac{1}{p-1}}\right]$$

$$= \frac{1}{p-1}\left(\left(\frac{a_0(t)}{\widehat{a}(t)}\right)^{\frac{1}{p-1}} x'''(t)\right)^{2-p} \frac{d}{dt}\left[\frac{a_0(t)}{\widehat{a}(t)} \phi(x'''(t))\right]$$

$$= -\frac{1}{p-1}\left(\left(\frac{a_0(t)}{\widehat{a}(t)}\right)^{\frac{1}{p-1}} x'''(t)\right)^{2-p} \frac{a_2(t)}{\widehat{a}(t)} \phi(x(g(t))). \tag{11}$$

From Lemma 2, we have

$$x(t) \geq \mathcal{A}_2(t)\left(\frac{a_0(t)}{\widehat{a}(t)}\right)^{\frac{1}{p-1}} x'''(t), \tag{12}$$

Since $x/\mathcal{A}_2$ is nonincreasing, we have that

$$\frac{x(g(t))}{\mathcal{A}_2(g(t))} \geq \frac{x(t)}{\mathcal{A}_2(t)},$$

which, with (12), gives

$$\left(\frac{x(g(t))}{\mathcal{A}_2(g(t))}\right)^{2-p} \leq \left(\left(\frac{a_0(t)}{\widehat{a}(t)}\right)^{\frac{1}{p-1}} x'''(t)\right)^{2-p}.$$

Thus, (11) becomes

$$\frac{d}{dt}\left[\left(\frac{a_0(t)}{\widehat{a}(t)}\right)^{\frac{1}{p-1}} x'''(t)\right] \leq -\frac{1}{p-1}\left(\frac{x(g(t))}{\mathcal{A}_2(g(t))}\right)^{2-p} \frac{a_2(t)}{\widehat{a}(t)} \phi(x(g(t)))$$

$$= -\frac{1}{p-1} \mathcal{A}_2^{p-2}(g(t)) \frac{a_2(t)}{\widehat{a}(t)} x(g(t)). \qquad (13)$$

From Lemma 2, we obtain

$$x(g(t)) \geq \frac{\mathcal{A}_2(g(t))}{\mathcal{A}_0(g(t))} x''(g(t)). \qquad (14)$$

Combining (13) and (14), we arrive at

$$\frac{d}{dt}\left[\left(\frac{a_0(t)}{\widehat{a}(t)}\right)^{\frac{1}{p-1}} x'''(t)\right] + \frac{1}{p-1} \frac{a_2(t)}{\widehat{a}(t)} \frac{\mathcal{A}_2^{p-1}(g(t))}{\mathcal{A}_0(g(t))} x''(g(t)) \leq 0.$$

Now, if we set $w := x'' > 0$, then w is a positive solution of the inequality

$$\frac{d}{dt}\left[\left(\frac{a_0(t)}{\widehat{a}(t)}\right)^{\frac{1}{p-1}} w'(t)\right] + \frac{1}{p-1} \frac{a_2(t)}{\widehat{a}(t)} \frac{\mathcal{A}_2^{p-1}(g(t))}{\mathcal{A}_0(g(t))} w(g(t)) \leq 0.$$

Using Corollary 1 in [26], the corresponding FDE (9) also has a positive solution; this is a contradiction.

Next, suppose first that x satisfies [C2]. Multiplying FDE (1) by $1/\widehat{a}(t)$, we find

$$\frac{d}{dt}\left[\frac{a_0(t)}{\widehat{a}(t)} \phi(x'''(t))\right] + \frac{a_2(t)}{\widehat{a}(t)} \phi(x(g(t))) = 0. \qquad (15)$$

Integrating (15) from t to ∞, we obtain

$$\frac{a_0(t)}{\widehat{a}(t)} \phi(x'''(t)) \geq \int_t^\infty \frac{a_2(\mathfrak{z})}{\widehat{a}(\mathfrak{z})} \phi(x(g(\mathfrak{z}))) d\mathfrak{z}$$

$$\geq \phi(x(g(t))) \int_t^\infty \frac{a_2(\mathfrak{z})}{\widehat{a}(\mathfrak{z})} d\mathfrak{z},$$

and then

$$x'''(t) \geq x(g(t)) \left[\frac{\widehat{a}(t)}{a_0(t)} \int_t^\infty \frac{a_2(\mathfrak{z})}{\widehat{a}(\mathfrak{z})} d\mathfrak{z}\right]^{\frac{1}{p-1}}.$$

By integrating from t to ∞, we obtain

$$-x''(t) \geq \int_t^\infty x(g(\tau)) \left[\frac{\widehat{a}(\tau)}{a_0(\tau)} \int_\tau^\infty \frac{a_2(\mathfrak{z})}{\widehat{a}(\mathfrak{z})} d\mathfrak{z}\right]^{\frac{1}{p-1}} d\tau$$

$$\geq x(g(t)) \int_t^\infty \left[\frac{\widehat{a}(\tau)}{a_0(\tau)} \int_\tau^\infty \frac{a_2(\mathfrak{z})}{\widehat{a}(\mathfrak{z})} d\mathfrak{z}\right]^{\frac{1}{p-1}} d\tau,$$

or

$$x''(t) + x(g(t)) \int_t^\infty \left[\frac{\widehat{a}(\tau)}{a_0(\tau)} \int_\tau^\infty \frac{a_2(\mathfrak{z})}{\widehat{a}(\mathfrak{z})} d\mathfrak{z}\right]^{\frac{1}{p-1}} d\tau \leq 0.$$

Then, x is a positive solution of this inequality. Using Corollary 1 in [26], the corresponding FDE (10) also has a positive solution; this is a contradiction.
The proof is complete. □

Corollary 1. Suppose that $p \geq 2$,

$$\alpha_0 := \liminf_{t \to \infty} \frac{A_0(t)}{A_0(g(t))} < \infty,$$

and

$$\alpha_1 := \liminf_{t \to \infty} \frac{t}{g(t)} < \infty.$$

FDE (1) is oscillatory if

$$\liminf_{t \to \infty} \left[\frac{a_2(t)}{\widehat{a}(t)} \left(\frac{a_0(t)}{\widehat{a}(t)} \right)^{\frac{1}{p-1}} A_0(t) A_2^{p-1}(g(t)) \right] > (p-1)\delta_0 \tag{16}$$

and

$$\liminf_{t \to \infty} \left[tg(t) \int_t^\infty \left[\frac{\widehat{a}(\tau)}{a_0(\tau)} \int_\tau^\infty \frac{a_2(\mathfrak{z})}{\widehat{a}(\mathfrak{z})} d\mathfrak{z} \right]^{\frac{1}{p-1}} d\tau \right] > \delta_1, \tag{17}$$

where

$$\delta_i = \max\left\{ \frac{\ell(1-\ell)}{\alpha_i^\ell} : \ell \in (0,1) \right\}, \text{ for } i = 0, 1.$$

Proof. Based on the converse hypothesis, we assume that FDE (1) has a nonoscillatory solution, which in turn inevitably leads to the existence of an eventually positive solution to this equation. Therefore, there is a $t_1 \in \mathbb{I}$ such that x satisfies [C1] or [C2] for $t \geq t_1$. As in the proof of Theorem 3, the second-order FDEs (9) and (10) have positive solutions. However, according to Theorem 1, conditions (16) and (17) confirm the oscillation of FDEs (9) and (10), respectively, which is a contradiction.
The proof is complete. □

The following corollary is obtained directly by setting $p = 2$ and $a_0(t) = 1$. This corollary studies the oscillation of the linear state of FDE (1).

Corollary 2. Suppose that

$$\alpha := \liminf_{t \to \infty} \frac{t}{g(t)} < \infty.$$

The FDE

$$\frac{d^4}{dt^4} x(t) + a_1(t) \frac{d^3}{dt^3} x(t) + a_2(t) x(g(t)) = 0$$

is oscillatory if

$$\liminf_{t \to \infty} \left[\frac{a_2(t)}{\widehat{a}^2(t)} A_0(t) A_2(g(t)) \right] > \delta$$

and

$$\liminf_{t \to \infty} \left[tg(t) \int_t^\infty \widehat{a}(\tau) \int_\tau^\infty \frac{a_2(\mathfrak{z})}{\widehat{a}(\mathfrak{z})} d\mathfrak{z} d\tau \right] > \delta,$$

where

$$\delta = \max\left\{ \frac{\ell(1-\ell)}{\alpha^\ell} : \ell \in (0,1) \right\}.$$

Example 1. Consider the FDE

$$\frac{d}{dt}\left[\frac{1}{t} \frac{d^3}{dt^3} x(t) \right] + \frac{1}{t^2} \frac{d^3}{dt^3} x(t) + \frac{c_0}{t^5} x(\lambda t) = 0, \tag{18}$$

where $t > 0$, $c_0 > 0$ and $\lambda \in (0,1)$. We note that $p = 2$, $\phi(t) = u$, $a_0(t) = 1/t$, $a_1(t) = 1/t^2$, $a_2(t) = c_0/t^5$, and $g(t) = \lambda t$. Thus, we have

$$\widehat{a}(t) = \frac{1}{t}, \ \mathcal{A}_0(t) = t, \ \mathcal{A}_1(t) = \frac{1}{2}t^2,$$

and

$$\mathcal{A}_2(t) = \frac{1}{6}t^3.$$

Moreover, from the definition of α_1 and α_2, we find that $\alpha_1 = \alpha_2 = 1/\lambda$.
Now, conditions (16) and (17) reduce to

$$\frac{\lambda^3}{6}c_0 > \delta_0$$

and

$$\lambda \frac{c_0}{6} > \delta_1,$$

where

$$\delta_i = \max\left\{ \ell(1-\ell)\lambda^\ell : \ell \in (0,1) \right\}, \text{ for } i = 0, 1.$$

Thus, using Corollary 1, FDE (18) is oscillatory if

$$\lambda^3 c_0 > 6\delta_0. \tag{19}$$

Remark 1. Using Theorem 2, FDE (18) is oscillatory if the second-order FDEs

$$\frac{d}{dt}\left(\frac{1}{t}\frac{d}{dt}w(t)\right) + \frac{\kappa c_0 \lambda^2}{2}\frac{1}{t^3}w(t) = 0 \tag{20}$$

and

$$\frac{d^2}{dt^2}w(t) + \frac{c_0 \lambda^2}{8}\frac{1}{t^2}w(t) = 0 \tag{21}$$

are oscillatory.
Now, From Theorem 1, FDEs (20) and (21) are oscillatory if

$$\frac{1}{8}\lambda^4 c_0 > \delta_2$$

and

$$\frac{1}{8}\lambda^3 c_0 > \delta_0$$

respectively, where

$$\delta_2 = \max\left\{ \ell(1-\ell)\lambda^{2\ell} : \ell \in (0,1) \right\}.$$

Therefore, FDE (18) is oscillatory if

$$c_0 > \max\left\{ \frac{8\delta_2}{\lambda^4}, \frac{8\delta_0}{\lambda^3} \right\}. \tag{22}$$

To compare the two criteria (19) and (22), we consider different values of parameter λ and determine the most efficient criterion through the following table.

We notice from Table 1 that Criterion (19) provides wider intervals for the parameter c_0, and this means that it is more efficient in testing the oscillation.

Table 1. The lower bounds of the parameter c_0 at which conditions (19) and (22) are satisfied.

λ	0.1	0.5	0.7	0.9
Criterion (19)	635.114	8.74015	3.68796	1.95338
Criterion (22)	5159.99	17.9293	6.01641	2.75110

3. Conclusions

Based on the comparison principle with equations of the second order, we established a new criterion of the Kneser type that confirms the oscillation of all solutions of fourth-order half-linear differential equations. After classifying the positive solutions according to their derivatives, we excluded the existence of positive solutions in each case separately. Then, we obtained a criterion that ensures the oscillation of the solutions to DE (1). By applying the new results to some examples and special cases, we clarified the importance of the new results. Extending our results to the neutral case is a suggested research point. Also, improving the monotonic properties of the studied equation can improve the oscillation criteria.

Author Contributions: Conceptualization, Y.A. and O.M.; methodology, Y.A. and O.M.; investigation, Y.A. and O.M.; writing—original draft preparation, Y.A. and O.M.; writing—review and editing, Y.A. and O.M. All authors have read and agreed to the published version of the manuscript.

Funding: This research received no external funding.

Acknowledgments: The authors express their sincere thanks and gratitude to the editor and anonymous reviewers for their comments, which are all valuable and very helpful for revising and improving the paper. The researchers would like to thank the Deanship of Scientific Research, Qassim University, for funding the publication of this project.

Conflicts of Interest: The authors declare no conflict of interest.

References

1. Hale, J.K. *Theory of Functional Differential Equations*; Springer: New York, NY, USA, 1977.
2. Alnafisah, Y.; Ahmed, H.M. Neutral delay Hilfer fractional integrodifferential equations with fractional brownian motion. *Evol. Equ. Control Theory* **2022**, *11*, 925–937. [CrossRef]
3. Mofarreh, F.; Khan, A.; Shah, R.; Abdeljabbar, A. A Comparative Analysis of Fractional-Order Fokker–Planck Equation. *Symmetry* **2023**, *15*, 430. [CrossRef]
4. Omar, O.A.; Alnafisah, Y.; Elbarkouky, R.A.; Ahmed, H.M. COVID-19 deterministic and stochastic modelling with optimized daily vaccinations in Saudi Arabia. *Results Phys.* **2021**, *28*, 104629. [CrossRef] [PubMed]
5. Yasmin, H.; Aljahdaly, N.H.; Saeed, A.M.; Shah, R. Probing Families of Optical Soliton Solutions in Fractional Perturbed Radhakrishnan–Kundu–Lakshmanan Model with Improved Versions of Extended Direct Algebraic Method. *Fractal Fract.* **2023**, *7*, 512. [CrossRef]
6. Aronsson, G.; Janfalk, U. On Hele-Shaw flow of power-law fluids. *Eur. J. Appl. Math.* **1992**, *3*, 343–366. [CrossRef]
7. Agarwal, R.P.; Bohner, M.; Li, W.-T. Nonoscillation and oscillation: Theory for functional differential equations. In *Monographs and Textbooks in Pure and Applied Mathematics*; Marcel Dekker, Inc.: New York, NY, USA, 2004; Volume 267.
8. Gyori, I.; Ladas, G. *Oscillation Theory of Delay Differential Equations with Applications*; Clarendon Press: Oxford, UK, 1991.
9. Erbe, L.H.; Kong, Q.; Zhong, B.G. *Oscillation Theory for Functional Differential Equations*; Marcel Dekker: New York, NY, USA, 1995.
10. Agarwal, R.P.; Grace, S.R.; O'Regan, D. *Oscillation Theory for Second Order Linear, Half-Linear, Superlinear and Sublinear Dynamic Equations*; Kluwer Academic Publishers: Dordrecht, The Netherlands, 2002.
11. Agarwal, R.P.; Grace, S.R.; O'Regan, D. *Oscillation Theory for Difference and Functional Differential Equations*; Kluwer Academic: Dordrecht, The Netherlands, 2000.
12. Onose, H. Forced oscillation for functional differential equations of fourth order. *Bull. Fac. Sci. Ibaraki Univ. Ser. A* **1979**, *11*, 57–63. [CrossRef]
13. Grace, S.R.; Agarwal, R.P.; Graef, J.R. Oscillation theorems for fourth order functional differential equations. *J. Appl. Math. Comput.* **2009**, *30*, 75–88. [CrossRef]
14. Wu, F. Existence of eventually positive solutions of fourth order quasilinear differential equations. *J. Math. Anal. Appl.* **2012**, *389*, 632–646. [CrossRef]
15. Kamo, K.I.; Usami, H. Oscillation theorems for fourth order quasilinear ordinary differential equations. *Stud. Sci. Math. Hung.* **2002**, *39*, 385–406. [CrossRef]

16. Zhang, C.; Li, T.; Suna, B.; Thandapani, E. On the oscillation of higher-order half-linear delay differential equations. *Appl. Math. Lett.* **2011**, *24*, 1618–1621. [CrossRef]
17. Zhang, C.; Agarwal, R.P.; Bohner, M.; Li, T. New results for oscillatory behavior of even-order half-linear delay differential equations. *Appl. Math. Lett.* **2013**, *26*, 179–183. [CrossRef]
18. Baculikova, B.; Dzurina, J.; Graef, J.R. On the oscillation of higher-order delay differential equations. *J. Math. Sci.* **2012**, *187*, 387–400. [CrossRef]
19. Grace, S.R. On the oscillatory and asymptotic behavior of damping functional differential equations. *Math. Jpn.* **1991**, *36*, 220–237.
20. Saker, S.H.; Pang, P.Y.; Agarwal, R.P. Oscillation theorem for second-order nonlinear functional differential equation with damping. *Dyn. Syst. Appl.* **2003**, *12*, 307–322.
21. Tunc, E.; Kaymaz, A. On oscillation of second-order linear neutral differential equations with damping term. *Dyn. Syst. Appl.* **2019**, *28*, 289–301. [CrossRef]
22. Graef, J.R.; Özdemir, O.; Kaymaz, A.; Tunc, E. Oscillation of damped second-order linear mixed neutral differential equations. *Monatsh. Math.* **2021**, *194*, 85–104. [CrossRef]
23. Jadlovská, J.; Džurina, J. Kneser-type oscillation criteria for second-order half-linear delay differential equations. *Appl. Math. Comput.* **2020**, *380*, 125289. [CrossRef]
24. Elabbasy, E.M.; Thandapani, E.; Moaaz, O.; Bazighifan, O. Oscillation of solutions to fourth-order delay differential equations with middle term. *Open J. Math. Sci.* **2019**, *3*, 191–197. [CrossRef]
25. Zhang, Q.; Liu, S.; Gao, L. Oscillation criteria for even-order half-linear functional differential equations with damping. *Appl. Math. Lett.* **2011**, *24*, 1709–1715. [CrossRef]
26. Kusano, T.; Naito, M. Comparison theorems for functional-differential equations with deviating arguments. *J. Math. Soc. Jpn.* **1981**, *33*, 509–532. [CrossRef]

Disclaimer/Publisher's Note: The statements, opinions and data contained in all publications are solely those of the individual author(s) and contributor(s) and not of MDPI and/or the editor(s). MDPI and/or the editor(s) disclaim responsibility for any injury to people or property resulting from any ideas, methods, instructions or products referred to in the content.

Article

Numerical Solution of Time-Fractional Schrödinger Equation by Using FDM

Moldir Serik, Rena Eskar * and Pengzhan Huang

College of Mathematics and Systems Science, Xinjiang University, Urumqi 830046, China; moldir114@163.com (M.S.); hpzh@xju.edu.cn (P.H.)
* Correspondence: renaeskar@xju.edu.cn

Abstract: In this paper, we first established a high-accuracy difference scheme for the time-fractional Schrödinger equation (TFSE), where the factional term is described in the Caputo derivative. We used the L1-2-3 formula to approximate the Caputo derivative, and the fourth-order compact finite difference scheme is utilized for discretizing the spatial term. The unconditional stability and convergence of the scheme in the maximum norm are proved. Finally, we verified the theoretical result with a numerical test.

Keywords: time-fractional Schrödinger equation; L1-2-3 formula; compact finite difference method; stability; Caputo derivative

MSC: 65M15; 65Y20

1. Introduction

In 1926, the Schrödinger equation was proposed by Schrödinger, who is a physicist from Austria [1], which combines the concept of matter wave with the wave equation to establish a second-order partial differential equation that describes the motion of microscopic particles, and its general form is as follows:

$$i\hbar \frac{\partial u}{\partial t} = -\frac{\hbar^2}{2m} \Delta u + Vu.$$

where u is the wave function, $\hbar$ is Planck constant, V is the potential function, m denotes the mass of the particle, and Δ represents the Laplace operator. In recent years, there have been many studies on the Schrödinger equation [2–10]. Researchers have found that fractional differential operators are non-local compared to integer differential operators and are very suitable for describing real-world processes of change with memory as well as hereditary properties. It has become one of the most important tools for describing all kinds of complex mechanical and physical behaviors. In 2004, Naber substituted the time term of the classical Schrödinger equation with the Caputo time-fractional derivative to propose the time-fractional Schrödinger equation (TFSE) [11], which describes the dependence of particle motion.

The TFSE is an integral-differential equation, and since it's very difficult to find the analytical solution, it has been a widely discussed hot topic to get a numerical solution of the TFSE with a smaller error and higher order. For example, Wei et al. proposed an LDG finite element method to solve the TFSE, which is implicit and fully discrete [12]. Garrappa R. et al. solved the TFSE based on the Krylov projection methods [13]. Liu et al. obtained the approximation solution of the TFSE based on the reproducing kernel theory and collocation method [14]. Zheng et al. presented a spectral collocation method for solving the TFSE [15].

Some L-type formulas have been exploited to replace the Caputo time-fractional term for discretizing the time derivative term and to reap the approximation solution of the

Citation: Serik, M.; Eskar, R.; Huang, P. Numerical Solution of Time-Fractional Schrödinger Equation by Using FDM. *Axioms* **2023**, *12*, 816. https://doi.org/10.3390/axioms12090816

Academic Editors: Behzad Djafari-Rouhani and Feliz Manuel Minhós

Received: 16 June 2023
Revised: 16 August 2023
Accepted: 22 August 2023
Published: 25 August 2023

Copyright: © 2023 by the authors. Licensee MDPI, Basel, Switzerland. This article is an open access article distributed under the terms and conditions of the Creative Commons Attribution (CC BY) license (https://creativecommons.org/licenses/by/4.0/).

TFSE. For example, Eskar, R. et al. used the L1 and L1-2 formulas to discretize the Caputo derivatives, and the compact difference scheme is exploited for the spatial terms to obtain the finite difference scheme [16]. Fei et al. constructed an implicit scheme by adopting the L2-1_σ formula to approximate the Caputo term; the weighted and shifted Grünwald formula is used for the spatial term [17]. Cen et al. also adopted the L2-1_σ formula on graded meshes for solving the TFKBE with an initial singularity [18]. Ding et al. solved a nonlinear TFSE by using the quintic non-polynomial spline in the spatial term and the L1 formula in the time term [19]. Mokhtari, R. et al. constructed three finite difference schemes by adopting different L-type formulas to approximate the Caputo derivatives in the time direction and the central difference format in the space direction, respectively. The accuracy of the three schemes are $O(\tau^{2-\alpha}+h^2), O(\tau^{3-\alpha}+h^2)$, and $O(\tau^3+h^2)$ [20], where $0 \leqslant \alpha \leqslant 1$, and τ (h) is time (spatial) step size. Hadhoud et al. received the approximation solution of the TFSE by using the L1 formula and proved the conditional stability of the technique [21].

In this paper, we use the L1-2-3 formula to approximate the Caputo derivative, and the fourth-order compact difference scheme is exploited to discretize the spatial derivative term for establishing a high-accuracy difference scheme, where the order in the time direction is 3 and the spatial direction is 4. Furthermore, we will prove the scheme is unconditionally stable and convergent in the maximum norm. At the end of the paper, a numerical test is given to prove the theoretical result.

2. Preliminaries

The following TFSE is considered:

$$i\frac{\partial^\alpha u(x,t)}{\partial t^\alpha} = \frac{\partial^2 u(x,t)}{\partial x^2} + f(x,t), \quad x \in \Omega = (0,L), \, t \in (0,T], \quad (1)$$

$$u(x,0) = \varphi(x), \quad x \in \Omega = [0,L], \quad (2)$$

$$u(0,t) = u(L,t) = \phi(t), \quad t \in [0,T]. \quad (3)$$

where $i = \sqrt{-1}$, $\alpha \in (0,1)$, T and L are positive real numbers, $u_0(x)$ and $f(x,t)$ are given functions, $\frac{\partial^\alpha u(x,t)}{\partial t^\alpha}$ is the Caputo derivative of order $\alpha \in (0,1)$, which is defined as follows [20]:

$$\frac{\partial^\alpha u(\cdot,t)}{\partial t^\alpha} = \frac{1}{\Gamma(1-\alpha)} \int_0^t \frac{u_s(\cdot,s)}{(t-s)^\alpha} ds.$$

In order to discretize the continuous problem, we first give a dissected grid of the solution region. Let $h = L/M$ and $\tau = T/N$ be the step sizes in the time and space directions, where M and N are two integers. Then $x_j = jh (j = 0,1,2,\cdots,M)$, $t^n = n\tau (n = 0,1,2,\cdots,N)$. Furthermore, we define a mesh that cover the domain $[0,L] \times [0,T]$. Let $\hat{U} = u_j^n$ is a grid function on the mesh. For any $u, v \in \hat{U}$, we introduce the following notations:

$$\delta_x u_{j+1/2}^n = \frac{u_{j+1}^n - u_j^n}{h}, \quad \delta_x u_{j-1/2}^n = \frac{u_j^n - u_{j-1}^n}{h}, \quad \delta_x^2 u_j^n = \frac{\delta_x u_{j+1/2}^n - \delta_x u_{j-1/2}^n}{h},$$

$$(u,v) = h\sum_{j=1}^{M-1} u_j \bar{v}_j, \quad ||u||^2 = (u,u), \quad ||u||_\infty = \max_{1 \leqslant j \leqslant M-1} |u_j|,$$

$$(u,v)_1 = h\sum_{j=0}^{M-1}(\delta_x u_{j+1/2})(\delta_x \bar{v}_{j+1/2}), \quad ||u||_1^2 = (u,u)_1,$$

where the $\bar{v}_j$ and $\bar{v}_{j+1/2}$ denote the complex-conjugate of v_j and $v_{j+1/2}$.

From the Taylor expansion, we have:

$$\delta_x^2 u_j^n = \frac{1}{h^2}(u_{j-1}^n - 2u_j^n + u_{j+1}^n)$$

$$= \frac{2}{h^2}\left(\frac{h^2 u''(x_j, t_n)}{2!} + \frac{h^4 u^{(4)}(x_j, t_n)}{4!}\right) + O(h^4)$$

$$= (1 + \frac{h^2}{12}\delta_x^2) u''(x_j, t_n) + O(h^4),$$

then, we get:

$$u''(x_j, t_n) = \frac{\delta_x^2}{(1 + \frac{h^2}{12}\delta_x^2)} u_j^n + O(h^4),$$

and we define the compact fourth-order difference formula as follow:

$$H u_j^n = (I + \frac{h^2}{12}\delta_x^2) u_j^n.$$

Definition 1 ([22]). *(The L1-2-3 formula). Assuming that $\alpha \in (0,1)$ and $u(x,t) \in C^{6,5}(\Omega \times [0,T])$. We have*

$$_0^C \mathcal{D}_t^\alpha u(\cdot, t^n) = \frac{1}{\tau^\alpha \Gamma(2-\alpha)}\left[d_0 u^n - \sum_{l=1}^{n-1}(d_{n-l-1} - d_{n-l}) u^l - d_{n-1} u^0\right], \qquad (4)$$

where u^n and u^0 are approximations of $u(\cdot, t^n)$ and $u(\cdot, t^0)$. And for $n = 1$,

$$d_0 = 1,$$

for $n = 2$,

$$d_l = \begin{cases} a_l + b_l, & l = 0 \\ a_l - b_{l-1}, & l = 1 \end{cases}$$

for $n = 3$,

$$d_l = \begin{cases} a_l + b_l + g_l, & l = 0 \\ a_l + b_l - b_{l-1} - 2g_{l-1}, & l = 1 \\ a_l - b_{l-1} + g_{l-2}, & l = 2 \end{cases}$$

and for $n \geq 4$,

$$d_l = \begin{cases} a_l + b_l + g_l, & l = 0 \\ a_l + b_l - b_{l-1} + g_l - 2g_{l-1}, & l = 1 \\ a_l + b_l - b_{l-1} + g_l - 2g_{l-1} + g_{l-2}, & 2 \leq l \leq n-3 \\ a_l + b_l - b_{l-1} - 2g_{l-1} + g_{l-2}, & l = n-2 \\ a_l - b_{l-1} + g_{l-2}, & l = n-1 \end{cases}$$

with

$$a_l = (l+1)^{1-\alpha} - l^{1-\alpha},$$

$$b_l = \frac{(l+1)^{2-\alpha} - l^{2-\alpha}}{2-\alpha} - \frac{(l+1)^{1-\alpha} - l^{1-\alpha}}{2},$$

$$g_l = \frac{(l+1)^{3-\alpha} - l^{3-\alpha}}{(2-\alpha)(3-\alpha)} - \frac{(l+1)^{1-\alpha} + 2l^{1-\alpha}}{6} - \frac{l^{2-\alpha}}{2-\alpha}.$$

Lemma 1 ([20]). *If $n \geqslant 4$, then we have:*
$$d_0 > |d_1|,$$
$$d_0 > d_2 \geqslant d_3 \geqslant \cdots \geqslant d_{n-1} > 0.$$

Lemma 2 ([20]). *For $d_j(j = 0, 1, 2)$, we have:*
$$d_0 > 1,$$
$$3d_0 + 2d_1 - 2d_2 > 2,$$
$$d_0 + d_1 - d_2 > 1/3.$$

Theorem 1 ([22]). *Let*
$$\epsilon_3(u(\cdot, t^n)) = \frac{\partial^\alpha u(\cdot, t^n)}{\partial t^\alpha} - {}_0^C\mathcal{D}_t^\alpha u(\cdot, t^n)$$
if $u(x, t) \in C^{6,5}(\Omega \times [0, T])$, then
$$|\epsilon_3(u(\cdot, t^1))| \leqslant \frac{\alpha}{2\Gamma(3-\alpha)} m_{tt} \tau^{2-\alpha},$$
$$|\epsilon_3(u(\cdot, t^2))| \leqslant \frac{\alpha}{3(1-\alpha)(2-\alpha)\Gamma(1-\alpha)} \left(\frac{1}{2} + \frac{1}{3-\alpha}\right) M_{ttt} \tau^{3-\alpha}$$
$$+ \frac{\alpha}{12\Gamma(1-\alpha)} (t^2 - t^1)^{-\alpha-1} M_{tt} \tau^3,$$
$$|\epsilon_3(u(\cdot, t^n))| \leqslant \frac{12\alpha}{\Gamma(1-\alpha)} (t^n - t^1)^{-\alpha-1} M_{tt} \tau^3 + \frac{\alpha}{8\Gamma(1-\alpha)} (t^n - t^2)^{-\alpha-1} M_{ttt} \tau^4$$
$$+ \frac{\alpha}{\Gamma(1-\alpha)} \left(\frac{1}{2} + \frac{1}{12} \frac{27 - 10\alpha + \alpha^2}{\prod_{i=1}^4 (\alpha - i)}\right) M_{tttt} \tau^{4-\alpha}, \quad n \geqslant 3$$

where
$$m_{tt} = \max_{0 \leqslant t \leqslant t^1} u_{tt}(\cdot, t), \quad M_{tt} = \max_{0 \leqslant t \leqslant t^1} |u_{tt}(\cdot, t)|, \quad M_{ttt} = \max_{0 \leqslant t \leqslant t^2} |u_{ttt}(\cdot, t)|, \quad M_{tttt} = \max_{0 \leqslant t \leqslant t^n} |u_{tttt}(\cdot, t)|.$$

Lemma 3 ([23]). *For any $u, v \in \hat{U}$, we have $(\delta_x^2 u, v) = -(u, v)_1$.*

Lemma 4 ([23]). *For any $u \in \hat{U}$, we have $||u||_\infty \leqslant h^{-1/2}||u||$.*

Lemma 5 ([24]). *For any $u \in \hat{U}$, we have $||u||_1^2 \leqslant \frac{4}{h^2}||u||^2$.*

Lemma 6. *For any $u \in \hat{U}$, we have $\frac{2}{3}||u||^2 \leqslant (Hu, u)$..*

Proof. Using Lemma 3 and Lemma 5, we have:
$$(Hu, u) = ((I + \frac{h^2}{12}\delta_x^2)u, u) = (u, u) + (\frac{h^2}{12}\delta_x^2 u, u)$$
$$= ||u||^2 - \frac{h^2}{12}(u, u)_1 = ||u||^2 - \frac{h^2}{12}||u||_1^2$$
$$\geqslant ||u||^2 - \frac{1}{3}||u||^2 = \frac{2}{3}||u||^2.$$

□

Lemma 7 ([25]). *Let $\{u^n\}$ and $\{v^n\}$ be nonnegative sequences, and c is a nonnegative constant, for all $n \geqslant 1$, if*

$$u^n \leqslant c + \sum_{l=0}^{n-1} u^l v^l,$$

then,

$$u^n \leqslant c \prod_{l=0}^{n-1}(1+v^n) \leqslant c \exp\left(\sum_{l=0}^{n-1} v^l\right).$$

Lemma 8 ([26]). *For any $u \in \hat{\mathcal{U}}$, we have $||u|| \leqslant \frac{L}{\sqrt{6}}||u||_1$.*

Lemma 9 ([27]). *For any $u \in \hat{\mathcal{U}}$, we have $(Hu, v) = (u, Hv)$.*

Lemma 10. *For any $u \in \hat{\mathcal{U}}$, we have $||Hu|| \leqslant \frac{4}{3}||u||$.*

Proof. Applying the inverse estimate $||\delta_x^2 u|| \leqslant \frac{4}{h^2}||u||$, we have:

$$||Hu|| = ||u + \frac{h^2}{12}\delta_x^2 u|| \leqslant ||u|| + \frac{h^2}{12}||\delta_x^2 u|| \leqslant ||u|| + \frac{1}{3}||u|| = \frac{4}{3}||u||.$$

□

3. Analysis of the Method

3.1. Construction of the Difference Scheme

To solve Equation (1), we discretize the time term by using the L1-2-3 formula, and the compact difference scheme is exploited for the spatial term, then we obtain the finite difference scheme as follows:

$$i_0^C \mathcal{D}_t^\alpha u_j^n = H^{-1}\delta_x^2 u_j^n + f_j^n, \quad 1 \leqslant j \leqslant M-1, \ 1 \leqslant n \leqslant N \tag{5}$$

$$u_j^0 = \varphi_j, \quad 0 \leqslant j \leqslant M \tag{6}$$

$$u_0^n = u_M^n = \phi^n, \quad 0 \leqslant n \leqslant N \tag{7}$$

where u_j^n is an approximation to $u(x_j, t^n)$, and $\varphi_j = \varphi(x_j)$, $\phi^n = \phi(t^n)$, $f_j^n = f(x_j, t^n)$. Since f_j^n has no effect on the discussion of the study that follows, for convenience, we assume $f_j^n = 0$.

3.2. Analysis of Stability

In this section, we will analyze the unconditional stability of the scheme (5) that was established in the previous subsection.

Theorem 2. *Difference scheme (5) is unconditionally stable.*

Proof. For $n = 1$, the inner product of Equation (5) and Hu^1 gives:

$$(i_0^C \mathcal{D}_t^\alpha u^1, Hu^1) = (H^{-1}\delta_x^2 u^1, Hu^1) = (\delta_x^2 u^1, u^1).$$

From the Lemma 3, we have:

$$i d_0 (Hu^1, u^1) - i d_0 (Hu^1, u^0) = -\mu(u^1, u^1)_1 = -\mu||u^1||_1^2,$$

where $\mu = \tau^\alpha \Gamma(2-\alpha)$.

According to the Lemma 6 and Cauchy-Schwarz inequality, we can obtain:

$$\frac{2}{3}||u^1||^2 \leqslant \frac{1}{4}||Hu^1||^2 + ||u^0||^2.$$

From Lemma 10, here is:
$$\frac{2}{3}||u^1||^2 \leqslant \frac{1}{3}||u^1||^2 + ||u^0||^2.$$

Eventually, we can get $||u^1|| \leqslant \sqrt{3}||u^0||$.

For $n = 2$, we can obtain the following equation by inner product of Equation (5) and Hu^2:
$$(i_0^C D_t^\alpha u^2, Hu^2) = (H^{-1}\delta_x^2 u^2, Hu^2) = (\delta_x^2 u^2, u^2).$$

From Lemma 3, we have:
$$id_0(Hu^2, u^2) - i(d_0 - d_1)(Hu^2, u^1) - id_1(Hu^2, u^0) = -\mu ||u^2||_1^2.$$

Further, we have:
$$d_0(Hu^2, u^2) \leqslant (d_0 - d_1)(Hu^2, u^1) + d_1(Hu^2, u^0).$$

Using the Lemma 6 and Cauchy-Schwarz inequality, we can obtain:
$$\frac{2}{3}d_0||u^2||^2 \leqslant (d_0 - d_1)(\frac{1}{4}||Hu^2||^2 + ||u^1||^2) + d_1(\frac{1}{4}||Hu^2||^2 + ||u^0||^2).$$

From Lemma 10, we can eventually obtain:
$$||u^2||^2 \leqslant \frac{3(d_0 - d_1)}{d_0}||u^1||^2 + \frac{3d_1}{d_0}||u^0||^2.$$

Then, for $\eta \geqslant 0$, we now have:
$$||u^2||^2 \leqslant \eta ||u^0||^2 + \sum_{l=0}^{1} v^l ||u^l||^2,$$

in which $v^0 = \frac{3d_1}{d_0}$, and $v^1 = \frac{3(d_0-d_1)}{d_0}$.

According to Lemma 1, $v^l > 0$, then using Lemma 7, we can obtain:
$$||u^2||^2 \leqslant \eta exp(\sum_{l=0}^{1} v^l)||u^0||^2 = \eta exp(3)||u^0||^2,$$

choosing $\eta \leqslant 3/exp(3)$ gives $||u^2|| \leqslant \sqrt{3}||u^0||$.

For $n \geqslant 3$, we can obtain the following equation by inner product of Equation (5) and Hu^n:
$$(i_0^C D_t^\alpha u^n, Hu^n) = (H^{-1}\delta_x^2 u^n, Hu^n) = (\delta_x^2 u^n, u^n).$$

From Lemma 3, we get:
$$id_0(Hu^n, u^n) - i\sum_{l=1}^{n-1}(d_{n-l-1} - d_{n-l})(Hu^n, u^l) - id_{n-1}(Hu^n, u^0) = -\mu ||u^n||_1^2.$$

Furthermore, we can obtain:
$$d_0(Hu^n, u^n) \leqslant \sum_{l=1}^{n-1}(d_{n-l-1} - d_{n-l})(Hu^n, u^l) + d_{n-1}(Hu^n, u^0).$$

Since only $d_1 - d_2$ is unknown positive or negative in $d_{n-l-1} - d_{n-l}$, for $l = 1, 2, \cdots, n-1$, so we discuss it in two cases.

Case1. If $d_2 < d_1$, from Lemma 6 and Cauchy-Schwarz inequality:

$$\frac{2}{3}d_0||u^n||^2 \leq \sum_{l=1}^{n-1}(d_{n-l-1} - d_{n-l})(\frac{1}{4}||Hu^n||^2 + ||u^l||^2) + d_{n-1}(\frac{1}{4}||Hu^n||^2 + ||u^0||^2).$$

From Lemma 10, we can obtain:

$$||u^n||^2 \leq \frac{3\sum_{l=1}^{n-1}(d_{n-l-1} - d_{n-l})}{d_0}||u^l||^2 + \frac{3d_{n-1}}{d_0}||u^0||^2.$$

Then, for $\eta \geq 0$, we now have:

$$||u^n||^2 \leq \eta||u^0||^2 + \sum_{l=0}^{n-1} v^l ||u^l||^2,$$

in which $v^0 = \frac{3d_{n-1}}{d_0}$, and $v^l = \frac{3(d_{n-l-1} - d_{n-l})}{d_0}$ for $l = 1, 2, \cdots, n-1$. According to Lemma 1, $v^l > 0$, then using Lemma 7:

$$||u^n||^2 \leq \eta \exp(\sum_{l=0}^{n-1} v^l)||u^0||^2 = \eta \exp(3)||u^0||^2,$$

choosing $\eta \leq 3/exp(3)$ gives $||u^n|| \leq \sqrt{3}||u^0||$.

Eventually, for $n \geq 1$, using Lemma 4, we have:

$$||u^n||_\infty \leq \sqrt{h}||u^n|| \leq \sqrt{3h}||u^0||.$$

Case2. If $d_2 > d_1$, then we have:

$$\frac{2}{3}d_0||u^n||^2 \leq \sum_{l=1, l \neq n-2}^{n-1}(d_{n-l-1} - d_{n-l})(Hu^n, u^l) + (d_2 - d_1)(Hu^n, u^{n-2}) + d_{n-1}(Hu^n, u^0).$$

From Lemma 6 and Cauchy-Schwarz inequality we can obtain:

$$\frac{2}{3}d_0||u^n||^2 \leq \sum_{l=1, l \neq n-2}^{n-1}(d_{n-l-1} - d_{n-l})(\frac{1}{8}||Hu^n||^2 + 2||u^l||^2) + (d_2 - d_1)(\frac{1}{8}||Hu^n||^2 + 2||u^{n-2}||^2)$$
$$+ d_{n-1}(\frac{1}{8}||Hu^n||^2 + 2||u^0||^2).$$

Furthermore, using Lemma 10 and Lemma 2, we have:

$$||u^n||^2 \leq \frac{12}{3d_0 - 2d_2 + 2d_1} \times (\sum_{l=1, l \neq n-2}^{n-1}(d_{n-l-1} - d_{n-l})||u^l||^2 + (d_2 - d_1)||u^{n-2}||^2 + d_{n-1}||u^0||^2)$$
$$\leq 6\sum_{l=1, l \neq n-2}^{n-1}(d_{n-l-1} - d_{n-l})||u^l||^2 + 6(d_2 - d_1)||u^{n-2}||^2 + 6d_{n-1}||u^0||^2.$$

Then, for $\eta \geq 0$, we now have:

$$||u^n||^2 \leq \eta||u^0||^2 + \sum_{l=0}^{n-1} v^l ||u^l||^2,$$

in which $v^0 = 6d_{n-1}$, $v^{n-2} = 6(d_2 - d_1)$, and $v^l = 6(d_{n-l-1} - d_{n-l})$ for $l = 1, 2, \cdots, n-3, n-1$.

According to Lemma 1, $v^l > 0$, then using Lemma 7, we can obtain:

$$||u^n||^2 \leqslant \eta exp(\sum_{l=0}^{n-1} v^l)||u^0||^2 = \eta exp(C)||u^0||^2,$$

where $C = 6(d_0 - 2d_1 + 2d_2)$, based on Lemma 1, $C > 0$. Choosing $\eta \leqslant 3/exp(C)$ gives $||u^n|| \leqslant \sqrt{3}||u^0||$.

Eventually, for $n \geqslant 1$, using Lemma 4, we have:

$$||u^n||_\infty \leqslant \sqrt{h}||u^n|| \leqslant \sqrt{3h}||u^0||.$$

In conclusion, scheme (5) is unconditionally stable. □

3.3. Analysis of Convergence

In the following, we consider the convergence of the difference scheme (5). The error equation holds:

$$e_j^n = u(x_j, t^n) - u_j^n, \tag{8}$$

where $u(x_j, t^n)$ denotes the exact solution of Equation (1), while u_j^n denotes the numerical solution.

Theorem 3. *Finite difference scheme (5) is always consistent with 3 order accuracy for $n > 2$, where $u \in C^{6,5}(\Omega \times [0, T])$.*

Proof. The local truncation error of the scheme (5) is:

$$T(x_j, t^n) = i_0^C D_t^\alpha u(x_j, t^n) - H^{-1}\delta_x^2 u(x_j, t^n) - f(x_j, t^n), \tag{9}$$

using Taylor expansion and Theorem 1, we have:

$$T(x_j, t^n) = i\frac{\partial^\alpha u(x_j, t^n)}{\partial t^\alpha} - \frac{\partial^2 u(x_j, t^n)}{\partial x^2} - i\epsilon_3(u(x_j, t^n)) + O(h^4)$$
$$= -i\epsilon_3(u(x_j, t^n)) + O(h^4).$$

Let $T_m = \max_{(x,t) \in \Omega \times I} |T(x,t)|$, then:

$$T_m \leqslant \begin{cases} \frac{M_{tt}}{2}\tau^{2-\alpha} + O(h^4), & t \in [0, t^1], \\ \frac{M_{tt}}{40}\tau^{2-\alpha} + \frac{M_{tt}}{3}\tau^{3-\alpha} + O(h^4), & t \in (t^1, t^2], \\ \frac{7M_{tt}}{2}\tau^3 + \frac{M_{tt}}{25}\tau^4 + \frac{M_{ttt}}{4}\tau^{4-\alpha} + O(h^4), & t \in (t^2, t^n]. \end{cases}$$

Obviously, for $n > 2$, $T_m = O(\tau^3 + h^4)$. Eventually, we have the following result:

$$||T_j^n|| \leqslant C_1(\tau^3 + h^4),$$

where C_1 is a positive integer. □

Theorem 4. *Finite difference scheme (5) is convergent if $u \in C^{4,4}(\Omega \times I)$.*

Proof. Subtracting Equation (5) from Equation (9) leads to:

$$T_j^n = i_0^C D_t^\alpha e_j^n - H^{-1}\delta_x^2 e_j^n. \tag{10}$$

Multiplying H on both sides of Equation (10), we have:

$$HT_j^n = i_0^C D_t^\alpha H e_j^n - \delta_x^2 e_j^n.$$

Taking the inner product with respect to e_j^n and fetching the real part, then the following equation holds:

$$-(\delta_x^2 e^n, e^n) = \text{Re}(HT^n, e^n).$$

By Lemma 3 and Lemma 8, we get:

$$6\|e^n\|^2 \leqslant L^2 \|e^n\|_1^2 = L^2 \text{Re}(HT^n, e^n) \leqslant L^2 |(HT^n, e^n)|.$$

Using Lemma 9, Cauchy-Schwarz inequality and Lemma 10, we can obtain:

$$6\|e^n\|^2 \leqslant L^2 |\frac{3}{4L^2}\|T^n\|^2 + \frac{L^2}{3}\|He^n\|^2| \leqslant \frac{L^4}{3}\|T^n\|^2 + \|e^n\|^2.$$

Further, we can get:

$$\|e^n\| \leqslant \frac{L^2}{\sqrt{15}}\|T^n\| \leqslant \frac{L^2}{\sqrt{15}} C_1(\tau^3 + h^4),$$

where Theorem 3 used. Eventually, we have:

$$\|e^n\| \leqslant C\left(\tau^3 + h^4\right),$$

where C is a positive integer. Therefore, for $n \geqslant 1$, finite difference scheme (5) is convergent when $u \in C^{6,5}(\Omega \times [0,T])$. □

4. Numerical Experiment

Furthermore, two numerical examples are given to demonstrate the theoretical analyses of the scheme (5). The following notations will be used when presenting the result,

$$L^\infty - error = \max_{0 \leqslant j \leqslant M, 0 \leqslant n \leqslant N} |e_j^n|.$$

$$Order = \log_2 \left[\frac{L^\infty - error(2h, \tau)}{L^\infty - error(h, \tau)} \right].$$

Example 1. *The one-dimensional TFSE is considered as follows:*

$$i\frac{\partial^\alpha u(x,t)}{\partial t^\alpha} = \frac{\partial^2 u(x,t)}{\partial x^2} + f(x,t), \quad x \in \Omega = (0,2),\ t \in (0,1],$$
$$u(x,0) = 0, \quad x \in [0,2],$$
$$u(0,t) = u(2,t) = 0, \quad t \in [0,1]$$

where $f(x,t) = \frac{2t^{2-\alpha}}{\Gamma(3-\alpha)}(i-1)\sin\pi x + (1+i)t^2\pi^2 \sin\pi x$, and the exact solution is given by

$$u(x,t) = (1+i)t^2 \sin\pi x.$$

Tables 1 and 2 indicate the maximum norm errors and the convergence orders in spatial direction. When taking different values of $\alpha(0.1, 0.5, 0.9)$ for $N = 2000$; we can know that the order of convergence in spatial direction is 4.

In Figure 1, we show the errors in the maximum norm for time direction attaining the third order of accuracy for $M = 2000$ for $\alpha = 0.1$ and $\alpha = 0.5$.

Table 1. Numerical error and convergence order in spatial direction for Example 1.

α	h	L^∞-Error	Order
	1/2	0.0395	-
	1/4	2.2777×10^{-3}	4.1107
0.1	1/8	1.4014×10^{-4}	4.0268
	1/16	8.7188×10^{-6}	4.0066
	1/32	5.4430×10^{-7}	4.0017
	1/2	0.0393	-
	1/4	2.2777×10^{-3}	4.1104
0.5	1/8	1.3974×10^{-4}	4.0258
	1/16	8.6938×10^{-6}	4.0066
	1/32	5.4273×10^{-7}	4.0017
	1/2	0.0396	-
	1/4	2.2935×10^{-3}	4.1108
0.9	1/8	1.4073×10^{-4}	4.0265
	1/16	8.7792×10^{-6}	4.0027
	1/32	5.7222×10^{-7}	3.9395

Table 2. Numerical error and convergence order in spatial direction for Example 2.

α	h	L^∞-Error	Order
	$\pi/2$	0.0240	-
	$\pi/4$	1.4026×10^{-3}	4.0953
0.1	$\pi/8$	8.6104×10^{-5}	4.0260
	$\pi/16$	5.3570×10^{-6}	4.0066
	$\pi/32$	3.3509×10^{-7}	3.9990
	$\pi/2$	0.0181	-
	$\pi/4$	1.0620×10^{-3}	4.0891
0.5	$\pi/8$	6.6241×10^{-5}	4.0028
	$\pi/16$	4.1390×10^{-6}	4.0004
	$\pi/32$	2.5174×10^{-7}	4.0393
	$\pi/2$	0.0117	-
	$\pi/4$	6.9124×10^{-4}	4.0856
0.9	$\pi/8$	4.4740×10^{-5}	3.9500
	$\pi/16$	2.7902×10^{-6}	4.0031
	$\pi/32$	1.7359×10^{-7}	4.0066

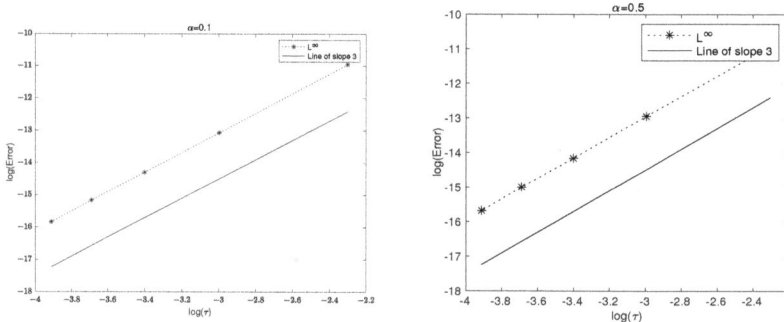

Figure 1. Convergence rates of numerical solutions at $M = 2000$ with different α for Example 1.

Figure 2 (Figure 3) represents the real (imaginary) part of the numerical solution and the exact solution for $\alpha = 0.7$, $h = 1/100$ and $\tau = 1/200$; it can be seen that our resulting numerical solution is very close to the exact solution.

Figure 4 gives the absolute modulus error between the numerical and exact solution when $M = 20$ and $N = 400$ for different $\alpha(0.2, 0.8)$, and we can observe that the error is very small.

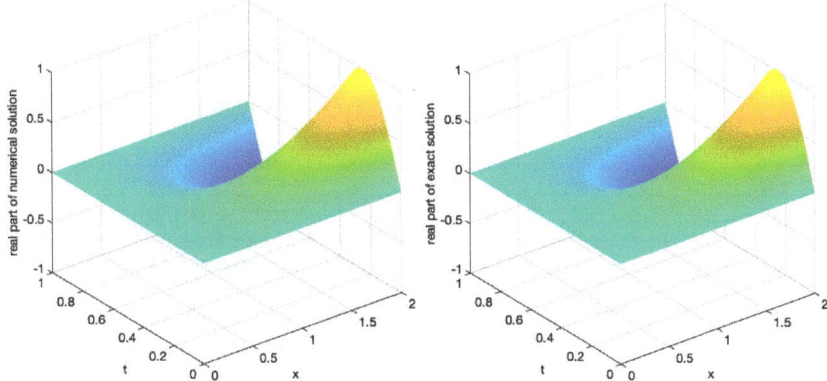

Figure 2. Real part of numerical solution and exact solution of Example 1.

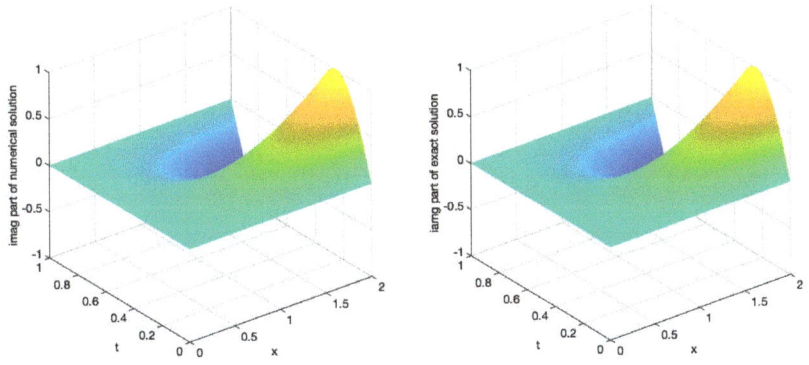

Figure 3. Imaginary part of numerical solution and exact solution of Example 1.

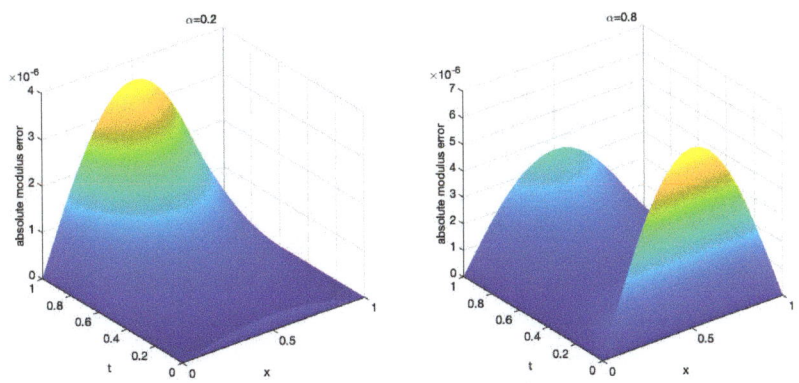

Figure 4. Absolute modulus error of Example1 for different α.

Example 2. The one-dimensional TFSE is considered as follows:

$$i\frac{\partial^\alpha u(x,t)}{\partial t^\alpha} = \frac{\partial^2 u(x,t)}{\partial x^2} + f(x,t), \quad x \in \Omega = (0, 2\pi), \ t \in (0, 1],$$
$$u(x,0) = 0, \quad x \in [0, 2\pi],$$
$$u(0,t) = u(2,t) = t^2, \quad t \in [0, 1]$$

where $f(x,t) = -\frac{2t^{2-\alpha}}{\Gamma(3-\alpha)} \sin x + t^2 \cos x + i(\frac{2t^{2-\alpha}}{\Gamma(3-\alpha)} \cos x + t^2 \sin x)$, and the exact solution is given by

$$u(x,t) = t^2(\cos x + i \sin x).$$

In Figure 5, we show the errors in the maximum norm for time direction attaining the third order of accuracy for $M = 2000$ for $\alpha = 0.1$ and $\alpha = 0.5$.

In Figure 6 (Figure 7), we plot the real (imaginary) part of the numerical solution and the exact solution for $\alpha = 0.3$, $h = \pi/100$ and $\tau = 1/200$, it can be seen that our resulting numerical solution gives a great approximation of the exact solution.

Figure 8 gives the absolute modulus error between the numerical and exact solution when $M = 20$ and $N = 400$ for different $\alpha(0.2, 0.8)$, and we can observe that the error is very small.

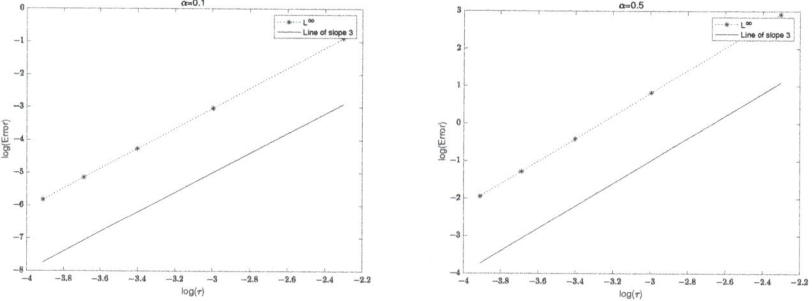

Figure 5. Convergence rates of numerical solutions at $M = 2000$ with different α for Example 2.

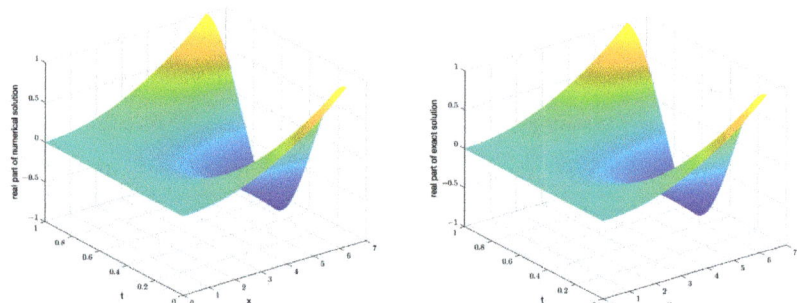

Figure 6. Real part of numerical solution and exact solution of Example 2.

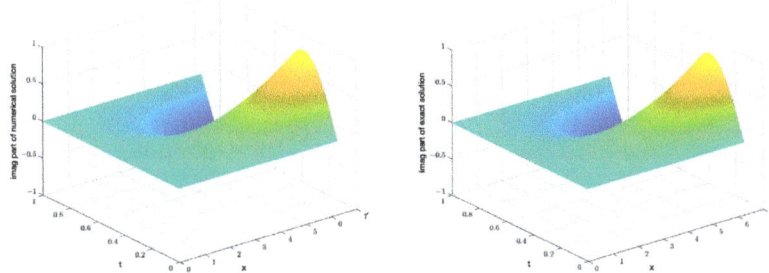

Figure 7. Imaginary part of numerical solution and exact solution of Example 2.

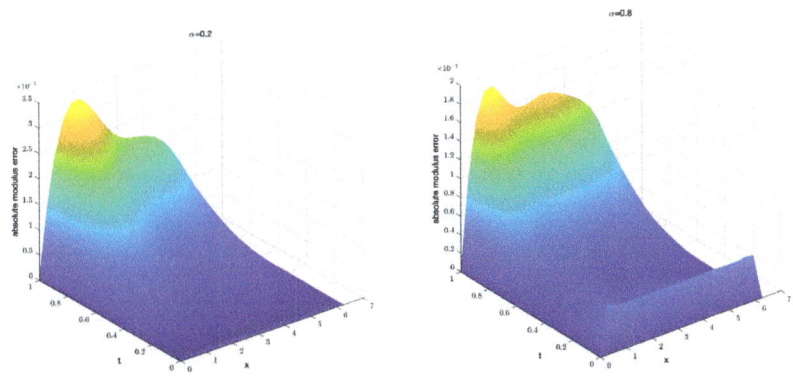

Figure 8. Absolute modulus error of Example 2 for different α.

Ref. [16] has used two L-type formulas to approximate the time fractional derivatives to establish two finite difference schemes, and the convergence orders are fourth order accuracy in the spatial direction and $2 - \alpha$ and $3 - \alpha$ in the temporal direction, respectively. The convergence order in the time direction for two schemes is shown in the Table 3:

Table 3. The convergence order in time direction [16].

α	τ	Example 1		Example 2	
		Order(L1)	Order(L1-2)	Order(L1)	Order(L1-2)
0.1	1/10	-	-	-	-
	1/20	1.768	3.042	1.764	3.010
	1/40	1.787	3.021	1.784	2.981
	1/80	1.802	3.010	1.800	2.965
0.5	1/10	-	-	-	-
	1/20	1.472	2.872	1.448	2.553
	1/40	1.480	2.699	1.468	2.524
	1/80	1.486	2.547	1.478	2.511
0.9	1/10	-	-	-	-
	1/20	1.089	1.397	1.051	2.086
	1/40	1.136	1.995	1.074	2.124
	1/80	1.157	2.162	1.087	2.100

By following Figures 1 and 5, we can know that with our method, we can achieve third order accuracy in the time direction, which is higher than [16].

5. Conclusions

In this paper, we first proposed a time-fractional Schrödinger equation with the Caputo time-fractional derivative of order $\alpha \in (0,1)$ for constructing the finite difference scheme to obtain the approximation solution of the equation; we approximated the Caputo derivative using the L1-2-3 formula to discretize the time term, and the spatial term is discretized by the fourth-order compact difference scheme; we then analyzed the unconditional stability of the scheme and also proved that the scheme is convergent in the maximum norm with an accuracy of $O(\tau^3 + h^4)$. At the end of this article, we give a numerical example to verify the theoretical result.

Author Contributions: Formal analysis, M.S. and R.E.; methodology, R.E. and P.H. All authors have read and agreed to the published version of the manuscript.

Funding: This research work was funded by Natural Science Foundation of Xinjiang Uygur Autonomous Region, 2021D01C068.

Institutional Review Board Statement: Not applicable.

Informed Consent Statement: Not applicable.

Data Availability Statement: Not applicable.

Conflicts of Interest: The authors declare no conflict of interest.

Abbreviations

TFSE	Time-fractional Schrödinger equation
LDG	Local discontinuous Galerkin
TFKBE	Time-fractional KdV Burgres' equation

References

1. Schrödinger, E. An undulatory theory of the mechanics of atoms and molecules. *Phys. Rev.* **1926**, *28*, 1049–1070. [CrossRef]
2. Chang, Q.; Jia, E.; Sun, W. Difference schemes for solving the generalized nonlinear Schrödinger equation. *J. Comput. Phys.* **1999**, *148*, 397–415. [CrossRef]
3. Dai, W. An unconditionally stable three-level explicit difference scheme for the Schrödinger equation with a variable coefficient. *SIAM J. Numer. Anal.* **1992**, *29*, 174–181. [CrossRef]
4. Ivanauskas, F.; Radziunas, M. On convergence and stability of the explicit difference method for solution of nonlinear Schrödinger equations. *SIAM J. Numer. Anal.* **1999**, *36*, 1466–1481. [CrossRef]
5. Nash, P.L.; Chen, L. Efficient finite difference solutions to the time-dependent Schrödinger equation. *J. Comput. Phys.* **1997**, *130*, 266–268. [CrossRef]
6. Sun, Z.; Wu, X. The stability and convergence of a difference scheme for the Schrödinger equation on an infinite domain by using artificial boundary conditions. *J. Comput. Phys.* **2006**, *214*, 209–223. [CrossRef]
7. Karakashian, O.A.; Akrivis, G.D.; Dougalis, V.A. On optimal order error estimates for the nonlinear Schrödinger equation. *SIAM J. Numer. Anal.* **1993**, *30*, 377–400. [CrossRef]
8. Bao, W.; Jaksch, D. An explicit unconditionally stable numerical method for solving damped nonlinear Schrödinger equations with a focusing nonlinearity. *SIAM J. Numer. Anal.* **2003**, *41*, 1406–1426. [CrossRef]
9. Li, B.; Fairweather, G.; Bialecki, B. Discrete-time orthogonal spline collocation methods for Schrödinger equations in two space variables. *SIAM J. Numer. Anal.* **1998**, *35*, 453–477. [CrossRef]
10. Robinson, M.P.; Fairweather, G. Orthogonal spline collocation methods for Schrödinger-type equations in one space variable. *Numer. Math.* **1994**, *68*, 355–376. [CrossRef]
11. Naber, M. Time fractional Schrödinger equation. *J. Math. Phys.* **2004**, *45*, 3339–3352. [CrossRef]
12. Wei, L.; He, Y.; Zhang, X.; Wang, S. Analysis of an implicit fully discrete local discontinuous Galerkin method for the time-fractional Schrödinger equation. *Finite Elem. Anal. Des.* **2012**, *59*, 28–34. [CrossRef]
13. Garrappa, R.; Moret, I.; Popolizio, M. Solving the time-fractional Schrödinger equation by Krylov projection methods. *J. Comput. Phys.* **2015**, *293*, 115–134. [CrossRef]
14. Liu, N.; Jiang, W. A numerical method for solving the time fractional Schrödinger equation. *Adv. Comput. Math.* **2018**, *44*, 1235–1248. [CrossRef]

15. Zheng, M.; Liu, F.; Jin, Z. The global analysis on the spectral collocation method for time fractional Schrödinger equation. *Appl. Math. Comput.* **2020**, *365*, 124689. [CrossRef]
16. Eskar, R.; Feng, X.; Kasim, E. On high-order compact schemes for the multidimensional time-fractional Schrödinger equation. *Adv. Differ. Equ.* **2020**, *1*, 1–18. [CrossRef]
17. Fei, M.; Wang, N.; Huang, C. A second-order implicit difference scheme for the nonlinear time-space fractional Schrödinger equation. *Appl. Numer. Math.* **2020**, *153*, 399–411. [CrossRef]
18. Cen, D.; Wang, Z.; Mo, Y. Second order difference schemes for time-fractional KdV–Burgers' equation with initial singularity. *Appl. Math. Lett.* **2021**, *112*, 106829. [CrossRef]
19. Ding, Q.; Wong, P.J.Y. Quintic non-polynomial spline for time-fractional nonlinear Schrödinger equation. *Adv. Differ. Equ.* **2020**, *46*, 1–27. [CrossRef]
20. Mokhtari, R.; Ramezani, M.; Haase, G. Stability and convergence analyses of the FDM based on some L-type formulae for solving the subdiffusion equation. *Numer. Math. Theor. Meth. Appl.* **2021**, *14*, 945–971.
21. Hadhoud, A.R.; Rageh, A.A.M.; Radwan, T. Computational solution of the time-fractional Schrödinger equation by using trigonometric B- Spline collocation method. *Fractal Fract.* **2022**, *6*, 127. [CrossRef]
22. Mokhtari, R.; Mostajeran, F. A high order formula to approximate the Caputo fractional derivative. *Commun. Appl. Math. Comput.* **2020**, *2*, 1–29. [CrossRef]
23. Xie, S.; Li, G.; Yi, S. Compact finite difference schemes with high accuracy for one-dimensional nonlinear Schrödinger equation. *Comput. Methods Appl. Mech. Eng.* **2009**, *198*, 1052–1060. [CrossRef]
24. Gao, Z.; Xie, S. Fourth-order alternating direction implicit compact finite difference schemes for two-dimensional Schrödinger equations. *Appl. Numer. Math.* **2011**, *61*, 593–614. [CrossRef]
25. Holte, J.M. Discrete Gronwall lemma and applications. *MAA-NCS Meet. Univ. North Dakota.* **2009**, *24*, 1–7.
26. Sun, Z. *The Numerical Methods for Partial Equations*; Science Press: Beijing, China, 2005; pp. 2–3. (In Chinese)
27. Wang, B.; Liang, D.; Sun, T. The conservative splitting high-order compact finite difference scheme for two-dimensional Schrödinger equations. *Int. J. Comput. Methods* **2017**, *14*, 1750079. [CrossRef]

Disclaimer/Publisher's Note: The statements, opinions and data contained in all publications are solely those of the individual author(s) and contributor(s) and not of MDPI and/or the editor(s). MDPI and/or the editor(s) disclaim responsibility for any injury to people or property resulting from any ideas, methods, instructions or products referred to in the content.

Article

Resolvent-Free Method for Solving Monotone Inclusions

Yan Tang [1,2] and Aviv Gibali [3,*]

[1] School of Mathematics and Statistics, Chongqing Technology and Business University, Chongqing 400067, China; tangyan@ctbu.edu.cn
[2] College of Mathematics, Sichuan University, Chengdu 610065, China
[3] Department of Mathematics, Braude College, Karmiel 2161002, Israel
* Correspondence: avivg@braude.ac.il

Abstract: In this work, we consider the monotone inclusion problem in real Hilbert spaces and propose a simple inertial method that does not include any evaluations of the associated resolvent and projection. Under suitable assumptions, we establish the strong convergence of the method to a minimal norm solution. Saddle points of minimax problems and critical points problems are considered as the applications. Numerical examples in finite- and infinite-dimensional spaces illustrate the performances of our scheme.

Keywords: monotone inclusion; resolvent free; minimax problems; critical point problems

MSC: 65K05; 65K10; 47H10; 47L25

Citation: Tang, Y.; Gibali, A. Resolvent-Free Method for Solving Monotone Inclusions. *Axioms* 2023, 12, 557. https://doi.org/10.3390/axioms12060557

Academic Editors: Patricia J. Y. Wong and Christopher Goodrich

Received: 19 April 2023
Revised: 27 May 2023
Accepted: 3 June 2023
Published: 5 June 2023

Copyright: © 2023 by the authors. Licensee MDPI, Basel, Switzerland. This article is an open access article distributed under the terms and conditions of the Creative Commons Attribution (CC BY) license (https://creativecommons.org/licenses/by/4.0/).

1. Introduction

Since Minty [1], and the many others to follow, such as [2–4], introduced the theory of the monotone operator, a large number of theoretical and practical developments have been presented. Pascali and Sburian [5] pointed out that the class of monotone operators is important, and due to the simple structure of the monotonicity condition, it can be handled easily. The *monotone inclusion problem* is one of the highlights due to its important significance in convex analysis and convex optimization problems, which includes convex minimization, monotone variational inequality, convex and concave minimax problems, linear programming problems and many others. For further information and applications, see, e.g., Bot and Csetnek [6], Korpelevich [7], Khanc et al. [8], Sicre et al. [9], Xu [10], Yin et al. [11] and the many references therein [12–15].

Let H be a real Hilbert space and $A : H \to H$ be a given operator with domain $Dom(A) = \{x \in H : Ax \neq \varnothing\}$. The *monotone inclusion problem* is formulated as finding a point x^* such that

$$0 \in Ax^*. \tag{1}$$

The monotonicity term of (1) refers to the monotonicity of A which means that for all $x, y \in H$,

$$\langle u - v, x - y \rangle \geq 0, u \in Ax, v \in Ay.$$

We denote the solution set of (1) by $\Omega = A^{-1}(0)$.

One of the simplest classical algorithms for solving the monotone inclusion problem (1) is the *proximal point* method of Martinet [16]. Given a maximal monotone mapping $A : H \to H$ and its associated resolvent $J_r^A = (I + rA)^{-1}$, the proximal point algorithm generates a sequence according to the update rule:

$$x_{n+1} = J_r^A x_n. \tag{2}$$

The proximal point algorithm, also known as the regularization algorithm, is a first-order optimization method that requires the function and gradient (subgradient) evaluations, and thus attracts much interest. For more relevant improvements and achievements on the regularization methods in Hilbert spaces, one can refer to [17–23].

One important application of monotone inclusions is the convex minimization problem. Given $C \subseteq R^n$ is a nonempty, closed and convex set and a continuously differentiable function f, the constrained minimization aims to find a point $x^* \in C$ such that

$$f(x^*) = \min_{x \in C} f(x). \tag{3}$$

Using some operator theory properties, it is known that x^* solves (3) if and only if $x^* = P_C(I - \lambda \nabla f)x^*$ for some $\lambda > 0$. This relationship translates to the projected gradient method:

$$x_{n+1} = P_C(x_n - \lambda \nabla f(x_n)),$$

where P_C is the metric projection onto C and ∇f is the gradient of f.

The projected gradient method calls for the evaluation of the projection onto the feasible set C as well as the gradient evaluation of f. This guarantees a reduction in the objective function while keeping the iterates feasible. With the set C as above and an operator $A : H \to H$, an important problem worth mentioning is the monotonic variational inequality problem, consisting of finding a point $x^* \in C$ such that

$$\langle Ax^*, x - x^* \rangle \geq 0 \text{ for all } x \in C. \tag{4}$$

Using the relationship between the projection P_C, the resolvent and the normal cone N_C of the set C, that is,

$$y = J_\lambda^{N_C}(x) \Leftrightarrow x \in y + \lambda N_C(y) \Leftrightarrow x - y \in \lambda N_C(y)$$
$$\Leftrightarrow \langle x - y, d - y \rangle \leq 0 \Leftrightarrow y = P_C x, \quad \forall d \in C,$$

we obtain the iterative step rule for solving (4)

$$x_{n+1} = P_C(x_n - \lambda A x_n). \tag{5}$$

Indeed, the mentioned optimization methods above now "dominate" in modern optimization algorithms based on first-order information (such as function values and radial/subgradient), and it can be predicted that they will become increasingly important as the scale of practical application problems increases. For excellent works, one can refer to Teboulle [24], Drusvyatskiy and Lewis [25], etc. However, it is undeniable that they are highly dependent on the structure of the given problem, and computationally, these methods rely on the ability to compute resolvents/projections per iteration; taking algorithm (5), for instance, the complexity of each step depends on the computation of the projection to the convex set C.

Hence, in this work, we wish to combine the popular inertial technology (see, e.g., Nesterov [26], Alvarez [27] and Alvarez–Attouch [28]) and establish a strong convergence iterative method that does not use resolvents or projections, and has good convergence properties due to the inertial technique.

The outline of this paper is as follows. In Section 2, we collect the definitions and results needed for our analysis. In Section 3, the resolvent/projection-free algorithm and its convergence analysis are presented. Later, in Section 4, we present two applications of the monotone inclusion problem, saddle points of the minimax problem and the critical points problem. Finally, in Section 5, numerical experiments illustrate the performances of our scheme in finite- and infinite-dimensional spaces.

2. Preliminaries

Let C be a nonempty, closed and convex subset of a real Hilbert space H equipped with the inner product $\langle \cdot, \cdot \rangle$. Denote the strong convergence to x of $\{x_n\}$ by $x_n \to x$, the ω-weak limit set of $\{x_n\}$ by

$$w_\omega(x_n) = \{x \in H : x_{n_j} \rightharpoonup x \text{ for some subsequence } \{x_{n_j}\} \text{ of } \{x_n\}\}.$$

We recall two useful properties of the norm:

$$\|x+y\|^2 \leq \|x\|^2 + 2\langle y, x+y \rangle; \tag{6}$$

$$\|\alpha x + \beta y + \gamma z\|^2 = \alpha\|x\|^2 + \beta\|y\|^2 + \gamma\|z\|^2 - \alpha\beta\|x-y\|^2 \\ - \beta\gamma\|y-z\|^2 - \alpha\gamma\|x-z\|^2, \tag{7}$$

for all $x, y, z \in H$ and $\alpha, \beta, \gamma \in \mathbb{R}$ such that $\alpha + \beta + \gamma = 1$.

Definition 1. *Let H be a real Hilbert space. An operator $A : H \to H$ is called μ-inverse strongly monotone (μ-ism) (or μ-cocoercive) if there exists a number $\mu > 0$ such that*

$$\langle x - y, Ax - Ay \rangle \geq \mu\|Ax - Ay\|^2.$$

Definition 2. *Let C be a nonempty, closed convex subset of H. The operator P_C is called the metric projection of H onto C: for every element $x \in H$, there is a unique nearest point $P_C x$ in C, such that*

$$\|x - P_C x\| = \min\{\|x - y\| : y \in C\}.$$

The characterization of the metric projection is

$$\langle x - P_C x, y - P_C x \rangle \leq 0, \forall x \in H, \forall y \in C. \tag{8}$$

Lemma 1 (Xu [29], Maingé [30]). *Assume that $\{a_n\}$ and $\{c_n\}$ are nonnegative real sequences such that*

$$a_{n+1} \leq (1 - \gamma_n)a_n + b_n + c_n, \quad \forall n \geq 0,$$

where $\{\gamma_n\}$ is a sequence in $(0,1)$ and $\{b_n\}$ is a real sequence. Provided that
(a) $\lim_{n\to\infty} \gamma_n = 0$, $\Sigma_{n=1}^\infty \gamma_n = \infty$; $\Sigma_{n=1}^\infty c_n < \infty$;
(b) $\limsup_{n\to\infty} \frac{b_n}{\gamma_n} \leq 0$.
Then, the limit of the sequence $\{a_n\}$ exists and $\lim_{n\to\infty} a_n = 0$.

Lemma 2 (see, e.g., Opial [31]). *Let H be a real Hilbert space and $\{x_n\}_{n=0}^\infty \subset H$ such that there exists a nonempty, closed and convex set $S \subset H$ satisfying the following:*
(1) *For every $z \in S$, $\lim_{n\to\infty} \|x_n - z\|$ exists;*
(2) *Any weak cluster point of $\{x_n\}_{n=0}^\infty$ belongs to S.*
Then, there exists $\bar{x} \in S$ such that $\{x_n\}_{n=0}^\infty$ converges weakly to $\bar{x}$.

Lemma 3 (see, e.g., Maingé [30]). *Let $\{\Gamma_n\}$ be a sequence of real numbers that does not decrease at infinity, in the sense that there exists a subsequence $\{\Gamma_{n_j}\}$ of $\{\Gamma_n\}$ such that $\Gamma_{n_j} < \Gamma_{n_j+1}$ for all $j \geq 0$. Also consider the sequence of integers $\{\sigma(n)\}_{n \geq n_0}$ defined by*

$$\sigma(n) = \max\{k \leq n : \Gamma_k \leq \Gamma_{k+1}\}.$$

Then, $\{\sigma(n)\}_{n \geq n_0}$ is a nondecreasing sequence verifying $\lim_{n\to\infty} \sigma(n) = \infty$ and, for all $n \geq n_0$,

$$\max\{\Gamma_{\sigma(n)}, \Gamma_n\} \leq \Gamma_{\sigma(n)+1}.$$

3. Main Result

We are concerned with the following monotone inclusion problem: finding $x^* \in H$ such that

$$0 \in Ax^*, \tag{9}$$

where A is a monotone-type operator on H.

Remark 1. *Clearly, if $y_n = z_n = x_n$ for some $n \geq 1$, then x_n is a solution of (9) and the iteration process is terminated in finite iterations. In general, the algorithm does not stop in finite iterations, and thus we assume that the algorithm generates an infinite sequence.*

Convergence Analysis

For the convergence analysis of our algorithm, we assume the following assumptions:

(A1) A is a continuous maximal monotone operator with cocoercive coefficient μ from H to H;

(A2) The solution set Ω of (9) is nonempty.

Theorem 1. *Suppose that the assumptions (A1)–(A2) hold. If the sequences $\{\alpha_n\}, \{\gamma_n\}$ are in $(0,1)$ and satisfy the following conditions:*

(B1) $\lim_{n \to \infty} \gamma_n = 0$, $\liminf (1 - \alpha_n - \gamma_n)\alpha_n > 0$ and $\sum_{n=1}^{\infty} \gamma_n = \infty$;

(B2) $\epsilon_n = o(\gamma_n)$.

Then, the recursion $\{x_n\}$ generated by Algorithm 1 converges strongly to an element p which is closest to 0 in Ω, that is, $p = P_\Omega(0)$.

Algorithm 1 Convergence Analysis

Initialization: Choose $\lambda_n \in (0, 2\mu)$, $\theta \in (0,1)$ and $\epsilon_n \in (0, \infty)$ such that $\sum_{n=1}^{\infty} \epsilon_n < \infty$, select arbitrary starting points $x_0, x_1 \in C$, and set $n = 1$.

Iterative Step: Given the iterates x_n and x_{n-1} for each $n \geq 1$, choose θ_n such that $0 < \theta_n < \bar{\theta}_n$, compute

$$\begin{cases} y_n = x_n + \theta_n(x_n - x_{n-1}), \\ z_n = y_n - \lambda_n A y_n, \\ x_{n+1} = (1 - \alpha_n - \gamma_n) y_n + \alpha_n z_n, \end{cases} \tag{10}$$

where

$$\bar{\theta}_n = \begin{cases} \min\{\theta, \epsilon_n[\max(\|x_n - x_{n-1}\|^2, \|x_n - x_{n-1}\|)]^{-1}\}, & x_n \neq x_{n-1}; \\ \theta, & else \end{cases}$$

Stopping Criterion: If $y_n = z_n$, then stop. Otherwise, set $n := n + 1$ and return to Iterative Step.

Proof. First, we prove that $\{x_n\}$ is bounded. Without the loss of the generality, let p be the closest element to 0 in Ω because $\Omega \neq \emptyset$. It follows from the cocoercivity of A with coefficient μ that

$$\langle Ax_n, x_n - p \rangle = \langle Ax_n - Ap, x_n - p \rangle \geq \mu \|Ax_n\|^2.$$

Taking into account the definition of y_n in the recursion (10), we have

$$\begin{aligned} \|y_n - p\| &= \|x_n + \theta_n(x_n - x_{n-1})pz\| \\ &\leq \|x_n - p\| + \theta_n \|x_n - x_{n-1}\|, \end{aligned}$$

and

$$\begin{aligned}
\|z_n - p\|^2 &= \|y_n - \lambda_n A y_n - p\|^2 \\
&= \|y_n - p\|^2 + \lambda_n^2 \|A y_n\|^2 - 2\lambda_n \langle A y_n, y_n - p \rangle \\
&\leq \|y_n - p\|^2 + \lambda_n^2 \|A y_n\|^2 - 2\mu \lambda_n \|A y_n\|^2 \\
&\leq \|y_n - p\|^2 + (\lambda_n - 2\mu)\lambda_n \|A y_n\|^2,
\end{aligned} \quad (11)$$

which implies that $\|z_n - p\| \leq \|y_n - p\|$. Furthermore, we have

$$\begin{aligned}
\|x_{n+1} - p\| &= \|(1 - \alpha_n - \gamma_n) y_n + \alpha_n z_n - p\| \\
&\leq (1 - \alpha_n - \gamma_n)\|y_n - p\| + \lambda_n^2 \|z_n - p\| + \gamma_n \|p\| \\
&\leq (1 - \gamma_n)\|y_n - p\| + \gamma_n \|p\| \\
&\leq (1 - \gamma_n)[\|x_n - p\| + \theta_n \|x_n - x_{n-1}\|] + \gamma_n \|p\| \\
&\leq (1 - \gamma_n)\|x_n - p\| + \gamma_n [\|p\| + \frac{\theta_n}{\gamma_n} \|x_n - x_{n-1}\|].
\end{aligned}$$

In view of the assumption on θ_n, we obtain $\theta_n \|x_n - x_{n-1}\| \leq \epsilon_n = o(\gamma_n)$, which entails that there exists some positive constant σ such that $\sigma = \sup \frac{\theta_n}{\gamma_n} \|x_n - x_{n-1}\|$; therefore,

$$\begin{aligned}
\|x_{n+1} - p\| &\leq (1 - \gamma_n)\|x_n - p\| + \gamma_n(\|p\| + \sigma) \\
&\leq \max\{\|x_0 - p\|, \|p\| + \sigma\},
\end{aligned}$$

namely, the sequence $\{x_n\}$ is bounded, and so are $\{y_n\}$ and $\{z_n\}$.

It follows from (10) and (11) that

$$\begin{aligned}
\|x_{n+1} - p\|^2 &= \|(1 - \alpha_n - \gamma_n) y_n + \alpha_n z_n - p\|^2 \\
&= \|(1 - \alpha_n - \gamma_n)(y_n - p) + \alpha_n (z_n - p) - \gamma_n p\|^2 \\
&\leq (1 - \alpha_n - \gamma_n)\|y_n - p\|^2 + \alpha_n \|z_n - p\|^2 + \gamma_n \|p\|^2 \\
&\quad - (1 - \alpha_n - \gamma_n)\alpha_n \|y_n - z_n\|^2 \\
&\leq (1 - \alpha_n - \gamma_n)\|y_n - p\|^2 + \alpha_n [\|y_n - p\|^2 + (\lambda_n - 2\mu)\lambda_n \|A y_n\|^2] \\
&\quad + \gamma_n \|p\|^2 - (1 - \alpha_n - \gamma_n)\alpha_n \|y_n - z_n\|^2 \\
&= (1 - \gamma_n)\|y_n - p\|^2 + \alpha_n (\lambda_n - 2\mu)\lambda_n \|A y_n\|^2 \\
&\quad + \gamma_n \|p\|^2 - (1 - \alpha_n - \gamma_n)\alpha_n \|y_n - z_n\|^2.
\end{aligned} \quad (12)$$

By using again the formation of y_n, we obtain

$$\begin{aligned}
\|y_n - p\|^2 &= \|x_n + \theta_n (x_n - x_{n-1}) - p\|^2 \\
&= \|(1 + \theta_n)(x_n - p) - \theta_n (x_{n-1} - p)\|^2 \\
&\leq (1 + \theta_n)\|x_n - p\|^2 - \theta_n \|x_{n-1} - p\|^2 + \theta_n(1 + \theta_n)\|x_n - x_{n-1}\|^2 \quad (13) \\
&\leq (1 + \theta_n)\|x_n - p\|^2 - \theta_n \|x_{n-1} - p\|^2 + 2\theta_n \|x_n - x_{n-1}\|^2.
\end{aligned}$$

Substituting (13) into (12), we have

$$\begin{aligned}
\|x_{n+1} - p\|^2 &\leq (1 - \gamma_n)[(1 + \theta_n)\|x_n - p\|^2 - \theta_n \|x_{n-1} - p\|^2 + 2\theta_n \|x_n - x_{n-1}\|^2] \\
&\quad + \alpha_n (\lambda_n - 2\mu)\lambda_n \|A y_n\|^2 + \gamma_n \|p\|^2 - (1 - \alpha_n - \gamma_n)\alpha_n \|y_n - z_n\|^2 \\
&= (1 - \gamma_n)[\|x_n - p\|^2 + \theta_n(\|x_n - p\|^2 - \|x_{n-1} - p)\|^2) \\
&\quad + 2\theta_n \|x_n - x_{n-1}\|^2] + \alpha_n (\lambda_n - 2\mu)\lambda_n \|A y_n\|^2 + \gamma_n \|p\|^2 \\
&\quad - (1 - \alpha_n - \gamma_n)\alpha_n \|y_n - z_n\|^2 \\
&= \|x_n - p\|^2 + \gamma_n(\|p\|^2 - \|x_n - p\|^2) + 2(1 - \gamma_n)\theta_n \|x_n - x_{n-1}\|^2 \\
&\quad + (1 - \gamma_n)\theta_n(\|x_n - p\|^2 - \|x_{n-1} - p)\|^2) + \alpha_n (\lambda_n - 2\mu)\lambda_n \|A y_n\|^2 \\
&\quad - (1 - \alpha_n - \gamma_n)\alpha_n \|y_n - z_n\|^2,
\end{aligned}$$

and transposing, we have

$$(1 - \alpha_n - \gamma_n)\alpha_n \|y_n - z_n\|^2 + \alpha_n(2\mu - \lambda_n)\lambda_n \|Ay_n\|^2$$
$$\leq (\|x_n - p\|^2 - \|x_{n+1} - p\|^2) + (1 - \gamma_n)\theta_n(\|x_n - p\|^2 - \|x_{n-1} - p)\|^2) \quad (14)$$
$$+ \gamma_n(\|p\|^2 - \|x_n - p\|^2) + 2(1 - \gamma_n)\theta_n \|x_n - x_{n-1}\|^2,$$

Here, two cases should be considered.

Case I. Assume that the sequence $\|x_n - p\|$ is decreasing, namely, there exists $N_0 > 0$ such that $\|x_{n+1} - p\| \leq \|x_n - p\|$ for each $n > N_0$, and then there is the limit of $\|x_n - p\|$ and $\lim_{n \to \infty}(\|x_{n+1} - p\| - \|x_n - p\|) = 0$. It turns out from (14) and the condition $(B1)$ that

$$(1 - \alpha_n - \gamma_n)\alpha_n \|y_n - z_n\|^2 \to 0; \quad \alpha_n(2\mu - \lambda_n)\lambda_n \|Ay_n\|^2 \to 0,$$

which implies that $\|y_n - z_n\|^2 \to 0$ and $\|Ay_n\|^2 \to 0$.

Furthermore, by the setting of u_n, we have $\|u_n - y_n\| = \alpha_n \|z_n - y_n\| \to 0$ and $\|x_{n+1} - u_n\| = \gamma_n \|y_n\| \to 0$, which together with $\|x_n - y_n\| = \theta_n \|x_n - x_{n-1}\| \to 0$ yields that

$$\|x_{n+1} - x_n\| \leq \|x_{n+1} - u_n\| + \|u_n - y_n\| + \|y_n - x_n\| \to 0.$$

Because $\{x_n\}$ is bounded, it follows from Eberlein–Shmulyan's theorem, for arbitrary point $q \in w_\omega(x_n)$, that there exits a subsequence $\{x_{n_j}\}$ of $\{x_n\}$ such that x_{n_j} converges weakly to q. By $\|x_n - y_n\| \to 0$, $\|Ay_n\|^2 \to 0$ and A is continuous, we have

$$0 = \lim_{n \to \infty} \|Ay_n\| = \lim_{j \to \infty} \|Ay_{n_j}\| = Aq,$$

which entails that $q \in A^{-1}(0)$. In view of the fact that the choice of q in $w_\omega(x_n)$ was arbitrary, we conclude that $w_\omega(x_n) \subset \Omega$, which makes Lemma 2 workable, that is, $\{x_n\}_{n=0}^\infty$ converges weakly to some point in Ω.

Now, we claim that $x_n \to p$, where $p = P_\Omega(0)$.

For this purpose, let $u_n = (1 - \alpha_n)y_n + \alpha_n z_n$, and then we have

$$\begin{aligned} x_{n+1} &= (1 - \alpha_n - \gamma_n)y_n + \alpha_n z_n = (1 - \gamma_n)u_n + \gamma_n(u_n - y_n) \\ &= (1 - \gamma_n)u_n + \gamma_n \alpha_n(z_n - y_n), \end{aligned}$$

which yields that

$$\begin{aligned} \|x_{n+1} - p\|^2 &= \|(1 - \gamma_n)u_n + \gamma_n \alpha_n(z_n - y_n) - p\|^2 \\ &= \|(1 - \gamma_n)(u_n - p) + \gamma_n \alpha_n(z_n - y_n) - \gamma_n p\|^2 \\ &\leq (1 - \gamma_n)^2 \|u_n - p\|^2 - 2\langle \gamma_n p - \gamma_n \alpha_n(z_n - y_n), x_{n+1} - z \rangle \\ &= (1 - \gamma_n)^2 \|u_n - p\|^2 - 2\gamma_n \alpha_n \langle y_n - z_n, x_{n+1} - p \rangle \quad (15) \\ &\quad + 2\gamma_n \langle -p, x_{n+1} - p \rangle. \end{aligned}$$

In addition, by using again the formation of $\{y_n\}$, we obtain

$$\begin{aligned} \|y_n - p\|^2 &= \|x_n + \theta_n(x_n - x_{n-1}) - p\|^2 \\ &= \|(1 + \theta_n)(x_n - p) - \theta_n(x_{n-1} - p)\|^2 \\ &\leq (1 + \theta_n)\|x_n - p\|^2 - \theta_n \|x_{n-1} - p\|^2 + \theta_n(1 + \theta_n)\|x_n - x_{n-1}\|^2 \\ &\leq (1 + \theta_n)\|x_n - p\|^2 - \theta_n \|x_{n-1} - p\|^2 + 2\theta_n \|x_n - x_{n-1}\|^2, \end{aligned}$$

and substituting the above inequality in (15), we have

$$
\begin{aligned}
\|x_{n+1} - p\|^2 &\leq (1-\gamma_n)^2\|y_n - p\|^2 - 2\gamma_n\alpha_n\langle y_n - z_n, x_{n+1} - p\rangle + 2\gamma_n\langle -p, x_{n+1} - p\rangle \\
&\leq (1-\gamma_n)^2[(1+\theta_n)\|x_n - p\|^2 - \theta_n\|x_{n-1} - p\|^2 + 2\theta_n\|x_n - x_{n-1}\|^2] \\
&\quad - 2\gamma_n\alpha_n\langle y_n - z_n, x_{n+1} - p\rangle + 2\gamma_n\langle -p, x_{n+1} - p\rangle \\
&\leq (1-\gamma_n)[\|x_n - p\|^2 + \theta_n(\|x_n - p\|^2 - \|x_{n-1} - p\|^2) + 2\theta_n\|x_n - x_{n-1}\|^2] \\
&\quad - 2\gamma_n\alpha_n\langle y_n - z_n, x_{n+1} - p\rangle + 2\gamma_n\langle -p, x_{n+1} - p\rangle \\
&\leq (1-\gamma_n)[\|x_n - p\|^2 + \theta_n\|x_n - x_{n-1}\| \cdot (\|x_n - p\| + \|x_{n-1} - p\|) \\
&\quad + 2\theta_n\|x_n - x_{n-1}\|^2] - 2\gamma_n\alpha_n\langle y_n - z_n, x_{n+1} - p\rangle + 2\gamma_n\langle -p, x_{n+1} - p\rangle \\
&\leq (1-\gamma_n)\|x_n - p\|^2 + \theta_n(1-\gamma_n)M\|x_n - x_{n-1}\| \\
&\quad + 2\gamma_n\langle -p, x_{n+1} - p\rangle - 2\gamma_n\alpha_n\langle y_n - z_n, x_{n+1} - p\rangle,
\end{aligned} \quad (16)
$$

where $M = \sup(\|x_n - p\| + \|x_{n-1} - p\| + 2\theta_n\|x_n - x_{n-1}\|)$.

Owing to $p = P_\Omega(0)$, we can infer that $\langle 0 - P_\Omega(0), y - P_\Omega(0)\rangle \leq 0$ for each $y \in \Omega$, so we have

$$\limsup\langle -p, x_{n+1} - p\rangle = \max_{q \in w_\omega(x_n)} \langle -p, q - p\rangle \leq 0.$$

In addition, from the assumption on $\{\theta_n\}$, we have

$$\sum_{n=1}^\infty \theta_n(1-\gamma_n)M\|x_n - x_{n-1}\| < \infty,$$

and from $y_n - z_n \to 0$, we have

$$\lim_{n\to\infty}\sup\{-2\gamma_n\alpha_n\langle y_n - z_n, x_{n+1} - p\rangle + 2\gamma_n\langle -p, x_{n+1} - p\rangle\}/\gamma_n \leq 0,$$

and therefore (16) enables Lemma 1 to be applicable to, namely, $\|x_n - p\| \to 0$.

Case II. If the sequence $\|x_n - p\|$ is not decreasing at infinity, in the sense that there exists a subsequence $\{\|x_{n_j} - p\|\}$ of $\{\|x_n - p\|\}$ such that $\|x_{n_j} - p\| \leq \|x_{n_{j+1}} - p\|$. Owing to Lemma 3, we can induce that $\|x_{\sigma(n)} - p\| \leq \|x_{\sigma(n)+1} - p\|$ and $\|x_n - p\| \leq \|x_{\sigma(n)+1} - p\|$, where $\sigma(n)$ is an indicator defined by $\sigma(n) = \max\{k \leq n : \|x_k - p\| \leq \|x_{k+1} - p\|\}$ and $\sigma(n) \to \infty$ as $n \to \infty$.

Taking into account the fact that the formula (14) still holds for each $\sigma(n)$, that is,

$$
\begin{aligned}
&(1-\alpha_{\sigma(n)}-\gamma_{\sigma(n)})\alpha_{\sigma(n)}\|y_\sigma(n) - z_\sigma(n)\|^2 + \alpha_{\sigma(n)}(2\mu - \lambda_{\sigma(n)})\lambda_{\sigma(n)}\|Ay_{\sigma(n)}\|^2 \\
&\leq (\|x_{\sigma(n)} - p\|^2 - \|x_{\sigma(n)+1} - p\|^2) + \gamma_{\sigma(n)}(\|p\|^2 - \|x_\sigma(n) - p\|^2) \\
&\quad + (1-\gamma_{\sigma(n)})\theta_{\sigma(n)}(\|x_{\sigma(n)} - p\|^2 - \|x_{\sigma(n)-1} - p\|^2) \\
&\quad + 2(1-\gamma_{\sigma(n)})\theta_{\sigma(n)}\|x_{\sigma(n)} - x_{\sigma(n)-1}\|^2 \\
&\leq \gamma_{\sigma(n)}(\|p\|^2 - \|x_{\sigma(n)} - p\|^2) + (1-\gamma_{\sigma(n)})\theta_{\sigma(n)}(\|x_{\sigma(n)} - p\|^2 - \|x_{\sigma(n)-1} - p)\|^2) \\
&\quad + 2(1-\gamma_{\sigma(n)})\theta_{\sigma(n)}\|x_{\sigma(n)} - x_{\sigma(n)-1}\|^2.
\end{aligned}
$$

In addition, from the theorem's assumptions (B_1) and (B_2) that

$$\|y_{\sigma(n)} - z_{\sigma(n)}\|^2 \to 0; \quad \|Ay_{\sigma(n)}\|^2 \to 0, \quad (17)$$

Similarly to the proofs of (16) in Case I, we have $w_\omega(x_n) \subset \Omega$ and

$$\limsup\langle -p, x_{\sigma(n)+1} - p\rangle \leq 0, \quad (18)$$

and

$$\begin{aligned}\|x_{\sigma(n)+1}-p\|^2 \leq\ & (1-\gamma_{\sigma(n)})\|x_{\sigma(n)}-p\|^2 + \theta_{\sigma(n)}(1-\gamma_{\sigma(n)})M\|x_{\sigma(n)}-x_{\sigma(n)-1}\| \\ & -2\gamma_{\sigma(n)}\alpha_{\sigma(n)}\langle y_{\sigma(n)}-z_{\sigma(n)},x_{\sigma(n)+1}-p\rangle \\ & +2\gamma_{\sigma(n)}\langle -p,x_{\sigma(n)+1}-p\rangle.\end{aligned} \quad (19)$$

Transposing again, we have

$$\begin{aligned}\gamma_{\sigma(n)}\|x_{\sigma(n)}-p\|^2 \leq\ & (\|x_{\sigma(n)}-p\|^2-\|x_{\sigma(n)+1}-p\|^2) + \theta_{\sigma(n)}(1-\gamma_{\sigma(n)})M \\ & \times \|x_{\sigma(n)}-x_{\sigma(n)-1}\| + 2\gamma_{\sigma(n)}\langle -p,x_{\sigma(n)+1}-p\rangle \\ & -2\gamma_{\sigma(n)}\alpha_{\sigma(n)}\langle y_{\sigma(n)}-z_{\sigma(n)},x_{\sigma(n)+1}-p\rangle \\ \leq\ & \theta_{\sigma(n)}(1-\gamma_{\sigma(n)})M\|x_{\sigma(n)}-x_{\sigma(n)-1}\| + 2\gamma_{\sigma(n)}\langle -p,x_{\sigma(n)+1}-p\rangle \\ & -2\gamma_{\sigma(n)}\alpha_{\sigma(n)}\langle y_{\sigma(n)}-z_{\sigma(n)},x_{\sigma(n)+1}-p\rangle,\end{aligned}$$

which amounts to

$$\begin{aligned}\|x_{\sigma(n)}-p\|^2 \leq\ & \frac{\theta_{\sigma(n)}}{\gamma_{\sigma(n)}}(1-\gamma_{\sigma(n)})M\|x_{\sigma(n)}-x_{\sigma(n)-1}\| + 2\langle -p,x_{\sigma(n)+1}-p\rangle \\ & -2\alpha_{\sigma(n)}\langle y_{\sigma(n)}-z_{\sigma(n)},x_{\sigma(n)+1}-p\rangle.\end{aligned} \quad (20)$$

Noting the grant of $\epsilon_{\sigma(n)}=o(\gamma_{\sigma(n)})$, we have $\frac{\theta_{\sigma(n)}}{\gamma_{\sigma(n)}}(1-\gamma_{\sigma(n)})M\|x_{\sigma(n)}-x_{\sigma(n)-1}\| \to 0$. Putting (18) and (17) into (20), it yields that $\|x_{\sigma(n)}-p\| \to 0$.

It follows from (19) that

$$\lim_{n\to\infty}\|x_{\sigma(n)+1}-p\| = \lim_{n\to\infty}\|x_{\sigma(n)}-p\|^2 = 0,$$

which makes Lemma 3 practicable, and hence

$$0 \leq \|x_n-p\| \leq \max\{\|x_n-p\|, \|x_{\sigma(n)}-p\|\} \leq \|x_{\sigma(n)+1}-p\| \to 0.$$

Consequently, the sequence $\{x_n\}$ converges strongly to p, which is the closest point to 0 in Ω. This completes the proof. □

Remark 2. *If the operator A is accretive with $\mu-$ cocoercivity or maximal monotone, then all the above results hold.*

4. Applications

4.1. Minimax Problem

Suppose H_1 and H_2 are two real Hilbert spaces, the general convex–concave minimax problem in a Hilbert space setting is illustrated as follows:

$$\min_{x\in Q}\max_{\lambda\in S} L(x,\lambda), \quad (21)$$

where Q and S are nonempty, closed and convex subsets of Hilbert spaces H_1 and H_2, respectively, and $L(x,\lambda)$ is convex in x (for each fixed $\lambda \in S$) and concave in λ (for each fixed $x \in Q$).

A solution $(x^*,\lambda^*) \in Q \times S$ of the minimax problem (21) is interpreted as a saddle point, satisfying the following inequality

$$L(x^*,\lambda) \leq L(x^*,\lambda^*) \leq L(x,\lambda^*), x\in Q, \lambda\in S,$$

which amounts to the fact that $x^* \in Q$ is a minimizer in Q of the function $L(\cdot,\lambda^*)$, and $\lambda^* \in S$ is a maximizer in S of the function $L(x^*,\cdot)$.

Minimax problems are an important modeling tool due to their ability to handle many important applications in machine learning, in particular, in generative adversarial nets (GANs), statistical learning, certification of robustness in deep learning and distributed computing. Some recent works can be seen in, e.g., Ataş [32], Ji-Zhao [33] and Hassanpour et al. [34].

For example, if we consider the standard convex programming problem,

$$\min f(x),$$
$$\text{s.t. } h_i(x) \leq 0, i = 1, 2, \ldots, l, \tag{22}$$

where f and h_i, $(i = 1, 2, \ldots, l)$ are convex functions. Using the Lagrange function L, the problem (22) can be reformulated as the following minimax problem (see, e.g., Qi and Sun [35]):

$$L(x, \lambda) = f(x) + \sum_i \lambda_i h_i(x). \tag{23}$$

It can be seen that $L(x, \lambda)$ in (23) is a convex–concave function on $Q \times S$, where

$$Q = \{x : h_i(x) \leq 0, i = 1, 2, \ldots, l\}, \quad S = \{\lambda : \lambda_i \geq 0, i = 1, 2, \ldots, l\},$$

and the Kuhn–Tucker vector (x^*, λ^*) of (22) is exactly the saddle point of Lagrangian function $L(x, \lambda)$ in (23).

Another nice example is the Tchebychev approximating problem that consists of finding (x, λ) such that

$$\min_{\lambda \in Q} \max_{x \in S} (g(x) - \lambda(x))^2,$$

that is, for given $g : S \subset \mathbb{R}^n \to \mathbb{R}$, finding $\lambda(x) \in Q$ approaching $g(x)$, where $\lambda : \mathbb{R}^n \to \mathbb{R}$ and Q is the space composed of the functions λ.

It is known that L has a saddle point if and only if

$$\min_{x \in Q} \max_{\lambda \in S} L(x, \lambda) = \max_{\lambda \in S} \min_{x \in Q} L(x, \lambda).$$

If L is convex–concave and differentiable, let $\nabla_x L(x, \lambda)$ and $-\nabla_\lambda L(x, \lambda)$ present the derivatives of L on x and λ, respectively, and then we have $\partial L(z) = [\nabla_x L(x, \lambda), -\nabla_\lambda L(x, \lambda)]^T$, where $z = (x, \lambda)$.

Note that ∂L is maximal monotone for the unconstrained case (i.e., $Q = H_1, S = H_2$), and finding a saddle point $z^* = (x^*, \lambda^*) \in Q \times S$ of L equals to solving the equation $\partial L(z^*) = 0$. For more details on the minimax problem and its solutions, one can refer to the von Neumann works from the 1920s and 1930s [36,37] and Ky Fan's minimax theorem [38].

Now, we consider minimax problems (21) under the unconstrained case, and let the solution set Ω of the minimax problem be nonempty. So, by taking $A = \partial L$, we can obtain the saddle point of the minimax problem in $H_1 \times H_2$ from the following results.

Theorem 2. *Let H_1 and H_2 be two real Hilbert spaces. Suppose that the function L is convex–concave and differentiable such that $\Omega \neq \emptyset$. Under the setting of the parameters in Algorithm 1, if the sequences $\{\alpha_n\}, \{\gamma_n\}, \{\epsilon_n\}$ are in $(0,1)$ and satisfying the conditions as in Theorem 1, then the sequence $\{z_n\}$ generated by the following scheme*

$$\begin{cases} y_n = z_n + \theta_n(z_n - z_{n-1}), \\ \bar{z}_n = y_n - \lambda_n \partial L(y_n), \\ z_{n+1} = (1 - \alpha_n - \gamma_n)y_n + \alpha_n \bar{z}_n, \end{cases} \tag{24}$$

converges strongly to the least norm element $z^* \in \Omega$, where $z_0 \in H_1 \times H_2$ and $z_1 \in H_1 \times H_2$ are two arbitrary initial points.

Proof. Noting that ∂L is maximal monotone, so letting A be ∂L in Algorithm 1, and following Theorem 1, we have the result. □

Indeed, if we denote $z_n = (x_n, \lambda_n) \in H_1 \times H_2$, then the recursions (24) specifically can be rewritten as follows for arbitrary initial points $x_0, x_1, \lambda_0, \lambda_1$,

$$\begin{cases} x'_n = x_n + \theta_n(x_n - x_{n-1}), \\ \lambda'_n = \lambda_n + \theta_n(\lambda_n - \lambda_{n-1}), \\ \bar{x}_n = x'_n - \nabla_x L(x'_n, \lambda'_n), \\ \bar{\lambda}_n = \lambda'_n + \nabla_\lambda L(x'_n, \lambda'_n), \\ x_{n+1} = (1 - \alpha_n - \gamma_n)x'_n + \alpha_n \bar{x}_n, \\ \lambda_{n+1} = (1 - \alpha_n - \gamma_n)\lambda'_n + \alpha_n \bar{\lambda}_n, \end{cases} \quad (25)$$

and the sequence pair (x_n, λ_n) converges strongly to an element $(x^*, \lambda^*) \in \Omega$ which is closest to $(0, 0)$.

4.2. Critical Points Problem

In this part, we focus on finding the critical points of the functional $F : H \to R \cup \{+\infty\}$ defined by

$$F := \Psi + \Phi, \quad (26)$$

where H is a real Hilbert space, the function $\Psi : H \to \mathbb{R} \cup \{+\infty\}$ is a proper, convex and lower semi-continuous function and $\Phi : H \to \mathbb{R}$ is a convex locally Lipschitz mapping.

A point x^* is said to be a critical point of $F = \Psi + \Phi$ if $x^* \in dom(\Psi)$ and if it satisfies

$$\Psi(x^*) - \Psi(v) \leq \Phi^\circ(x^*, v - x^*),$$

where Φ° is the generalized directional derivative of Φ at $x^* \in C$ in the direction $v \in H$ which is defined by

$$\Phi^\circ(x^*, v) = \limsup_{\substack{t \downarrow 0 \\ w \to x^*}} \frac{\Phi(w + tv) - \Phi(w)}{t}.$$

Critical point theory is a powerful theoretical tool, which has been greatly developed in recent years and has been widely used in many fields, such as differential equations, operations research optimization and so on. For some recent works on the applications of critical point theory, we can refer to Trushnikov et al. [39], Turgut et al. [40] and therein.

A typical instance is finding the solution of the impulsive differential equation model existing in the fields of medicine, biology, rocket and aerospace motion and optimization theory which can be transformed into finding the critical point of some functional.

Specifically, we consider the following impulsive differential equation:

$$\begin{cases} -\ddot{q}(t) = \lambda q(t) + f(t, q(t)), t \in (s_{k-1}, s_k), \\ \triangle \dot{q}(s_k) = g_k(q(s_k^-)), k = 1, 2, \cdots, \end{cases} \quad (27)$$

where $k \in \mathbb{Z}, \lambda \geq 0, q(t) \in \mathbb{R}^n, \triangle \dot{q}(s_k) = \dot{q}(s_k^+) - \dot{q}(s_k^-), \dot{q}(s_k^\pm) = \lim_{t \to s_k^\pm} \dot{q}(t), f(t, q) = grad_q I(t, q), I(t, q) \in C^1(\mathbb{R} \times \mathbb{R}^n, \mathbb{R}), g_k(q) = grad_q G_k(q), G_k \in C^1(\mathbb{R}^n, \mathbb{R})$. In addition, there exist $m \in \mathbb{N}$ and $T \in \mathbb{R}^+$ such that $0 = s_0 < s_1 < s_2 < \ldots < s_m = T, s_{k+m} = s_k + T, g_{k+m} = g_k$ holds for all $k \in \mathbb{Z}$.

Let $H = \{q \in \mathbb{R} \to \mathbb{R}^n | q$ be absolute continuous, $\dot{q} \in L^2((0, T), \mathbb{R}^n), q(t) = q(t + T), t \in \mathbb{R}\}$ and the norm $\|\cdot\|$ is induced by the inner product $\langle q, p \rangle = \int_0^T \dot{q}(t)\dot{p}(t) + q(t)p(t)dt, \forall p, q \in H$.

Denote $K = \{1, 2, \cdots, m\}$, and the functional on H is defined as

$$F(q) = \int_0^T \frac{1}{2}|\dot{q}|^2 - \frac{1}{2}\lambda q^2 - I(t, q)dt + \sum_{k \in K} G_k(q(s_k)),$$

and then the periodic solution of the system (27) corresponds to the critical point of the functional F one to one.

If the functional F in (26) satisfies the Palais–Smale compact conditions and F is bounded from below, then there exists a critical point x^* such that $F(x^*) = \inf_{u \in H} F(u)$ (see, e.g., Motreanu and Panagiotopoulos [41]). From Fermat's theorem, one can refer that the critical point x^* is a solution of the inclusion (see, e.g., Moameni [42]),

$$0 \in \partial \Psi(x^*) + \partial_c \Phi(x^*),$$

where $\partial_c \Phi(\cdot)$ is the generalized derivative of Φ defined as

$$\partial_c \Phi(u) = \{u^* \in H^*; \Phi^\circ(u,v) \geq \langle u^*, v \rangle, \forall v \in H\}.$$

From Clarke [43], $\partial_c \Phi$ carries bounded sets of H into bounded sets of H^* and is hemicontinuous. Moreover, we can infer that $\partial_c \Phi$ is a monotone mapping because Φ is convex, which makes Browder ([17], Theorem 2) applicable, namely, $\partial \Psi + \partial_c \Phi$ is a maximal monotone mapping. Denoted by Ω is the critical points set of the problem (26). By taking $A = \partial \Psi + \partial_c \Phi$, we have the following result.

Theorem 3. *Let H be a real Hilbert space. Suppose that $F : H \to (-\infty, \infty]$ is of the form (26), bounded from below and satisfying the Palais–Smale compact conditions such that $\Omega \neq \emptyset$. Under the setting of the parameters in Algorithm 1, if $\{\alpha_n\}$, $\{\gamma_n\}$, $\{\epsilon_n\}$ are the sequences in $(0,1)$ satisfying the conditions as in Theorem 1, then the sequence $\{z_n\}$ generated by the following schemes*

$$\begin{cases} y_n = z_n + \theta_n(z_n - z_{n-1}), \\ \bar{z}_n = y_n - \lambda_n(\partial \Psi + \partial_c \Phi)(y_n), \\ z_{n+1} = (1 - \alpha_n - \gamma_n)y_n + \alpha_n \bar{z}_n, \end{cases} \quad (28)$$

converges strongly to an element $\bar{x} \in \Omega$ which is closest to 0.

5. Numerical Examples

In this section, we present numerical examples in finite- and infinite-dimensional spaces to illustrate the applicability, efficiency and stability of Algorithm 1. All the codes for the results are written in Matlab R2016b and are performed on an LG dual-core personal computer.

Example 1. *Here, we test the effectiveness of our algorithm in finite-dimensional space which does not need super high dimensions. For the purpose, let $H = \mathbb{R}^6$, and define the monotone operators A as follows:*

$$A = \begin{pmatrix} 6 & 0 & 0 & 0 & 0 & 0 \\ 0 & 7 & 0 & 0 & 0 & 0 \\ 0 & 0 & 8 & 0 & 0 & 0 \\ 0 & 0 & 0 & 3 & 0 & 0 \\ 0 & 0 & 0 & 0 & 4 & 0 \\ 0 & 0 & 0 & 0 & 0 & 1 \end{pmatrix} \quad (29)$$

it is easy to verify that the cocoercivity coefficient $\mu = \frac{1}{8}$, so we set $\lambda_n = \frac{1}{8} - \frac{1}{10n}$.

Next, let us compare our Algorithm 1 with the regularization method. Specifically, the regularization algorithm (RM) is considered as

$$\begin{cases} y_n = x_n + \theta_n(x_n - x_{n-1}), \\ z_n = J_r^A y_n, \\ x_{n+1} = (1 - \alpha_n - \gamma_n)y_n + \alpha_n z_n. \end{cases}$$

As for the components, both our Algorithm 1 and the regularization method (RM), initial points x_0, x_1 are generated randomly by Matlab , inertial coefficient θ_n is chosen to satisfy that if $\theta > \epsilon_n \times (\max(\|x_{n-1} - x_n\|, \|x_{n-1} - x_n\|^2))$, then $\theta_n = 1/((n+2)^2 \times (\max(\|x_{n-1} - x_n\|, \|x_{n-1} - x_n\|^2)))$; otherwise, $\theta_n = \frac{\theta}{2}$, where $\theta = 0.6$, $\epsilon_n = 1/(n+1)^2$, $\gamma_n = 1/(10n)$. The experimental results are listed in Figure 1. Moreover, the iterations and convergence rate of Algorithm 1 for different values of $\{\alpha_n\}$ are presented in Table 1.

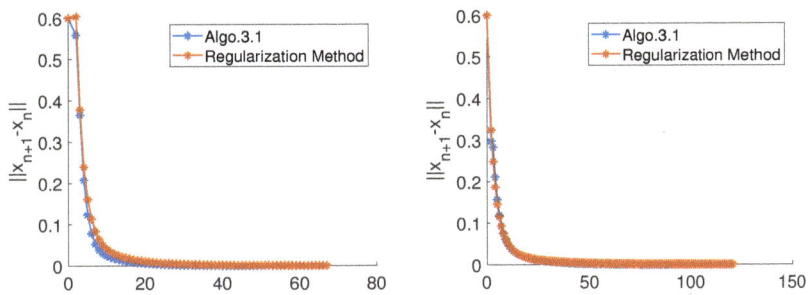

Figure 1. Algorithm 1 and the Regularization Method.

Table 1. Example 1 Numerical Results for Algorithm 1 and Regularization Method.

	Algorithm 1				Regularization Method		
$\{\alpha_n\}$	CPU Time	Iter.	$\frac{\|x_{n+1}-x^*\|}{\|x_{n+1}-x_0\|}$	r	CPU Time	Iter.	$\frac{\|x_{n+1}-x^*\|}{\|x_{n+1}-x_0\|}$
$1 - \frac{1}{100n}$	0.0201	42	6.1691×10^{-04}	0.1	0.0324	63	5.3741×10^{-04}
$\frac{1}{2} - \frac{1}{100n}$	0.0594	88	9.159×10^{-04}	0.05	0.0530	115	0.0013
$\frac{1}{8} - \frac{1}{100n}$	0.0422	276	0.0039	0.01	0.2205	367	0.0078

Example 2. *Now, we measure our Algorithm 1 in $H = L_2[0,1]$ with $\|\cdot\| = (\int_0^1 x^2(t)dt)^{\frac{1}{2}}$. Define the mappings A by $A(x)(t) := 2x(t)/3$ for all $x(t) \in L_2[0,1]$, and then it can be shown that A is $\frac{3}{2}$-cocoercive monotone mapping. All the parameters θ_n, θ, λ_n, ϵ_n and γ_n are chosen as in Example 1. The stop criterion is $\|x_{n+1} - x_n\| \leq 10^{-6}$. We test Algorithm 1 for the following three different initial points:*

Case I: $x_0 = 2t^3 e^{5t}$, $x_1 = \sin(3t)e^t/100$;
Case II: $x_0 = \sin(-3t) + \cos(-5t)/2$, $x_1 = 2t\sin(3t)e^{-5t}/200$;
Case III: $x_0 = 2t\sin(3t)e^{-5t}/200$, $x_1 = e^t - e^{-2t}$.

In addition, we also test the regularization method as illustrated in Example 1, and the tendency of the sequence is proposed in Figures 2 and 3 and Table 2.

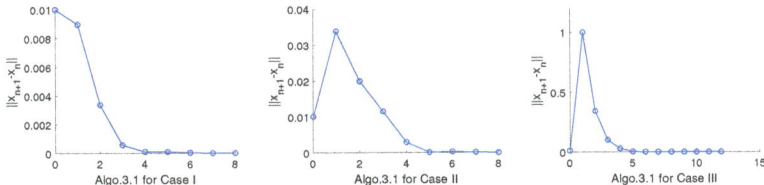

Figure 2. Algorithm 1 for Case I, Case II, Case III in Example 2.

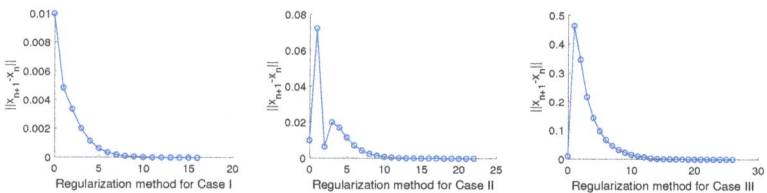

Figure 3. Regularization Method for Case I, Case II, Case III in Example 2.

Table 2. Example 2 Numerical Results for Algorithm 1 and Regularization Method.

	Case I		Case II		Case III	
	Algorithm 1	RM	Algorithm 1	RM	Algorithm 1	RM
CPU time	2.64	5.28	4.29	8.6	3.62	7.59
Iteration Number	9	17	9	23	13	27

6. Conclusions

The proximal point method (regularization method) and projection-based method are two classical and significant methods for solving monotone inclusions, variational inequalities and related problems.

However, the evaluations of resolvents/projections in these methods heavily rely on the structure of the given problem, and in the general case, this might seriously affect the computational effort of the given method. Thus, motivated by the ideas of Chidume et al. [44], Alvarez [28], Alvarez–Attouch [27] and Zegeye [45], we present a simple strong convergence method that avoids the need to compute resolvents/projections.

We present several theoretical applications such as minimax problems and critical point problems, as well as some numerical experiments illustrating the performances of our scheme.

Author Contributions: All authors contributed equally to this work. All authors read and approved the final manuscript.

Funding: This article was funded by the National Natural Science Foundation of China (12071316) and the Natural Science Foundation of Chongqing (cstc2021jcyj-msxmX0177).

Conflicts of Interest: The authors declare no conflict of interest.

References

1. Minty, G.J. Monotone (nonlinear)operators in Hilbert spaces. *Duke Math. J.* **1962**, *29*, 341–346. [CrossRef]
2. Browder, F. The solvability of nonlinear functional equations. *Duke Math. J.* **1963**, *30*, 557–566. [CrossRef]
3. Leray, J.; Lions, J. Quelques résultats de Višik sur les problèmes elliptiques non linéares par les méthodes de Minty-Browder. *Bull. Soc. Math. Fr.* **1965**, *93*, 97–107. [CrossRef]
4. Minty, G.J. On a monotonicity method for the solution of non-linear equations in Banach spaces. *Proc. Nat. Acad. Sci. USA* 1963, *50*, 1038–1041. [CrossRef] [PubMed]
5. Pascali, D.; Sburian, S. *Nonlinear Mappings of Monotone Type*; Editura Academia Bucuresti: Bucharest, Romania, 1978; p. 101.
6. Bot, R.I.; Csetnek, E.R. An inertial forward-backward-forward primal-dual splitting algorithm for solving monotone inclusion problems. *Numer. Algorithms* **2016**, *71*, 519–540. [CrossRef]
7. Korpelevich, G.M. The extragradient method for finding saddle points and other problems. *Ekonomika i Matematicheskie Metody* **1976**, *12*, 747–756.
8. Khan, S.A.; Suantai, S.; Cholamjiak, W. Shrinking projection methods involving inertial forward–backward splitting methods for inclusion problems. *Rev. Real Acad. Cienc. Exactas Fis. Nat. A Mat.* **2019**, *113*, 645–656. [CrossRef]
9. Sicre, M.R. On the complexity of a hybrid proximal extragradient projective method for solving monotone inclusion problems. *Comput. Optim. Appl.* **2020**, *76*, 991–1019. [CrossRef]
10. Xu, H.K. A regularization method for the proximal point algorithm. *J. Glob. Optim.* **2006**, *36*, 115–125. [CrossRef]

11. Yin, J.H.; Jian, J.B.; Jiang, X.Z.; Liu, M.X.; Wang, L.Z. A hybrid three-term conjugate gradient projection method for constrained nonlinear monotone equations with applications. *Numer. Algorithms* **2021**, *88*, 389–418. [CrossRef]
12. Berinde, V. *Iterative Approximation of Fixed Points*; Lecture Notes in Mathematics; Springer: London, UK, 2007.
13. Chidume, C.E. An approximation method for monotone Lipshitz operators in Hilbert spaces. *J. Austral. Math. Soc. Ser.* **1986**, *A 41*, 59–63. [CrossRef]
14. Kačurovskii, R.I. On monotone operators and convex functionals. *Usp. Mat. Nauk.* **1960**, *15*, 213–215.
15. Zarantonello, E.H. *Solving Functional Equations by Contractive Averaging*; Technical Report #160; U. S. Army Mathematics Research Center: Madison, WI, USA, 1960.
16. Martinet, B. Regularisation d'inequations variationnelles par approximations successives. *Rev. Fr. Inform. Rech. Oper.* **1970**, *4*, 154–158.
17. Browder, F.E. Nonlinear maximal monotone operators in Banach space. *Math. Annalen* **1968**, *175*, 89–113. [CrossRef]
18. Bruck, R.E., Jr. A strongly convergent iterative method for the solution of $0 \in Ux$ for a maximal monotone operator U in Hilbert space. *J. Math. Anal. Appl.* **1974**, *48*, 114–126. [CrossRef]
19. Boikanyo, O.A.; Morosanu, G. A proximal point algorithm converging strongly for general errors. *Optim. Lett.* **2010**, *4*, 635–641. [CrossRef]
20. Khatibzadeh, H. Some Remarks on the Proximal Point Algorithm. *J. Optim. Theory Appl.* **2012**, *153*, 769–778. [CrossRef]
21. Rockafellar, R.T. Monotone operators and the proximal point algorithm. *SIAM J. Control Optim.* **1976**, *14*, 877–898. [CrossRef]
22. Shehu, Y. Single projection algorithm for variational inequalities in Banach spaces with applications to contact problems. *Acta Math Sci.* **2020**, *40B*, 1045–1063. [CrossRef]
23. Yao, Y.H.; Shahzad, N. Strong convergence of a proximal point algorithm with general errors. *Optim. Lett.* **2012**, *6*, 621–628. [CrossRef]
24. Teboulle, M. A simplified view of first order methods for optimization. *Math. Program. Ser. B* **2018**, *170*, 67–96. [CrossRef]
25. Drusvyatskiy, D.; Lewis, A.S. Error bounds, quadratic growth, and linear convergence of proximal methods. *Math. Oper. Res.* **2018**, *43*, 919–948. [CrossRef]
26. Nesterov, Y. *Introductory Lectures on Convex Optimization*; Cluwer: Baltimore, MD, USA, 2004.
27. Alvarez, F. Weak convergence of a relaxed and inertial hybrid projection-proximal point algorithm for maximal monotone operators in Hilbert spaces. *SIAM J. Optim.* **2004**, *14*, 773–782. [CrossRef]
28. Alvarez, F.; Attouch, H. An inertial proximal method for maximal monotone operators via discretization of a nonlinear oscillator with damping. *Set-Valued Anal.* **2001**, *9*, 3–11. [CrossRef]
29. Xu, H.K. Iterative algorithms for nonliear operators. *J. Lond. Math. Soc.* **2002**, *66*, 240–256. [CrossRef]
30. Maingé, P.E. Approximation methods for common fixed points of nonexpansive mappingn Hilbert spaces. *J. Math. Anal. Appl.* **2007**, *325*, 469–479. [CrossRef]
31. Opial, Z. Weak convergence of the sequence of successive approximations for nonexpansive mappings. *Bull Amer Math Soc.* **1967**, *73*, 591–597. [CrossRef]
32. Ataş, İ. Comparison of deep convolution and least squares GANs for diabetic retinopathy image synthesis. *Neural Comput. Appl.* **2023**, *35*, 14431–14448. [CrossRef]
33. Ji, M.M.; Zhao, P. Image restoration based on the minimax-concave and the overlapping group sparsity. *Signal Image Video Process.* **2023**, *17*, 1733–1741. [CrossRef]
34. Hassanpour, H.; Hosseinzadeh, E.; Moodi, M. Solving intuitionistic fuzzy multi-objective linear programming problem and its application in supply chain management. *Appl. Math.* **2023**, *68*, 269–287. [CrossRef]
35. Qi, L.Q.; Sun, W.Y. *Nonconvex Optimization and Its Applications*; Book Series (NOIA, Volume 4), Minimax and Applications; Kluwer Academic Publishers: London, UK, 1995, pp. 55–67. [CrossRef]
36. von Neumann, J. Zur Theorie der Gesellschaftsspiele. *Math. Ann.* **1928**, *100*, 295–320. [CrossRef]
37. von Neumann, J. Uber ein bkonomisches Gleichungssystem und eine Verallgemeinerung des Brouwerschen Fixpunktsatzes, *Ergebn. Math. Kolloqu. Wien* **1935**, *8*, 73–83. [CrossRef]
38. Fan, K. *A minimax inequality and applications*. In Inequalities, III; Shisha, O., Ed.; Academic Press: San Diego, CA, USA, 1972; pp. 103–113.
39. Trushnikov, D.N.; Krotova, E.L.; Starikov, S.S.; Musikhin, N.A.; Varushkin, S.V.; Matveev, E.V. Solving the inverse problem of surface reconstruction during electron beam surfacing. *Russ. J. Nondestruct. Test.* **2023**, *59*, 240–250.
40. Turgut, O.E.; Turgut, M.S.; Kirtepe, E. A systematic review of the emerging metaheuristic algorithms on solving complex optimization problems. *Neural Comput. Appl.* **2023**, *35*, 14275–14378.
41. Motreanu, D.; Panagiotopoulos, P.D. *Minimax Theorems and Qualitative Properties of the Solutions of Hemivariational Inequalities*; Nonconvex Optimization and Its Applications; Kluwer Academic: New York, NY, USA, 1999. [CrossRef]
42. Moameni, A. Critical point theory on convex subsets with applications in differential equations and analysis. *J. Math. Pures. Appl.* **2020**, *141*, 266–315.
43. Clarke, F. *Functional Analysis Calculus of Variations and Optimal Control*; Springer: London, UK, 2013; pp. 193–209.

44. Chidume, C.E.; Osilike, M.O. Iterative solutions of nonlinear accretive operator equations in arbitrary Banach spaces. *Nonlinear Anal. Theory Methods Appl.* **1999**, *36*, 863–872. [CrossRef]
45. Zegeye, H. Strong convergence theorems for maximal monotone mappings in Banach spaces. *J. Math. Anal. Appl.* **2008**, *343*, 663–671. [CrossRef]

Disclaimer/Publisher's Note: The statements, opinions and data contained in all publications are solely those of the individual author(s) and contributor(s) and not of MDPI and/or the editor(s). MDPI and/or the editor(s) disclaim responsibility for any injury to people or property resulting from any ideas, methods, instructions or products referred to in the content.

Article

Recent Results on Expansive-Type Evolution and Difference Equations: A Survey

Behzad Djafari Rouhani [1,*] and Mohsen Rahimi Piranfar [2]

[1] Department of Mathematical Sciences, University of Texas at El Paso, 500 W. University Ave., El Paso, TX 79968, USA
[2] Department of Mathematics, Institute for Advanced Studies in Basic Sciences (IASBS), Zanjan P.O. Box 45195-1159, Iran; m.piranfar@gmail.com
* Correspondence: behzad@utep.edu

Abstract: In this survey, we review some old and new results initiated with the study of expansive mappings. From a variational perspective, we study the convergence analysis of expansive and almost-expansive curves and sequences governed by an evolution equation of the monotone or non-monotone type. Finally, we propose two well-defined algorithms to remedy the shortcomings concerning the ill-posedness of expansive-type evolution systems.

Keywords: first-order evolution equation; asymptotic behavior; maximal monotone operator; difference equation; periodic solution; expansive-type gradient system

MSC: 47H05; 47H25; 39A12; 37A30; 39A23

1. Introduction

Let H be a real Hilbert space, with an inner product $\langle \cdot, \cdot \rangle$, induced norm $\|\cdot\|$, and identity operator I. The study of the existence and approximation of solutions to nonlinear equations is an important topic and an active field of research in nonlinear analysis. However, nonlinear equations, even with strong restrictive conditions imposed, may not have a solution. An important case is the question raised by L. Nirenberg.

Let $D \subset H$. A self-mapping $T : D \to D$ is said to be expansive (expanding) if

$$\|x - y\| \leq \|Tx - Ty\|, \quad \forall x, y \in D.$$

Nirenberg's question states: "Is any continuous expansive mapping $T : H \to H$ such that $T(H)$ has nonempty interior, surjective?" [1]. This question can be formulated as whether for every continuous expansive mapping T and every $u \in H$, does the equation $T(x) = u$ have a solution? In spite of the strong conditions in Nirenberg's question, one may think that the answer is positive; however, recently, Ives and Preiss [2] answered this question negatively. Indeed, they provided a counterexample in $L^2(0, +\infty)$, which gives a negative answer to Nirenberg's problem even in general separable Hilbert spaces. This question had been already asked for more general spaces, such as Banach spaces, where Morel and Steinlein [3] constructed a counterexample in l^1. In any case, before this negative answer, many attempts to solve this question ended up giving affirmative answers to Nirenberg's question under additional conditions. Among them, we point out [4], where the interior of the range of the expansive mapping is assumed to be unbounded. For more results, see [5–8].

From a variational point of view, one can find a correspondence between expansive mappings and nonexpansive operators. We will get back to this correspondence, but before going further. Let us review briefly some classical results on nonexpansive mappings and their variational analysis. A mapping $T : D \subset H \to H$ is nonexpansive if

$$\|Tx - Ty\| \leq \|x - y\| \quad \forall x, y \in D,$$

where D is a nonempty subset of H. Nonexpansive mappings are generalizations of contractions (with a Lipschitz constant $k < 1$); however, their behaviors can be extremely different. One of the basic problems for nonlinear mappings concerns the following:

$$\text{find } x \in D \text{ such that } T(x) = x.$$

Every solution to the above problem is called a fixed point of T, and the set of all fixed points of T is denoted by Fix(T). If T is nonexpansive, then Fix(T) is closed and convex. The most important properties of contractions are described by the celebrated Banach contraction principle:

Theorem 1 ([9]). *Let $D \subset H$, and let $T : D \to D$ be a contraction. Then, (i) T has a unique fixed point, say p, and (ii) for each $x \in D$, $\lim_{n \to +\infty} T^n(x) = p$.*

This theorem does not hold for nonexpansive mappings without any additional conditions. The following theorem, which extends the first part of Banach's contraction principle, was independently proved in 1965 by Browder [10], Kirk [11] and Göhde [12]. We state the theorem here in Hilbert space to stay in the framework of our paper; however, the theorem is proved in more general Banach spaces.

Theorem 2. *Suppose that $T : D \to D$ is a nonexpansive mapping, where D is a nonempty, closed and convex subset of H. Then, T has a fixed point, and the set of all fixed points of T, which may not be a singleton, is closed and convex.*

The second part of Banach's contraction principle does not hold for nonexpansive mappings either. Indeed, according to Banach's contraction principle, all orbits of a contraction T converge to the unique fixed point of T, while orbits of a nonexpansive mapping may not converge at all. Baillon, in 1975, proved that the Cesaro means of the Picard iterates of any nonexpansive mapping T always converge weakly to a fixed point of T, provided that Fix$(T) \neq \emptyset$.

Theorem 3. *Let D be a nonempty, closed, and convex subset of H, and T be a nonexpansive mapping from D into itself. If the set Fix(T) is nonempty, then for each $x \in D$, the Cesaro means*

$$S_n(x) = \frac{1}{n} \sum_{k=1}^{n-1} T^k x,$$

converge weakly to some $y \in \text{Fix}(T)$.

For more details, we refer the reader to [13] and the beautiful books by Goebel and Kirk [14], and by Goebel and Reich [15].

If D is not convex, then Fix(T) may be empty, and then Baillon's proof is not applicable anymore. To avoid the convexity assumption on D, Djafari Rouhani [16,17] introduced the notions of nonexpansive and almost-nonexpansive sequences and curves.

In this survey, after reviewing some backgrounds on nonexpnasive curves and related notions, we take an expansive-type variational approach to problems of the form

$$\text{find } x \in D \text{ such that } 0 \in A(x),$$

where $A : D \subset H \rightrightarrows H$ is a (possibly multivalued) nonlinear operator.

Section 3, briefly, provides some intuition and backgrounds on the celebrated steepest-descent method and its monotone generalizations. In Section 4, we review some definitions and results on expansive curves. Applying the results in Section 4, Section 5 describes the asymptotic behavior of an expansive-type quasi-autonomous system. In Section 6, we recall discrete versions of the definitions and propositions in Section 4 and apply them to study the asymptotic behavior of an almost-nonexpansive sequence. Section 7 studies the periodic behavior of the expansive sequence described in Section 6. Section 8 is devoted to the study of continuous- and discrete-time non-monotone expansive-type dynamics. As will be seen later, the system considered in Section 5 is "strongly ill-posed". In Section 9, we introduce new well-posed expansive-type systems, which yield weak and strong convergence to zeros of any maximal monotone operator.

Notation 1. *Let u be a curve in H, and $C \subset H$.*

(i) *Convergence in weak and strong topologies are, respectively, denoted by $\rightharpoonup$ and $\to$.*
(ii) $\overline{\mathrm{conv}}(C)$ *denotes the closed convex hull of C.*
(iii) $\omega_w(u)$ *denotes the set of all sequential weak limit points of u.*
(iv) $L(u) = \{q \in H : \lim_{t \to +\infty} \|u(t) - q\| \text{ exists}\}$.
(v) *The weighted average of u is $\sigma_T := \frac{1}{T} \int_0^T u(t) dt$.*

2. Nonexpansive and Almost-Nonexpansive Curves

We recall the following definition from [17]:

Definition 1. *(i) The curve $u(t)$ in H is nonexpansive if for all $r, s, h \geq 0$, we have $\|u(r+h) - u(s+h)\| \leq \|u(r) - u(s)\|$.*

(ii) $u(t)$ is an almost-nonexpansive curve if for all $r, s, h \geq 0$, we have $\|u(r+h) - u(s+h)\|^2 \leq \|u(r) - u(s)\|^2 + \varepsilon(r,s)$, where $\lim_{r,s \to +\infty} \varepsilon(r,s) = 0$.

The following concept introduced in [18] will play an important role:

Definition 2. *Given a bounded curve $u(t)$ in H, the asymptotic center c of $u(t)$ is defined as follows: for every $q \in H$, let $\phi(q) = \limsup_{t \to +\infty} \|u(t) - q\|^2$. Then, ϕ is a continuous and strictly convex function on H, satisfying $\phi(q) \to +\infty$ as $\|q\| \to +\infty$. Therefore, ϕ achieves its minimum on H at a unique point c called the asymptotic center of the curve $u(t)$.*

To the best of our knowledge, Edelstein [18] was the first one who applied the technique of an asymptotic center to fixed-point theory. Combining the notion of nonexpansive curves and the concept of an asymptotic center, Djafari Rouhani proved theorems regarding the asymptotic behavior of nonexpansive and almost-nonexpansive curves without assuming the existence of a fixed point.

Theorem 4 ([17]). *Let $u(t)$ be an almost-nonexpansive curve in H. Then, the following are equivalent:*

(i) $L(u) \neq \emptyset$.
(ii) $\liminf_{T \to +\infty} \|\sigma_T\| < +\infty$.
(iii) σ_T *converges weakly to $p \in H$.*

Moreover, under these conditions, we have:

- $\overline{\mathrm{conv}}(\omega_w(u)) \cap L(u) = \{p\}$.
- p *is the asymptotic center of the curve $u(t)$.*

Browder and Petryshyn [19] introduced the notion of asymptotically regular mappings. A mapping $T : D \to D$ is (weakly) asymptotically regular on D if

$$(T^{n+1}x - T^n x \rightharpoonup 0) \quad T^{n+1}x - T^n x \to 0, \quad \forall x \in D.$$

They also showed that if $T: D \to D$ is nonexpansive, then for every $0 < \lambda < 1$, $T_\lambda = \lambda I + (1-\lambda)T$ is asymptotically regular, and $\text{Fix}(T_\lambda) = \text{Fix}(T)$. Djafari Rouhani extended the notion of asymptotically regular mappings to curves in H:

Definition 3. *(i) The curve $u(t)$ in H is asymptotically regular if for all $h > 0$, $u(t+h) - u(t) \to 0$ as $t \to +\infty$.*

(ii) $u(t)$ is a weakly asymptotically regular curve in H if $u(t+h) - u(t) \rightharpoonup 0$ as $t \to +\infty$.

The following theorem provides sufficient conditions for the weak convergence of asymptotically regular almost-nonexpansive curves:

Theorem 5 ([17]). *Let $u(t)$ be a weakly asymptotically regular almost-nonexpansive curve in H. Then, the following are equivalent:*

(i) $L(u(t)) \neq \emptyset$.
(ii) $\liminf_{t \to +\infty} \|u(t)\| < +\infty$.
(iii) $u(t)$ converges weakly to $p \in H$.

3. A Steepest-Descent-like Method

For a smooth function $\phi: H \to \mathbb{R}$, the gradient operator $\nabla \phi$ shows the direction of steepest ascent of a particle traveling along the graph of ϕ, hence $-\nabla \phi$ shows the direction of steepest descent. If we consider the curve $u(t)$ as the position of a particle in time t, then the above discussion shows that if the velocity vector $\dot{u}(t)$ equals the value of $-\nabla \phi$ at $u(t)$, then $u(t)$ travels along the steepest-descent direction on the graph of ϕ. In this case, if ϕ has a minimum point, then it may happen that $u(t)$ goes to a minimum point of ϕ. This leads to one of the most celebrated methods in optimization:

Let ϕ be convex with a nonempty set of minimizers. Then, every solution trajectory to the following system

$$\dot{u}(t) = -\nabla \phi(u(t)), \tag{1}$$

converges weakly to a minimizer of ϕ. This method is called the steepest-descent method. A counterexample due to Baillon [20,21] shows that, in general, solutions to the above system may not be strongly convergent in H; see also [22] (Proposition 3.3). Generalizations of this method to nonsmooth and monotone cases were studied by several authors in the 1970s. If $A^{-1}(0)$ is nonempty, Baillon and Brézis [23,24] proved the weak convergence of the mean of solutions to the following system:

$$-\dot{u}(t) \in Au(t), \tag{2}$$

where A is a maximal monotone operator in H and $u(0) = u_0 \in \overline{D(A)}$ is arbitrary. Bruck [25] established the weak convergence of solutions to (2) with an additional condition on A, which is called demipositivity. Motivated by the approach of nonexpansive curves, Djafari Rouhani studied the convergence analysis of a quasi-autonomous version of (2) without assuming $A^{-1}(0)$ to be nonempty.

Theorem 6 ([17]). *If u is a weak solution (for the notion of weak and strong solutions, see [26]) of the system*

$$\begin{cases} -\dot{u}(t) \in Au(t) + f(t), \\ u(0) = u_0 \in \overline{D(A)}, \end{cases} \tag{3}$$

on every interval $[0, T]$, and satisfies $\sup_{t>0} \|u(t)\| < +\infty$, and if $f - f_\infty \in L^1((0, +\infty); H)$ for some $f_\infty \in H$, then $\sigma_T = (1/T) \int_0^T u(t) dt$ converges weakly to the asymptotic center of the curve $u(t)$.

The following theorems, respectively, study the weak and strong convergence of trajectories of (3).

Theorem 7 ([17]). *If u is a weak solution of the system (3) on every interval $[0, T]$, and satisfies $\sup_{t>0} \|u(t)\| < +\infty$ and for all $h \geq 0$, $u(t+h) - u(t) \rightharpoonup 0$ as $t \to +\infty$, and if $f - f_\infty \in L^1((0, +\infty); H)$ for some $f_\infty \in H$, then $u(t)$ converges weakly as $t \to +\infty$ to the asymptotic center of the curve $u(t)$.*

Theorem 8 ([17]). *If u is a weak solution of the system (3) on every interval $[0, T]$, and satisfies $\lim_{t \to +\infty} \langle u(t), u(t+h) \rangle = \alpha(h)$ exists uniformly in $h \geq 0$, then $\sigma_T = (1/T) \int_0^T u(t) dt$ converges strongly as $T \to +\infty$ to the asymptotic center of the curve $u(t)$.*

4. Expansive Curves and Autonomous Systems

Now, we are in a position to go back to expansive mappings. In general, contrary to nonexpansive mappings, an expansive mapping may not be continuous. As we have seen, the set of fixed points of a nonexpansive mapping may be empty, but it always remains closed and convex. Djafari Rouhani [27] provided examples to show that there are expansive self-mappings of the closed unit ball of H, namely empty, nonconvex, or nonclosed sets of fixed points. The first mean ergodic theorem for expansive mappings was proved by Djafari Rouhani [27]. A continuous time approach to the orbits of an expansive mapping was considered by Djafari Rouhani, and introduced as the notion of expansive curves.

Definition 4. *An expansive curve u in H is a curve satisfying $\|u(t+h) - u(s+h)\| \geq \|u(t) - u(s)\|$ for all $s, t, h \geq 0$.*

Expansive curves inherit many properties of orbits of expansive mappings, including the lack of convexity and lack of closedness of the set of their fixed points. In any case, the following two sets, which can be defined for any curve, are closed and convex (or empty) sets.

$$F_1(u) = \{q \in H : \|u(t) - q\| \text{ is nonincreasing;}\}$$
$$E_1(u) = \{q \in H : \|u(t) - q\| \text{ is nondecreasing.}\}$$

The following theorem describes the ergodic, weak, and strong convergence of expansive curves in H:

Theorem 9 ([27]). *Let u be an expansive curve in H and $\sigma_T = \frac{1}{T} \int_0^T u(t) dt$ for $T > 0$.*

(i) *If $\liminf_{T \to +\infty} \|\sigma_T\| < +\infty$ and $\|u(t)\| = o(\sqrt{t})$, then the weak limit q of any weakly convergent subsequence of σ_T belongs to E_1.*

(ii) *If in addition to (i), $\liminf_{t \to +\infty} \|u(t)\| < +\infty$, then u is a bounded curve and σ_T converges weakly to the asymptotic center p of $u(t)$. Moreover we have $p = \lim_{t \to +\infty} P_{E_1} u(t)$.*

(iii) *If in addition to (ii), u is weakly asymptotically regular, then $u(t)$ converges weakly to p as $t \to +\infty$.*

(iv) *If $\lim_{t \to +\infty} \|u(t)\|$ exists, then σ_T converges strongly to the asymptotic center p of $u(t)$, and moreover in addition to $p = \lim_{t \to +\infty} P_{E_1} u(t)$, we have $p = P_K 0$, where $K_t = \overline{\text{conv}}\{u(s); s \geq t\}$ and $K = \cap_{t \geq 0} K_t$.*

Now, let A be a monotone operator in H. If u is weak solution of

$$\begin{cases} \dot{u}(t) \in Au(t), \\ u(0) = u_0, \end{cases} \quad (4)$$

on $[0, T]$ for every $T > 0$, then u is an expansive curve in H [27] (Lemma 5.3); hence, Theorem 9 describes the asymptotic behavior of any weak solution to (4). Unfortunately, the system (4) is "strongly ill-posed". For example, consider the simple linear case of $A = -\Delta$ with Dirishlet boundary conditions, which yields the heat equation with final Cauchy data and is not solvable in general. In Section 9, we try to fix this problem.

5. Almost-Expansive Curves and Quasi-Autonomous Evolution Systems

By introducing an expansive counterpart to the notion of almost-nonexpansive curves, we will be able to study the asymptotic behavior of solutions to (4) for the quasi-autonomous case. Before going further, let us first recall the definition of an almost-expansive curve and a description of its asymptotic behavior from [28].

Definition 5. *The curve u in H is called almost expansive if*

$$\limsup_{s,t \to +\infty} \left[\sup_{h \geq 0} (\|u(s) - u(t)\|^2 - \|u(s+h) - u(t+h)\|^2) \right] \leq 0,$$

where for every $\varepsilon > 0$, there exists $t_0 \geq 0$, such that for all $s, t \geq t_0$, and for all $h \geq 0$, we have

$$\|u(s) - u(t)\|^2 \leq \|u(s+h) - u(t+h)\|^2 + \varepsilon.$$

We note that if u is bounded, then this definition is equivalent to

$$\limsup_{s,t \to +\infty} \sup_{h \geq 0} (\|u(s) - u(t)\| - \|u(s+h) - u(t+h)\|) \leq 0.$$

The following theorem describes the ergodic, weak, and strong convergence of almost-expansive curves in H.

Theorem 10 ([27]). *Let u be an almost expansive curve in H.*

(i) *If $\liminf_{T \to +\infty} \|\sigma_T\| < +\infty$ and $\|u(t)\| = o(\sqrt{t})$, then either the weak limit q of any weakly convergent subsequence σ_{T_n} of σ_T belongs to $L(u)$ or $\|u(t)\| \to +\infty$ as $t \to +\infty$.*
(ii) *If in addition to (i), $\liminf_{t \to +\infty} \|u(t)\| < +\infty$, then u is bounded and σ_T converges weakly as $T \to +\infty$ to the asymptotic center p of u.*
(iii) *Assuming the conditions in (ii), $u(t)$ converges weakly as $t \to +\infty$ to the asymptotic center p of u if, and only if, u is weakly asymptotically regular.*
(iv) *If $0 \in L(u)$, then σ_T converges strongly as $T \to +\infty$ to the asymptotic center p of u. Moreover, we have $p = P_K 0$, where $K_t = \overline{\text{conv}}\{u(s); s \geq t\}$ and $K = \cap_{t \geq 0} K_t$.*
(v) *If u is asymptotically regular, then $\lim_{t \to +\infty} u(t) = p = P_K 0$, where p is the asymptotic center of u and $K_t = \overline{\text{conv}}\{u(s); s \geq t\}$ and $K = \cap_{t \geq 0} K_t$.*

The following proposition relates the asymptotic behavior of expansive-type evolution equations to that of almost-expansive curves.

Proposition 1 ([28]). *If u is a weak solution of*

$$\begin{cases} \dot{u}(t) + f(t) \in Au(t), \\ u(0) = u_0, \end{cases} \quad (5)$$

on $[0, T]$ for every $T > 0$, and if $\sup_{t \geq 0} \|u(t)\| < +\infty$ and

$$\lim_{s,r \to +\infty} \int_s^{+\infty} \|f(\theta + (r-s)) - f(\theta)\| d\theta = 0,$$

then the curve u is almost expansive in H.

Therefore, similar to the expansive case, one can apply the results on the asymptotic behavior of almost-expansive curves to describe the asymptotic behavior of solutions to (5).

Theorem 11 ([28]). *Assume u is a weak solution of (5) on every interval $[0, T]$ and $\sup_{t \geq 0} \|u(t)\| < +\infty$. Assume $f - f_\infty \in L^1((0, +\infty); H)$ for some $f_\infty \in H$. Then, the following hold:*

(i) $\sigma_T \rightharpoonup p$ *as $T \to +\infty$, where p is the asymptotic center of u.*

(ii) $u(t) \rightharpoonup p$ as $t \to +\infty$, if and only if u is weakly asymptotically regular.
(iii) If $\lim_{t \to +\infty} \|u(t)\|$ exists, then $\lim_{T \to +\infty} \sigma_T = p = P_K 0$, where K is as defined above.
(iv) $\lim_{t \to +\infty} u(t) = p = P_K 0$ if and only if u is asymptotically regular.

6. Expansive-Type Difference Equations

As we have already explained, the dissipative systems of the form (3) have a unique weak solution, whereas for solutions to (4), neither existence nor uniqueness is guaranteed. A similar situation occurs for the backward discretization of (4):

$$u_{n+1} - u_n \in \lambda_n A u_{n+1}.$$

Hence, we consider the following forward discretization:

$$u_{n+1} - u_n \in \lambda_n A u_n, \tag{6}$$

which is always well defined.

Similar to the continuous case, by introducing the notion of almost-expansive sequences and studying their asymptotic behavior under some suitable conditions, we describe the asymptotic behavior of the solution to (6).

Definition 6. *A sequence u_n in H is said to be almost-expansive if for all $i, j, k \geq 0$, we have*

$$\limsup_{i,j \to \infty} \left[\sup_{k \geq 0} (\|u_i - u_j\|^2 - \|u_{i+k} - u_{j+k}\|^2) \right] \leq 0.$$

i.e., $\forall \varepsilon > 0$, $\exists N_0$ such that $\forall i, j \geq N_0$, $\forall k \geq 0$, $\|u_i - u_j\|^2 \leq \|u_{i+k} - u_{j+k}\|^2 + \varepsilon$.

We note that if u_n is bounded, then this definition is equivalent to

$$\limsup_{i,j \to \infty} \left[\sup_{k \geq 0} (\|u_i - u_j\| - \|u_{i+k} - u_{j+k}\|) \right] \leq 0.$$

The sequence of averages of u_n is denoted by s_n and defined by $s_n = \frac{1}{n} \sum_{k=0}^{n-1} u_k$. The following theorem provides a discrete version of Theorem 10.

Theorem 12 ([27]). *Let u_n be an almost expansive sequence in H.*
(i) *If $\liminf_{n \to +\infty} \|s_n\| < +\infty$ and $\|u_n\| = o(\sqrt{t})$, then either the weak limit q of any weakly convergent subsequence s_{n_k} of s_n belongs to $L(u_n)$ or $\|u_n\| \to +\infty$ as $n \to +\infty$.*
(ii) *If in addition to (i), $\liminf_{n \to +\infty} \|u_n\| < +\infty$, then u_n is bounded and s_n converges weakly as $n \to +\infty$, to the asymptotic center p of u_n.*
(iii) *Assuming the conditions in (ii), u_n converges weakly as $n \to +\infty$ to the asymptotic center p of u_n, if and only if u_n is weakly asymptotically regular.*
(iv) *If $0 \in L(u_n)$, then s_n converges strongly as $n \to +\infty$ to the asymptotic center p of u_n. Moreover, we have $p = P_K 0$, where $K_n = \overline{\text{conv}}\{u_k; k \geq n\}$ and $K = \cap_{n \geq 0} K_n$.*
(v) *If u_n is asymptotically regular, then $\lim_{n \to +\infty} u_n = p = P_K 0$, where p is the asymptotic center of u_n, and K is defined above.*

We still need an additional condition for the sequence u_n governed by (6) to be almost expansive.

Proposition 2 ([29]). *Let λ_n be a nondecreasing sequence of positive numbers, such that*

$$\limsup_{\substack{j \geq i \\ i,j \to +\infty}} \sum_{l=i}^{+\infty} \left(\frac{\lambda_{(j-i)+l}}{\lambda_l} - 1 \right) = 0. \tag{7}$$

If u_n is a bounded solution to (6), then u_n is almost expansive.

Note that the condition (7) in the above proposition is in particular satisfied if $\sup_{n\geq 1} \lambda_n \leq \lambda$ for some $\lambda > 0$, and $\frac{\lambda}{a_n+1} \leq \lambda_n$ for some $a_n \in l^1$. For example, the sequence $\lambda_n = \frac{n^2}{1+n^2}$ satisfies the conditions of the above proposition. Now, we are in a position to apply our results on almost-expansive sequences to describe the asymptotic behavior of the sequence u_n governed by (6).

Theorem 13 ([29]). *Assume that λ_n is a nondecreasing sequence satisfying the condition (7), and u_n is a bounded solution to (6). Then, the following hold:*
- (i) $s_n \rightharpoonup p$, as $n \to +\infty$, where p is the asymptotic center of u_n.
- (ii) $u_n \rightharpoonup p$, as $n \to +\infty$ if and only if u is weakly asymptotically regular.
- (iii) If $\lim_{n\to+\infty} \|u_n\|$ exists, then $\lim_{n\to+\infty} s_n = p = P_K 0$, where K is as defined above.
- (iv) $\lim_{n\to+\infty} u_n = p = P_K 0$ if and only if u_n is asymptotically regular.

In the following theorem, by assuming the zero set of A to be nonempty, we can obtain stronger results:

Theorem 14 ([29]). *Let u_n be the sequence generated by (6), where $A^{-1}(0) \neq \emptyset$ and $\liminf_{n\to+\infty} \lambda_n \geq \lambda$ for some $\lambda > 0$. If u_n is bounded, then there exists some $p \in A^{-1}(0)$, such that $u_n \rightharpoonup p$ as $n \to +\infty$. Otherwise, $\|u_n\| \to +\infty$ as $n \to +\infty$.*

Note that if the step size λ_n goes to infinity as $n \to +\infty$, then the existence of a bounded solution to (6) implies that $A^{-1}(0) \neq \emptyset$. In fact, let u_n be a bounded solution to (6) and $b_n = \frac{u_{n+1}-u_n}{\lambda_n}$. Clearly, $b_n \in Au_n$ and $b_n \to 0$. Since u_n is bounded, there exist some $q \in H$ and a subsequence u_{n_k}, such that $u_{n_k} \rightharpoonup q$ as $k \to +\infty$. Now, the maximality of A implies that $q \in A^{-1}(0)$.

7. Periodic Solutions in Discrete Time

In this section, we will need the following extended version of expansive mappings

Definition 7. *The mapping $T : D(T) \subset H \to H$ is said to be α-expansive if*

$$\alpha \|x-y\| \leq \|Tx - Ty\|, \quad \forall x, y \in D(T).$$

If $\alpha = 1$, we say that T is expansive.

Clearly, letting $\alpha = 1$, the above definition coincides with the definition of an expansive mapping, and if $T : H \to H$ is α-expansive, then T^{-1} exists and it is $\frac{1}{\alpha}$-Lipschitz continuous. The following theorem provides sufficient conditions for the system (6) to have a periodic solution.

Theorem 15 ([29]). *Suppose that A is a single-valued and maximal strongly monotone operator in H. If λ_n is a periodic sequence with period N, then there exists an N-periodic solution to (6).*

The above theorem does not hold for a general maximal monotone operator A; not even for subdifferentials of proper, convex and lower semicontinuous functions, nor for inverse strongly monotone operators. To see this, let $A : \mathbb{R} \to \mathbb{R}$ be the constant function $A \equiv 1$, and $\lambda_n \equiv 1$. Then, (6) reduces to $u_{n+1} = u_n + 1$, which shows that the sequence u_n tends to $+\infty$, as $n \to +\infty$, for all $u_0 \in \mathbb{R}$. Therefore, it does not have a periodic solution. However, assuming (6) has a periodic solution, is it possible that (6) has another solution (by starting from a different initial point) that behaves differently? The following theorem answers this question.

Theorem 16 ([29]). *Assume that A is a single-valued and maximal monotone operator in H, and the sequence λ_n is periodic with period N. If (6) has an N-periodic solution w_n, then every bounded solution to (6) is also periodic with period N and differs from w_n by an additive constant.*

In general, the existence of periodic solutions does not imply the boundedness of all solutions to (6). For this, let $D = [0,1]$, $A = (I - P_D)$, and $\lambda_n \equiv 1$. Then, (6) reduces to $u_{n+1} = 2u_n - P_D u_n$. If we choose $u_0 = 0$, then $u_n \equiv 0$, which is a periodic solution with period N for all $N \in \mathbb{N}$. However, if we choose $u_0 = 2$, then $u_{n+1} = 2u_n - 1$, which clearly goes to $+\infty$, as $n \to +\infty$.

8. A Gradient System of Expansive Type

In this section, we consider a particular case of non-monotone operators. This case is motivated by the prominent example of a maximal monotone operator that is the subdifferential of a proper, convex, and lower semicontinuous function. A quasiconvex function is an extension of a convex function, which has found many applications in economics [30]. Unlike the convex case, quasiconvex functions do not have a convex epigraph, but have convex sublevel sets. This is stated formally in the following definition:

Definition 8. *(i) A function $\phi : H \to (-\infty, +\infty]$ is quasiconvex if*

$$\phi(\lambda x + (1-\lambda)y) \leq \max\{\phi(x), \phi(y)\}, \quad \forall x, y \in H \text{ and } \forall \lambda \in [0,1].$$

(ii) A function $\phi : H \to (-\infty, +\infty]$ is strongly quasiconvex if there is $\alpha > 0$ such that

$$\phi(\lambda x + (1-\lambda)y) \leq \max\{\phi(x), \phi(y)\} - \alpha\lambda(1-\lambda)\|x - y\|^2, \quad \forall x, y \in H \text{ and } \forall \lambda \in [0,1].$$

The notion of a subdifferential has been generalized for nonconvex functions by many authors. Nevertheless, in any circumstance, the subdifferential operator of a quasiconvex function is not monotone. However, in the case where the quasiconvex function $\phi : H \to \mathbb{R}$ is Gâteaux differentiable, then the following characterization holds:

ϕ is quasiconvex on $H \Leftrightarrow (\forall x, y \in H, \ \phi(y) \leq \phi(x) \Rightarrow \langle \nabla \phi(x), x - y \rangle \geq 0)$.

This characterization will be useful in the rest of this section to make up for the lack of monotonicity.

We consider the expansive system governed by the non-monotone operator $\nabla \phi$, where $\phi : H \to \mathbb{R}$ is a differentiable quasiconvex function. Indeed, as in [31], we consider the following differential equation

$$\dot{u}(t) = \nabla \phi(u(t)) + f(t), \quad t \in [0, +\infty), \tag{8}$$

where $\phi : H \to \mathbb{R}$ is a differentiable quasiconvex function, such that $\nabla \phi$ is Lipschitz continuous and $f \in W^{1,1}((0, +\infty); H)$. The Cauchy–Lipschitz theorem implies the existence of a unique solution of the system (8) with an initial condition, where $\nabla \phi$ is Lipschitz continuous. In order to study the asymptotic behavior of solutions to systems of the form (8), the authors in [31] introduced the following set for a function ϕ along a curve u:

$$L_\phi(u) = \{y \in H : \exists T > 0 \text{ s.t. } \phi(y) \leq \phi(u(t)) \ \forall t \geq T\}.$$

Denoting the set of all global minimizers of ϕ by Argmin ϕ, then Argmin $\phi \subset L_\phi(u)$. The following proposition shows that if u is a solution to (8), then $L_\phi(u) \subset L(u)$.

Proposition 3 ([31]). *Let $u(t)$ be a solution to (8). For an arbitrary interval $[a,b]$, where $b \geq a \geq 0$, and each $y \in L_\phi(u)$, we have*

$$\|u(a) - y\| \leq \|u(b) - y\| + \int_a^b \|f(t)\| dt,$$

and therefore $\lim_{t \to +\infty} \|u(t) - y\|$ exists (it may be infinite).

Proposition 4 ([31]). *Let $u(t)$ be a solution to (8). If $\liminf_{t \to +\infty} \|u(t)\| < +\infty$, then*
(i) $\lim_{t \to +\infty} \nabla \phi(u(t)) = 0$.
(ii) $\lim_{t \to +\infty} \phi(u(t))$ *exists and is finite.*
(iii) $L_\phi(u) \neq \emptyset$.
(iv) u *is bounded.*

The following theorem describes the asymptotic behavior of solutions to (8).

Theorem 17 ([31]). *Let $u(t)$ be a solution to (8). If $\liminf_{t \to +\infty} \|u(t)\| < +\infty$, then there exists some $p \in (\nabla \phi)^{-1}(0)$, such that $u(t) \rightharpoonup p$ as $t \to +\infty$, and if $p \notin \operatorname{Argmin} \phi$, the convergence is strong. If $u(t)$ is unbounded, then $\|u(t)\| \to +\infty$ as $t \to +\infty$.*

Note that the above theorem shows that if $(\nabla \phi)^{-1}(0) = \emptyset$, then for any solution to (8), we have $\lim_{t \to +\infty} \|u(t)\| = +\infty$.

The following two theorems provide sufficient conditions for the strong convergence of solutions to (8).

Theorem 18 ([31]). *With either one of the following assumptions, bounded solutions to (8) converge strongly to some point in $(\nabla \phi)^{-1}(0)$:*
(i) *Sublevel sets of ϕ are compact.*
(ii) $\operatorname{int} L_\phi(u) \neq \emptyset$.

Theorem 19 ([31]). *Assume that $\phi : H \to \mathbb{R}$ is a strongly quasiconvex function and $u(t)$ is a bounded solution to (8). Then, $\operatorname{Argmin} \phi$ is a singleton and $u(t)$ converges strongly to the unique minimizer of ϕ.*

For a differentiable quasiconvex function $\phi : H \to \mathbb{R}$ whose gradient $\nabla \phi$ is Lipschitz continuous with Lipschitz constant K, as in Section 6, we consider the forward finite-difference discrete version of (8), which yields a well-defined sequence:

$$u_{n+1} - u_n = \lambda_n \nabla \phi(u_n) + f_n, \tag{9}$$

where the sequence f_n belongs to l^1 and $\lambda_n \geq \varepsilon$ for some $\varepsilon > 0$.

In order to study the asymptotic behavior of u_n, we define the following discrete version of $L_\phi(u)$:

$$L_\phi(u_n) = \{y \in H : \exists N > 0 \text{ s.t. } \phi(y) \leq \phi(u_n) \ \forall n \geq N\}.$$

The following proposition is a discrete version of Proposition 3.

Proposition 5 ([31]). *Let u_n be the sequence generated by (9). For each $y \in L_\phi(u_n)$, and $k < m$, we have*

$$\|u_k - y\| \leq \|u_m - y\| + \sum_{n=k}^{m-1} \|f_n\|, \tag{10}$$

and consequently $\lim_{n \to +\infty} \|u_n - y\|$ exists (it may be infinite).

Proposition 6 ([31]). *Let u_n be a solution to (9), such that $\liminf_{n\to+\infty} \|u_n\| < +\infty$. Then, $L_\phi(u_n)$ is nonempty if and only if $\lim_{n\to+\infty} \phi(u_n)$ exists, and in this case u_n is bounded.*

If ϕ is convex, we can omit the Lipschtz continuity condition on $\nabla \phi$ in Proposition 6.

Proposition 7 ([31]). *Assume that u_n is a solution to (9), such that $\liminf_{n\to+\infty} \|u_n\| < +\infty$. If either one of the following conditions is satisfied, then $L_\phi(u_n)$ is nonempty.*
(i) ϕ is convex and the sequence of step sizes λ_n is bounded above.
(ii) $\limsup_{n\to+\infty} \lambda_n < \frac{2}{K}$.

In the continuous case, we showed that if $\liminf_{t\to+\infty} \|u(t)\| < +\infty$, then $L_\phi(u) \neq \emptyset$. However, in the discrete case, it remains an open problem whether without any additional assumption that $\liminf_{n\to+\infty} \|u_n\| < +\infty$ implies that $L_\phi(u_n)$ is nonempty.

The following theorems describe the weak and strong convergence of solutions to (9).

Theorem 20 ([31]). *Assume that u_n is the sequence given by (9), and $L_\phi(u_n) \neq \emptyset$. If $\liminf_{n\to+\infty} \|u_n\| < +\infty$, then there is some $p \in (\nabla \phi)^{-1}(0)$, such that $u_n \rightharpoonup p$ as $n \to +\infty$, and if $p \notin \text{Argmin } \phi$, the convergence is strong. If u_n is not bounded, then $\|u_n\| \to +\infty$, as $n \to +\infty$.*

Theorem 21 ([31]). *Let u_n be a bounded sequence, which satisfies (9), and let $L(u_n) \neq \emptyset$. If either one of the following assumptions holds, then u_n converges strongly to some point in $(\nabla \phi)^{-1}(0)$:*
(i) Sublevel sets of ϕ are compact.
(ii) $\text{int } L_\phi(u_n) \neq \emptyset$.

Example 1. *Assume that $\phi : \mathbb{R} \to \mathbb{R}$ is defined by $\phi(x) = \arctan(x^3)$ and consider (9) with $\lambda_n = \frac{2}{3}n$ and $f_n \equiv 0$. Then, it is easy to see that all the assumptions of Theorem 21 are satisfied. In Table 1, we compare 1000 iterations u_n generated by (9) starting from two different initial points, namely $u_0 = -0.5$ and $u_0 = 1$. The numerical results show that for $u_0 = -0.5$, $u_n \to 0 \in (\nabla \phi)^{-1}(0)$, and for $u_0 = 1$, u_n slowly goes to infinity.*

Table 1. Comparing 1000 iterations u_n with different initial points.

n	u_n	u_n
0	-0.5	1
1	-0.00769231	2
10	-0.00404869	3.63765
20	-0.00171074	4.68854
30	-0.0008858	5.46951
40	-0.000533135	6.11128
50	-0.000354164	6.66517
60	-0.000251763	7.15741
70	-0.000187942	7.60348
80	-0.000145564	8.01339
90	-0.000116023	8.39404
100	-0.0000946225	8.7504
1000	-9.94968×10^{-7}	21.8786

9. Some New Results

As we have seen in Section 4, given a maximal monotone operator, expansive systems of the form (4) may be "strongly ill-posed" in general. In this section, we consider a special class of maximal monotone operators that induces well-posed expansive evolution systems. Motivated by this, we propose an expansive-type approach for the approximation of zeros of any maximal monotone operator.

9.1. Weak Convergence

We start with the following definition:

Definition 9. *Let $\lambda > 0$. The operator $A : H \to H$ is said to be λ-inverse strongly monotone if*

$$\lambda \|A(x) - A(y)\|^2 \leq \langle A(x) - A(y), x - y \rangle, \quad \forall x, y \in H.$$

Clearly, a λ-inverse strongly monotone operator is $\frac{1}{\lambda}$-Lipschitz.

Let $A : H \to H$ be a λ-inverse strongly monotone operator, such that $A^{-1}(0) \neq \emptyset$. Consider the following differential equation:

$$\begin{cases} \dot{u}(t) = Au(t), \\ u(0) = x \in H. \end{cases} \quad (11)$$

Since A is Lipschitz, then the Cauchy–Lipschitz theorem guarantees that there exists a unique solution to (11). The following Lemma is due to Z. Opial [32], and is an effective tool in the convergence analysis of curves in the weak topology.

Lemma 1. *Let $u : [0, +\infty) \to H$, and let $S \subset H$ be nonempty. Assume that*
(i) For every $y \in S$, $\lim_{t \to +\infty} \|u(t) - y\|$ exists;
(ii) Every sequential weak limit point of u belongs to S.
Then, there exists $p \in S$, such that $u(t) \rightharpoonup p$ as $t \to +\infty$.

Theorem 22. *Assume that u is a strong solution to (11). If u is unbounded, then $\|u(t)\| \to +\infty$, as $t \to +\infty$. If u is bounded, then there exists some $p \in A^{-1}(0)$, such that $u(t) \rightharpoonup p$ as $t \to +\infty$.*

Proof. Let $y \in A^{-1}(0)$ and $h_y(t) = \frac{1}{2}\|u(t) - y\|^2$. By the monotonicity of A we have:

$$\dot{h}_y(t) = \langle \dot{u}(t), u(t) - y \rangle = \langle Au(t), u(t) - y \rangle \geq 0.$$

Hence, $h_y(t)$ is nondecreasing. If $u(t)$ is unbounded then $h_y(t) \to +\infty$ is as $t \to +\infty$, which implies that $\|u(t)\| \to +\infty$ is as $t \to +\infty$. If $u(t)$ is bounded, then $\lim_{t \to +\infty} h_y(t)$ exists. Multiplying both sides of (11) by $u(t) - y$ and then using the fact that A is λ-inverse strongly monotone, we obtain:

$$\dot{h}_y(t) = \langle \dot{u}(t), u(t) - y \rangle = \langle Au(t), u(t) - y \rangle \geq \lambda \|Au(t)\|^2. \quad (12)$$

Replacing $Au(t)$ with $\dot{u}(t)$ in (12) and then integrating both sides of (12) on $[0, t]$, we obtain:

$$\lambda \int_0^t \|\dot{u}(\tau)\|^2 d\tau \leq h_y(t) - h_y(0).$$

Since $\lim_{t \to +\infty} h_y(t)$ exists, the above inequality implies that $\dot{u} \in L^2([0, +\infty), H)$. On the other hand, since u is bounded and A is Lipschitz, (11) yields $\dot{u}$ and is bounded, and hence u is Lipschitz. Now, since $\ddot{u}$ is the composition of two Lipschitz mappings, $\dot{u}$ is Lipschitz too. This implies that $\dot{u}$ is uniformly continuous. This together with $\dot{u} \in L^2([0, +\infty), H)$ yields $\lim_{t \to +\infty} \dot{u}(t) = 0$ and hence by (11), $\lim_{t \to +\infty} Au(t) = 0$. Now, let q be a weak cluster point of $u(t)$. There exists a sequence $t_n \subset [0, +\infty)$, such that $t_n \to +\infty$ as $n \to +\infty$, and $u(t_n) \rightharpoonup q$ as $n \to +\infty$. From the maximality of A, we have $q \in A^{-1}(0)$. Now an easy application of Opial's Lemma concludes the proof. □

Let A be an arbitrary maximal monotone operator, and $\lambda > 0$. The resolvent of A of index λ is the single-valued operator $J_\lambda^A = (I + \lambda A)^{-1}$, which is nonexpansive and everywhere defined. The Yosida approximation of A of index λ is $A_\lambda = \frac{1}{\lambda}(I - J_\lambda^A)$. A straightforward calculation shows that the Yosida approximation of index λ is λ-inverse and strongly monotone, and $A_\lambda^{-1}(0) = A^{-1}(0)$. Therefore, the Cauchy–Lipschitz theorem implies that the differential equation

$$\dot{u}(t) = A_\lambda(u(t)), \tag{13}$$

with an initial condition $u(0) = u_0 \in H$ is well defined. Therefore, by Theorem 22, if $u_\lambda(t)$ is a solution to (13) that remains bounded, then $u_\lambda(t)$ converges weakly to a zero of A, otherwise $u_\lambda(t)$ goes to infinity in the norm as $t \to +\infty$.

9.2. Strong Convergence via Tikhonov Regularization

In this subsection, we propose well-posed dynamics that approximate zeros of an arbitrary maximal monotone operator A in strong topology. For this purpose, let us assume that $\alpha : [0, +\infty) \to (0, +\infty)$ is absolutely continuous on every finite interval, and define $A_t = A + \alpha(t)I$. Hence, A_t is onto, and due to the strong monotonicity of A_t, the zero set of A_t is a singleton. Let $\xi(t)$ denote the unique zero of A_t. We call $\xi(t)$ the central path of A corresponding to $\alpha(t)$.

Lemma 2 ([33]). *Let A be a maximal monotone operator, let $\alpha(t)$ be a positive function, and let $\xi(t)$ be the central path corresponding to A and $\alpha(t)$. If $A^{-1}(0) \neq \emptyset$, then $\xi(t)$ is bounded. Moreover, if $\lim_{t \to +\infty} \alpha(t) = 0$, then $\xi(t)$ converges strongly to the least norm element in $A^{-1}(0)$.*

Since $\xi(t) = J^A_{\frac{1}{\alpha(t)}}(0)$, by the resolvent identity, we have

$$\|\xi(t+\delta) - \xi(t)\| = \left\|J^A_{\frac{1}{\alpha(t)}}\left(\left(1 - \frac{\alpha(t)}{\alpha(t+\delta)}\right)\xi(t)\right) - J^A_{\frac{1}{\alpha(t)}}(0)\right\| \leq \left\|\left(1 - \frac{\alpha(t)}{\alpha(t+\delta)}\right)\xi(t)\right\|.$$

If $A^{-1}(0) \neq \emptyset$, then Lemma 2 implies that $\xi(t)$ is bounded. The boundedness of $\xi(t)$ and the absolute continuity of $\alpha(t)$ on every finite interval together with the above inequality implies that $\xi(t)$ is absolutely continuous on every finite interval, since $\alpha(t)$ does not take the value zero, therefore it is bounded away from zero. Hence, $\xi(t)$ is almost everywhere differentiable. Dividing both sides of the above inequality by δ and then letting $\delta \to 0$, we obtain

$$\|\dot{\xi}(t)\| \leq \frac{|\dot{\alpha}(t)|}{\alpha(t)}\|\xi(t)\|, \quad \text{a.e. } t \geq 0. \tag{14}$$

Theorem 23. *Let $\alpha : [0, +\infty) \to (0, +\infty)$ be absolutely continuous on every finite interval, such that*

(i) $\lim_{t \to +\infty} \alpha(t) = 0$;

(ii) $\lim_{t \to +\infty} \frac{\dot{\alpha}(t)}{\alpha(t)^2} = 0$;

(iii) $\int_0^{+\infty} \alpha(t)dt = +\infty$.

Let $A : H \rightrightarrows H$ be maximal monotone with a nonempty zero set. Then, every bounded (possible) solution to the following differential equation

$$\begin{cases} \dot{u}(t) = A(u(t)) + \alpha(t)u(t), \\ u(0) = u_0 \in H, \end{cases} \tag{15}$$

converges strongly to the zero of A with minimal norm.

Proof. Let $h(t) = \frac{1}{2}\|u(t) - \xi(t)\|^2$. We have

$$\dot{h}(t) = \langle \dot{u}(t) - \dot{\xi}(t), u(t) - \xi(t) \rangle,$$

hence
$$\dot{h}(t) + \langle \dot{\xi}(t), u(t) - \xi(t) \rangle = \langle A(u(t)) - A(\xi(t)), u(t) - \xi(t) \rangle + \alpha(t)\|u(t) - \xi(t)\|^2,$$

By applying the Cauchy–Schuartz inequality and the monotonicity of A, we obtain
$$2\alpha(t)h(t) \leq \dot{h}(t) + M\|\dot{\xi}(t)\|, \tag{16}$$

where $M = \sup_{t>0} \|u(t) - \xi(t)\|$. Multiplying both sides of (16) by $e^{-E(t)}$, where $E(t) = \int_0^t \alpha(\tau)d\tau$, we get:

$$-M\frac{\|\dot{\xi}(t)\|}{\alpha(t)}\alpha(t)e^{-E(t)} \leq e^{-E(t)}\dot{h}(t) - \alpha(t)e^{-E(t)}h(t),$$

Then,
$$M\frac{\|\dot{\xi}(t)\|}{\alpha(t)}\frac{d}{dt}\left(e^{-E(t)}\right) \leq \frac{d}{dt}\left(e^{-E(t)}h(t)\right).$$

Integrating the above inequality on $[s,t]$, we get
$$m(s)\left(e^{-E(t)} - e^{-E(s)}\right) \leq e^{-E(t)}h(t) - e^{-E(s)}h(s),$$

where $m(s) = M\inf_{t \geq s} \frac{\|\dot{\xi}(t)\|}{\alpha(t)}$. Letting $t \to +\infty$ in the above inequality, since $h(t)$ is bounded and $\lim_{t \to +\infty} E(t) = +\infty$, we obtain
$$e^{-E(s)}h(s) \leq e^{-E(s)}m(s) \leq e^{-E(s)}M\frac{\|\dot{\xi}(s)\|}{\alpha(s)}.$$

Multiplying the above inequality by $e^{E(s)}$, and applying (14), we obtain
$$h(s) \leq M\frac{|\dot{\alpha}(s)|}{\alpha(s)^2}\|\xi(s)\|.$$

Now, letting $s \to +\infty$, we conclude the result by applying (ii) and Lemma 2. □

Remark 1. *By applying a nonautonomous version of the Cauchy–Lipschitz theorem, the following Tikhonov regularization system has a unique solution.*

$$\begin{cases} \dot{u} = A_\lambda(u(t)) + \alpha(t)u(t), \\ u(0) = u_0 \in H. \end{cases} \tag{17}$$

Therefore, by Theorem 23, the system (17) provides a continuous time-expansive method to approximate the zero with the least norm of any maximal monotone operator A.

Author Contributions: Writing—original draft, B.D.R. and M.R.P. All authors have read and agreed to the published version of the manuscript.

Funding: This research received no external funding.

Data Availability Statement: Not applicable.

Conflicts of Interest: The authors declare no conflict of interest.

References

1. Nirenberg, L. *Topics in Nonlinear Functional Analysis*; Lecture Notes; Courant Institute of Mathematical Sciences, New York University: New York, NY, USA, 1974.
2. Ives, D.; Preiss, D. Solution to a problem of Nirenberg concerning expanding maps. *Proc. Am. Math. Soc.* **2021**, *149*, 301–310. [CrossRef]
3. Morel, J.; Steinlein, H. On a problem of Nirenberg concerning expanding maps. *J. Funct. Anal.* **1984**, *59*, 145–150. [CrossRef]
4. Asfaw, T.M. A Positive Answer on Nirenberg's Problem on Expansive Mappings in Hilbert Spaces. *Abstr. Appl. Anal.* **2022**, *2022*, 9487405. [CrossRef]
5. Hernández, J.E.; Nashed, M.Z. Global invertibility of expanding maps. *Proc. Am. Math. Soc.* **1992**, *116*, 285–291. [CrossRef]
6. Kartsatos, A.G. On the connection between the existence of zeros and the asymptotic behavior of resolvents of maximal monotone operators in reflexive Banach spaces. *Trans. Am. Math. Soc.* **1998**, *350*, 3967–3987. [CrossRef]
7. Szczepański, J. A new result on the Nirenberg problem for expanding maps. *Nonlinear Anal.* **2001**, *43*, 91–99. [CrossRef]
8. Xiang, T. Notes on expansive mappings and a partial answer to Nirenberg's problem. *Electron. J. Differ. Equ.* **2013**, *2013*, 1–16.
9. Banach, S. Sur les opérations dans les ensembles abstraits et leurs applications. *Fund. Math.* **1922**, *3*, 133–181. [CrossRef]
10. Browder, F.E. Nonexpansive nonlinear operators in a Banach space. *Proc. Nat. Acad. Sci. USA* **1965**, *54*, 1041–1044. [CrossRef]
11. Kirk, W.A. A fixed point theorem for mappings which do not increase distances. *Am. Math. Mon.* **1965**, *72*, 1004–1006. [CrossRef]
12. Göhde, D. Zum Prinzip der kontraktiven Abbildung. *Math. Nachr.* **1965**, *30*, 251–258. [CrossRef]
13. Reich, S. Almost convergence and nonlinear ergodic theorems. *J. Approx. Theory* **1978**, *24*, 269–272. [CrossRef]
14. Goebel, K.; Kirk, W.A. *Topics in Metric Fixed Point Theory, Cambridge Studies in Advanced Mathematics*; Cambridge University Press: Cambridge, UK, 1990; Volume 28.
15. Goebel, K.; Reich, S. *Uniform Convexity, Hyperbolic Geometry, and Nonexpansive Mappings, Monographs and Textbooks in Pure and Applied Mathematics*; Marcel Dekker: New York, NY, USA, 1984; Volume 83.
16. Rouhani, B.D. Asymptotic behaviour of almost nonexpansive sequences in a Hilbert space. *J. Math. Anal. Appl.* **1990**, *151*, 226–235. [CrossRef]
17. Rouhani, B.D. Asymptotic behaviour of quasi-autonomous dissipative systems in Hilbert spaces. *J. Math. Anal. Appl.* **1990**, *147*, 465–476. [CrossRef]
18. Edelstein, M. The construction of an asymptotic center with a fixed-point property. *Bull. Am. Math. Soc.* **1972**, *78*, 206–208. [CrossRef]
19. Browder, F.E.; Petryshyn, V.W. The solution by iteration of nonlinear functional equations in Banach spaces. *Bull. Amer. Math. Soc.* **1966**, *72*, 571–576. [CrossRef]
20. Baillon, J.-B. Un exemple concernant le comportement asymptotique de la solution du problème $du/dt + \partial\phi(u) \ni 0$. *J. Funct. Anal.* **1978**, *28*, 369–376. [CrossRef]
21. Baillon, J.-B. Ph.D. Thèse, Université Paris VI, Paris, France, 1978.
22. Attouch, H.; Baillon, J.-B. Weak versus strong convergence of a regularized Newton dynamic for maximal monotone operators. *Vietnam J. Math.* **2018**, *46*, 177–195. [CrossRef]
23. Baillon, J.-B. Un théorème de type ergodique pour les contractions non linéaires dans un espace de Hilbert. *C. R. Acad. Sci. Paris* **1975**, *280*, 1511–1514.
24. Baillon, J.-B.; Brézis, H. Une remarque sur le comportement asymptotique des semi-groupes non linéaires. *Houston J. Math.* **1976**, *2*, 5–7.
25. Bruck, R.E. Asymptotic convergence of nonlinear contraction semigroups in Hilbert space. *J. Func. Anal.* **1975**, *18*, 15–26. [CrossRef]
26. Brézis, H. *Opérateurs Maximaux Monotones et Semi-Groupes de Contractions Dans les Espaces de Hilbert*; Elsevier: Amsterdam, The Netherlands, 1973.
27. Rouhani, B.D. Ergodic theorems for expansive maps and applications to evolution systems in Hilbert spaces. *Nonlinear Anal.* **2001**, *47*, 4827–4834. [CrossRef]
28. Rouhani, B.D. Asymptotic behavior of quasi-autonomous expansive type evolution systems in a Hilbert space. *Nonlinear Dyn.* **2004**, *35*, 287–297. [CrossRef]
29. Rouhani, B.D.; Piranfar, M.R. Asymptotic behavior and periodic solutions to a first order expansive type difference equation. *Dyn. Contin. Discrete Impuls. Syst. Ser. A Math. Anal.* **2020**, *27*, 325–337.
30. Cambini, A.; Martein, L. *Generalized Convexity and Optimization, Lecture Notes in Economics and Mathematical System*; Springer: Berlin/Heidelberg, Germany, 2009; Volume 616.
31. Rouhani, B.D.; Piranfar, M.R. Asymptotic behavior for a qasi-autonomous gradient system of expansive type governed by a quasiconvex function. *Electron. J. Differ. Equ.* **2021**, *15*, 1–13.
32. Opial, Z. Weak convergence of the sequence of successive approximations for nonexpansive mappings. *Bull. Am. Math. Soc.* **1967**, *73*, 591–597. [CrossRef]
33. Cominetti, R.; Peypouquet, J.; Sorin, S. Strong asymptotic convergence of evolution equations governed by maximal monotone operators with Tikhonov regularization. *J. Differ. Equ.* **2008**, *245*, 3753–3763. [CrossRef]

Disclaimer/Publisher's Note: The statements, opinions and data contained in all publications are solely those of the individual author(s) and contributor(s) and not of MDPI and/or the editor(s). MDPI and/or the editor(s) disclaim responsibility for any injury to people or property resulting from any ideas, methods, instructions or products referred to in the content.

Article

A Mathematical Model for Zika Virus Infection and Microcephaly Risk Considering Sexual and Vertical Transmission

Mahmoud A. Ibrahim [1,2,*] and Attila Dénes [1]

[1] National Laboratory for Health Security, Bolyai Institute, University of Szeged, Aradi vértanúk tere 1, 6720 Szeged, Hungary
[2] Department of Mathematics, Faculty of Science, Mansoura University, Mansoura 35516, Egypt
* Correspondence: mibrahim@math.u-szeged.hu

Abstract: We establish a compartmental model for Zika virus disease transmission, with particular attention paid to microcephaly, the main threat of the disease. To this end, we consider separate microcephaly-related compartments for affected infants, as well as the role of asymptomatic carriers, the influence of seasonality and transmission through sexual contact. We determine the basic reproduction number of the corresponding time-dependent model and time-constant model and study the dependence of this value on the mosquito-related parameters. In addition, we demonstrate the global stability of the disease-free periodic solution if $\mathcal{R}_0 < 1$, whereas the disease persists when $\mathcal{R}_0 > 1$. We fit our model to data from Colombia between 2015 and 2017 as a case study. The fitting is used to figure out how sexual transmission affects the number of cases among women as well as the number of microcephaly cases. Our sensitivity analyses conclude that the most effective ways to prevent Zika-related microcephaly cases are preventing mosquito bites and controlling mosquito populations, as well as providing protection during sexual contact.

Keywords: non-autonomous epidemic model; Zika fever; microcephaly; basic reproduction number

MSC: 34C23; 34C25; 34C60; 37N25; 92D25; 92D30

1. Introduction

Zika fever or Zika virus disease (ZIKV) is an arthropod-borne disease caused by a *Flavivirus*, mainly spread by infected female mosquito bites. The species responsible for transmission are primarily *Aedes aegypti* and *Aedes albopictus* [1]. Unlike other arboviruses, Zika can also be transmitted via sexual contact, primarily from males to females [2]. Evidence shows that ZIKV remains in semen up to six months, which is longer than it can remain in other bodily fluids. This means that the disease can still be transmitted several months after recovery [3]. The most common way for Zika to be transmitted is from a pregnant woman to her child. This has been shown to cause microcephaly and other serious fetal brain deficiencies although, historically, Zika fever was thought to have mild symptoms in humans, such as moderate fever, conjunctivitis, rash and joint discomfort. The Zika virus was first isolated in 1947 in a rhesus monkey in the Zika forest (Uganda). It was shown that the virus is transmitted between primates and mosquitoes, especially the mosquito species *Aedes africanus* [4]. At the end of 2015, the European Centre for Disease Prevention and Control published a study on the possible connection between Zika fever, congenital microcephaly and Guillain–Barré syndrome [5,6]. For example, in Brazil, 2782 microcephaly cases were reported in the year following the emergence of Zika fever, while there were only 147 and 167 cases in the two preceding years [7]. ZIKV was found to have been transmitted intrauterine for the first time in Brazil, in the uteri of two pregnant women whose fetuses were born with microcephaly. In Colombia, a total of 19,993 female pregnant women with presumed Zika virus disease were recorded from the start of the epidemic up to week 33 of 2017, of whom 6365 were laboratory-confirmed with Zika virus infection [8,9]. In total, 1415 occurrences of microcephaly and other congenital disorders of the central nervous system were recorded in Colombia between the first week of 2016 and week 33 of 2017. Among these, 196 were laboratory-confirmed as being associated with Zika virus infection. The number of cases having microcephaly reveals an increasing trend in 2016, reaching its high in week 28. Whereas the number of cases has been decreasing since, in comparison to the same period 2014 and 2015, the trend has nevertheless shown a greater number of cases. In [10], the authors confirmed the link between microcephaly and congenital Zika infection based on a case–control investigation in 2016. The study [11], using data from national reporting databases in Brazil, also confirmed that congenital Zika infection, in particular in the first six months of pregnancy, can be linked with microcephaly and with other birth defects. Ref. [12] found that the number of Guillain–Barré syndrome patients increased parallelly with the number of Zika cases, while microcephaly cases appeared five months after the beginning of the outbreak, showing a functional relationship between the transmission of Zika fever and the increase of microcephaly and Guillain–Barré syndrome cases. Microcephaly was linked to other problems, such as miscarriage, stillbirth and other birth defects [13].

Several researchers have studied the dynamics of the Zika virus spread using mathematical models. Ref. [14] established a compartmental model that includes mosquito-borne spread and sexual transmission as well. In this paper, males and females were not differentiated. Ref. [15] formulated and analysed five compartmental models of Zika transmission, modelling heterogeneity in sexual transmission in several different ways. Saad-Roy, Ma and van den Driessche [16] introduced a model differentiating humans w.r.t. their sex and sexual activity. Some studies also consider the changes in the weather and climate in the models, see, e.g., [17–21]. A model for the transmission of the ZIKV presented in [22] also includes the effect of the periodicity of weather. This model included time-dependent mosquito parameters. The global dynamics are determined by the basic reproduction number $\mathcal{R}_0$: the disease-free equilibrium is shown to be globally asymptotically stable if $\mathcal{R}_0 < 1$, whereas when $\mathcal{R}_0 > 1$ the disease persists in the population. The model studied in [23] incorporated vertical transmission of the Zika virus among humans, the birth of newborns having microcephaly and asymptomatic carriers of the virus. In [24], a non-autonomous model was developed that took into account the majority of the important aspects of Zika spread: vector-borne and sexual transmission, the prolonged time of infectiousness following recovery, the role of asymptomatically infected persons, and the significance of weather seasonality. As the main concern regarding Zika infections is the possibility of malformations in newborns, a particular emphasis was put on the assessment of the effect of the epidemic on women.

In the current study, we extend the compartmental model described in [24] by taking into account the vertical transmission of Zika to the fetus in the early stages of pregnancy in order to better estimate the risk of microcephaly due to Zika. We determine the basic reproduction number of the corresponding time-dependent model using different methods. In addition, we demonstrate the global stability of the disease-free periodic solution in the case $\mathcal{R}_0 < 1$, whereas the disease persists when $\mathcal{R}_0 > 1$. To support the theoretical conclusions, numerical simulations are provided. In addition, we fit our model to data from Colombia between 2015 and 2017 as a case study.

2. Methods
2.1. Seasonal Compartmental Model

To account for sexual, vector-borne and vertical transmission, we divided the whole human population N_h into three categories: adult females, denoted by N_f, adult males, denoted by N_m, and children, denoted by N_c and consisting of newly born babies and children under puberty. In order to simplify our model, we do not introduce separate compartments for pregnant women, but we assume that a constant percentage of women (in any of the adult female compartments) is pregnant at any time t. Susceptible humans (S_f, S_m and S_c) are those who can be infected by the Zika virus. Once having contracted the disease, individuals progress to the exposed compartment (E_f, E_m and E_c), and these persons do not have any symptoms yet. If a person has been exposed to the Zika virus but has not yet developed symptoms or been confirmed as infected, they can still potentially spread the virus to others. This is because the virus can be present in the blood (viraemia) and semen (virusemenia) of an infected person for a period of time before symptoms appear [14,25]. Following the incubation time, exposed humans transfer to one of the symptomatically infected classes (I_f^s, I_m^s, I_c^s) and the asymptomatically infected compartments (I_f^a, I_m^a, I_c^a), based on whether that person shows symptoms or not. Both asymptomatically and symptomatically infected adult males progress to the convalescent class (I_m^r) which includes individuals who have recovered from the disease but are still able to spread it through sexual contact. For adult females, we introduce the compartment I_f^r. A percentage of those in I_f^r are those recovered mothers who had Zika during their pregnancy. Children of women who were previously infected by Zika might develop microcephaly and be born into the M_c class, or they might be born healthy and thus arrive at the recovered compartment R_c. To incorporate the time from infection of the mother to birth, we introduce a time delay (τ), which in our model is given as a constant delay based on the average time between infection and delivery of mothers who have given birth to babies with microcephaly. Adults enter the recovered classes (R_f, R_m) after the convalescent phase. Infected mothers' children who are born healthy will move to the recovered compartment R_c, while those who develop microcephaly will move to compartment M_c. The Zika virus only causes microcephaly during pregnancy and not after birth in non-infected children. It only affects the developing fetal brain leading to abnormal brain development and microcephaly in some newborns. Children who were not infected during pregnancy are not at risk of developing microcephaly [26]. Once the infected children have recovered, they will be transferred to the recovered compartment. We point out that the infectious classes (E, I^s, I^a, I^r) also differ in terms of recovery and transmission rates. We introduce three mosquito compartments: susceptible (S_v), exposed (E_v) and infected (I_v). Figure 1 depicts the model's transmission diagram.

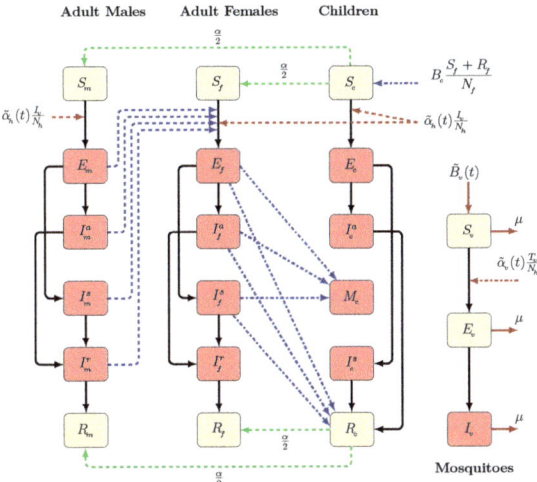

Figure 1. The dynamics of the spread of the Zika virus, taking into account three human groups, and sexual, vertical and vectorial transmission. Adult males, adult females, children and mosquitoes are denoted by the lower indices m, f, c and v, respectively. Yellow nodes denote non-infectious and red nodes denote infectious compartments. The disease progression is depicted by black, solid arrows. The direction of sexual transmission from adult males to adult females is shown by blue dashed arrows, while blue dash–dotted arrows illustrate the direction of vertical infection from adult females to their children. Green dashed arrows show the direction of the maturation from child to adult. Red dashed lines show the direction of mosquito-to-human transmission.

The total human population is $N_h(t) = N_f(t) + N_m(t) + N_c(t)$ and the total population for each group is given as:

$$N_f(t) = S_f(t) + E_f(t) + I_f^a(t) + I_f^s(t) + I_f^r(t) + R_f(t),$$
$$N_m(t) = S_m(t) + E_m(t) + I_m^a(t) + I_m^s(t) + I_m^r(t) + R_m(t),$$
$$N_c(t) = S_c(t) + E_c(t) + I_c^a(t) + I_c^s(t) + M_c(t) + R_c(t),$$

while the total mosquito population is given by $N_v(t) = S_v(t) + E_v(t) + I_v(t)$.

In accordance with the transmission diagram in Figure 1 and the parameter description given in Table 1, the mathematical model takes the form

$$\text{Adult females}\begin{cases} S'_f(t) = \frac{\alpha}{2}S_c(t) - \beta\frac{T_h(t)}{N_f(t)}S_f(t) - \tilde{\alpha}_h(t)\frac{I_v(t)}{N_h(t)}S_f(t) - dS_f(t), \\ E'_f(t) = \beta\frac{T_h(t)}{N_f(t)}S_f(t) + \tilde{\alpha}_h(t)\frac{I_v(t)}{N_h(t)}S_f(t) - (\nu_h + d)E_f(t), \\ I_f^{a\prime}(t) = \theta\nu_h E_f(t) - \gamma_a I_f^a(t) - dI_f^a(t), \\ I_f^{s\prime}(t) = (1-\theta)\nu_h E_f(t) - \gamma_s I_f^s(t) - dI_f^s(t), \\ I_f^{r\prime}(t) = \gamma_a I_f^a(t) + \gamma_s I_f^s(t) - \gamma_r I_f^r(t) - dI_f^r(t), \\ R'_f(t) = \frac{\alpha}{2}R_c(t) + \gamma_r I_f^r(t) - dR_f(t), \end{cases}$$

$$\text{Adult males}\begin{cases} S'_m(t) = \frac{\alpha}{2}S_c(t) - \tilde{\alpha}_h(t)\frac{I_v(t)}{N_h(t)}S_m(t) - dS_m(t), \\ E'_m(t) = \tilde{\alpha}_h(t)\frac{I_v(t)}{N_h(t)}S_m(t) - (\nu_h + d)E_m(t), \\ I_m^{a\prime}(t) = \theta\nu_h E_m(t) - \gamma_a I_m^a(t) - dI_m^a(t), \\ I_m^{s\prime}(t) = (1-\theta)\nu_h E_m(t) - \gamma_s I_m^s(t) - dI_m^s(t), \\ I_m^{r\prime}(t) = \gamma_a I_m^a(t) + \gamma_s I_m^s(t) - \gamma_r I_m^r(t) - dI_m^r(t), \\ R'_m(t) = \frac{\alpha}{2}R_c(t) + \gamma_r I_m^r(t) - dR_m(t), \end{cases}$$

$$\text{Children}\begin{cases} S'_c(t) = B_c\frac{S_f(t-\tau)+R_f(t-\tau)}{N_f(t-\tau)}e^{-\xi\tau} - \tilde{\alpha}_h(t)\frac{I_v(t)}{N_h(t)}S_c(t) - \alpha S_c(t) - \xi S_c(t), \\ E'_c(t) = \tilde{\alpha}_h(t)\frac{I_v(t)}{N_h(t)}S_c(t) - \nu_h E_c(t) - \xi E_c(t), \\ I_c^{a\prime}(t) = \theta\nu_h E_c(t) - \gamma_a I_c^a(t) - \xi I_c^a(t), \\ I_c^{s\prime}(t) = (1-\theta)\nu_h E_c(t) - \gamma_s I_c^s(t) - \xi I_c^s(t), \\ M'_c(t) = (1-p)B_c\frac{E_f(t-\tau)+I_f^a(t-\tau)+I_f^s(t-\tau)}{N_f(t-\tau)}e^{-\xi\tau} - \xi M_c(t), \\ R'_c(t) = pB_c\frac{E_f(t-\tau)+I_f^a(t-\tau)+I_f^s(t-\tau)}{N_f(t-\tau)}e^{-\xi\tau} + \gamma_a I_c^a(t) + \gamma_s I_c^s(t) - \alpha R_c(t) - \xi R_c(t), \end{cases}$$

$$\text{Mosquitoes}\begin{cases} S'_v(t) = \tilde{B}_v(t) - \tilde{\alpha}_v(t)\frac{T_v(t)}{N_h(t)}S_v(t) - \mu S_v(t), \\ E'_v(t) = \tilde{\alpha}_v(t)\frac{T_v(t)}{N_h(t)}S_v(t) - (\nu_v + \mu)E_v(t), \\ I'_v(t) = \nu_v E_v(t) - \mu I_v(t), \end{cases}$$

(1)

where

$$T_h(t) = \kappa_e E_m(t) + \kappa_a I_m^a(t) + I_m^s(t) + \kappa_r I_m^r(t),$$
$$T_v(t) = \eta_e\left(E_f(t) + E_m(t) + E_c(t)\right) + \eta_a\left(I_f^a(t) + I_m^a(t) + I_c^a(t)\right) + I_f^s(t) + I_m^s(t) + I_c^s(t),$$

and all other parameter descriptions are summarized in Table 1. In particular, B_c and ξ are children's birth and death rates, d is the adult death rate and β is the rate at which symptomatic males spread the disease to susceptible females; β multiplied by κ_e, κ_a and κ_r yields the rates at which exposed, asymptotically infected and convalescent men spread the disease to women, respectively. The fraction of asymptomatically infected individuals is represented by θ.

Table 1. Description of the model (1) parameters.

Parameter	Description
B_c	Natural birth rate of children
ζ	Natural death rate of children
α	Maturation rate
d	Natural death rate of adults
β	Transmission rate from human to human
α_h	Baseline value of mosquito-to-human transfer rate
α_v	Baseline value of humans-to-mosquito transfer rate
θ	Ratio of asymptomatic infections
$\kappa_e, \kappa_a, \kappa_r$	Relative transmissibility of exposed humans to infectious humans
η_e, η_a	Relative transmissibility of infectious human to mosquitoes
γ_a	Progression rate from I^a to I^r
γ_s	Progression rate from I^s to I^r
γ_r	Recovery rate of convalescent humans
ν_h	Human incubation rate
ν_v	Incubation rate in mosquitoes
B_v	Baseline value of mosquito birth rate
μ	Mosquito death rate
p	Fraction of children who have recovered
$1-p$	Fraction of children who have microcephaly
a, b	Seasonality parameters
τ	Constant delay

Humans have a latent period of $1/\nu$ length and the infection periods are as follows: $1/\gamma_a, 1/\gamma_s$ and $1/\gamma_s$. The period $1/\gamma_r$ represents the length of time that recovered men are still infectious through sexual contact and recovered women are still infectious during pregnancy. The functions $\tilde{\alpha}_h(t)$, $\tilde{\alpha}_v(t)$ and $\tilde{B}_v(t)$ represent, respectively, the transmission rate from an infected mosquito to a susceptible person, the transmission rate from an infected human to a susceptible mosquito and the birth rate of mosquitoes. These functions are considered to be time-periodic, with one year serving as the period and following for instance [22,24,27] they are expected to be of the form $\alpha_h \cdot \left(\sin\left(\frac{2\pi}{P}t + b\right) + a\right)$, $\alpha_v \cdot \left(\sin\left(\frac{2\pi}{P}t + b\right) + a\right)$ and $B_v \cdot \left(\sin\left(\frac{2\pi}{P}t + b\right) + a\right)$ where P represents the length of the period, a and b are free adjustment parameters, and α_h, α_v, B_v denote the (constant) baseline values of the time-dependent parameters, respectively. Just like in the case of human-to-human transmission, we also introduce the modification parameters η_e, η_a for the infectiousness of exposed and asymptomatically infected people, respectively. We have $1/\nu_v$ for the length of the latent period for mosquitoes, while the average life span of mosquitoes is given by $1/\mu$.

2.2. Zika Fever and Microcephaly Cases Data

The public and freely available weekly ZIKV confirmed cases were collected from the National Health Institute of Colombia [28–30] and Pan American Health Organization [31,32]. We focus our analysis on 2015–2017 confirmed ZIKV cases since the start of the epidemic on week 33 of 2015 up to week 33 of 2017, while for microcephaly we use the data starting from week 33 of 2015 up to week 3 of 2017. There was a delay between the mother's infection and the delivery which caused the lag time between the peaks observed in the number of symptomatically infected cases and microcephaly cases. Figure 2a shows the weekly confirmed cases of the 2015–2017 ZIKV outbreak in Colombia. Figure 2b shows the weekly confirmed microcephaly cases of 2015–2017 in Colombia.

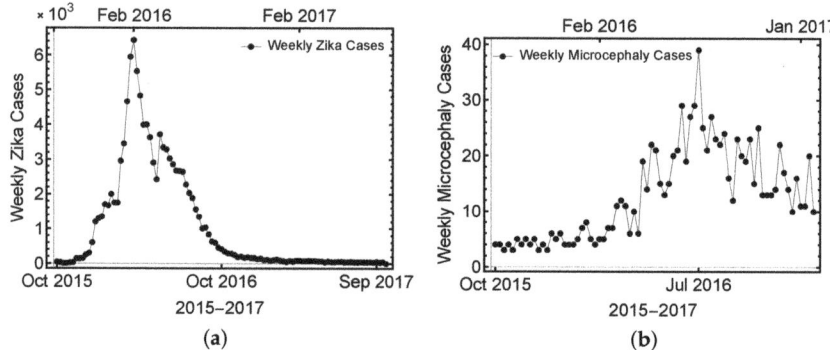

Figure 2. Colombia, weekly distribution of ZIKV and microcephaly cases, 2015–2017. (**a**) Weekly Zika cases. (**b**) Weekly microcephaly cases.

2.3. Parameter Estimation, Sensitivity and Reproduction Numbers

To calculate the parameters of model (1) providing the most satisfactory fit to data, we use Latin hypercube sampling. This sampling method is used to simultaneously measure the variance in various parameter values (see, e.g., [33] for details). The main idea of the method is to generate a representative sample set from the ranges for all fitted parameters. To obtain a representative sample set of size m, the parameter ranges are divided into m equal subintervals and one point is selected from each subinterval. After obtaining the m lists of samples, they are combined randomly into m-tuples. For each element of this sample set, the solutions of the model (1) are numerically calculated. Finally, we apply the least squares method to find the parameters providing the best fit. In order to classify the parameters w.r.t. their influence on the number of microcephaly cases, we employ partial rank correlation coefficients estimation (PRCC, see, e.g., [34]), to perform sensitivity analysis. When we change the parameters within the predetermined ranges, the PRCC-based sensitivity analysis assesses the impact of the parameters on the response function (in our case, the number of microcephaly cases). Higher positive (or negative) PRCC values indicate that a parameter has a positive (or negative) correlation with the outcome function.

The basic reproduction number ($\mathcal{R}_0$) of a periodic mathematical model can be determined as the spectral radius of a linear integral operator on a set of time-dependent functions (see [35], for details). Although the value of $\mathcal{R}_0$ cannot be computed analytically, there are methods to do it numerically (see, e.g., [36] for details). There are also interesting results from calculating the basic reproduction number as a time average for the corresponding periodic model. Setting the time-dependent parameters (mosquito birth rate and bite rates) to constant yields the formula for the time-average basic reproduction number, which can be found in (12). In addition to the basic reproduction number ($\mathcal{R}_0$), the instantaneous reproduction rate, $\mathcal{R}_{inst}$, which measures the average number of secondary cases per infectious case in a population, can be computed by multiplying $\mathcal{R}_0$ by the size of the susceptible percentage of the host population.

3. Results

3.1. Threshold Dynamics

We present some notations for studying the existence of solutions to the system (1) as well as the uniqueness of those solutions. For a certain continuous ω-periodic function $h(t)$, we introduce $\hat{h} = \sup_{t \in [0,\omega)} h(t)$.

Let

$$C := C([-\tau, 0], \mathbb{R}^6) \times \mathbb{R}^{15},$$
$$C^+ := C([-\tau, 0], \mathbb{R}^6_+) \times \mathbb{R}^{15}_+.$$

Thus (C, C^+) defines an ordered Banach space together with the maximum norm. If $x = (x_1, x_2, \ldots, X_{21}) : [-\tau, \sigma] \to \mathbb{R}_+^{21}$ is continuous function with $\sigma > 0$, then, for any $t \in [0, \sigma)$, we define $x_t \in C$ to be $x_t(\theta) = (x_1(t+\theta), x_2(t+\theta), x_3(t+\theta), x_4(t+\theta), x_5(t+\theta), x_6(t+\theta), x_7(t), x_8(t), \ldots, x_{21}(t))$, $\forall \theta \in [-\tau, 0]$.

Define
$$\Omega := \left\{ \phi \in C^+ : \begin{array}{l} \phi_i(\theta) \geq 0, \; i = \{1, 2, \ldots, 6\}, \; \forall \theta \in [-\tau, 0], \\ \phi_j \geq 0, \; j = \{7, 8, \ldots, 21\}. \end{array} \right\}.$$

Lemma 1. *Equation (1) has a unique non-negative bounded solution $u(t, \phi)$ on $[0, \infty)$ with $u_0 = \phi$, for any $\phi \in \Omega$, such that $u_t(\phi) \in \Omega$ for all $t \geq 0$.*

Proof. We introduce the following matrix function $\tilde{f}(t, \phi)$, for any $\phi = (\phi_1, \phi_2, \ldots, \phi_{21}) \in \Omega$, as follows:

$$\tilde{f}(t, \phi) = \begin{pmatrix} \frac{\alpha}{2}\phi_{13}(0) - \beta \frac{T_h(0)}{N_f}\phi_1(0) - \frac{\tilde{\alpha}_h(t)\phi_{21}(0)}{N_h}\phi_1(0) - d\phi_1(0) \\ \beta \frac{T_h(0)}{N_f}\phi_1(0) + \frac{\tilde{\alpha}_h(t)\phi_{21}(0)}{N_h}\phi_1(0) - (\nu_h + d)\phi_2(0) \\ \theta \nu_h \phi_2(0) - \gamma_a \phi_3(0) - d\phi_3(0) \\ (1-\theta)\nu_h \phi_2(0) - \gamma_s \phi_4(0) - d\phi_4(0) \\ \gamma_a \phi_3(0) + \gamma_s \phi_4(0) - \gamma_r \phi_5(0) - d\phi_5(0) \\ \frac{\alpha}{2}\phi_{18}(0) + \gamma_r \phi_5(0) - d\phi_6(0) \\ \frac{\alpha}{2}\phi_{13}(0) - \frac{\tilde{\alpha}_h(t)\phi_{21}(0)}{N_h}\phi_7(0) - d\phi_7(0) \\ \frac{\tilde{\alpha}_h(t)\phi_{21}(0)}{N_h}\phi_7(0) - (\nu_h + d)\phi_8(0) \\ \theta \nu_h \phi_8(0) - \gamma_a \phi_9(0) - d\phi_9(0) \\ (1-\theta)\nu_h \phi_8(0) - \gamma_s \phi_{10}(0) - d\phi_{10}(0) \\ \gamma_a \phi_9(0) + \gamma_s \phi_{10}(0) - \gamma_r \phi_{11}(0) - d\phi_{11}(0) \\ \frac{\alpha}{2}\phi_{18}(0) + \gamma_r \phi_{11}(0) - d\phi_{12}(0) \\ B_c \frac{\phi_1(-\tau) + \phi_6(-\tau)}{N_f} e^{-\xi\tau} - \frac{\tilde{\alpha}_h(t)\phi_{21}(0)}{N_h}\phi_{13}(0) - \alpha\phi_{13}(0) - \xi\phi_{13}(0) \\ \frac{\tilde{\alpha}_h(t)\phi_{21}(0)}{N_h}\phi_{13}(0) - \nu_h \phi_{14}(0) - \xi\phi_{14}(0) \\ \theta \nu_h \phi_{14}(0) - \gamma_a \phi_{15}(0) - \xi\phi_{15}(0) \\ (1-\theta)\nu_h \phi_{14}(0) - \gamma_s \phi_{16}(0) - \xi\phi_{16}(0) \\ (1-p) B_c \frac{\phi_2(-\tau) + \phi_3(-\tau) + \phi_4(-\tau)}{N_f} e^{-\xi\tau} - \xi\phi_{17}(0) \\ p B_c \frac{\phi_2(-\tau) + \phi_3(-\tau) + \phi_4(-\tau)}{N_f} e^{-\xi\tau} + \gamma_a \phi_{15}(0) + \gamma_s \phi_{16}(0) - \alpha\phi_{18}(0) - \xi\phi_{18}(0) \\ \tilde{B}_v(t) - \tilde{\alpha}_v(t) \frac{T_v(0)}{N_h}\phi_{19}(0) - \mu\phi_{19}(0) \\ \tilde{\alpha}_v(t) \frac{T_v(0)}{N_h}\phi_{19}(0) - (\nu_v + \mu)\phi_{20}(0) \\ \nu_v \phi_{20}(0) - \mu\phi_{21}(0) \end{pmatrix},$$

where

$T_h(0) = \kappa_e \phi_8(0) + \kappa_a \phi_9(0) + \phi_{10}(0) + \kappa_r \phi_{11}(0),$
$T_v(0) = \eta_e(\phi_2(0) + \phi_8(0) + \phi_{14}(0)) + \eta_a(\phi_3(0) + \phi_9(0) + \phi_{15}(0)) + \phi_4(0) + \phi_{10}(0) + \phi_{16}(0).$

Notice that $\tilde{f}(t, \phi)$ is continuous in $(t, \phi) \in \mathbb{R}_+ \times \Omega$ and $\tilde{f}(t, \phi)$ is Lipschitz in ϕ on each compact subset of Ω. Therefore, by [37] (Theorems 2.2.1 and 2.2.3) (1) has a unique solution $u(t, \phi)$ on its maximal interval $[0, \sigma_\phi)$ of existence with $u_0 = \phi$.

Let $\phi = (\phi_1, \phi_2, \ldots, \phi_{21}) \in \Omega$. If $\phi_{13} = 0$, then $\tilde{f}_{13}(t, \phi) \geq 0$. If $\phi_{17} = 0$, then $\tilde{f}_{17}(t, \phi) \geq 0$. If $\phi_{18} = 0$, then $\tilde{f}_{18}(t, \phi) \geq 0$. If $\phi_i = 0$ for some $i = \{1, 2, \ldots, 21\}$, then $\tilde{f}_i(t, \phi) \geq 0$. Obviously, the total number of humans, represented by $N_h(t)$, abides by:

$$N_h'(t) = B_c e^{-\xi \tau} - \xi N_c(t) - d N_f(t) - d N_m(t) \geq B_c e^{-\xi \tau} - (\xi + 2d) N_h(t).$$

It is important to note that the linear equation $\frac{dy}{dt} = B_c e^{-\xi \tau} - (\xi + 2d) y(t)$ has a globally stable equilibrium $\frac{B_c e^{-\xi \tau}}{\xi + 2d}$ and for any $0 < \delta < \frac{B_c e^{-\xi \tau}}{\xi + 2d}$, $\frac{dy}{dt}|_{y=\delta} = B_c e^{-\xi \tau} - (\xi + 2d)\delta > 0$. As a result, if $y(0) \geq \delta$, then $y(t) \geq \delta$ holds true for all $t \geq 0$. Based on the comparison principle, if $N_h(0) = \sum_{i=1}^{18} \phi_i(0) \geq \delta$, then $N_h(t) \geq \delta$. Then by [38] (Theorem 5.2.1 and Remark 5.2.1), the unique solution $u(t, \phi)$ of (1) with $u_0 = \phi$ satisfies $u_t(\phi) \in \Omega$ for all $t \in [0, \sigma_\phi)$.

From (1), we obtain

$$N_h'(t) = B_c e^{-\xi \tau} - \xi N_c(t) - d N_f(t) - d N_m(t) \leq B_c e^{-\xi \tau} - \xi N_h(t), \quad (2)$$

where $\tilde{\xi} \leq d$. Clearly, $N_v(t)$ satisfies

$$N_v'(t) = \tilde{B}_v(t) - \mu N_v(t) \leq \hat{\tilde{B}}_v - \mu N_v(t), \forall t \in [0, \sigma_\phi).$$

Hence, $N_h(t)$ and $N_v(t)$ are ultimately bounded on $[0, \sigma_\phi)$. By [37] (Theorem 2.3.1), it follows that $\sigma_\phi = \infty$. When $N_h(t) > \max\{\frac{B_c e^{-\xi \tau}}{\xi + 2d}, \frac{\hat{\tilde{B}}_v}{\mu}\}$ and $N_v(t) > \max\{\frac{B_c e^{-\xi \tau}}{\xi + 2d}, \frac{\hat{\tilde{B}}_v}{\mu}\}$, we have

$$\frac{dN_h(t)}{dt} < 0 \quad \text{and} \quad \frac{dN_v(t)}{dt} < 0.$$

This implies that all solutions are uniformly bounded. □

Next, we investigate the existence and uniqueness of the disease-free periodic solution of system (1). Define

$$\psi = (S_f(0), E_f(0), I_f^a(0), I_f^s(0), I_f^r(0), R_f(0), S_m(0), E_m(0), I_m^a(0), I_m^s(0), I_m^r(0), R_m(0), S_c(0), E_c(0),$$
$$I_c^a(0), I_c^s(0), M_c(0), R_c(0), S_v(0), E_v(0), I_v(0)) \in \mathbb{R}_+^{21}.$$

When there is no disease present, with a positive initial condition $\psi \in \mathbb{R}_+^{21}$, we have the following system

$$\begin{aligned} S_f'(t) &= \frac{\alpha}{2} S_c(t) - d S_f(t), \\ S_m'(t) &= \frac{\alpha}{2} S_c(t) - d S_m(t), \\ S_c'(t) &= B_c e^{-\xi \tau} - \xi S_c(t) \end{aligned} \quad (3)$$

from the last equation of system (3) we can derive

$$S_c(t) = S_c(0) e^{-\xi t} + \frac{B_c e^{-\xi \tau}}{\xi}(1 - e^{-\xi t}). \quad (4)$$

with an arbitrary initial value $S_c(0)$. Equation (4) has a unique equilibrium $S_c^* = \frac{B_c e^{-\xi \tau}}{\xi}$ in $\mathbb{R}_+$. Consequently, $|S_c(t) - S_c^*| \to 0$ as $t \to \infty$ and S_c^* is globally attractive on $\mathbb{R}_+$. Therefore, system (3) has a unique equilibrium $(S_f^*, S_m^*, S_c^*) = (\frac{\alpha B_c e^{-\xi \tau}}{2 d \xi}, \frac{\alpha B_c e^{-\xi \tau}}{2 d \xi}, \frac{B_c e^{-\xi \tau}}{\xi})$.

To get the disease-free periodic equilibrium of (1), consider the following equation:

$$\frac{dS_v(t)}{dt} = \tilde{B}_v(t) - \mu S_v(t). \quad (5)$$

It is clear that (5) admits a single positive ω-periodic solution $S_v^*(t)$ given by

$$S_v^*(t) = \left[\int_0^t \tilde{B}_v(r)e^{\mu r}dr + \frac{\int_0^\omega \tilde{B}_v(r)e^{\mu r}dr}{e^{\mu t}-1}\right]e^{-\mu},$$

that is globally attractive in $\mathbb{R}$ and, hence, (1) has a single disease-free periodic solution

$$E_0 = (S_f^*, 0, 0, 0, 0, 0, S_m^*, 0, 0, 0, 0, 0, S_c^*, 0, 0, 0, 0, 0, S_v^*(t), 0, 0). \tag{6}$$

3.1.1. Basic Reproduction Numbers

By linearizing system (1) at the disease-free periodic solution E_0, we get the periodic linear system for the infective variables as follows:

$$\begin{cases} E_f'(t) = \beta T_h(t) + \frac{\tilde{\alpha}_h(t)I_v(t)}{N_h^*}S_f^* - (\nu_h + d)E_f(t), \\ I_f^{a'}(t) = \theta \nu_h E_f(t) - \gamma_a I_f^a(t) - dI_f^a(t), \\ I_f^{s'}(t) = (1-\theta)\nu_h E_f(t) - \gamma_s I_f^s(t) - dI_f^s(t), \\ I_f^{r'}(t) = \gamma_a I_f^a(t) + \gamma_s I_f^s(t) - \gamma_r I_f^r(t) - dI_f^r(t), \end{cases}$$

$$\begin{cases} E_m'(t) = \frac{\tilde{\alpha}_h(t)I_v(t)}{N_h^*}S_m^* - (\nu_h + d)E_m(t), \\ I_m^{a'}(t) = \theta \nu_h E_m(t) - \gamma_a I_m^a(t) - dI_m^a(t), \\ I_m^{s'}(t) = (1-\theta)\nu_h E_m(t) - \gamma_s I_m^s(t) - dI_m^s(t), \\ I_m^{r'}(t) = \gamma_a I_m^a(t) + \gamma_s I_m^s(t) - \gamma_r I_m^r(t) - dI_m^r(t), \end{cases} \tag{7}$$

$$\begin{cases} E_c'(t) = \frac{\tilde{\alpha}_h(t)I_v(t)}{N_h^*}S_c^* - \nu_h E_c(t) - \xi E_c(t), \\ I_c^{a'}(t) = \theta \nu_h E_c(t) - \gamma_a I_c^a(t) - \xi I_c^a(t), \\ I_c^{s'}(t) = (1-\theta)\nu_h E_c(t) - \gamma_s I_c^s(t) - \xi I_c^s(t), \\ M_c'(t) = (1-p)B_c\frac{E_f(t-\tau)+I_f^a(t-\tau)+I_f^s(t-\tau)}{N_f^*}e^{-\xi\tau} - \xi M_c(t), \end{cases}$$

$$\begin{cases} E_v'(t) = \tilde{\alpha}_v(t)\frac{T_v(t)}{N_h^*}S_v^*(t) - (\nu_v + \mu)E_v(t), \\ I_v'(t) = \nu_v E_v(t) - \mu I_v(t). \end{cases}$$

Let $C := C([-\tau, 0], \mathbb{R}^4) \times \mathbb{R}^{10}$. Assume that $v = (v_1, v_2, \ldots, v_{14}) : [-\tau, \sigma] \to \mathbb{R}^{14}$ is a continuous function with $\sigma > 0$, we define $v_t \in C$ by

$$v_t(\theta) = (v_1(t+\theta), v_2(t+\theta), v_3(t+\theta), v_4(t+\theta), v_5(t), v_6(t), \ldots, v_{14}(t)), \forall \theta \in [-\tau, 0],$$

for any $t \in [0, \sigma)$. Define a map $F : \mathbb{R} \to \mathcal{L}(C, \mathbb{R}^{14})$ and a matrix function $V(t)$ as follows:

$$F(t)\phi = \begin{bmatrix} \beta\left(\kappa_e\phi_8(0)+\kappa_a\phi_9(0)+\phi_{10}(0)+\kappa_r\phi_{11}(0)\right)+\tilde{\alpha}_h(t)\frac{\phi_{14}(0)}{N_h^*}S^* \\ 0 \\ 0 \\ 0 \\ \frac{\tilde{\alpha}_h(t)\phi_{14}(0)}{N_h^*}S_m^* \\ 0 \\ 0 \\ 0 \\ \frac{\tilde{\alpha}_h(t)\phi_{14}(0)}{N_h^*}S_c^* \\ 0 \\ 0 \\ 0 \\ \tilde{\alpha}_v(t)\frac{\eta_e(\phi_2(0)+\phi_8(0)+\phi_{14}(0))+\eta_a(\phi_3(0)+\phi_9(0)+\phi_{15}(0))+\phi_4(0)+\phi_{10}(0)+\phi_{16}(0)}{N_h^*}S_v^*(t) \\ 0 \end{bmatrix},$$

$$V(t) = \begin{bmatrix}
v_h+d & 0 & 0 & 0 & 0 & 0 & 0 & 0 & 0 & 0 & 0 & 0 & 0 & 0 \\
-\theta v_h & \gamma_a+d & 0 & 0 & 0 & 0 & 0 & 0 & 0 & 0 & 0 & 0 & 0 & 0 \\
-(1-\theta)v_h & -\gamma_a & \gamma_s+d & 0 & 0 & 0 & 0 & 0 & 0 & 0 & 0 & 0 & 0 & 0 \\
0 & -\gamma_s & -\gamma_s & \gamma_r & 0 & 0 & 0 & 0 & 0 & 0 & 0 & 0 & 0 & 0 \\
0 & 0 & 0 & 0 & v_h+d & 0 & 0 & 0 & 0 & 0 & 0 & 0 & 0 & 0 \\
0 & 0 & 0 & 0 & -\theta v_h & \gamma_a+d & 0 & 0 & 0 & 0 & 0 & 0 & 0 & 0 \\
0 & 0 & 0 & 0 & -(1-\theta)v_h & -\gamma_a & \gamma_s+d & 0 & 0 & 0 & 0 & 0 & 0 & 0 \\
0 & 0 & 0 & 0 & 0 & -\gamma_a & -\gamma_s & \gamma_r & 0 & 0 & 0 & 0 & 0 & 0 \\
0 & 0 & 0 & 0 & 0 & 0 & 0 & 0 & v_h+\xi & 0 & 0 & 0 & 0 & 0 \\
0 & 0 & 0 & 0 & 0 & 0 & 0 & 0 & -\theta v_h & \gamma_a+\xi & 0 & 0 & 0 & 0 \\
0 & 0 & 0 & 0 & 0 & 0 & 0 & 0 & -(1-\theta)v_h & -\gamma_a & \gamma_s+\xi & 0 & 0 & 0 \\
-\frac{(1-p)P_c}{N_f^*} & -\frac{(1-p)P_c}{N_f^*} & -\frac{(1-p)P_c}{N_f^*} & 0 & 0 & 0 & 0 & 0 & 0 & 0 & 0 & \xi & 0 & 0 \\
0 & 0 & 0 & 0 & 0 & 0 & 0 & 0 & 0 & 0 & 0 & 0 & v_h+\mu & 0 \\
0 & 0 & 0 & 0 & 0 & 0 & 0 & 0 & 0 & 0 & 0 & 0 & -v_h & \mu
\end{bmatrix}.$$

System (7) can be written as:

$$\frac{dv(t)}{dt} = F(t)v_t - V(t)v(t), \quad \forall \geqslant 0. \tag{8}$$

Assume $Z(t,s), t \geqslant s$ to be the evolution operator of the linear ω-periodic system

$$\frac{dz}{dt} = -V(t)z. \tag{9}$$

That is, for each $s \in \mathbb{R}$, the 14×14 matrix $Z(t,s)$ satisfies

$$\frac{d}{dt}Z(t,s) = -V(t)Z(t,s), \quad \forall t \geqslant s, \ Z(s,s) = I,$$

where I is the 14×14 identity matrix.

Following Zhao [39] (Section 2), we suppose that the initial distribution of infectious individuals is $v(t)$, ω-periodic in s. $F(t-s)v_{t-s}$ is the distribution of newly infected individuals at time $t-s$, which is formed by the infectious individuals who were presented throughout the time period $[t-s-\tau, t-s]$ for any $s \geqslant 0$. Then $Z(t,t-s)F(t-s)v_{t-s}$ provides the distribution of those infected individuals who were newly infected at time $t-s$ and remain infected at time t. It concludes that

$$\int_0^\infty Z(t,t-s)F(t-s)v_{t-s}ds = \int_0^\infty Z(t,t-s)F(t-s)v(t-s+.)ds,$$

represents the distribution of accumulative new infections at time t caused by all those infected people raised at a time previous to t.

Let C_ω stands for the ordered Banach space of all ω-periodic functions from $\mathbb{R}$ to $\mathbb{R}^{14}$, that has the maximum norm $\|.\|_\infty$ and the positive cone

$$C_\omega^+ := \{v \in C_\omega : v(t) \geqslant 0, \forall t \in \mathbb{R}\}.$$

Then, a linear operator $\mathcal{L} : C_\omega \to C_\omega$ can be defined as

$$[\mathcal{L}v](t) = \int_0^\infty Z(t,t-s)F(t-s)v(t-s+.)ds, \forall t \in \mathbb{R}, \ v \in C_\omega. \tag{10}$$

As stated in [39], the basic reproduction number is defined as $\mathcal{R}_0 := \rho(\mathcal{L})$. Let $\bar{P}(t)$ be the solution map of (7) for any $t \geqslant 0$ and, hence, $\bar{P}(t)\phi = u_t(\phi)$, where $u(t,\phi)$ is the unique solution of (7) with $u_0 = \phi \in C$. Thus, $\bar{P} := \bar{P}(\omega)$ is the Poincaré map associated with (7). Assume $\rho(\bar{P})$ is the spectral radius of $\bar{P}$. By [39] (Theorem 2.1), we have the following lemma.

Lemma 2. $\mathcal{R}_0 - 1$ has the same sign as $\rho(\bar{P}) - 1$.

These results suggest that $\mathcal{R}_0$ is a critical value for the disease local spread, as well as that the stability of the zero solution of system (7) depends on the sign of $\mathcal{R}_0 - 1$.

3.1.2. Derivation of the Time-Average Reproduction Number

In model (1) the delay τ was introduced to take account of the delay between the infection of the mother and the delivery which caused the lag time between the peaks observed on symptomatically infected cases and microcephaly cases. By setting $\tau = 0$, we can use the general approach established in [40] to calculate a formula for the time-average reproduction number $[\mathcal{R}_0]$ of (1).

We calculate a formula for the basic reproduction number $\mathcal{R}_0^A$ of the autonomous model obtained from (1) by setting the time-dependent parameters (mosquito birth $\tilde{B}_v(t) \equiv B_v$) and biting rates ($\tilde{\alpha}_h(t) \equiv \alpha_h$ and $\tilde{\alpha}_v(t) \equiv \alpha_v$) to constant. Given the infectious states E_f, I_f^a, I_f^s, I_f^r, E_m, I_m^a, I_m^s, I_m^r, E_c, I_c^a, I_c^s, E_v and I_v in (1) and substituting the values in

$$E_0 = \left(S_f^*, 0, 0, 0, 0, 0, S_m^*, 0, 0, 0, 0, 0, S_c^*, 0, 0, 0, 0, 0, S_v^*, 0, 0\right)$$
$$= \left(\frac{\alpha B_c}{2d(\xi + \alpha)}, 0, 0, 0, 0, 0, \frac{\alpha B_c}{2d(\xi + \alpha)}, 0, 0, 0, 0, 0, \frac{B_c}{\xi + \alpha}, 0, 0, 0, 0, 0, \frac{B_v}{\mu}, 0, 0\right),$$

we compute the matrices F and V for the new infection terms and the remaining transfer terms. These two matrices are, respectively, given by

$$F = \begin{bmatrix} 0 & 0 & 0 & 0 & \beta\kappa_e & \beta\kappa_a & \beta & \beta\kappa_r & 0 & 0 & 0 & 0 & 0 & \frac{\alpha_h S_f^*}{N_h^*} \\ 0 & 0 & 0 & 0 & 0 & 0 & 0 & 0 & 0 & 0 & 0 & 0 & 0 & 0 \\ 0 & 0 & 0 & 0 & 0 & 0 & 0 & 0 & 0 & 0 & 0 & 0 & 0 & 0 \\ 0 & 0 & 0 & 0 & 0 & 0 & 0 & 0 & 0 & 0 & 0 & 0 & 0 & 0 \\ 0 & 0 & 0 & 0 & 0 & 0 & 0 & 0 & 0 & 0 & 0 & 0 & 0 & \frac{\alpha_h S_m^*}{N_h^*} \\ 0 & 0 & 0 & 0 & 0 & 0 & 0 & 0 & 0 & 0 & 0 & 0 & 0 & 0 \\ 0 & 0 & 0 & 0 & 0 & 0 & 0 & 0 & 0 & 0 & 0 & 0 & 0 & 0 \\ 0 & 0 & 0 & 0 & 0 & 0 & 0 & 0 & 0 & 0 & 0 & 0 & 0 & 0 \\ 0 & 0 & 0 & 0 & 0 & 0 & 0 & 0 & 0 & 0 & 0 & 0 & 0 & \frac{\alpha_h S_c^*}{N_h^*} \\ 0 & 0 & 0 & 0 & 0 & 0 & 0 & 0 & 0 & 0 & 0 & 0 & 0 & 0 \\ 0 & 0 & 0 & 0 & 0 & 0 & 0 & 0 & 0 & 0 & 0 & 0 & 0 & 0 \\ \frac{\alpha_v \eta_e S_v^*}{N_h^*} & \frac{\alpha_v \eta_a S_v^*}{N_h^*} & \frac{\alpha_v S_v^*}{N_h^*} & 0 & \frac{\alpha_v \eta_e S_v^*}{N_h^*} & \frac{\alpha_v \eta_a S_v^*}{N_h^*} & \frac{\alpha_v S_v^*}{N_h^*} & 0 & \frac{\alpha_v \eta_e S_v^*}{N_h^*} & \frac{\alpha_v \eta_a S_v^*}{N_h^*} & \frac{\alpha_v S_v^*}{N_h^*} & 0 & 0 & 0 \\ 0 & 0 & 0 & 0 & 0 & 0 & 0 & 0 & 0 & 0 & 0 & 0 & 0 & 0 \end{bmatrix}$$

and

$$V = \begin{bmatrix} d+\nu_h & 0 & 0 & 0 & 0 & 0 & 0 & 0 & 0 & 0 & 0 & 0 & 0 & 0 \\ -\theta\nu_h & \gamma_a+d & 0 & 0 & 0 & 0 & 0 & 0 & 0 & 0 & 0 & 0 & 0 & 0 \\ -(1-\theta)\nu_h & 0 & \gamma_s+d & 0 & 0 & 0 & 0 & 0 & 0 & 0 & 0 & 0 & 0 & 0 \\ 0 & -\gamma_a & -\gamma_s & \gamma_r+d & 0 & 0 & 0 & 0 & 0 & 0 & 0 & 0 & 0 & 0 \\ 0 & 0 & 0 & 0 & d+\nu_h & 0 & 0 & 0 & 0 & 0 & 0 & 0 & 0 & 0 \\ 0 & 0 & 0 & 0 & -\theta\nu_h & \gamma_a+d & 0 & 0 & 0 & 0 & 0 & 0 & 0 & 0 \\ 0 & 0 & 0 & 0 & -(1-\theta)\nu_h & 0 & \gamma_s+d & 0 & 0 & 0 & 0 & 0 & 0 & 0 \\ 0 & 0 & 0 & 0 & 0 & -\gamma_a & -\gamma_s & \gamma_r+d & 0 & 0 & 0 & 0 & 0 & 0 \\ 0 & 0 & 0 & 0 & 0 & 0 & 0 & 0 & \xi+\nu_h & 0 & 0 & 0 & 0 & 0 \\ 0 & 0 & 0 & 0 & 0 & 0 & 0 & 0 & -\theta\nu_h & \gamma_a+\xi & 0 & 0 & 0 & 0 \\ 0 & 0 & 0 & 0 & 0 & 0 & 0 & 0 & -(1-\theta)\nu_h & 0 & \gamma_s+\xi & 0 & 0 & 0 \\ \frac{(p-1)B_c}{N_f^*} & \frac{(p-1)B_c}{N_f^*} & \frac{(p-1)B_c}{N_f^*} & 0 & 0 & 0 & 0 & 0 & 0 & 0 & 0 & \xi & 0 & 0 \\ 0 & 0 & 0 & 0 & 0 & 0 & 0 & 0 & 0 & 0 & 0 & 0 & \mu+\nu_v & 0 \\ 0 & 0 & 0 & 0 & 0 & 0 & 0 & 0 & 0 & 0 & 0 & 0 & -\nu_v & \mu \end{bmatrix},$$

hence the next generation matrix FV^{-1} has the following characteristic polynomial:

$$\lambda^{11}\left(\lambda^3 - (R_{fv}R_{vf} + R_{vm}R_{mv} + R_{vc}R_{cv})\lambda - R_{mf}R_{fv}R_{vm}\right) = 0$$

where

$$R_{mf} = \frac{\beta \kappa_e}{d+v_h} + \frac{\theta \beta \kappa_a v_h}{(d+\gamma_a)(d+v_h)} + \frac{(1-\theta)\beta v_h}{(d+\gamma_s)(d+v_h)} + \frac{\beta \kappa_r v_h (\gamma_a \gamma_s + \theta \gamma_a d + (1-\theta)\gamma_s d)}{(d+\gamma_a)(d+\gamma_s)(d+\gamma_r)(d+v_h)}$$

$$R_{fv} = R_{mv} = \frac{\alpha_v \eta e S_v^*}{(d+v_h)N_h^*} + \frac{\theta \alpha_v \eta_a v_h S_v^*}{(d+\gamma_a)(d+v_h)N_h^*} + \frac{(1-\theta)\alpha_v v_h S_v^*}{(d+\gamma_a)(d+v_h)N_h^*},$$

$$R_{cv} = \frac{\alpha_v \eta e S_v^*}{(\xi+v_h)N_h^*} + \frac{\theta \alpha_v \eta_a v_h S_v^*}{(\xi+\gamma_a)(\xi+v_h)N_h^*} + \frac{(1-\theta)\alpha_v v_h S_v^*}{(\xi+\gamma_s)(\xi+v_h)N_h^*},$$

$$R_{vf} = R_{vm} = \frac{\alpha}{2d}R_{vc} = \frac{\alpha}{2d}\frac{\alpha_h v_v B_c}{\mu(\xi+\alpha)(\mu+v_v)N_h^*},$$

The characteristic polynomial, therefore, takes the form

$$2d\lambda^3 - 2R_{vc}(dR_{cv} + \alpha R_{fv})\lambda - \alpha R_{mf}R_{fv}R_{vc} = 0.$$

Following [40], $\mathcal{R}_0^A$ is the spectral radius of FV^{-1}. Accordingly, $\mathcal{R}_0^A$ corresponds to the dominant eigenvalue given by the root of the cubic equation

$$\mathcal{R}_0^A = \frac{2R_{vc}(dR_{cv}+\alpha R_{fv})}{3\sqrt[3]{6}\left(\sqrt{(9d^2\alpha R_{fv}R_{mf}R_{cv})^2 - 48R_{vc}^3(dR_{cv}+\alpha R_{fv})^3} - 9d^2\alpha R_{fv}R_{mf}R_{cv}\right)^{1/3}} \\ + \frac{\left(\sqrt{(9d^2\alpha R_{fv}R_{mf}R_{cv})^2 - 48R_{vc}^3(dR_{cv}+\alpha R_{fv})^3} - 9d^2\alpha R_{fv}R_{mf}R_{cv}\right)^{1/3}}{3\sqrt[3]{36}d}, \quad (11)$$

where R_{mf} is the basic reproduction number corresponding to sexual transmission and R_{fv}, R_{cv}, R_{vc} are the reproductive numbers relevant to vector-borne transmission.

We derive the formula for $[\mathcal{R}_0]$ (the time-average reproduction number) of the corresponding non-autonomous model (1) by using the following remark presented in [36].

Remark 1. *Given a continuous ω-periodic function $q(t)$, its average is defined as*

$$[q] := \frac{1}{\omega}\int_0^\omega q(t)\,dt.$$

Then, $[\mathcal{R}_0]$ is given by

$$[\mathcal{R}_0] = \frac{2[R_{vc}]\bigl(d[R_{cv}]+\alpha[R_{fv}]\bigr)}{3\sqrt[3]{6}\left(\sqrt{(9d^2\alpha[R_{fv}]R_{mf}[R_{cv}])^2 - 48[R_{vc}]^3(d[R_{cv}]+\alpha[R_{fv}])^3} - 9d^2\alpha[R_{fv}]R_{mf}[R_{cv}]\right)^{\frac{1}{3}}} \\ + \frac{\left(\sqrt{(9d^2\alpha[R_{fv}]R_{mf}[R_{cv}])^2 - 48[R_{vc}]^3(d[R_{cv}]+\alpha[R_{fv}])^3} - 9d^2\alpha[R_{fv}]R_{mf}[R_{cv}]\right)^{\frac{1}{3}}}{3\sqrt[3]{36}d}, \quad (12)$$

where

$$[R_{fv}] = \frac{\eta_e[\tilde{\alpha}_v][\tilde{B}_v]}{\mu(d+v_h)N_h^*} + \frac{\theta \eta_a v_h[\tilde{\alpha}_v][\tilde{B}_v]}{\mu(d+\gamma_a)(d+v_h)N_h^*} + \frac{(1-\theta)v_h[\tilde{\alpha}_v][\tilde{B}_v]}{\mu(d+\gamma_a)(d+v_h)N_h^*},$$

$$[R_{cv}] = \frac{\eta_e[\tilde{\alpha}_v][\tilde{B}_v]}{\mu(\xi+v_h)N_h^*} + \frac{\theta \eta_a v_h[\tilde{\alpha}_v][\tilde{B}_v]}{\mu(\xi+\gamma_a)(\xi+v_h)N_h^*} + \frac{(1-\theta)v_h[\tilde{\alpha}_v][\tilde{B}_v]}{\mu(\xi+\gamma_a)(\xi+v_h)N_h^*},$$

$$[R_{vc}] = \frac{B_c v_v[\tilde{\alpha}_h]}{\mu(\xi+\alpha)(\mu+v_v)N_h^*}.$$

3.1.3. Global Dynamics

In terms of $\mathcal{R}_0$, we investigate the global dynamics of (1). We employ the theory of monotone semiflows developed in [41] (Section 2.3). Then, we continue with a new phase space on which (7) eventually forms a strongly monotone periodic semiflow. We prove that, if $\mathcal{R}_0 < 1$, then the unique disease-free equilibrium is globally asymptotically stable and the disease dies out, while, if $\mathcal{R}_0 > 1$, the infection persists and there exists at least an ω-periodic solution of (1).

Define
$$Y := C([-\tau, 0], \mathbb{R}^4) \times \mathbb{R}^{10} \text{ and } Y_+ := C([-\tau, 0], \mathbb{R}^4_+) \times \mathbb{R}^{10}_+.$$

The following lemma can be obtained by using the method of steps.

Lemma 3. *For any $\phi \in Y_+$ and for all $t \geqslant 0$, system (7) has a unique non-negative solution $v(t, \phi)$ with $v_0 = \phi$.*

Assume that $P(t)$ is the solution map of system (1) on Y for any given $t \geqslant 0$. Therefore, $P := P(\omega)$ is the Poincaré map corresponding to the linear Equation (7) and $\rho(\bar{P}) = \rho(P)$ by using Lou and Zhao [42] (Lemma 3.8).

Define
$$X := C([-\tau, 0], \mathbb{R}^6_+) \times \mathbb{R}^{15}_+,$$
$$X_0 := \{\phi = (\phi_1, \phi_2, \ldots, \phi_{21}) \in X : \phi_i(0) > 0, \, i = 2, 3, 4, 5, 8, 9, 10, 11, 14, 15, 16, 20, 21\},$$
$$\partial X_0 := X \setminus X_0 = \{\phi \in X : \phi_i(0) = 0, \, i = 2, 3, 4, 5, 8, 9, 10, 11, 14, 15, 16, 20, 21\}.$$

Theorem 1. *The subsequent statements are valid:*

(i) *If $\rho(P) < 1$, the disease-free periodic solution E_0 defined by (6) is globally attractive for system (1) in X.*

(ii) *If $\rho(P) > 1$, then system (1) admits a positive ω-periodic solution and there exists a positive constant $\kappa > 0$ such that any solution $u(t, \phi)$ of system (1) for all initial values $\phi \in X_0$ satisfies*

$$\liminf_{t \to \infty} \left(E_f(t, \phi), I_f^a(t, \phi), I_f^s(t, \phi), I_f^r(t, \phi), E_m(t, \phi), I_m^a(t, \phi), I_m^s(t, \phi), I_m^r(t, \phi), E_c(t, \phi), \right.$$
$$\left. I_c^a(t, \phi), I_c^s(t, \phi), E_v(t, \phi), I_v(t, \phi) \right)^T \geqslant (\kappa, \kappa, \kappa, \kappa, \kappa, \kappa, \kappa, \kappa, \kappa, \kappa, \kappa, \kappa, \kappa)^T.$$

Proof. If $\rho(P) < 1$, let $v(t, \phi)$ and $w(t, \psi)$ be the unique solutions of (7) with $v_0 = \phi$ and $w_0 = \psi$, respectively, for any ψ and ϕ in Y_+ with $\phi \geqslant \psi$. Smith [38] (Theorem 5.1.1) implies that $v(t, \phi) \geqslant v(t, \psi)$ for all $t \geqslant 0$ and. hence, $P : Y_+ \to Y_+$ is monotone for all $t \geqslant 0$. Consider $\phi, \psi \in Y$ satisfy $\phi > \psi$ and represent $v(t, \phi) = (\bar{x}_1(t), \bar{x}_2(t), \ldots, \bar{x}_{14}(t))$ and $w(t, \psi) = (x_1(t), x_2(t), \ldots, x_{14}(t))$. By applying a simple comparison argument on each interval $[n\tau, (n+1)\tau], n \in \mathbb{N}$, it is possible to demonstrate that $\bar{x}_i(t) > x_i(t)$ for all $t > t_0, i = \{1, 2, 3, 4\}$. The next step is to demonstrate that $P(t)$ becomes eventually strongly monotone. We assume, without losing generality, that $\phi_{14} > \psi_{14}$.

Claim 1. *There exists $t_0 \in [0, \tau]$ s.t. $\bar{x}_1(t) > x_1(t), \forall t \geqslant t_0$.*

First, for some $t_0 \in [0, \tau]$, we show that $\bar{x}_1(t_0) > x_1(t_0)$. If not, then for each $t_0 \in [0, \tau]$, $\bar{x}_1(t) = x_1(t)$ and, consequently, $\frac{d\bar{x}_1(t)}{dt} = \frac{dx_1(t)}{dt}$ for all $t_0 \in (0, \tau)$. Then, we get

$$\tilde{\alpha}_h(t) \frac{S_f^*}{N_h^*} (\bar{x}_{14}(t) - x_{14}(t)) - (\nu_h + d)(\bar{x}_1(t) - x_1(t)) = 0.$$

It is observed that $\bar{x}_1(t) = x_1(t)$ and $\bar{x}_{14}(t) = x_{14}(t)$ for all $t_0 \in [0, \tau]$, then $\phi_{14}(\theta) = \psi_{14}(\theta)$ for all $t_0 \in [0, \tau]$, which contradicts the hypothesis that $\phi_{14} > \psi_{14}$.

Let $g_1(t,x) := \tilde{\alpha}_h(t)\frac{S_f^*}{N_h^*}x_{14}(t) - (\nu_h + d)x(t)$. Then, we have

$$\frac{d\bar{x}_1(t)}{dt} = \tilde{\alpha}_h(t)\frac{S_f^*}{N_h^*}\bar{x}_{14}(t) - (\nu_h + d)\bar{x}_1(t)$$

$$\geq \tilde{\alpha}_h(t)\frac{S_f^*}{N_h^*}x_{14}(t) - (\nu_h + d)\bar{x}_1(t)$$

$$= g_1(t, \bar{x}_1(t)),$$

we obtain $\frac{d\bar{x}_1(t)}{dt} - g_1(t, \bar{x}_1(t)) \geq 0 = \frac{dx_1(t)}{dt} - g_1(t, x_1(t))\ \forall t \geq t_0$. Since $\bar{x}_1(t_0) > x_1(t_0)$, the comparison theorem [43] (Theorem 4) indicates that $\bar{x}_1(t) > x_1(t), \forall t \geq t_0$.

Claim 2. $\bar{x}_2(t) > x_2(t), \forall t \geq t_0 + \tau$.
Let $g_2(t,x) := \theta\nu_h x_1(t) - (\gamma_a + d)x(t)$. Then we have

$$\frac{d\bar{x}_2(t)}{dt} = \theta\nu_h \bar{x}_1(t) - (\gamma_a + d)\bar{x}_2(t)$$

$$\geq \theta\nu_h x_1(t) - (\gamma_a + d)\bar{x}_2(t)$$

$$= g_2(t, \bar{x}_2(t)),$$

and, hence, $\frac{d\bar{x}_2(t)}{dt} - g_2(t, \bar{x}_2(t)) \geq 0 = \frac{dx_2(t)}{dt} - g_2(t, x_2(t))\ \forall t > t_0$. It follows from [43] (Theorem 4) that $\bar{x}_2(t) > x_2(t)$ for all $t > t_0 + \tau$.

Claim 3. $\bar{x}_3(t) > x_3(t)$ for all $t \geq t_0$.
Let $g_3(t,x) := (1-\theta)\nu_h x_1(t) - (\gamma_s + d)x(t)$, Then we have

$$\frac{d\bar{x}_3}{dt} = (1-\theta)\nu_h \bar{x}_1(t) - (\gamma_s + d)\bar{x}_3(t)$$

$$\geq (1-\theta)\nu_h x_1(t) - (\gamma_s + d)\bar{x}_3(t)$$

$$= g_3(t, \bar{x}_3(t)),$$

and hence, $\frac{d\bar{x}_3(t)}{dt} - g_3(t, \bar{x}_3(t)) \geq 0 = \frac{dx_3(t)}{dt} - g_3(t, x_3(t))\ \forall t > t_0$. It follows from [43] (Theorem 4) that $\bar{x}_3(t) > x_3(t)$ for all $t > t_0$.

Claim 4. $\bar{x}_4(t) > x_4(t)$ for all $t \geq t_0$.
Let $g_4(t,x) := \gamma_a x_2(t) + \gamma_s x_3(t) - (\gamma_r + d)x(t)$. Then we have

$$\frac{d\bar{x}_4}{dt} = \gamma_a \bar{x}_2(t) + \gamma_s \bar{x}_3(t) - (\gamma_r + d)\bar{x}_4(t)$$

$$\geq \gamma_a x_2(t) + \gamma_s x_3(t) - (\gamma_r + d)\bar{x}_4(t)$$

$$= g_4(t, \bar{x}_4(t)),$$

and therefore, $\frac{d\bar{x}_3(t)}{dt} - g_3(t, \bar{x}_3(t)) \geq 0 = \frac{dx_3(t)}{dt} - g_3(t, x_3(t))\ \forall t > t_0$. It follows from [43] (Theorem 4) that $\bar{x}_3(t) > x_3(t)$ for all $t > t_0$.

Claim i ($i = 5, 6, \ldots, 14$). $\bar{x}_i(t) > x_i(t), i = 5, 6, \ldots, 14$ for all $t \geq t_0$.
In a similar way to the previous four claims, we can show that $\bar{x}_i(t) > x_i(t), i = 5, 6, \ldots, 14$ for all $t \geq t_0$.

Given two positive real numbers a and b, we write $a \gg b$ if and only if a is much greater than b. If we take into consideration the claims made above, we arrive at

$$(\bar{x}_1(t), \bar{x}_2(t), \ldots, \bar{x}_{14}(t)) \gg (x_1(t), x_2(t), \ldots, x_{14}(t)), \quad \forall t > t_0 + \tau.$$

Because $t_0 \in [0, \tau]$, it can be shown that

$$(\bar{x}_{1t}, \bar{x}_{2t}, \ldots, \bar{x}_{14t}) \gg (x_{1t}, x_{2t}, \ldots, x_{14t}), \quad \forall t > 2\tau,$$

that is $v_t(\phi) \gg w_t(\psi)$ for all $t > 2\tau$. Hence, it follows that $P(t)$ is strongly monotone for any $t > 2\tau$.

According to [37] (Theorem 3.6.1), the linear operator $\bar{P}(t)$ is compact on Y_+ for any $t \geqslant 2\tau$. Hence, $P(t)$ is compact and strongly monotone on Y for $t \geqslant 2\tau$. Select a positive integer $n_0 > 0$ such that $n_0 \omega > 2\tau$. Given that $P^{n_0 \omega} = P(n_0 \omega)$, it follows from [44] (Lemma 3.1) that $\rho(P)$ is a simple eigenvalue of P with a strongly positive eigenvector and the modulus of any additional eigenvalue is smaller than $\rho(P)$. By [45] (Lemma 1), there is a positive ω-periodic function $\bar{v}(t) = (\bar{v}_1(t), \bar{v}_2(t), \ldots, \bar{v}_{14}(t))^T$ s.t. $v^*(t) = e^{\lambda t} \bar{v}(t)$ is a positive solution of (7) where $\lambda = \frac{\ln \rho(P)}{\omega}$.

Assume the linear periodic system with parameter ϵ:

$$\begin{aligned}
E_f'(t) &= \beta T_h(t) + \tilde{\alpha}_h(t) I_v(t) \frac{S_f^*}{N_h^* - \epsilon} - (\nu_h + d) E_f(t), \\
I_f^{a\prime}(t) &= \theta \nu_h E_f(t) - \gamma_a I_f^a(t) - d I_f^a(t), \\
I_f^{s\prime}(t) &= (1 - \theta) \nu_h E_f(t) - \gamma_s I_f^s(t) - d I_f^s(t), \\
I_f^{r\prime}(t) &= \gamma_a I_f^a(t) + \gamma_s I_f^s(t) - \gamma_r I_f^r(t) - d I_f^r(t), \\
E_m'(t) &= \tilde{\alpha}_h(t) I_v(t) \frac{S_m^*}{N_h^* - \epsilon} - (\nu_h + d) E_m(t), \\
I_m^{a\prime}(t) &= \theta \nu_h E_m(t) - \gamma_a I_m^a(t) - d I_m^a(t), \\
I_m^{s\prime}(t) &= (1 - \theta) \nu_h E_m(t) - \gamma_s I_m^s(t) - d I_m^s(t), \\
I_m^{r\prime}(t) &= \gamma_a I_m^a(t) + \gamma_s I_m^s(t) - \gamma_r I_m^r(t) - d I_m^r(t), \\
E_c'(t) &= \tilde{\alpha}_h(t) I_v(t) \frac{S_c^*}{N_h^* - \epsilon} - \nu_h E_c(t) - \xi E_c(t), \\
I_c^{a\prime}(t) &= \theta \nu_h E_c(t) - \gamma_a I_c^a(t) - \xi I_c^a(t), \\
I_c^{s\prime}(t) &= (1 - \theta) \nu_h E_c(t) - \gamma_s I_c^s(t) - \xi I_c^s(t), \\
M_c'(t) &= (1 - p) B_c \frac{E_f(t - \tau) + I_f^a(t - \tau) + I_f^s(t - \tau)}{N_f^* - \epsilon} e^{-\xi \tau} - \xi M_c(t), \\
E_v'(t) &= \tilde{\alpha}_v(t) T_v(t) \frac{S_v^*(t) + \epsilon}{N_h^* - \epsilon} - (\nu_v + \mu) E_v(t), \\
I_v'(t) &= \nu_v E_v(t) - \mu I_v(t).
\end{aligned} \qquad (13)$$

Assume that $P_\epsilon(t)$ is the solution map of system (13) on Y_+ and $P_\epsilon := P_\epsilon(\omega)$. Since $\lim_{\epsilon \to 0} \rho(P_\epsilon) = \rho(P) < 1$, we can choose a small enough $\epsilon > 0$ s.t. $\rho(P_\epsilon) < 1$. It is straightforward to demonstrate that $P_\epsilon(t)$ is also compact and eventually strongly monotone on Y. Then, there exists a positive ω-periodic function $v_\epsilon(t) = (v_{\epsilon_1}(t), v_{\epsilon_2}(t), \ldots, v_{\epsilon_{14}}(t))$ such that $u_\epsilon(t) = e^{\frac{\ln \rho(P_\epsilon)}{\omega} t} v_\epsilon(t)$ is a positive solution of (13). As a result,

$$\lim_{t \to \infty} u_\epsilon(t) = 0.$$

Clearly, $S_v(t)$ satisfies $S_v'(t) = \tilde{B}_v(t) - \mu S_v(t)$; it has a globally attractive ω-periodic solution $S_v^*(t)$. Then there is a large enough integer $T_1 > 0$ s.t. $T_1 \omega > \tau$ and $S_v^*(t) - \epsilon \leqslant S_v(t) \leqslant S_v^*(t) + \epsilon$ for all $t \geqslant T_1 \omega$. Then we have

$$\begin{aligned}
E_f'(t) &\leq \beta T_h(t) + \tilde{\alpha}_h(t) I_v(t) \frac{S_f^*}{N_h^* - \epsilon} - (\nu_h + d) E_f(t), \\
I_f^{a\prime}(t) &\leq \theta \nu_h E_f(t) - \gamma_a I_f^a(t) - d I_f^a(t), \\
I_f^{s\prime}(t) &\leq (1 - \theta) \nu_h E_f(t) - \gamma_s I_f^s(t) - d I_f^s(t),
\end{aligned}$$

$$I_f^{r\prime}(t) \leq \gamma_a I_f^a(t) + \gamma_s I_f^s(t) - \gamma_r I_f^r(t) - dI_f^r(t),$$

$$E_m'(t) \leq \tilde{\alpha}_h(t) I_v(t) \frac{S_m^*}{N_h^* - \epsilon} - (\nu_h + d)E_m(t),$$

$$I_m^{a\prime}(t) \leq \theta \nu_h E_m(t) - \gamma_a I_m^a(t) - dI_m^a(t),$$

$$I_m^{s\prime}(t) \leq (1-\theta)\nu_h E_m(t) - \gamma_s I_m^s(t) - dI_m^s(t),$$

$$I_m^{r\prime}(t) \leq \gamma_a I_m^a(t) + \gamma_s I_m^s(t) - \gamma_r I_m^r(t) - dI_m^r(t),$$

$$E_c'(t) \leq \tilde{\alpha}_h(t) I_v(t) \frac{S_c^*}{N_h^* - \epsilon} - \nu_h E_c(t) - \xi E_c(t),$$

$$I_c^{a\prime}(t) \leq \theta \nu_h E_c(t) - \gamma_a I_c^a(t) - \xi I_c^a(t),$$

$$I_c^{s\prime}(t) \leq (1-\theta)\nu_h E_c(t) - \gamma_s I_c^s(t) - \xi I_c^s(t),$$

$$M_c'(t) \leq (1-p)B_c \frac{E_f(t-\tau) + I_f^a(t-\tau) + I_f^s(t-\tau)}{N_f^* - \epsilon} e^{-\xi \tau} - \xi M_c(t),$$

$$E_v'(t) \leq \tilde{\alpha}_v(t) T_v(t) \frac{S_v^*(t) + \epsilon}{N_h^* - \epsilon} - (\nu_v + \mu)E_v(t),$$

$$I_v'(t) \leq \nu_v E_v(t) - \mu I_v(t),$$

for all $t \geq T_1 \omega$. Choose a sufficiently large number $K > 0$ such that

$$\left(E_f(t,\phi), I_f^a(t,\phi), I_f^s(t,\phi), I_f^r(t,\phi), E_m(t,\phi), I_m^a(t,\phi), I_m^s(t,\phi), I_m^r(t,\phi), E_c(t,\phi), I_c^a(t,\phi), I_c^s(t,\phi),\right.$$
$$\left. E_v(t,\phi), I_v(t,\phi)\right) \leq K u_\epsilon(t),$$

for all $t \in [T_1\omega, T_1\omega + \tau]$. By using [38] (Theorem 5.1.1), $\forall\, t \geq T_1 \omega + \tau$, we obtain

$$\lim_{t \to \infty} \left(E_f(t,\phi), I_f^a(t,\phi), I_f^s(t,\phi), I_f^r(t,\phi), E_m(t,\phi), I_m^a(t,\phi), I_m^s(t,\phi), I_m^r(t,\phi), E_c(t,\phi), I_c^a(t,\phi),\right.$$
$$\left. I_c^s(t,\phi), E_v(t,\phi), I_v(t,\phi)\right)^T = (0,0,0,0,0,0,0,0,0,0,0,0,0)^T.$$

Furthermore, it follows from the chain transitive sets arguments (see, [46] (Theorem 3.6) and [47] (Theorem 2.5)) that $\lim_{t\to\infty}(S_f(t) - S_f^*) = 0$, $\lim_{t\to\infty} R_f(t) = 0$, $\lim_{t\to\infty}(S_m(t) - S_m^*) = 0$, $\lim_{t\to\infty} R_m(t) = 0$, $\lim_{t\to\infty}(S_c(t) - S_c^*) = 0$, $\lim_{t\to\infty} R_c(t) = 0$ and $\lim_{t\to\infty}(S_v(t) - S_v^*(t)) = 0$. This completes the proof of the first statement.

For the sake of simplicity, we only show the main steps of the proof of the second statement when $\rho(P) > 1$. In this case, we employ the persistence theory for periodic semiflows.

Let $Q(t): X \to X$ be the solution maps of (1) on X, that is, $Q(t)\psi = u_t(\phi)$, $t \geq 0$, where $u(t,\phi)$ is the unique solution of (1) satisfying $u_0 = \phi \in X$. Therefore, $Q := Q(\omega)$ is the Poincaré map associated with (1). From (1), it follows that $Q(t)X_0 \subseteq X_0$ for all $t \geq 0$. It is important to note that a map Q is point dissipative if there exists a bounded set B such that, for each $x \in \mathbb{R}^n$, there is an integer $n_0 = n_0(x)$ such that $Q^n x \in B$ for $n \geq n_0$. Therefore, the discrete-time system $\{Q^n : X \to X\}_{n \geq 0}$ is point dissipative by Lemma 1 and from [37] (Theorem 3.6.1), $Q(t)$ is compact for each $t \geq \tau$, and, then, Q^n is compact for enough large n. According to [39] (Theorem 1.1.3), Q has a global attractor.

Next, we demonstrate that Q is uniformly persistent w.r.t. $(X_0, \partial X_0)$. Let $M = (S_f^*, 0, 0, 0, 0, 0, S_m^*, 0, 0, 0, 0, 0, S_c^*, 0, 0, 0, 0, 0, S_v^*, 0, 0)$, where $S_v^* = S_v^*(\xi)$ for all $\xi \in [-\tau, 0]$. Define

$$M_\partial := \{\phi \in \partial X_0 : Q^n(\phi) \in \partial X_0, \forall n \geq 0\}$$
$$= \{\phi \in \partial X_0 : \phi_i(0) = 0, i = 2, 3, 4, 5, 8, 9, 10, 11, 14, 15, 16, 20, 21\}.$$

For any given $\phi \in M_\partial$, we see that $Q^n(\phi) \to M$ as $n \to \infty$ by using the theory of internally chain transitive sets (see [39] (Theorems 1.2.1 and 1.2.2) and [42]). From the above discussion, it is clear that M is an isolated invariant set for Q in X, and $W^s(M) \cap X_0 = \varnothing$, where $W^s(M)$ is the stable set of M for Q. By the acyclicity theory on uniform persistence for maps (see [39] (Theorem 1.3.1 and Remark 1.3.1)), it follows that $Q : X \to X$ is uniformly persistent w.r.t. $(X_0, \partial X_0)$ where there exists $\kappa_0 > 0$ s.t.

$$\liminf_{n \to \infty} d(Q^n(\phi), \partial X_0) \geq \kappa_0, \forall \phi \in X_0.$$

As a result, $Q : X_0 \to X_0$ has a compact global attractor A_0 by [39] (Theorem 4.5). For any $\phi \in A_0$, we have $\phi_i(0) > 0$ for all $i = \{2,3,4,5,8,9,10,11,14,15,16,20,21\}$. Let $B_0 := \bigcup_{t \in [0,\omega]} Q(t)A_0$. Then $\phi_i(0) > 0$, $i = \{2,3,4,5,8,9,10,11,14,15,16,20,21\}$, for all $\phi \in B_0$. Furthermore, $B_0 \subseteq X_0$ and $\lim_{t \to \infty} d(Q(t)\phi, B_0) = 0$ for all $\phi \in X_0$. The attractiveness of B_0 completes the proof. □

Following the statements in [48] (Lemma 3.8), we get $\rho(P) = \rho(\bar{P})$. Using Lemma 2 and Theorem 1, we have the subsequent result.

Theorem 2. *The following statements are valid:*
1. *If $\mathcal{R}_0 < 1$, then the disease-free periodic solution E_0 defined by (6) is globally attractive for system (1) in X.*
2. *If $\mathcal{R}_0 > 1$, then system (1) admits a positive ω-periodic solution and there exists a positive constant $\kappa > 0$ such that any solution $u(t, \phi)$ of system (1) for all initial values $\phi \in X_0$ satisfies*

$$\liminf_{t \to \infty} \left(E_f(t,\phi), I_f^a(t,\phi), I_f^s(t,\phi), I_f^r(t,\phi), E_m(t,\phi), I_m^a(t,\phi), I_m^s(t,\phi), I_m^r(t,\phi), E_c(t,\phi), \right.$$
$$\left. I_c^a(t,\phi), I_c^s(t,\phi), E_v(t,\phi), I_v(t,\phi) \right)^T \geq (\kappa, \kappa, \kappa, \kappa, \kappa, \kappa, \kappa, \kappa, \kappa, \kappa, \kappa, \kappa, \kappa)^T.$$

3.2. Numerical Results

Figure 3a is in accordance with the analytical results noting that the disease-free equilibrium E_0 is globally asymptotically stable if $\mathcal{R}_0 < 1$. According to Theorem 1, Equation (1) is persistent w.r.t. the infective compartments if $\mathcal{R}_0 > 1$. Figure 3b indicates the disease persistence if $\mathcal{R}_0 > 1$.

3.2.1. Parameter Estimation for Colombia

By employing the method explained in Section 2.3, we fitted our system to symptomatically infected and microcephaly data in Colombia, 2015–17. Figure 2 shows the weekly confirmed ZIKV cases of the 2015–2017 outbreak and the weekly microcephaly cases of 2015–2017 from Colombia with parameter values are given in Table 2. Figure 4a depicts model (1) fitted to symptomatically infected data and Figure 4b illustrates model (1) fitted to microcephaly data from Colombia, showing a reasonably good fit.

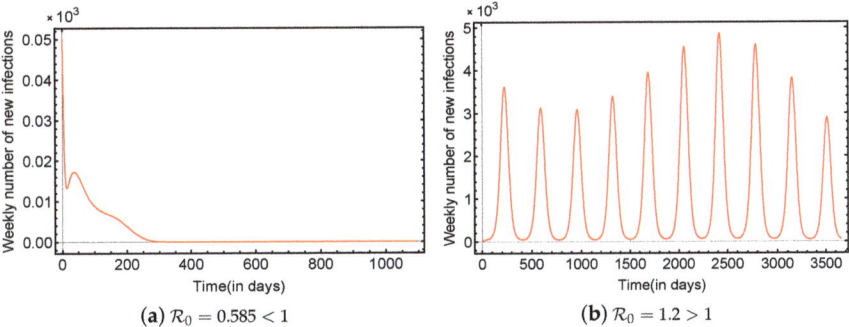

Figure 3. Weekly number of Zika new infections in (**a**) when $\mathcal{R}_0 = 0.585 < 1$, $\alpha_h = 0.112$, $\alpha_v = 1.2$ and $B_v = 41,400$, and in (**b**) when $\mathcal{R}_0 = 1.2 > 1$, $\alpha_h = 0.185$, $\alpha_v = 0.139$ and $B_v = 95,000$. The rest of the parameter values are given in Table 2.

Table 2. Parameters, ranges and fitted values of model (1) in the case of Colombia.

Parameter	Range	Value Symptomatically Infected	Value Microcephaly	Source
B_c	–	1826.81	1826.81	[49]
ζ	$\frac{1}{22 \times 365} - \frac{1}{14 \times 365}$	$\frac{1}{16.98 \times 365}$	$\frac{1}{18.68 \times 365}$	[23]
d	–	0.0000368	0.0000368	[49]
α	$\frac{1}{18 \times 365} - \frac{1}{12 \times 365}$	$\frac{1}{16.52 \times 365}$	$\frac{1}{17.56 \times 365}$	[23]
β	0.01–0.1	0.029	0.029	[14,24]
α_h	0.03–0.75	0.382	0.283	[50,51]
α_v	0.09–0.75	0.227	0.227	[50,51]
θ	0.75–0.9	0.822	0.853	[14,24,52]
κ_e	0.2–0.9	0.654	0.845	[14,24]
κ_a	0.2–0.8	0.505	0.509	[14,24]
κ_r	0.2–0.8	0.493	0.309	[14,24]
η_e	0.2–0.7	0.653	0.518	[14,24]
η_a	0.2–0.7	0.471	0.672	[14,24]
γ_a	0.05–0.4	0.2907	0.2907	[14,24]
γ_s	0.2–0.5	0.421	0.2268	[53]
γ_r	0.03–0.09	0.0652	0.0719	[54,55]
ν_h	0.1–0.5	0.35	0.209	[53]
ν_v	0.08–0.125	0.0911	0.115	[51,56]
B_v	500–100,000	18,000	51,047	Fitted
$1/\mu$	7–35	10.169	10.169	[51]
p	0.9–1	0.95	0.95	Fitted
a	1–10	1.8674	4.0325	Fitted
b	1–365	269.4	348.3	Fitted
τ	1–270	160	200	[31,32]

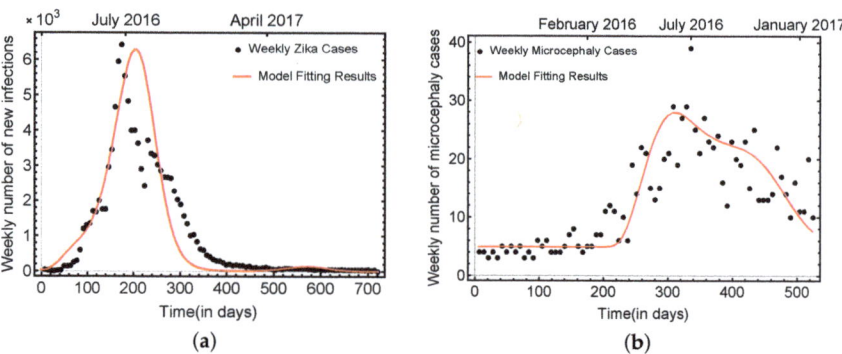

Figure 4. The model (1) fits Colombian data between 2015 and 2017, with parameter values shown in Table 2. (**a**) Number of symptomatically infected. (**b**) Number of microcephaly cases.

3.2.2. The Impact of Sexual Transmission

Our model (1) allows us to estimate the effect of sexual transmission on infectious cases. Figure 5 depicts the number of symptomatically infected individuals in Colombia and the number of symptomatically infected estimated by our model ignoring sexual transmission. The results suggest that sexual transmission, a phenomenon previously unknown in mosquito-borne diseases, increased the total number of cases by several hundred.

Utilizing our model (1), we compare the symptomatic cases in adult females and the microcephaly cases with the corresponding numbers without sexual transmission (see Figure 6). Moreover, we observe a noticeable increase in the number of symptomatic cases in adult females and microcephaly cases with sexual transmission compared to those without it. This indicates that sexual transmission is playing a crucial role in spreading the disease to this specific group of individuals. The results of our simulations suggest that sexual transmission is a significant contributor to the spread of the disease, and it should be taken into account in the development of effective control and prevention strategies. Using our model, we estimate that 9–18% of the total number of microcephaly cases in Colombia could be linked to Zika infection caused by sexual transmission.

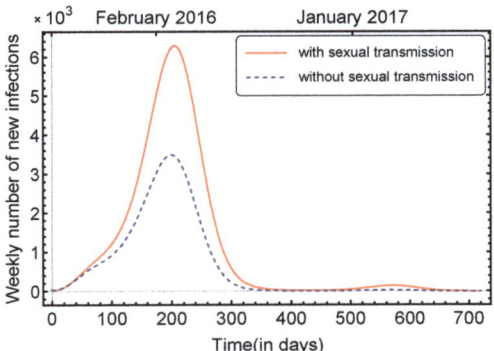

Figure 5. Number of the symptomatically infected and estimated number of symptomatically infected humans in the absence of sexual transmission.

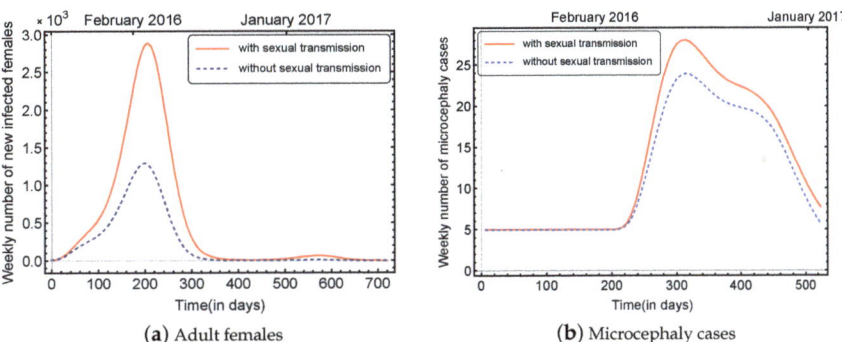

Figure 6. Number of symptomatically infected adult females and estimated number of symptomatically infected adult females without sexual transmission in (**a**), and in (**b**) the number of microcephaly cases and estimated number of microcephaly cases without sexual transmission.

3.2.3. Sensitivity Analysis and Reproduction Numbers

To evaluate the dependency of the microcephaly number of cases on the controllable parameters of the model, we perform sensitivity analysis utilizing PRCC analysis. In Figure 7, we demonstrate the comparison of the PRCC values obtained for the parameters $\alpha_h, \alpha_v, \beta, B_v$ and μ. The result of the sensitivity analysis suggests that the most crucial factors in the transmission of the disease, and consequently in the elevation of the number of microcephaly cases, are birth and death rates of mosquitoes. In comparison with these, the transmission rates, including sexual transmission, seem to have a somewhat smaller effect; however, they are still important factors in the transmission of Zika fever, as can also be seen from the simulations of the previous subsection. Based on the sensitivity analysis, we can assess that the most efficient ways to prevent Zika-related microcephaly cases are mosquito control and defence against mosquito bites.

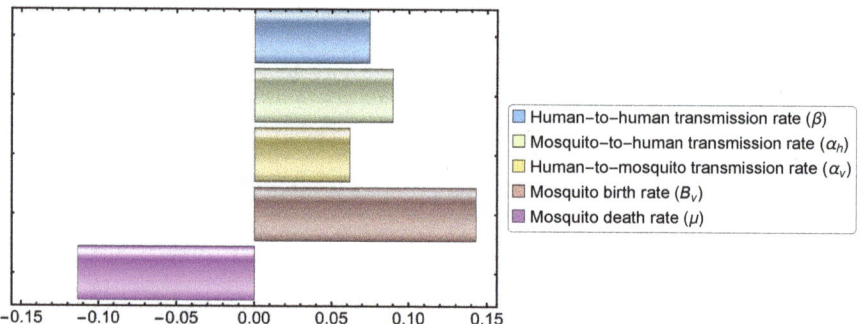

Figure 7. Partial rank correlation coefficients of the five parameters which can be subject to control measures. Parameters with positive (or negative) PRCC are positively (or negatively) correlated with the total number of cases.

Using the method established in [36], we obtained numerically $\mathcal{R}_0 \approx 0.974$ in the case of Colombia, as per the fact that the disease disappeared. We deduce a Formula (12) for the basic reproduction number, which provides the time-average reproduction number of the associated time-varying model (1) in any time point by substituting the values of the parameters into it, where the value of the time-dependent parameters is always taken at that given time point t. Moreover, Formula (11) provides us with the basic reproduction number of the associated time-constant model. To evaluate the dependence of the time-average basic reproduction number on the three controllable model parameters ($[\tilde{B}_v], [\tilde{\alpha}_h], [\tilde{\alpha}_v]$), the contour plots of the time-average reproduction number, $[\mathcal{R}_0]$, in terms of mosquito birth rate and mosquito-to-human transmission rate (left panel) and human-to-mosquito transmission rate (right panel), are shown in Figure 8, respectively. Similarly, the contour plots of the basic reproduction number, $\mathcal{R}_0^A$, of the autonomous model are given in Figure 9. The rest of the parameters are set as obtained in the fitting of symptomatically infected cases in Table 2. Figures 8 and 9 illustrate that the most significant measures to control the transmission of Zika involve decreasing mosquito birth rate, decreasing mosquito bites, personal bite surveillance and sexual contact protection.

Figure 10 shows the instantaneous reproduction number along with the number of symptomatically infected in Colombia, 2015–2017, showing that the number of infected individuals begins to decline when the instantaneous reproduction number goes below 1. The highest value of the instantaneous reproduction number is calculated to be about $\mathcal{R}_{inst} \approx 1.25$; this value can be contrasted with previous estimates. The authors in [16] estimated $\mathcal{R}_{inst} \approx 1.4$ for Brazil. Furthermore, the authors in [24] estimated $\mathcal{R}_{inst} \approx 1.47$ in Costa Rica, while in Suriname $\mathcal{R}_{inst} \approx 1.45$. These values are close to our results.

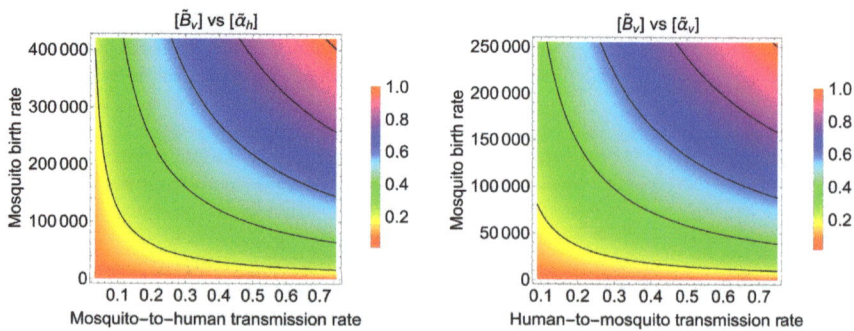

Figure 8. The contour plot of $[\mathcal{R}_0]$ as a function of $[\tilde{B}_v]$ and one of the three controllable parameters: mosquito-to-human transmission rate ($[\tilde{\alpha}_h]$) and human-to-mosquito transmission rate ($[\tilde{\alpha}_v]$).

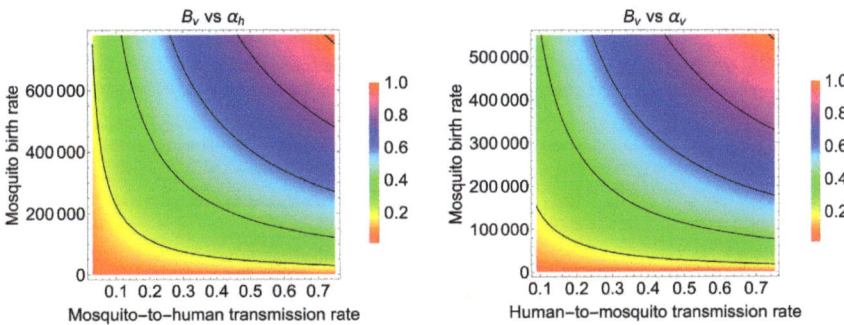

Figure 9. The contour plot of $\mathcal{R}_0^A$ as a function of B_v and one of the three controllable parameters: mosquito-to-human transmission rate (α_h) and human-to-mosquito transmission rate (α_v).

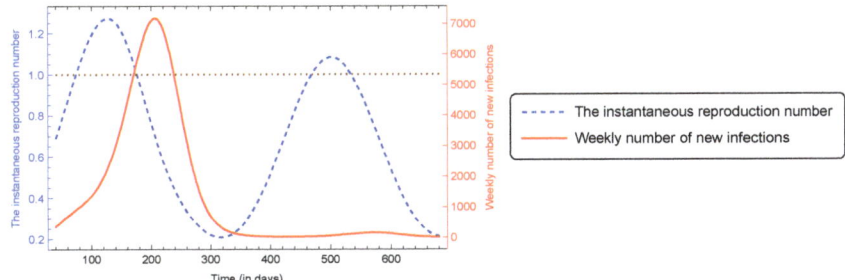

Figure 10. The instantaneous reproduction number and the number of symptomatically infected in Colombia, 2015–2017.

4. Discussion

We have developed a mathematical model for Zika virus disease transmission, with the particular aim of providing a better understanding of the effect on the most important health risk created by this disease, i.e., microcephaly. In our model, we tried to include most of the relevant characteristics of the Zika virus disease, namely, by improving our model given in [24], we consider both transmission ways (vectorial and sexual transmission), the role of asymptomatic carriers and time-dependent mosquito-related parameters due to the seasonality of weather. Our model also has its limitations: we have assumed an equal percentage of pregnant women in all female compartments, which might be different from reality. Furthermore, we have made the technical simplification of taking the time delay, τ, as a constant. Although periodic functions are a rather efficient tool to model the roughly periodic change of weather, they are, of course, unable to exactly describe the variance of weather. It is essential to acknowledge that the existence of a large number of parameters and broad intervals for their possible values makes it unlikely to identify a single set of parameters that precisely fits the data of the epidemic. The objective instead is to provide a credible estimate of the actual scenario and establish ranges for each parameter such that the true values have a high probability of falling within these intervals. This way, we can have a better understanding of the dynamics of the epidemic and make informed decisions accordingly.

We have established that the global dynamics of the system are described by the reproduction number: if $\mathcal{R}_0 < 1$, namely, we have shown global asymptotic stability of the disease-free periodic solution E_0, in this case, the disease goes extinct. If $\mathcal{R}_0 > 1$, the disease becomes endemic in the population. We also provided numerical simulations in accordance with these theoretical results (see Figure 3).

As an example of the application of the model, we fitted it to the number of Zika cases and the number of microcephaly cases in Colombia. Using the results of the fitting and partial rank correlation coefficients analysis, we tried to assess which phenomena are the main drivers of the increase in microcephaly cases. We have estimated the contribution of sexual transmission to the increase in the number of cases to find that about 9–18% of the microcephaly cases might be attributed to this sexual transmission, a novel phenomenon for mosquito-borne diseases. Our results indicate that the sexual transmission rate increases the number of infected adult females and consequently increases the risk of microcephaly due to vertical transmission.

The basic reproduction number of the time-periodic model, the instantaneous reproduction number and the time-dependent reproduction number were calculated. The results are consistent with the extinction of the ZIKV epidemic in Colombia. By calculating both the time-average reproduction number for the time-period model and the reproduction number of the time-constant model, we determine the dependency of the basic reproduction number on the model's controllable parameters. We obtain that mosquito birth and biting rates are the most significant factors in the transmission of Zika and the increase of microcephaly cases after the end of the outbreak in Colombia; however, the sexual transmission rate also has an important impact on the spread of the disease.

Based on our results, we may conclude that mosquito control, protection against mosquito bites and sexual contact protection during the pregnancy period are the most successful ways to prevent Zika-related microcephaly cases.

Author Contributions: Conceptualization, M.A.I. and A.D.; methodology, M.A.I. and A.D.; software, M.A.I. and A.D.; validation, M.A.I. and A.D.; formal analysis, M.A.I.; investigation, M.A.I. and A.D.; writing—original draft preparation, M.A.I. and A.D.; writing—review and editing, M.A.I. and A.D.; visualization, M.A.I. and A.D. All authors have read and agreed to the published version of the manuscript.

Funding: This research was supported by project TKP2021-NVA-09, implemented with the support provided by the Ministry of Innovation and Technology of Hungary from the National Research, Development and Innovation Fund, financed under the TKP2021-NVA funding scheme. M. A. Ibrahim was supported by project no. 129877 of the National Research, Development and Innovation Office of Hungary, financed under the KKP_19 funding scheme and by a fellowship from the Egyptian government in the long-term mission system. A. Dénes acknowledges the support of the National Laboratory for Health Security, RRF-2.3.1-21-2022-00006 and of projects no. 128363 and no. 125119 of the National Research, Development and Innovation Office of Hungary, financed under the PD_18 and SNN_17 funding schemes, respectively.

Institutional Review Board Statement: Not applicable.

Informed Consent Statement: Not applicable.

Data Availability Statement: Not applicable.

Conflicts of Interest: The authors declare no conflict of interest.

References

1. Petersen, L.R.; Jamieson, D.J.; Powers, A.M.; Honein, M.A. Zika virus. *N. Engl. J. Med.* **2016**, *374*, 1552–1563. [CrossRef] [PubMed]
2. Magalhaes, T.; Foy, B.D.; Marques, E.T.; Ebel, G.D.; Weger-Lucarelli, J. Mosquito-borne and sexual transmission of Zika virus: Recent developments and future directions. *Virus Res.* **2018**, *254*, 1–9. [CrossRef] [PubMed]
3. Mead, P.S.; Duggal, N.K.; Hook, S.A.; Delorey, M.; Fischer, M.; Olzenak McGuire, D.; Becksted, H.; Max, R.J.; Anishchenko, M.; Schwartz, A.M.; et al. Zika virus shedding in semen of symptomatic infected men. *N. Engl. J. Med.* **2018**, *378*, 1377–1385. [CrossRef] [PubMed]
4. Dick, G.W.; Kitchen, S.F.; Haddow, A.J. Zika virus (I). Isolations and serological specificity. *Trans. R. Soc. Trop. Med. Hyg.* **1952**, *46*, 509–520. [CrossRef] [PubMed]

5. World Health Organization. Zika Virus, Microcephaly and Guillain–Barré Syndrome. Situation Report. Available online: http://apps.who.int/iris/bitstream/handle/10665/204961/zikasitrep_7Apr2016_eng.pdf (accessed on 15 February 2023).
6. European Centre for Disease Prevention and Control. Zika Virus Epidemic in the Americas: Potential Association with Microcephaly and Guillain–Barré (2015) Rapid Risk Assessment. Available online: ecdc.europa.eu/en/publications/Publications/zika-virus-americas-association-with-microcephaly-rapid-risk-assessment.pdf (accessed on 15 February 2023).
7. Romero, S. Alarm Spreads in Brazil over a Virus and a Surge in Malformed Infants. Available online: https://www.nytimes.com/2015/12/31/world/americas/alarm-spreads-in-brazil-over-a-virus-and-a-surge-in-malformed-infants.html?smid=nytcore-ipad-share&smprod=nytcore-ipad&_r=1 (accessed on 15 February 2023).
8. Colombia National Institute of Health. Epidemiological Bulletin. EW 52 of 2016. Available online: http://www.ins.gov.co/boletinepidemiologico/Boletn%20Epidemiolgico/2016%20Bolet%C3%ADn%20epidemiol%C3%B3gico%20semana%2052%20-.pdf (accessed on 15 February 2023).
9. Colombia National Institute of Health. Epidemiological Bulletin. EW 33 of 2017. Available online: http://www.ins.gov.co/boletinepidemiologico/Boletn%20Epidemiolgico/2017%20Bolet%C3%ADn%20epidemiol%C3%B3gico%20semana%2033.pdf (accessed on 15 February 2023).
10. de Araújo, T.V.B.; Ximenes, R.A.A.; de Barros Miranda-Filho, D.; Souza, W.V.; Montarroyos, U.R.; de Melo, A.P.L.; Valongueiro, S.; de Albuquerque, M.F.P.M.; Braga, C.; Filho, S.P.B.; et al. Association between microcephaly, Zika virus infection, and other risk factors in Brazil: Final report of a case-control study. *Lancet Infect. Dis.* **2018**, *18*, 328–336. [PubMed]
11. Brady, O.J.; Osgood-Zimmerman, A.; Kassebaum, N.J.; Ray, S.E.; de Araújo, V.E.; da Nóbrega, A.A.; Frutuoso, L.C.; Lecca, R.C.; Stevens, A.; Zoca de Oliveira, B.; et al. The association between Zika virus infection and microcephaly in Brazil 2015–2017: An observational analysis of over 4 million births. *PLoS Med.* **2019**, *16*, e1002755. [CrossRef] [PubMed]
12. Méndez, N.; Oviedo-Pastrana, M.; Mattar, S.; Caicedo-Castro, I.; Arrieta, G. Zika virus disease, microcephaly and Guillain-Barré syndrome in Colombia: Epidemiological situation during 21 months of the Zika virus outbreak, 2015–2017. *Arch. Public Health* **2017**, *75*, 65 . [CrossRef]
13. Song, B.H.; Yun, S.I.; Woolley, M.; Lee, Y.M. Zika virus: History, epidemiology, transmission, and clinical presentation. *J. Neuroimmunol.* **2017**, *308*, 50–64. [CrossRef]
14. Gao, D.; Lou, Y.; He, D.; Porco, T.C.; Kuang, Y.; Chowell, G.; Ruan, S. Prevention and control of Zika as a mosquito-borne and sexually transmitted disease: A mathematical modeling analysis. *Sci. Rep.* **2016**, *6*, 28070. [CrossRef]
15. Sasmal, S.K.; Ghosh, I.; Huppert, A.; Chattopadhyay, J. Modeling the spread of Zika virus in a stage-structured population: Effect of sexual transmission. *Bull. Math. Biol.* **2018**, *80*, 3038–3067. [CrossRef]
16. Saad-Roy, C.; Ma, J.; Van den Driessche, P. The effect of sexual transmission on Zika virus dynamics. *J. Math. Biol.* **2018**, *77*, 1917–1941. [CrossRef]
17. Caminade, C.; Turner, J.; Metelmann, S.; Hesson, J.C.; Blagrove, M.S.; Solomon, T.; Morse, A.P.; Baylis, M. Global risk model for vector-borne transmission of Zika virus reveals the role of El Niño 2015. *Proc. Natl. Acad. Sci. USA* **2017**, *114*, 119–124. [CrossRef] [PubMed]
18. Mordecai, E.A.; Cohen, J.M.; Evans, M.V.; Gudapati, P.; Johnson, L.R.; Lippi, C.A.; Miazgowicz, K.; Murdock, C.C.; Rohr, J.R.; Ryan, S.J.; et al. Detecting the impact of temperature on transmission of Zika, dengue, and chikungunya using mechanistic models. *PLoS Neglected Trop. Dis.* **2017**, *11*, e0005568. [CrossRef] [PubMed]
19. Wang, W.; Zhou, M.; Zhang, T.; Feng, Z. Dynamics of a Zika virus transmission model with seasonality and periodic delays. *Commun. Nonlinear Sci. Numer. Simul.* **2023**, *116*, 106830. [CrossRef]
20. Zhu, G.; Shi, Y.; Li, Y.; Xiao, G.; Xiao, J.; Liu, Q. Model-Based Projection of Zika Infection Risk with Temperature Effect: A Case Study in Southeast Asia. *Bull. Math. Biol.* **2022**, *84*, 92. [CrossRef]
21. Suparit, P.; Wiratsudakul, A.; Modchang, C. A mathematical model for Zika virus transmission dynamics with a time-dependent mosquito biting rate. *Theor. Biol. Med Model.* **2018**, *15*, 11. [CrossRef]
22. Ibrahim, M.A.; Dénes, A. Threshold dynamics in a model for Zika virus disease with seasonality. *Bull. Math. Biol.* **2021**, *83*, 27. [CrossRef]
23. Agusto, F.B.; Bewick, S.; Fagan, W. Mathematical model of Zika virus with vertical transmission. *Infect. Dis. Model.* **2017**, *2*, 244–267. [CrossRef]
24. Dénes, A.; Ibrahim, M.A.; Oluoch, L.; Tekeli, M.; Tekeli, T. Impact of weather seasonality and sexual transmission on the spread of Zika fever. *Sci. Rep.* **2019**, *9*, 17055. [CrossRef]
25. Foy, B.D.; Kobylinski, K.C.; Foy, J.L.C.; Blitvich, B.J.; da Rosa, A.T.; Haddow, A.D.; Lanciotti, R.S.; Tesh, R.B. Probable non-vector-borne transmission of Zika virus, Colorado, USA. *Emerg. Infect. Dis.* **2011**, *17*, 880. [CrossRef]
26. Centers for Disease Control and Prevention, National Center on Birth Defects and Developmental Disabilities. Facts about Microcephaly. Available online: www.cdc.gov/ncbddd/birthdefects/microcephaly.html (accessed on 15 February 2023).
27. Bakary, T.; Boureima, S.; Sado, T. A mathematical model of malaria transmission in a periodic environment. *J. Biol. Dyn.* **2018**, *12*, 400–432. [CrossRef]

28. Instituto Nacional de Salud (Colombia). Boletín Epidemiológico. Bogotá, D. C.: 2017. Available online: http://www.ins.gov.co/boletin-epidemiologico/Paginas/default.aspx (accessed on 15 February 2023).
29. Ministerio de Salud y Protección Social—Instituto Nacional de Salud (Colombia) Circular Conjunta Externa N° 00000061 de 2015. Vigilancia de la Fiebre por Virus Zika (ZIKV) en su fase II Epidémica y Fortalecimiento de la Prevención de la Fiebre por Virus Zika en Grupos de Riesgo. Bogotá, D.C. 2017. Available online: http://www.ins.gov.co/Noticias/ZIKA/Circular%20Conj%20061%202015%20Fiebre%20zika.pdf (accessed on 15 February 2023).
30. Ministerio de Salud y Protección Social—Instituto Nacional de Salud (Colombia). Protocolo de Vigilancia en Salud Pública: Enfermedad por Virus Zika. Bogotá, D.C. 2017. Available online: http://bvs.minsa.gob.pe/local/MINSA/3449.pdf (accessed on 15 February 2023).
31. Pan American Health Organization. Countries and Territories with Autochthonous Transmission of Zika Virus in the Americas Reported in 2015–2017. Available online: https://www.paho.org/hq/index.php?option=com_Content&view=article&id=11603:countries-and-territories-with-autochthonous-transmission-of-zika-virus-in-the-americas-reported-in-2015-2017&Itemid=41696&lang=en (accessed on 15 February 2023).
32. Pan American Health Organization. Zika–Epidemiological Report Colombia. Available online: https://www.paho.org/hq/dmdocuments/2017/2017-phe-zika-situation-report-col.pdf (accessed on 15 February 2023).
33. McKay, M.D.; Beckman, R.J.; Conover, W.J. A comparison of three methods for selecting values of input variables in the analysis of output from a computer code. *Technometrics* **2000**, *42*, 55–61. [CrossRef]
34. Blower, S.M.; Dowlatabadi, H. Sensitivity and uncertainty analysis of complex models of disease transmission: An HIV model, as an example. *Int. Stat. Rev. Int. Stat.* **1994**, *62*, 229–243. [CrossRef]
35. Wang, W.; Zhao, X.Q. Threshold dynamics for compartmental epidemic models in periodic environments. *J. Dyn. Differ. Equations* **2008**, *20*, 699–717. [CrossRef]
36. Mitchell, C.; Kribs, C. A comparison of methods for calculating the basic reproductive number for periodic epidemic systems. *Bull. Math. Biol.* **2017**, *79*, 1846–1869. [CrossRef] [PubMed]
37. Hale, J.K.; Lunel, S.M.V. *Introduction to Functional Differential Equations*; Springer Science & Business Media: New York, NY, USA, 2013; Volume 99.
38. Smith, H.L. *Monotone Dynamical Systems: An Introduction to the Theory of Competitive and Cooperative Systems: An Introduction to the Theory of Competitive and Cooperative Systems*; American Mathematical Society: Providence, RI, USA, 2008.
39. Zhao, X.Q. Basic reproduction ratios for periodic compartmental models with time delay. *J. Dyn. Differ. Equations* **2017**, *29*, 67–82. [CrossRef]
40. Diekmann, O.; Heesterbeek, J.; Roberts, M.G. The construction of next-generation matrices for compartmental epidemic models. *J. R. Soc. Interface* **2010**, *7*, 873–885. [CrossRef]
41. Zhao, X.Q. *Dynamical Systems in Population Biology*; Springer: Cham, Switzerland, 2003; Volume 16.
42. Lou, Y.; Zhao, X.Q. A theoretical approach to understanding population dynamics with seasonal developmental durations. *J. Nonlinear Sci.* **2017**, *27*, 573–603. [CrossRef]
43. Walter, W. On strongly monotone flows. *Ann. Pol. Math.* **1997**, *66*, 269–274. [CrossRef]
44. Liang, X.; Zhao, X.Q. Asymptotic speeds of spread and traveling waves for monotone semiflows with applications. *Commun. Pure Appl. Math. J. Issued Courant Inst. Math. Sci.* **2007**, *60*, 1–40. [CrossRef]
45. Wang, X.; Zhao, X.Q. Dynamics of a time-delayed Lyme disease model with seasonality. *SIAM J. Appl. Dyn. Syst.* **2017**, *16*, 853–881. [CrossRef]
46. Wang, X.; Zhao, X.Q. A periodic vector-bias malaria model with incubation period. *SIAM J. Appl. Math.* **2017**, *77*, 181–201. [CrossRef]
47. Zhang, Y.; Zhao, X.Q. A reaction-diffusion Lyme disease model with seasonality. *SIAM J. Appl. Math.* **2013**, *73*, 2077–2099. [CrossRef]
48. Xu, D.; Zhao, X.Q. Dynamics in a periodic competitive model with stage structure. *J. Math. Anal. Appl.* **2005**, *311*, 417–438. [CrossRef]
49. World Health Organization. WHO Global Health Observatory Data Repository. Crude Birth and Death Rate. Data by Country. Available online: http://apps.who.int/gho/data/node.main.CBDR107?lang=en (accessed on 15 February 2023).
50. Chikaki, E.; Ishikawa, H. A dengue transmission model in Thailand considering sequential infections with all four serotypes. *J. Infect. Dev. Ctries.* **2009**, *3*, 711–722. [CrossRef] [PubMed]
51. Andraud, M.; Hens, N.; Marais, C.; Beutels, P. Dynamic epidemiological models for dengue transmission: A systematic review of structural approaches. *PLoS ONE* **2012**, *7*, e49085. [CrossRef] [PubMed]
52. Duffy, M.R.; Chen, T.H.; Hancock, W.T.; Powers, A.M.; Kool, J.L.; Lanciotti, R.S.; Pretrick, M.; Marfel, M.; Holzbauer, S.; Dubray, C.; et al. Zika virus outbreak on Yap Island, federated states of Micronesia. *N. Engl. J. Med.* **2009**, *360*, 2536–2543. [CrossRef] [PubMed]
53. Bearcroft, W. Zika virus infection experimentally induced in a human volunteer. *Trans. R. Soc. Trop. Med. Hyg.* **1956**, *50*, 442–448. [CrossRef]
54. Gourinat, A.C.; O'Connor, O.; Calvez, E.; Goarant, C.; Dupont-Rouzeyrol, M. Detection of Zika virus in urine. *Emerg. Infect. Dis.* **2015**, *21*, 84. [CrossRef]

55. Musso, D.; Roche, C.; Robin, E.; Nhan, T.; Teissier, A.; Cao-Lormeau, V.M. Potential sexual transmission of Zika virus. *Emerg. Infect. Dis.* **2015**, *21*, 359. [CrossRef]
56. Boorman, J.; Porterfield, J. A simple Technique for Infection of Mosquitoes with Viruses. Transmission of Zika Virus. *Trans. R. Soc. Trop. Med. Hyg.* **1956**, *50*, 238–242. [CrossRef] [PubMed]

Disclaimer/Publisher's Note: The statements, opinions and data contained in all publications are solely those of the individual author(s) and contributor(s) and not of MDPI and/or the editor(s). MDPI and/or the editor(s) disclaim responsibility for any injury to people or property resulting from any ideas, methods, instructions or products referred to in the content.

Article

An Inertial Subgradient Extragradient Method for Approximating Solutions to Equilibrium Problems in Hadamard Manifolds

Olawale Kazeem Oyewole and Simeon Reich *

Department of Mathematics, The Technion—Israel Institute of Technology, Haifa 32000, Israel
* Correspondence: sreich@technion.ac.il

Abstract: In this work, we are concerned with the iterative approximation of solutions to equilibrium problems in the framework of Hadamard manifolds. We introduce a subgradient extragradient type method with a self-adaptive step size. The use of a step size which is allowed to increase per iteration is to avoid the dependence of our method on the Lipschitz constant of the underlying operator as has been the case in recent articles in this direction. In general, operators satisfying weak monotonicity conditions seem to be more applicable in practice. By using inertial and viscosity techniques, we establish a convergence result for solving a pseudomonotone equilibrium problem under some appropriate conditions. As applications, we use our method to solve some theoretical optimization problems. Finally, we present some numerical illustrations in order to demonstrate the quantitative efficacy and superiority of our proposed method over a previous method present in the literature.

Keywords: equilibrium problem; extragradient method; Hadamard manifold; pseudomonotone operator; Riemannian manifold

MSC: 47H09; 49J25; 65K10; 90C25

Citation: Oyewole, O.K.; Reich, S. An Inertial Subgradient Extragradient Method for Approximating Solutions to Equilibrium Problems in Hadamard Manifolds. *Axioms* **2023**, *12*, 256. https://doi.org/10.3390/axioms12030256

Academic Editor: Behzad Djafari-Rouhani

Received: 12 December 2022
Revised: 22 February 2023
Accepted: 23 February 2023
Published: 1 March 2023

Copyright: © 2023 by the authors. Licensee MDPI, Basel, Switzerland. This article is an open access article distributed under the terms and conditions of the Creative Commons Attribution (CC BY) license (https://creativecommons.org/licenses/by/4.0/).

1. Introduction

The minimax inequality introduced in 1972 by Ky Fan [1], later renamed as Equilibrium Problem (EP), plays a major role in many fields and provides a unified framework for the study of variational inequalities, game theory, mathematical economics, fixed point theory and optimization theory. The use of the term equilibrium problem is credited to the 1994 paper by Blum and Oetlli [2], which followed an earlier article by Muu and Oetlli [3]. In the latter paper, three standard examples of the EP were given, viz: fixed point, convex minimization and variational inequality problems. The EP also includes as examples, convex differentiable optimization, complementarity, saddle point and Nash equilibrium problem [2,3]. Let $g : K \times K \to \mathbb{R}$ be a bifunction such that $g(x,x) = 0$ for all $x \in K$, where K is a nonempty subset of a topological space X. Then, the EP calls for finding a point $x \in K$ such that

$$g(x,y) \geq 0 \quad \forall y \in K.$$

The study of variational inequality, equilibrium and other related optimization problems has recently received considerable attention from researchers in the framework of Riemannian manifolds. Thus, methods and ideas have been extended from linear settings to this more general setting. These generalizations become necessary because of the advantages they bring forth. For example, nonconvex optimization problems can easily be transformed into problems of convex type by choosing a suitable Riemannian metric [4–6]. Another advantage of this extension is that constrained optimization problems can be viewed as unconstrained ones [4,6–8]. As a result, classical methods for solving optimization problems have been extended from linear frameworks to Riemannian manifolds. In 2012, Colao et al. [9] studied equilibrium problems on Hadamard manifolds in the following setting: Let K be a nonempty, closed and convex subset of an Hadamard manifold M and let $g : K \times K \to \mathbb{R}$ be a bifunction satisfying $g(x,x) = 0$ for all $x \in M$. An equilibrium problem (EP, for short) on a manifold consists of finding

$$x \in K \text{ such that } g(x,y) \geq 0 \quad \forall y \in K. \tag{1}$$

We denote by $Sol(g, K)$ the solution set of the EP (1). By developing and proving Fan's KKM Lemma, Colao et al. [9] studied the existence of solutions to the EP in the framework of Hadamard spaces. For many other studies and results in this direction, see, for example, [10–12].

The development of an effective iterative algorithm for approximating solutions to optimization problems is another interesting area of research in nonlinear analysis and optimization theory. Iterative approximation of solutions to equilibrium problems in any setting, whether linear or nonlinear, includes, for example, the use of the Extragradient Method (EGM) proposed by Korpelevich [13]. The EGM was initially used for solving saddle point problems. It was later adapted for solving variational inequality and then equilibrium problems. Inspired by the EGM and the perceived drawbacks of the method, Censor et al. [14] introduced the Subgradient Extragradient Method (SEGM), which has since been used for solving both variational and equilibrium problems. For solving EPs, Tran et al. [15] introduced an extragradient-like method for approximating solutions to pseudomonotone equilibrium problems. Using an alternative approach, Nguyen et al. [16] introduced a method for finding common solutions to fixed point and equilibrium problems, which is based on the extragradient method proposed in [15]. More recently, Rehman et al. [17] introduced an inertial subgradient extragradient algorithm for solving equilibrium problems. Using a viscosity approach, they proved a strong convergence theorem for an algorithm approximating solutions to EPs with pseudomonotone bifunctions. For more contributions regarding methods for solving EPs in linear settings, see, for example, [12,18–21].

We note that several of the methods discussed above have been extended to EPs on Hadamard manifolds. The first work of Colao et al. [9] was followed by those of Salahuddin [10] and Li et al. [21]. Neto et al. [22] extended the result of Nguyen et al. [16] to this setting by considering the following algorithm: Given $\lambda_n > 0$, compute

$$\begin{cases} y_n = \arg\min_{z \in M}\{g(x_n,z) + \frac{1}{2\lambda_n}d^2(x_n,z)\}, \\ x_{n+1} = \arg\min_{z \in M}\{g(y_n,z) + \frac{1}{2\lambda_n}d^2(x_n,z)\}, \end{cases}$$

where $0 \leq \lambda_n < \mu < \min\{\frac{1}{c_1}, \frac{1}{c_2}\}$, and $c_1 > 0$ and $c_2 > 0$ are the Lipschitz constants of the bifunction g. Fan et al. [23] proposed an explicit extragradient method for solving pseudomonotone equilibrium problems on Hadamard manifolds. Their method uses a variable step size which is monotonically decreasing. These authors proved a convergence theorem for their method and also established an R-linear convergence result for the proposed method. Very recently, Ali-Akbari [24] has introduced a subgradient extragradient algorithm for approximating solutions to EPs on Hadamard manifolds and has proved a convergence theorem for approximating solutions to pseudomonotone equilibrium problems. This theorem depends on the Lipschitz constants of the corresponding bifunctions.

The inertial technique finds crucial application in the construction of effective and accelerated algorithms in fixed point and optimization theory (see, for instance, [25,26]). In this method, the next iterate is determined by two preceding iterates (x_{n-1} and x_n) and an inertial parameter θ_n which controls the momentum $x_n - x_{n-1}$. For more recent developments regarding inertial algorithms, we refer the readers to [25,27,28] and to references therein. At this point, we recall that the viscosity method due to Moudafi [29] for a nonexpansive mapping S and a given strict contraction f over K is given by $x_0 \in K$ and $x_{n+1} = \beta_n f(x_n) + (1 - \beta_n)Sx_n$, $n \geq 0$, where the sequence $\{\beta_n\} \subset (0, 1)$ converges to zero. The viscosity method has also been adapted to the framework of Hadamard manifolds

(see [30,31]). In this setting, the sequence $\{x_n\}$ starting with an arbitrary point $x_0 \in K$ is given by
$$x_{n+1} = \exp_{f(x_n)}(1-\beta_n)\exp^{-1}_{f(x_n)} Sx_n \ \forall n \geq 0.$$

Motivated by the subgradient method of [14], the viscosity approach [30–32], and by Rehman et al. [17,27] and Ali-Akbari [24], we introduce an inertial subgradient extragradient algorithm for approximating solutions to equilibrium problems on Hadamard manifolds. Employing the viscosity technique, we propose an algorithm for approximating solutions to pseudomonotone equilibrium problems and establish a convergence theorem for it. The proposed algorithm uses a self-adaptive step length which is allowed to increase during the execution of the method. In this way, dependence of the method on the Lipschitz constants is dispensed with. In order to be more precise, we now highlight the following advantages of our result over previous results announced in this direction in the literature:

(i) The method in the present paper uses an adaptive step size which is allowed to increase from iteration to iteration unlike the method in [23,33], where the step sizes decrease monotonically, and the method of [17,24,27], which relies on the Lipschitz condition imposed on the bifunction. Since the relevant Lipschitz constants can be difficult to estimate, this affects the efficiency of the method;

(ii) We note that the sequence of control parameters of the viscosity step of our method is only required to be non-summable. This differs from [30,32], where an extra condition (that the difference between successive parameters be summable) is imposed;

(iii) The use of the inertial technique makes the convergence of our algorithm faster than that of the method used in [23,24];

(iv) Our result is obtained in the framework of an Hadamard manifold unlike the results of [15–17], which were obtained in real Hilbert spaces.

The rest of our paper is organized as follows: First, we recall some useful definitions and preliminary results in Section 2. In Section 3, we introduce our proposed method, state our main result and present its convergence analysis. Two applications are presented in Section 4. In Section 5, we present the results of a numerical experiment which shows the efficiency of our method. We provide some concluding remarks in Section 6.

2. Preliminaries

Let M be an m-dimensional manifold, let $x \in M$ and let T_xM be the tangent space of M at $x \in M$. We denote by $TM = \bigcup_{x \in M} T_xM$ the tangent bundle of M. An inner product $\mathcal{R}\langle \cdot, \cdot \rangle$ is called a Riemannian metric on M if $\langle \cdot, \cdot \rangle_x : T_xM \times T_xM \to \mathbb{R}$ is an inner product for all $x \in M$. The corresponding norm induced by the inner product $\mathcal{R}_x\langle \cdot, \cdot \rangle$ on T_xM is denoted by $\| \cdot \|_x$. We will drop the subscript x and adopt $\| \cdot \|$ for the corresponding norm induced by the inner product. A differentiable manifold M endowed with a Riemannian metric $\mathcal{R}\langle \cdot, \cdot \rangle$ is called a Riemannian manifold. In what follows, we denote the Riemannian metric $\mathcal{R}\langle \cdot, \cdot \rangle$ by $\langle \cdot, \cdot \rangle$ when no confusion arises. Given a piecewise smooth curve $\gamma : [a_1, a_2] \to M$ joining x to y (that is, $\gamma(a_1) = x$ and $\gamma(a_2) = y$), we define the length $l(\gamma)$ of γ by $l(\gamma) := \int_{a_1}^{a_2} \|\gamma'(t)\| dt$. The Riemannian distance $d(x,y)$ is the minimal length over the set of all such curves joining x to y. The metric topology induced by d coincides with the original topology on M. We denote by ∇ the Levi–Civita connection associated with the Riemannian metric [34].

Let γ be a smooth curve in M. A vector field X along γ is said to be parallel if $\nabla_{\gamma'}X = \mathbf{0}$, where $\mathbf{0}$ is the zero tangent vector. If γ' itself is parallel along γ, then we say that γ is a geodesic and $\|\gamma'\|$ is a constant. If $\|\gamma'\| = 1$, then the geodesic γ is said to be normalized. A geodesic joining x to y in M is called a minimizing geodesic if its length equals $d(x,y)$. A Riemannian manifold M equipped with a Riemannian distance d is a metric space (M,d). A Riemannian manifold M is said to be complete if for all $x \in M$, all geodesics emanating from x are defined for all $t \in \mathbb{R}$. The Hopf–Rinow theorem [34] posits that if M is complete, then any pair of points in M can be joined by a minimizing geodesic. Moreover, if (M,d) is a complete metric space, then every bounded and closed subset of M is compact. If M is a complete Riemannian manifold, then the exponential map $\exp_x : T_x M \to M$ at $x \in M$ is defined by

$$\exp_x v := \gamma_v(1, x) \quad \forall v \in T_x M,$$

where $\gamma_v(\cdot, x)$ is the geodesic starting from x with velocity v (that is, $\gamma_v(0, x) = x$ and $\gamma'_v(0, x) = v$). Then, for any t, we have $\exp_x tv = \gamma_v(t, x)$ and $\exp_x 0 = \gamma_v(0, x) = x$. Note that the mapping $\exp_x$ is differentiable on $T_x M$ for every $x \in M$. The exponential map $\exp_x$ has an inverse $\exp_x^{-1} : M \to T_x M$. For any $x, y \in M$, we have $d(x, y) = \| \exp_y^{-1} x \| = \| \exp_x^{-1} y \|$ (see [34] for more details). The parallel transport $P_{\gamma, \gamma(a_2), \gamma(a_1)} : T_{\gamma(a_1)} M \to T_{\gamma(a_2)} M$ on the tangent bundle TM along $\gamma : [a_1, a_2] \to \mathbb{R}$ with respect to ∇ is defined by

$$P_{\gamma, \gamma(a_2), \gamma(a_1)} v = F(\gamma(a_2)), \quad \forall a_1, a_2 \in \mathbb{R} \text{ and } v \in T_{\gamma(a_1)} M,$$

where F is the unique vector field such that $\nabla_{\gamma'(t)} F = \mathbf{0}$ for all $t \in [a_1, a_2]$ and $F(\gamma(a_1)) = v$. If γ is a minimizing geodesic joining x to y, then we write $P_{y,x}$ instead of $P_{\gamma, y, x}$. Note that for every $a_1, a_2, r, s \in \mathbb{R}$, we have

$$P_{\gamma(s), \gamma(r)} \circ P_{\gamma(r), \gamma(a_1)} = P_{\gamma(s), \gamma(a_1)} \text{ and } P_{\gamma(a_2), \gamma(a_1)}^{-1} = P_{\gamma(a_1), \gamma(a_2)}.$$

Additionally, $P_{\gamma(a_2), \gamma(a_1)}$ is an isometry from $T_{\gamma(a_1)} M$ to $T_{\gamma(a_2)} M$, that is, the parallel transport preserves the inner product

$$\langle P_{\gamma(a_2), \gamma(a_1)}(u), P_{\gamma(a_2), \gamma(a_1)}(v) \rangle_{\gamma(a_2)} = \langle u, v \rangle_{\gamma(a_1)}, \quad \forall u, v \in T_{\gamma(a_1)} M. \tag{2}$$

We now give some examples of Hadamard manifolds.
Space 1: Let $\mathbb{R}_{++} = \{x \in \mathbb{R} : x > 0\}$ and $M = (\mathbb{R}_{++}, \langle \cdot, \cdot \rangle)$ be the Riemannian manifold equipped with the inner product $\langle x, y \rangle = xy \ \forall x, y \in \mathbb{R}$. Since the sectional curvature of M is zero [35], M is an Hadamard manifold. Let $x, y \in M$ and $v \in T_x M$ with $\|v\|_2 = 1$. Then, $d(x, y) = |\ln x - \ln y|$, $\exp_x tv = xe^{\frac{vx}{t}}$, $t \in (0, +\infty)$, and $\exp_x^{-1} y = x \ln y - x \ln x$.
Space 2: Let $\mathbb{R}_{++}^m$ be the product space $\mathbb{R}_{++}^m := \{(x_1, x_2, \cdots, x_m) : x_i \in \mathbb{R}_{++}, i = 1, 2, \cdots, m\}$. Let $M = ((R)_+ +, \langle \cdot, \cdot \rangle)$ be the m-dimensional Hadamard manifold with the Riemannian metric $\langle p, q \rangle = p^T q$ and the distance $d(x, y) = |\ln \frac{x}{y}| = |\ln \sum_{i=1}^m \frac{x_i}{y_i}|$, where $x, y \in M$ with $x = \{x_i\}_{i=1}^m$ and $y = \{y_i\}_{i=1}^m$.
Space 3: See [36]. Let $M = \mathbb{H}^n$ be the n dimensional hyperbolic space of constant sectional curvature $k = -1$. The metric of $\mathbb{H}^n$ is induced from the Lorentz metric $\{\cdot, \cdot\}$ and will be denoted by the same symbol. Consider the following model for $\mathbb{H}^n$:

$$\mathbb{H}^n = \{\xi = \xi^1, \xi^2, \cdots, \xi^{n+1} \in \mathbb{R}^{n+1} : \xi^{n+1} > 0 \text{ and } \{\xi, \xi\} = -1\}.$$

Let $x, y \in \mathbb{H}^n$ and $v \in T_x \mathbb{H}^n$. Then, a normalized geodesic γ_x starting from $\gamma_x(0) = x$ is defined by

$$\gamma_x(t) = (\cosh t) x + (\sinh t) v.$$

We have $\{u, x\} = 0$ for all $u \in T_x \mathbb{H}^n$. Also,

$$\exp_x^{-1} y = \cosh^{-1}(\{x, y\}) \frac{y + \{x, y\} x}{\sqrt{\{x, y\}^2 - 1}}.$$

A subset $K \subset M$ is said to be convex if for any two points $x, y \in K$, the geodesic γ joining x to y is contained in K. That is, if $\gamma : [a_1, a_2] \to M$ is a geodesic such that $x = \gamma(a_1)$ and $y = \gamma(a_2)$, then $\gamma((1 - t) a_1 + t a_2) \in K$ for all $t \in [0, 1]$. A complete simply connected Riemannian manifold of non-positive sectional curvature is called an Hadamard manifold. We denote by M a finite dimensional Hadamard manifold. Henceforth, unless otherwise stated, we represent by K a nonempty, closed and convex subset of M.

We now collect some results and definitions which we shall use in the next section.

Proposition 1 ([34]). *Let $x \in M$. The exponential mapping $\exp_x : T_x M \to M$ is a diffeomorphism. For any two points $x, y \in M$, there exists a unique normalized geodesic joining x to y, which is given by*
$$\gamma(t) = \exp_x t \exp_x^{-1} y \quad \forall\, t \in [0,1].$$

A geodesic triangle $\Delta(p,q,r)$ of a Riemannian manifold M is a set containing three points p, q, r and three minimizing geodesics joining these points.

Proposition 2 ([34]). *Let $\Delta(p,q,r)$ be a geodesic triangle in M. Then,*
$$d^2(p,q) + d^2(q,r) - 2\langle \exp_q^{-1} p, \exp_q^{-1} r \rangle \leq d^2(r,q) \tag{3}$$

and
$$d^2(p,q) \leq \langle \exp_p^{-1} r, \exp_p^{-1} q \rangle + \langle \exp_q^{-1} r, \exp_q^{-1} p \rangle. \tag{4}$$

Moreover, if θ is the angle at p, then we have
$$\langle \exp_p^{-1} q, \exp_p^{-1} r \rangle = d(q,p) d(p,r) \cos\theta.$$

Also,
$$\| \exp_p^{-1} q \|^2 = \langle \exp_p^{-1} q, \exp_p^{-1} q \rangle = d^2(p,q).$$

For any $x \in M$ and $K \subset M$, there exists a unique point $y \in K$ such that $d(x,y) \leq d(x,z)$ for all $z \in K$. This unique point y is called the nearest point projection of x onto the closed and convex set K and is denoted $P_K(x)$.

Lemma 1 ([37]). *For any $x \in M$, there exists a unique nearest point projection $y = P_K(x)$. Furthermore, the following inequality holds:*
$$\langle \exp_y^{-1} x, \exp_y^{-1} z \rangle \leq 0 \quad \forall\, z \in K.$$

We call a mapping $f : M \to M$ a ψ-contraction if
$$d(f(x), f(y)) \leq \psi(d(x,y)) \quad \forall\, x, y \in M,$$

where $\psi : [0, +\infty) \to [0, +\infty)$ is a function satisfying the following two conditions:
(i) $\psi(s) < s$ for all $s > 0$;
(ii) ψ is continuous.

Remark 1. (a) $\psi(s) = \frac{s}{s+1}$ *for all $s \geq 0$ satisfies conditions (i) and (ii) above.*
(b) *If $\psi(s) = ks$ for all $s \geq 0$ and $k \in (0,1)$, then f is a ψ-contraction mapping with a Lipschitz constant k.*
(c) *Any ψ-contraction mapping is nonexpansive.*

Any ψ-contraction belongs to the class of mappings introduced by Boyd and Wong [38] who established the existence and uniqueness of a fixed point for mappings in this class in the framework of complete metric spaces.

The next lemma presents the relationship between triangles in $\mathbb{R}^2$ and geodesic triangles in Riemannian manifolds (see [39]).

Lemma 2 ([39]). *Let $\Delta(u_1, u_2, u_3)$ be a geodesic triangle in M. Then, there exists a triangle $\Delta(\bar{u}_1, \bar{u}_2, \bar{u}_3)$ corresponding to $\Delta(u_1, u_2, u_3)$, such that $d(u_i, u_{i+1}) = \|\bar{u}_i - \bar{u}_{i+1}\|$ with the indices taking modulo 3. This triangle is unique up to isometries of $\mathbb{R}^2$.*

The triangle $\Delta(\bar{u}_1, \bar{u}_2, \bar{u}_3)$ in Lemma 2 is called the comparison triangle for $\Delta(u_1, u_2, u_3) \subset M$. The points $\bar{u}_1, \bar{u}_2$ and $\bar{u}_3$ are called comparison points to the points u_1, u_2 and u_3 in M.

A function $h : M \to \mathbb{R}$ is said to be geodesic if for any geodesic $\gamma \in M$, the composition $h \circ \gamma : [u, v] \to \mathbb{R}$ is convex, that is,

$$h \circ \gamma(\lambda u + (1 - \lambda)v) \leq \lambda h \circ \gamma(u) + (1 - \lambda)h \circ \gamma(v), \ u, v \in \mathbb{R}, \lambda \in [0, 1].$$

The subdifferential of a function $h : M \to \mathbb{R}$ at a point $x \in M$ is given by

$$\partial h(x) := \{z \in T_x M : h(y) \geq h(x) + \langle z, \exp_x^{-1} y\rangle \ \forall y \in M\}.$$

The convex function h is called subdifferentiable at a point $x \in M$ if the set $\partial h(x)$ is nonempty. The elements of $\partial h(x)$ are called the subgradients of h at x. The set $\partial h(x)$ is closed and convex, and it is known to be nonempty if h is convex on M. We denote by $\partial_2 h$ the partial derivative of h at the second argument, that is, $\partial_2 h(x, \cdot)$ for all $x \in M$. The normal cone, denoted N_K, is defined at a point $x \in M$ by

$$N_K(x) := \{z \in T_x M : \langle z, \exp_x^{-1} y\rangle \leq 0 \ \forall y \in K\}.$$

Lemma 3 ([20]). *Let $x_0 \in M$ and $\{x_n\} \subset M$ be such that $x_n \to x_0$. Then, for any $y \in M$, we have $\exp_{x_n}^{-1} y \to \exp_{x_0}^{-1} y$ and $\exp_y^{-1} x_n \to \exp_y^{-1} x_0$;*

The following definitions can be found in [40]. Let K be a nonempty, closed and convex subset of M. A bifunction $g : M \times M \to \mathbb{R}$ is said to be

(i) Monotone on K if
$$g(x, y) + g(y, x) \leq 0 \ \forall x, y \in K;$$

(ii) Pseudomontone on K if
$$g(x, y) \geq 0 \Rightarrow g(y, x) \leq 0 \ \forall x, y \in K;$$

(iii) Lipschitz-type continuous if there exist constants $c_1 > 0$ and $c_2 > 0$, such that
$$g(x, y) + g(y, z) \geq g(x, z) - c_1 d^2(x, y) - c_2 d^2(y, z) \ \forall x, y, z \in K.$$

For solving EP (1), we make the following assumptions concerning g on K:

(A1) g is pseudomonotone on K and $g(x, x) = 0$ for all $x \in M$;
(A2) $g(\cdot, y)$ is upper semicontinuous for all $y \in M$;
(A3) $g(x, \cdot)$ is convex and subdifferentiable for all fixed $x \in M$;
(A4) g satisfies a Lipschitz-type condition on M.

The following propositions (see [41]) are very useful in our convergence analysis:

Proposition 3. *Let M be an Hadamard manifold and $d : M \times M :\to \mathbb{R}$ be the distance function. Then, the function d is convex with respect to the product Riemannian metric. In other words, given any pair of geodesics $\gamma_1 : [0, 1] \to M$ and $\gamma_2 : [0, 1] \to M$, then for all $t \in [0, 1]$, we have*

$$d(\gamma_1(t), \gamma_2(t)) \leq (1 - t)d(\gamma_1(0), \gamma_2(0)) + t d(\gamma_1(1), \gamma_2(1)).$$

In particular, for each $y \in M$, the function $d(\cdot, y) : M \to \mathbb{R}$ is a convex function.

Proposition 4. *Let M be an Hadamard manifold and $x \in M$. Let $\rho_x(y) = \frac{1}{2}d^2(x, y)$. Then, $\rho_x(y)$ is strictly convex and its gradient at y is given by*

$$\partial \rho_x(y) = -\exp_y^{-1} x.$$

Proposition 5. *Let K be a nonempty convex subset of an Hadamard manifold M and let $h : K \to \mathbb{R}$ be a proper, convex and lower semicontinuous function on K. Then, a point x solves the convex minimization problem*

$$\min_{x \in K} h(x)$$

if and only if $0 \in \partial h(x) + N_K(x)$.

Lemma 4 ([42]). *Let $u, v \in \mathbb{R}^n$ and $\lambda \in [0,1]$. Then, the following relations hold:*
(i) $\|\lambda u + (1-\lambda)v\|^2 = \lambda \|u\|^2 + (1-\lambda)\|v\|^2 - \lambda(1-\lambda)\|u-v\|^2$;
(ii) $\|u \pm v\|^2 = \|u\|^2 \pm 2\langle u, v \rangle + \|v\|^2$;
(iii) $\|u + v\|^2 \leq \|u\|^2 + 2\langle v, u+v \rangle$.

Lemma 5 ([43]). *Let $\{u_n\}$ be a sequence of non-negative real numbers, $\{\alpha_n\}$ be a sequence of real numbers in $(0,1)$ such that $\sum_{n=1}^{\infty} \alpha_n = \infty$ and $\{v_n\}$ be a sequence of real numbers. Assume that*

$$u_{n+1} \leq (1-\alpha_n)u_n + \alpha_n v_n \quad \forall\, n \geq 1.$$

If $\limsup_{k \to \infty} v_{n_k} \leq 0$ for every subsequence $\{u_{n_k}\}$ of $\{u_n\}$ satisfying the condition

$$\liminf_{k \to \infty}(u_{n_k+1} - u_{n_k}) \geq 0,$$

then $\lim_{n \to \infty} u_n = 0$.

3. Main Result

In this section, we first propose a convergent algorithm for approximating a solution to the EP (1) and then present its convergence analysis. Let $f : M \to M$ be a ψ-contraction where $\psi : [0, +\infty) \to [0, +\infty)$ is a continuous and increasing function satisfying $\psi(0) = 0$ and $\psi(s) < s$ for all $s > 0$. The solution set $Sol(g, K)$ is closed and convex [9,10]. We assume that $Sol(g, K)$ is nonempty.

Assume $\{\epsilon_n\}$ is a positive sequence such that $\epsilon_n = \circ(\beta_n)$, that is, $\lim_{n \to \infty} \frac{\epsilon_n}{\beta_n} = 0$, where β_n is a sequence in $(0,1)$ satisfying

(C1) $\lim_{n \to \infty} \beta_n = 0$ and $\sum_{n=1}^{\infty} \beta_n = \infty$.

Remark 2. *We observe that Algorithm 1 provides us with a self-adaptive method where the step length can increase from iteration to iteration unlike the monotone decreasing sequence of step lengths in [17]. By this construction, the dependence of the bifunction g on the Lipschitz constants is dispensed with.*

Algorithm 1: Inertial subgradient extragradient method for solving EP (ISEMEP)

Initialization: Choose $x_0, x_1 \in K$, $\lambda_1 > 0$, $\mu \in (0,1)$, a non-negative sequence of real numbers $\{\delta_n\}$ such that $\sum_{n=1}^{\infty} \delta_n < +\infty$ and $\theta > 0$.

Step 1: Given x_n, x_{n-1} and λ_n, choose θ_n such that $\theta_n \in [0, \bar{\theta}_n]$, where

$$\bar{\theta}_n = \begin{cases} \min\left\{\theta, \frac{\epsilon_n}{d(x_n, x_{n-1})}\right\}, & \text{if } x_n \neq x_{n-1}, \\ \theta, & \text{otherwise.} \end{cases}$$

Compute

$$\begin{cases} w_n = \exp_{x_n}(\theta_n \exp_{x_n}^{-1} x_{n-1}), \\ y_n = \arg\min_{y \in M}\left\{g(w_n, y) + \frac{1}{2\lambda_n} d^2(w_n, y)\right\}, \end{cases} \quad (5)$$

If $y_n = w_n$, then stop. Otherwise, go to the next step.

Step 2: Define the half-space T_n by

$$T_n := \{y \in M : \langle \exp_{y_n}^{-1} w_n - \lambda_n v_n, \exp_{y_n}^{-1} y \rangle \leq 0\}$$

with $v_n \in \partial_2 g(w_n, y_n)$ and compute

$$z_n = \arg\min_{y \in T_n}\left\{g(y_n, y) + \frac{1}{2\lambda_n} d^2(w_n, y)\right\}. \quad (6)$$

Step 3: Compute

$$x_{n+1} = \gamma_n(1-\beta_n) \quad \forall n \geq 0, \quad (7)$$

where $\gamma_n : [0,1] \to M$ is the geodesic joining $f(x_n)$ to z_n, that is, $\gamma_n(0) = f(x_n)$ and $\gamma_n(1) = z_n$ for all $n \geq 0$.

$$\lambda_{n+1} = \begin{cases} \min\left\{\lambda_n + \delta_n, \frac{\mu[d^2(y_n, w_n) + d^2(z_n, y_n)]}{2[g(w_n, z_n) - g(w_n, y_n) - g(y_n, z_n)]}\right\}, & g(w_n, z_n) - g(w_n, y_n) - g(y_n, z_n) > 0, \\ \lambda_n + \delta_n, & \text{otherwise.} \end{cases} \quad (8)$$

Set $n := n+1$ and return to **Step 1**.

Lemma 6. *Let $\{\lambda_n\}$ be the sequence given by (8). Then, $\lim_{n\to\infty} \lambda_n = \lambda$ with*

$$\min\left\{\frac{\mu}{2\max\{c_1, c_2\}}, \lambda_1\right\} \leq \lambda \leq \lambda_1 + \delta,$$

where $\delta = \sum_{n=0}^{\infty} \delta_n$.

Proof. Assume (A4) holds, then there exist c_1 and c_2 such that

$$g(w_n, z_n) - g(w_n, y_n) - g(y_n, z_n) \leq c_1 d^2(y_n, w_n) + c_2 d^2(z_n, y_n)$$
$$\leq \max\{c_1, c_2\}(d^2(y_n, w_n) + d^2(z_n, y_n)).$$

Thus,

$$\frac{\mu(d^2(y_n, w_n) + d^2(z_n, y_n))}{2(g(w_n, z_n) - g(w_n, y_n) - g(y_n, z_n))} \geq \frac{\mu}{2\max\{c_1, c_2\}}.$$

Using induction, we obtain

$$\min\left\{\frac{\mu}{2\max\{c_1,c_2\}}, \lambda_1\right\} \leq \lambda_n \leq \lambda_1 + \delta.$$

It is not difficult to show that $\lim_{n\to\infty} \lambda_n = \lambda$. Therefore, the convergence of $\{\lambda_n\}$ implies that

$$\min\left\{\frac{\mu}{2\max\{c_1,c_2\}}, \lambda_1\right\} \leq \lambda \leq \lambda_1 + \delta.$$

□

Lemma 7. *The sequence $\{x_n\}$ defined recursively by Algorithm 1 satisfies the inequality*

$$d^2(z_n, p) \leq d^2(w_n, p) - \left(1 - \frac{\mu\lambda_n}{\lambda_{n+1}}\right)[d^2(w_n, y_n) + d^2(y_n, z_n)].$$

Proof. Let $p \in Sol(g, K)$. Using the definition of z_n and Proposition 5, we find that

$$0 \in \partial_2\left\{g(y_n, y) + \frac{1}{2\lambda_n}d^2(w_n, y)\right\}(z_n) + N_{T_n}(z_n).$$

There exist $a_n \in \partial_2 g(y_n, z_n)$ and $b_n \in N_{T_n}(z_n)$ such that

$$\lambda_n a_n - \exp_{z_n}^{-1} w_n + b_n = 0.$$

Hence, for all $y \in T_n$, we obtain

$$\lambda_n \langle a_n, \exp_{y_n}^{-1} y\rangle = \langle \exp_{z_n}^{-1} w_n, \exp_{z_n}^{-1} y\rangle - \langle b_n, \exp_{z_n}^{-1} y\rangle.$$

Since $b_n \in N_{T_n}(z_n)$, we have $\langle b_n, \exp_{z_n}^{-1} y\rangle \leq 0$ for all $y \in T_n$. Therefore,

$$\langle \exp_{z_n}^{-1} w_n, \exp_{z_n}^{-1} y\rangle \leq \lambda_n \langle a_n, \exp_{z_n}^{-1} y\rangle \quad \forall y \in T_n. \tag{9}$$

From the definition of the subdifferential and the fact that $a_n \in \partial_2 g(y_n, z_n)$, it follows that

$$\langle a_n, \exp_{y_n}^{-1} y\rangle \leq g(y_n, y) - g(y_n, z_n) \quad \forall y \in M. \tag{10}$$

We obtain from (9) and (10) that

$$\langle \exp_{z_n}^{-1} w_n, \exp_{z_n}^{-1} y\rangle \leq \lambda_n(g(y_n, y) - g(y_n, z_n)) \quad \forall y \in T_n. \tag{11}$$

Let $y = p$ in (11). We have

$$\langle \exp_{z_n}^{-1} w_n, \exp_{z_n}^{-1} p\rangle \leq \lambda_n(g(y_n, p) - g(y_n, z_n)).$$

Since $p \in Sol(g, K)$, we have $g(p, y_n) \geq 0$. If follows from the pseudomonotonicity of g that $g(y_n, p) \leq 0$. Thus, we obtain

$$\langle \exp_{z_n}^{-1} w_n, \exp_{z_n}^{-1} p\rangle \leq -\lambda_n g(y_n, z_n). \tag{12}$$

It is easy to from (8), that

$$-g(y_n, z_n) \leq \frac{\mu}{2\lambda_{n+1}}d^2(y_n, w_n) + \frac{\mu}{2\lambda_{n+1}}d^2(y_n, z_n) - g(w_n, z_n) + g(w_n, y_n),$$

which implies, since $\lambda_n > 0$, that

$$-\lambda_n g(y_n, z_n) \leq \frac{\mu \lambda_n d^2(y_n, w_n)}{2\lambda_{n+1}} + \frac{\mu \lambda_n d^2(y_n, z_n)}{2\lambda_{n+1}} - \lambda_n [g(w_n, z_n) - g(w_n, y_n)]. \quad (13)$$

It follows from $z_n \in T_n$ that $\langle \exp_{y_n}^{-1} w_n - \lambda_n v_n, \exp_{y_n}^{-1} z_n \rangle \leq 0$, which implies that

$$\langle \exp_{y_n}^{-1} w_n, \exp_{y_n}^{-1} z_n \rangle \leq \lambda_n \langle v_n, \exp_{y_n}^{-1} z_n \rangle. \quad (14)$$

Since $v_n \in \partial_2 g(w_n, y_n)$, it follows from the definition of the subdifferential that

$$\langle v_n, \exp_{y_n}^{-1} y \rangle \leq g(w_n, y) - g(w_n, y_n).$$

Setting $y = z_n$ in the above inequality, we have

$$\langle v_n, \exp_{y_n}^{-1} z_n \rangle \leq g(w_n, z_n) - g(w_n, y_n).$$

Thus, it follows from above inequality and (14) that

$$\langle \exp_{y_n}^{-1} w_n, \exp_{y_n}^{-1} z_n \rangle \leq \lambda_n [g(w_n, z_n) - g(w_n, y_n)]. \quad (15)$$

Combining (12), (13) and (15), we obtain

$$\langle \exp_{z_n}^{-1} w_n, \exp_{y_n}^{-1} p \rangle \leq \frac{\mu \lambda_n d^2(y_n, w_n)}{2\lambda_{n+1}} + \frac{\mu \lambda_n d^2(z_n, y_n)}{2\lambda_{n+1}} - \langle \exp_{y_n}^{-1} w_n, \exp_{y_n}^{-1} z_n \rangle. \quad (16)$$

Using Equation (3) and Proposition 2, we obtain

$$d^2(w_n, z_n) + d^2(z_n, p) - d^2(w_n, p) \leq 2\langle \exp_{z_n}^{-1} w_n, \exp_{z_n}^{-1} p \rangle$$

and

$$-2\langle \exp_{y_n}^{-1} w_n, \exp_{y_n}^{-1} z_n \rangle \leq d^2(w_n, z_n) - d^2(w_n, y_n) - d^2(z_n, y_n).$$

Using this in (16), we obtain

$$d^2(w_n, z_n) + d^2(z_n, p) - d^2(w_n, p) \leq \frac{\mu \lambda_n d^2(w_n, y_n)}{\lambda_{n+1}} + \frac{\mu \lambda_n d^2(z_n, y_n)}{\lambda_{n+1}} + d^2(w_n, z_n) - d^2(w_n, y_n) - d^2(z_n, y_n).$$

Therefore, we have

$$d^2(z_n, p) \leq d^2(w_n, p) - \left(1 - \frac{\mu \lambda_n}{\lambda_{n+1}}\right)[d^2(w_n, y_n) + d^2(z_n, y_n)]. \quad (17)$$

□

Lemma 8. *Let $f : K \to K$ be a ψ-contraction and assume that*

$$0 < \kappa := \sup\left\{\frac{\psi(d(x_n, q))}{d(x_n, q)} : x_n \neq q, \; n \geq 0, \; q \in Sol(g, K)\right\} < 1.$$

Then, the sequence $\{x_n\}$ generated by Algorithm 1 is bounded.

Proof. Fix $n \geq 1$ and $p \in Sol(g, K)$, and consider the geodesic triangles $\Delta(w_n, x_n, p)$ and $\Delta(x_n, x_{n-1}, p)$ with the comparison triangles $\Delta(w'_n, x'_n, p')$ and $\Delta(x'_n, x'_{n-1}, p')$. Then, by Lemma 2, we have $d(w_n, p) = \|w'_n - p'\|$, $d(x_n, p) = \|x'_n - p'\|$ and $d(x_n, x_{n-1}) =$

$\|x'_n - x'_{n-1}\|$. Recall from Algorithm 1 that $w_n = \exp_{x_n} \theta_n \exp^{-1}_{x_n} x_{n-1}$. The comparison point of w_n is $w'_n = x'_n + \theta_n(x'_{n-1} - x'_n)$. Thus, we obtain

$$\begin{aligned} d(w_n, p) &= \|w'_n - p'\| \\ &= \|x'_n + \theta_n(x'_{n-1} - x'_n) - p'\| \\ &\leq \|x'_n - p'\| + \theta_n\|x'_n - x'_{n-1}\| \\ &= \|x'_n - p'\| + \beta_n \cdot \frac{\theta_n}{\beta_n}\|x'_n - x'_{n-1}\|. \end{aligned} \quad (18)$$

Since $\frac{\theta_n}{\beta_n}\|x'_n - x'_{n-1}\| = \frac{\theta_n}{\beta_n}d(x_n, x_{n-1}) \to 0$ as $n \to \infty$, there exists a constant $M_1 > 0$ such that $\frac{\theta_n}{\beta_n}d(x_n, x_{n-1}) = \frac{\theta_n}{\beta_n}\|x'_n - x'_{n-1}\| \leq M_1 \ \forall n \geq 1$. Hence, we obtain

$$d(w_n, p) \leq d(x_n, p) + \beta_n M_1. \quad (19)$$

It is not difficult to see that

$$d^2(w_n, p) \leq d^2(x_n, p) + 2\theta_n d(x_n, p)d(x_n, x_{n-1}) + \theta_n^2 d^2(x_n, x_{n-1}). \quad (20)$$

Next, using the definition of x_{n+1}, the convexity of the Riemannian distance and (17), we see that

$$\begin{aligned} d(x_{n+1}, p) &= d(\gamma_n(1 - \beta_n), p) \\ &\leq \beta_n d(\gamma_n(0), p) + (1 - \beta_n)d(\gamma_n(1), p) \\ &= \beta_n d(f(x_n), p) + (1 - \beta_n)d(z_n, p) \\ &\leq \beta_n(d(f(x_n), f(p)) + d(f(p), p)) + (1 - \beta_n)d(w_n, p) \\ &\leq \beta_n \psi(d(x_n, p)) + \beta_n d(f(p), p) + (1 - \beta_n)d(w_n, p). \end{aligned}$$

Since $0 < \kappa = \sup\{\frac{\psi(d(x_n,q))}{d(x_n,q)} : x_n \neq q, \ n \geq 0, \ q \in Sol(g, K)\} < 1$, we find that

$$\begin{aligned} d(x_{n+1}, p) &\leq \beta_n \kappa d(x_n, p) + (1 - \beta_n)d(w_n, p) + \beta_n d(f(p), p) \\ &\leq \beta_n \kappa d(x_n, p) + (1 - \beta_n)[d(x_n, p) + \beta_n M_1] + \beta_n d(f(p), p) \\ &= (1 - \beta_n(1 - \kappa))d(x_n, p) + \beta_n(1 - \beta_n)M_1 + \beta_n d(f(p), p) \\ &\leq \max\left\{d(x_n, p), \frac{M_1 + d(f(p), p)}{1 - \kappa}\right\} \\ &\quad \vdots \\ &\leq \max\left\{d(x_0, p), \frac{M_1 + d(f(p), p)}{1 - \kappa}\right\}. \end{aligned} \quad (21)$$

$$(22)$$

Hence, the sequence $\{x_n\}$ is bounded. Consequently, the sequences $\{w_n\}$, $\{y_n\}$ and $\{z_n\}$ are bounded too. □

Theorem 1. *Let $f : K \to K$ be a ψ-contraction and assume conditions (A1)–(A4) hold. If $0 < \kappa = \sup\{\frac{\psi(d(x_n,q))}{d(x_n,q)} : x_n \neq q, \ n \geq 0, \ q \in Sol(g, K)\} < 1$, then the sequence $\{x_n\}$ generated by Algorithm 1 converges to a point $p \in Sol(g, K)$, where $p = P_{Sol(g,K)}f(p)$ and $P_{Sol(g,K)}$ is the nearest point projection of K onto $Sol(g, K)$.*

Proof. Let $p \in Sol(g, K)$ satisfy $p = P_{Sol(g,K)}f(p)$. Note that this fixed point equation has a unique solution by the Boyd–Wong fixed point theorem [38]. Fix $n \geq 1$ and let $w = f(x_n)$, $z = z_n$ and $y = f(p)$. Consider the following geodesic triangles with their respective comparison triangles in $\mathbb{R}^2$: $\Delta(w, z, p)$ and $\Delta(w', z', p')$, $\Delta(y, z, w)$ and $\Delta(y', z', w')$, $\Delta(y, z, p)$

and $\Delta(y', z', p')$. By Lemma 2, we have $d(w, z) = \|w' - z'\|$, $d(w, y) = \|w' - y'\|$, $d(w, p) = \|w' - p'\|$, $d(z, y) = \|z' - y'\|$ and $d(y, p) = \|y' - p'\|$. From the definition of x_{n+1}, we have

$$x_{n+1} = \exp_w(1 - \beta_n) \exp_w^{-1} z.$$

The comparison point of x_{n+1} in $\mathbb{R}^2$ is $x'_{n+1} = \beta_n w' + (1 - \beta_n) z'$. Let α and α' denote the angles at p and p' in the triangles $\Delta(y, x_{n+1}, p)$ and $\Delta(y', x'_{n+1}, p')$, respectively. Then, we have $\alpha \leq \alpha'$ and $\cos \alpha' \leq \cos \alpha$. Using Lemma 4 and the property of f, we obtain

$$\begin{aligned} d^2(x_{n+1}, p) &\leq \|x'_{n+1} - p'\|^2 \\ &= \|\beta_n(w' - p') + (1 - \beta_n)(y' - p')\|^2 \\ &\leq \|\beta_n(w' - y') + (1 - \beta_n)(z' - p')\|^2 + 2\beta_n \langle x'_{n+1} - p', y' - p' \rangle \\ &\leq (1 - \beta_n)\|z' - p'\|^2 + \beta_n \|w' - y'\|^2 + 2\beta_n \|x'_{n+1} - p'\| \|y' - p'\| \cos \alpha' \\ &\leq (1 - \beta_n) d^2(z, p) + \beta_n d^2(w, y) + 2\beta_n d(x_{n+1}, p) d(y, p) \cos \alpha \\ &= (1 - \beta_n) d^2(z_n, p) + \beta_n d^2(f(x_n), f(p)) + 2\beta_n d(x_{n+1}, p) d(f(p), p) \cos \alpha. \end{aligned}$$

Since $d(x_{n+1}, p) d(f(p), p) \cos \alpha = \langle \exp_p^{-1} f(p), \exp_p^{-1} x_{n+1} \rangle$ and $0 < \kappa = \sup\{\frac{\psi(d(x_n, q))}{d(x_n, q)} : x_n \neq q, n \geq 0, q \in \text{Sol}(g, K)\} < 1$, using (20), we obtain

$$\begin{aligned} d^2(x_{n+1}, p) &\leq (1 - \beta_n) d^2(z_n, p) + \beta_n \psi(d^2(x_n, p)) + 2\beta_n \langle \exp_p^{-1} f(p), \exp_p^{-1} x_{n+1} \rangle \\ &\leq (1 - \beta_n) d^2(w_n, p) - (1 - \beta_n)\left(1 - \frac{\mu \lambda_n}{\lambda_{n+1}}\right)[d^2(y_n, w_n) + d^2(z_n, y_n)] + \beta_n \psi(d^2(x_n, p)) \\ &\quad + 2\beta_n \langle \exp_p^{-1} f(p), \exp_p^{-1} x_{n+1} \rangle \\ &= [1 - \beta_n(1 - \kappa)] d^2(x_n, p) + \beta_n(1 - \kappa) b_n - (1 - \beta_n)\left(1 - \frac{\mu \lambda_n}{\lambda_{n+1}}\right)[d^2(y_n, w_n) + d^2(z_n, y_n)], \end{aligned} \quad (23)$$

where

$$b_n = \frac{1}{1 - \kappa}\left(2 \langle \exp_p^{-1} f(p), \exp_p^{-1} x_{n+1} \rangle + \frac{2\theta_n}{\beta_n} d(x_n, p) d(x_n, x_{n-1}) + \frac{\theta_n^2}{\beta_n} d^2(x_n, x_{n-1})\right).$$

It follows from (23) that

$$(1 - \beta_n)\left(1 - \frac{\mu \lambda_n}{\lambda_{n+1}}\right)[d^2(y_n, w_n) + d^2(z_n, y_n)] \leq d^2(x_n, p) - d^2(x_{n+1}, p) + \beta_n(1 - \kappa)M', \quad (24)$$

where $M' = \sup_{n \in \mathbb{N}} b_n$. We claim that $d(x_n, p) \to 0$ as $n \to \infty$. To prove this, set $a_n = d(x_n, p)$ and $d_n = \beta_n(1 - \kappa)$. It is easy to see from (23) that the sequence $\{a_n\}$ satisfies

$$a_{n+1} \leq (1 - d_n) a_n + d_n b_n. \quad (25)$$

Next, we claim that $\limsup_{k \to \infty} b_{n_k} \leq 0$ whenever there exists a subsequence $\{a_{n_k}\}$ of $\{a_n\}$ satisfying

$$\liminf_{k \to \infty} (a_{n_k+1} - a_{n_k}) \geq 0.$$

To prove this, assume the existence of such a subsequence $\{a_{n_k}\}$. Then, by using (24), we have

$$\begin{aligned} \limsup_{k \to \infty}(1 - \beta_{n_k})\left(1 - \frac{\mu \lambda_{n_k}}{\lambda_{n_k+1}}\right)[d^2(y_{n_k}, w_{n_k}) + d^2(z_{n_k}, y_{n_k})] &\leq \limsup_{k \to \infty}(a_{n_k} - a_{n_k+1}) + (1 - \kappa) M' \lim_{k \to \infty} \beta_{n_k} \\ &= -\liminf_{k \to \infty}(a_{n_k+1} - a_{n_k}) \\ &\leq 0. \end{aligned}$$

Note that $\lambda_n \to \lambda$ as $n \to \infty$ and that $\mu \in (0,1)$. Hence, there exists $N \geq 0$ such that for all $n \geq N$, $0 < \frac{\mu \lambda_n}{\lambda_{n+1}} < 1$. That is, $\lim_{n \to \infty} \left(1 - \frac{\mu \lambda_n}{\lambda_{n+1}}\right) = 1 - \mu > 0$.
This, in its turn, implies that

$$\lim_{k \to \infty} d(y_{n_k}, w_{n_k}) = 0 = \lim_{k \to \infty} d(z_{n_k}, y_{n_k}). \tag{26}$$

By replacing p with x_{n_k} in (18), it is not difficult to see that

$$\lim_{k \to \infty} d(w_{n_k}, x_{n_k}) \leq \lim_{k \to \infty} \beta_{n_k} \cdot \frac{\theta_{n_k}}{\beta_{n_k}} \|x'_{n_k} - x'_{n_k-1}\|$$
$$= \lim_{k \to \infty} \beta_{n_k} \cdot \frac{\theta_{n_k}}{\beta_{n_k}} d(x_{n_k}, x_{n_k-1})$$
$$= 0. \tag{27}$$

Using the triangle inequality, we obtain

$$d(y_{n_k}, x_{n_k}) \leq d(y_{n_k}, w_{n_k}) + d(w_{n_k}, x_{n_k}),$$
$$d(z_{n_k}, x_{n_k}) \leq d(z_{n_k}, y_{n_k}) + d(y_{n_k}, x_{n_k}).$$

Using (26) and (27), we obtain

$$d(y_{n_k}, x_{n_k}), \ d(z_{n_k}, x_{n_k}) \to 0 \text{ as } k \to \infty. \tag{28}$$

By employing the convexity of the Riemannian distance, we have

$$d(x_{n+1}, z_n) = d(\gamma_n(1 - \beta_n), z_n)$$
$$\leq \beta_n d(\gamma_n(0), z_n) + (1 - \beta_n) d(\gamma_n(1), z_n)$$
$$\leq \beta_n d(f(x_n), z_n) + (1 - \beta_n) d(z_n, z_n)$$
$$\leq \beta_n d(f(x_n), z_n). \tag{29}$$

Thus, it follows from (C1) that

$$\lim_{k \to \infty} d(x_{n_k+1}, z_{n_k}) = 0.$$

When combined with (28), we obtain

$$\lim_{k \to \infty} d(x_{n_k+1}, x_{n_k}) = 0. \tag{30}$$

Now, we claim that $\limsup_{k \to \infty} b_{n_k} \leq 0$. To see this, we only need to show that

$$\limsup_{k \to \infty} \langle \exp_p^{-1} f(p), \exp_p^{-1} x_{n_k+1} \rangle \leq 0.$$

Since $\{x_{n_k}\}$ is bounded, there exists a subsequence $\{x_{n_{k_j}}\}$ of $\{x_{n_k}\}$ which converges to $q \in M$ such that

$$\lim_{j \to \infty} \langle \exp_p^{-1} f(p), \exp_p^{-1} x_{n_{k_j}} \rangle = \limsup_{k \to \infty} \langle \exp_p^{-1} f(p), \exp_p^{-1} x_{n_k} \rangle$$
$$= \langle \exp_p^{-1} f(p), \exp_p^{-1} q \rangle. \tag{31}$$

Since $x_{n_{k_j}} \to q$, it follows from (28) that $y_{n_{k_j}}, z_{n_{k_j}} \to q$. Using (11), we see that

$$\lambda_n g(y_n, y) - \lambda_n g(y_n, z_n) \geq \langle \exp_{z_n}^{-1} w_n, \exp_{z_n}^{-1} y \rangle \quad \forall y \in T_n,$$

which implies, in view of (13), that

$$\lambda_n g(y_n, y) \geq \lambda_n g(y_n, z_n) + \langle \exp_{z_n}^{-1} w_n, \exp_{z_n}^{-1} y \rangle$$
$$\geq -\frac{\mu \lambda_n}{2\lambda_{n+1}} \left(d^2(y_n, w_n) + d^2(z_n, y_n) \right) + \lambda_n (g(w_n, z_n) - g(w_n, y_n)) + \langle \exp_{z_n}^{-1} w_n, \exp_{z_n}^{-1} y \rangle.$$

Using (15), we obtain

$$\lambda_{n_k} g(y_{n_k}, y) \geq -\frac{\mu \lambda_{n_k}}{2\lambda_{n_k+1}} \left(d^2(y_{n_k}, w_{n_k}) + d^2(z_{n_k}, y_{n_k}) \right) + \langle \exp_{z_{n_k}}^{-1} w_{n_k}, \exp_{z_{n_k}}^{-1} y \rangle + \langle \exp_{y_{n_k}}^{-1} w_{n_k}, \exp_{y_{n_k}}^{-1} z_{n_k} \rangle. \tag{32}$$

Passing to the limit in (32) with n_k replaced by n_{k_j}, and using $\lambda_n \to \lambda > 0$, condition (A2), Lemma 3 and $y_{n_{k_j}} \to q$, we find that

$$g(q, y) \geq \limsup_{j \to \infty} g(y_{n_{k_j}}, y) \geq 0 \quad \forall y \in T_n.$$

Since $K \subset T_n$, we see that $g(q, y) \geq 0 \quad \forall y \in K$, which implies that $q \in Sol(g, K)$. Finally, from $p = P_{Sol(g,K)} f(p)$, (30), (31) and Lemma 1, it follows that

$$\lim_{j \to \infty} \langle \exp_p^{-1} f(p), \exp_p^{-1} x_{n_{k_j}+1} \rangle = \limsup_{k \to \infty} \langle \exp_p^{-1} f(p), \exp_p^{-1} x_{n_k+1} \rangle$$
$$= \langle \exp_p^{-1} f(p), \exp_p^{-1} q \rangle$$
$$\leq 0.$$

Hence, we conclude by applying Lemma 5 to (25) that the sequence $\{x_n\}$ converges to $p \in Sol(g, K)$, as asserted. □

4. Applications

In this section, we apply our main result to some theoretical optimization problems.

4.1. An Application to Solving Variational Inequality Problems

Suppose

$$g(x, y) = \begin{cases} \langle Gx, \exp_x^{-1} y \rangle, & \text{if } x, y \in K, \\ +\infty, & \text{otherwise,} \end{cases}$$

where $G : K \to M$ is a mapping. Then, the equilibrium problem (1) concurs with the following variational inequality (VIP) (see [44]):

$$\text{Find } x \in K \text{ such that } \langle Gx, \exp_x^{-1} y \rangle \geq 0 \quad \forall y \in K. \tag{33}$$

We denote the set of solutions of VIP (33) as $VIP(G, K)$. The mapping $G : K \to M$ is said to be pseudomonotone if

$$\langle Gx, \exp_x^{-1} y \rangle \geq 0 \Rightarrow \langle Gy, \exp_x^{-1} y \rangle \geq 0, \ x, y \in K.$$

Assume that the function G satisfies the following conditions:

(V1) The function G is pseudomonotone on K with $VIP(G, K) \neq \emptyset$;
(V2) G is L-Lipschitz continous, that is,

$$\|P_{y,x} Gx - Gy\| \leq \|x - y\|, \ x, y \in K,$$

where $P_{y,x}$ is a parallel transport (see [7,45]);
(V3) $\limsup_{n \to \infty} \langle Gx_n, \exp_{x_n}^{-1} y \rangle \leq \langle Gp, \exp_p^{-1} y \rangle$ for every $y \in K$ and $\{x_n\} \subset K$ such that $x_n \to p$.

By replacing the proximal term $\arg\min_{y \in M}\{g(x,y) + \frac{1}{2\lambda_n}d^2(x,y)\}$ with $P_K(\exp_x(-\lambda_n G(x)))$, where P_K is the metric projection of M onto K in Algorithm 1, we have the following method for approximating a point in $VIP(G,K)$:

In this setting, we have the following convergence theorem for approximating a solution to the VIP (33).

Theorem 2. *Let $f : K \to K$ be a ψ-contraction and $G : K \to M$ be a pseudomonotone operator satisfying conditions V1–V3. If $0 < \kappa = \sup\{\frac{\psi(d(x_n,q))}{d(x_n,q)} : x_n \neq q, n \geq 0, q \in VIP(G,K)\} < 1$, then the sequence $\{x_n\}$ generated by Algorithm 2 converges to an element $p \in VIP(G,K)$ which satisfies $p = P_{VIP(G,K)}f(p)$.*

Algorithm 2: Inertial subgradient extragradient method for solving VIP(ISEMVIP)

Initialization: Choose $x_0, x_1 \in K$, $\lambda_1 > 0$, $\mu \in (0,1)$, a non-negative sequence of real numbers $\{\delta_n\}$ such that $\sum_{n=0}^{\infty} \delta_n < +\infty$ and $\theta > 0$.

Step 1: Given x_n, x_{n-1} and λ_n, choose θ_n such that $\theta_n \in [0, \bar{\theta}_n]$, where

$$\bar{\theta}_n = \begin{cases} \min\left\{\theta, \frac{\epsilon_n}{d(x_n, x_{n-1})}\right\}, & \text{if } x_n \neq x_{n-1}, \\ \theta, & \text{otherwise.} \end{cases}$$

Compute

$$\begin{cases} w_n = \exp_{x_n}(\theta_n \exp_{x_n}^{-1} x_{n-1}), \\ y_n = P_K(\exp_{w_n}(-\lambda_n G(w_n))). \end{cases} \tag{34}$$

If $y_n = w_n$, then stop. Otherwise, go to the next step.

Step 2: Compute $v_n = Gw_n$ and define the half-space T_n by

$$T_n := \{y \in M : \langle \exp_{y_n}^{-1} w_n - \lambda_n v_n, \exp_{y_n}^{-1} y \rangle \leq 0\}$$

with $v_n \in \partial_2 g(w_n, y_n)$ and compute

$$z_n = P_{T_n}(\exp_{w_n}(-\lambda_n G(w_n))). \tag{35}$$

Step 3: *Compute*

$$x_{n+1} = \gamma_n(1 - \beta_n) \quad \forall n \geq 0, \tag{36}$$

where $\gamma_n : [0,1] \to M$ is the geodesic joining $f(x_n)$ to z_n, that is, $\gamma_n(0) = f(x_n)$ and $\gamma_n(1) = z_n$ for all $n \geq 0$.

$$\lambda_{n+1} = \begin{cases} \min\left\{\lambda_n + \delta_n, \frac{\mu[d^2(y_n, w_n) + d^2(z_n, y_n)]}{2[\langle P_{y_n, w_n} G(w_n) - G(y_n), z_n - y_n \rangle]}\right\}, & \langle P_{y_n, w_n} G(w_n) - G(y_n), z_n - y_n \rangle > 0, \\ \lambda_n + \delta_n, & \text{otherwise.} \end{cases} \tag{37}$$

Set $n := n + 1$ and return to **Step 1**.

Remark 3. Note that Algorithm 2 is a direct application of Algorithm 1 to a variational inequality problem and that the projection onto the half-space T_n in Algorithm 2 can be calculated in closed form without the need to use a minimization algorithm for computing z_n in Algorithm 1 for solving equilibrium problems. For a closed-form formula for computing the metric projection onto T_n, (see for example, [46]).

4.2. An Application to Solving Convex Optimization Problems

Consider the convex optimization problem (COP)

$$\left\{ \min_{x \in K} h(x), \right. \tag{38}$$

where h is a proper lower semicontinuous convex function of M into $(-\infty, +\infty]$ such that K is contained in the effective domain of h, that is, $K \subset \text{dom} h := \{x \in M : h(x) < +\infty\}$. The set of solutions to COP (38) is denoted by $COP(h, K)$. Let the bifunction $g : K \times K \to \mathbb{R}$ be defined by $g(x, y) := h(y) - h(x)$. Then, $g(x, y)$ satisfies conditions (A1)–(A4) and $COP(h, K) = Sol(g, K)$. Let $Prox_{\lambda h}$ be the proximal operator of the function h of parameter $\lambda > 0$ let ∇h denote the gradient of h. Using the term $Prox_{\lambda h}(\exp_x(-\lambda \nabla h(x)))$ in place of $\arg \min_{y \in M} \{g(x, y) + \frac{1}{2\lambda_n} d^2(x, y)\}$ in Algorithm 1, we obtain a method for minimizing the function h.

5. Numerical Example

In this section, we present some numerical illustrations of our main result. All codes were written in Matlab 2017b computed on a Personal Computer (PC) Core i5 at 2.0 GHz and 8.00 GB RAM.

Example 1. *We consider an extension of the Nash equilibrium model introduced in [7,47]. In this problem, the bifunction $g : K \times K \to \mathbb{R}$ is given by*

$$g(x, y) = \langle Px + Qy + p, y - x \rangle.$$

Let M be Space 2 above and let $K \subset M$ be given by

$$K = \{x = (x_1, x_2, \cdots, x_m) : 1 \leq x_i \leq 100, \ i = 1, 2, \cdots, m\}.$$

Let $x, y \in K$, and let $p = (p_1, p_2, \cdots, p_m)^T \in \mathbb{R}^m$ be chosen randomly with elements in $[1, m]$. The matrices P and Q are two square matrices of order m such that Q is symmetric positive semidefinite and $Q - P$ is negative semidefinite. It is known (see [7]) that g is pseudomonotone and satisfies (A2) with Lipschitz constants $c_1 = c_2 = \frac{1}{2}\|Q - P\|$ (see [15], Lemma 6.2). Assumptions (A3) and (A4) are also satisfied (see [48]). Thus, our main theorem is fully compatible with this example. Setting $\delta_n = \frac{1}{2n+7}$, $\beta_n = \frac{1}{n+1}$, $\epsilon_n = \frac{1}{n^{1.1}}$, $\mu = 0.5$ and $\lambda_1 = 10^{-3}$, we compare our method with (Algorithm 1) of Fan et al. [23]. The comparisons are made for some values of m using $\|x_{n+1} - x_n\|^2 = 10^{-4}$ as the stopping criterion. The results for this example are presented in Table 1 and Figure 1.

Table 1. Computation results for Example 1.

		Algorithm 1	Fan et al. Alg.
$m = 20$	No of Iter.	23	39
	CPU time (s)	0.0013	2.9229
$m = 30$	No of Iter.	23	43
	CPU time (s)	0.0130	3.6771
$m = 50$	No of Iter.	41	53
	CPU time (s)	0.0050	5.8712
$m = 60$	No of Iter.	35	40
	CPU time (s)	0.0050	5.8712

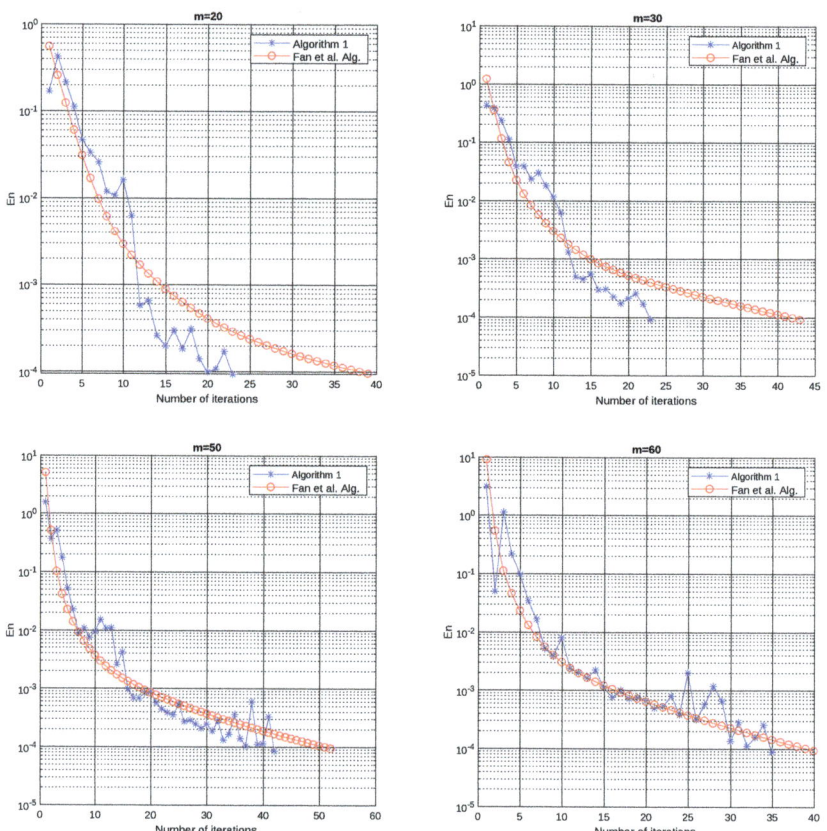

Figure 1. Example 1, **Top left**: $m = 20$; **Top right**: $m = 30$; **Bottom left**: $m = 50$; **Bottom right**: $m = 60$.

Example 2. *Let M be Space 2 above. We consider an example of a variational inequality and present a numerical comparison of Algorithm 1 through its adaptation to VI with (Algorithm 1) of Fan et al. [23]. The following example has been considered by authors in many recent articles (see, for example, [49]). Let the mapping $F : E \to M$ be defined by*

$$F(x) = \begin{pmatrix} 0.5x_1x_2 - 2x_2 - 10^7 \\ -4x_1 + 0.1x_2^2 - 10^7 \end{pmatrix}$$

where $x = (x_1, x_2)$ and $K := \{x \in \mathbb{R}^2 : (x_1 - 2)^2 + (x_2 - 2)^2 \leq 1\}$. It is known that the mapping F is pseudomonotone on K and L-Lipschitz continuous with $L = 5$. For this example, we let $\beta_n = \frac{1}{n+1}$, $\delta_n = \frac{1}{2n+1}$, $\theta_n = \frac{1}{3}$, $\epsilon_n = \frac{1}{n^{1.2}}$ and $\lambda_1 = 10^{-8}$. Using $\|x_{n+1} - x_n\|^2 = 10^{-4}$ as the stopping criterion, we compare Algorithm 1 and **Fan et al. alg.** *for different initial values of x_0 and x_1. The results for this example are presented in Figure 2 and Table 2.*

(Case 1) $x_0 = [0.5, 1]$ *and* $x_1 = [1, 2]'$;
(Case 2) $x_0 = [2, -1]$ *and* $x_1 = [1, -2]'$;
(Case 3) $x_0 = [1.2, 1.5]$ *and* $x_1 = [0, 0.5]'$;
(Case 4) $x_0 = [0.3, 0.5]$ *and* $x_1 = [-0.9, -0.7]'$.

Table 2. Computation result for Example 2.

		Algorithm 1	Fan et al. Alg.
Case 1	No of Iter.	15	29
	CPU time (s)	0.0013	2.9229
Case 2	No of Iter.	17	29
	CPU time (s)	0.0130	3.6771
Case 3	No of Iter.	15	22
	CPU time (s)	0.0050	5.8712
Case 4	No of Iter.	15	17
	CPU time (s)	0.0050	5.8712

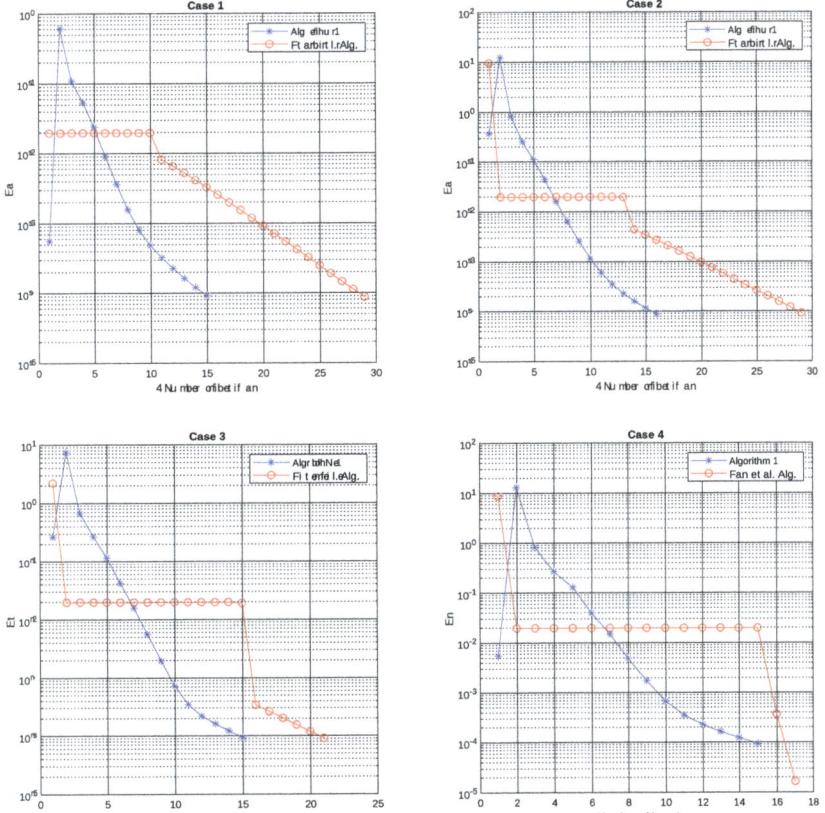

Figure 2. Example 2, **Top left**: Case 1; **Top right**: Case 2; **Bottom left**: Case 3; **Bottom right**: Case 4.

6. Conclusions

In this paper, we introduced an inertial subgradient extragradient method for approximating solutions to equilibrium problems in the framework of Hadamard manifolds. Since we use self-adaptive step sizes which are allowed to increase from iteration to iteration, our method does not require knowledge of the Lipschitz constant of the cost operator. A convergence result was proved by using a viscosity technique with mild conditions on the control parameters involved for generating the sequence of the approximants. We also provided two theoretical applications of our result. Furthermore, we presented some numerical experiments which illustrate the performance of the method we proposed. By way of comparison to another method presented for the same subject in Fan et al. [23], we displayed the competitiveness of our Algorithm. The authors intend to consider more examples in Hadamard manifolds in future works.

Author Contributions: Conceptualization, O.K.O. and S.R.; methodology, O.K.O. and S.R.; software, O.K.O.; validation, S.R.; funding acquisition, S.R. All authors have read and agreed to the published version of the manuscript.

Funding: Simeon Reich was partially supported by the Israel Science Foundation (Grant 820/17), by the Fund for the Promotion of Research at the Technion and by the Technion General Research Fund.

Acknowledgments: Both authors are very grateful to the editors and to five anonymous referees for their useful comments and helpful suggestions.

Conflicts of Interest: The authors declare no conflict of interest.

References

1. Fan, K. A Minimax Inequality and Its Application. In *Inequalities*; Shisha, O., Ed.; Academic: New York, NY, USA, 1972; Volume 3, pp. 103–113.
2. Blum, E.; Oettli, W. From optimization and variational inequalities to equilibrium problems. *Math. Stud.* **1994**, *63*, 123–145.
3. Muu, L.; Oettli, W. Convergence of an adaptive penalty scheme for finding constrained equilibria. *Nonlinear Anal.* **1992**, *18*, 1159–1166. [CrossRef]
4. Rapcsák, T. Geodesic convexity in nonlinear optimization. *J. Optim. Theory Appl.* **1991**, *69*, 169–183. [CrossRef]
5. Rapcsák, T. *Nonconvex Optimization and Its Applications, Smooth Nonlinear Optimization in Rn*; Kluwer Academic Publishers: Dordrecht, The Netherlands, 1997.
6. Udriste, C. *Convex Functions and Optimization Methods on Riemannian Manifolds, Mathematics and Its Applications*; Kluwer Academic: Norwell, MA, USA, 1994; Volume 297.
7. Khammahawong, K.; Kumam, P.; Chaipunya, P.; Yao, J.; Wen, C.; Jirakitpuwapat, W. An extragradient algorithm for strongly pseudomonotone equilibrium problems on Hadamard manifolds. *Thai J. Math.* **2020**, *18*, 350–371.
8. Upadhyay, B.; Ghosh, A.; Mishra, P.; Treanţă, S. Optimality conditions and duality for multiobjective semi-infinite programming problems on Hadamard manifolds using generalized geodesic convexity. *RAIRO-Oper. Res.* **2022**, *56*, 2037–2065. [CrossRef]
9. Colao, V.; López, G.; Marino, G.; Martín-Márquez, V. Equilibrium problems in Hadamard manifolds. *J. Math. Anal. Appl.* **2012**, *388*, 61–77. [CrossRef]
10. Salahuddin, S. The existence of solution for equilibrium problems in Hadamard manifolds. *Trans. A. Razmadze Math. Inst.* **2017**, *171*, 381–388. [CrossRef]
11. Tang, G.; Zhou, L.; Huang, N. Existence results for a class of hemivariational inequality problems on Hadamard manifolds. *Optimization* **2016**, *65*, 1451–1461. [CrossRef]
12. Zhou, L.-W.; Huang, N.-J. Existence of solutions for vector optimization on Hadamard manifolds. *J. Optim. Theory Appl.* **2013**, *157*, 44–53. [CrossRef]
13. Korpelevich, G. An extragradient method for finding saddle points and for other problems. *Ekon. Mat. Metody.* **1976**, *12*, 747–756.
14. Censor, Y.; Gibali, A.; Reich, S. The subgradient extragradient method for solving variational inequalities in Hilbert spaces. *J. Optim. Theory Appl.* **2011**, *148*, 318–335. [CrossRef] [PubMed]
15. Tran, D.; Dung, M.; Nguyen, V. Extragradient algorithms extended to equilibrium problems. *Optimization* **2008**, *57*, 749–776. [CrossRef]
16. Nguyen, T.; Strodiot, J.; Nguyen, V. Hybrid methods for solving simultaneously an equilibrium problem and countably many fixed point problems in a Hilbert space. *J. Optim. Theory Appl.* **2014**, *160*, 809–831. [CrossRef]
17. Rehman, H.; Kumam, P.; Sitthithakerngkiet, K. Viscosity-type method for solving pseudomonotone equilibrium problems in a real Hilbert space with applications. *AIMS Math.* **2021**, *6*, 1538–1560. [CrossRef]
18. Ceng, L.; Li, X.; Qin, X. Parallel proximal point methods for systems of vector optimization problems on Hadamard manifolds without convexity. *Optimization* **2020**, *69*, 357–383. [CrossRef]
19. Hieu, D.V.; Quy, P.K.; Vy, L.V. Explicit iterative algorithms for solving equilibrium problems. *Calcolo* **2019**, *56*, 11. [CrossRef]
20. Li, C.; López, G.; Martín-Márquez, V. Monotone vector fields and the proximal point algorithm on Hadamard manifolds. *J. Lond. Math. Soc.* **2009**, *79*, 663–683. [CrossRef]
21. Li, C.; Yao, J. Variational inequalities for set-valued vector fields on Riemannian manifolds: Convexity of the solution set and the proximal point algorithm. *SIAM J. Control Optim.* **2012**, *50*, 2486–2514. [CrossRef]
22. Neto, J.C.; Santos, P.; Soares, P. An extragradient method for equilibrium problems on Hadamard manifolds. *Optim. Lett.* **2016**, *10*, 1327–1336. [CrossRef]

23. Fan, J.; Tan, B.; Li, S. An explicit extragradient algorithm for equilibrium problems on Hadamard manifolds. *Comp. Appl. Math.* **2021**, *40*, 68. [CrossRef]
24. Ali-Akbari, M. A subgradient extragradient method for equilibrium problems on Hadamard manifolds. *Int. J. Nonlinear Anal. Appl.* **2022**, *13*, 75–84.
25. Alvarez, F.; Attouch, H. An inertial proximal method for maximal monotone operators via discretization of a nonlinear oscillator with damping. *Set-Valued Anal.* **2001**, *9*, 3–11. [CrossRef]
26. Polyak, B. Some methods of speeding up the convergence of iterarive methods. *Zh. Vychisl. Mat. Mat. Fiz.* **1964**, *4*, 1–17.
27. Rehman, H.; Kumam, P.; Gibali, A.; Kumam, W. Convergence analysis of a general inertial projection-type method for solving pseudomonotone equilibrium problems with applications. *J. Ineq. Appl.* **2021**, *2021*, 63. [CrossRef]
28. Oyewole, O.; Izuchukwu, C.; Okeke, C.; Mewomo, O. Inertial approximation method for split variational inclusion problem in Banach spaces. *Int. J. Nonlinear Anal. Appl.* **2020**, *11*, 285–304.
29. Moudafi, A. Viscosity approximation methods for fixed-points problems. *J. Math. Anal. Appl.* **2000**, *241*, 46–55. [CrossRef]
30. Al-Homidan, S.; Ansari, Q.; Babu, F.; Yao, J.-C. Viscosity method with a f-contraction mapping for hierarchical variational inequalities on Hadamard manifolds. *Fixed Point Theory* **2020**, *21*, 561–584. [CrossRef]
31. Huang, S. Approximations with weak contractions in Hadamard manifolds. *Linear Nonlinear Anal.* **2015**, *1*, 317–328.
32. Dilshad, M.; Khan, A.; Akram, M. Splitting type viscosity methods for inclusion and fixed point problems on Hadamard manifolds. *AIMS Math.* **2021**, *6*, 5205–5221. [CrossRef]
33. Thong, D.; Hieu, D. Some extragradient-viscosity algorithms for solving variational inequality problems and fixed point problems. *Numer. Algorithms* **2019**, *82*, 761–789. [CrossRef]
34. Sakai, T. *Riemannian Geometry. Vol. 149, Translations of Mathematical Monographs*; American Mathematical Society: Providence, RI, USA, 1996.
35. Ansari, Q.; Babu, F.; Yao, J. Regularization of proximal point algorithms in Hadamard manifolds. *J. Fixed Point Theory Appl.* **2019**, *21*, 25. [CrossRef]
36. Ferreira, O.; Perez, L.L.; Nemeth, S. Singularities of monotone vector fields and an extragradient algorithm. *J. Glob. Optim.* **2005**, *31*, 133–151. [CrossRef]
37. Wang, J.; López, G.; Martín-Márquez, V.; Li, C. Monotone and accretive vector fields on Riemannian manifolds. *J. Optim. Theory Appl.* **2010**, *146*, 691–708. [CrossRef]
38. Boyd, D.; Wong, J. On nonlinear contractions. *Proc. Am. Math. Soc.* **1969**, *20*, 335–341. [CrossRef]
39. Bridson, M.; Haefliger, A. *Metric Spaces of Non-Positive Curvature. Grundlehren der Mathematischen Wissenschaften (Fundamental Principles of Mathematical Sciences)*; Springer: Berlin, Germany, 1999; Volume 319. [CrossRef]
40. Mastroeni, G. On auxiliary principle for equilibrium problems. In *Equilibrium Problems and Variational Models*; Nonconvex Optimization and Its Applications; Kluwer Academic: Norwell, MA, USA, 2003; Volume 68; pp. 289–298.
41. Ferreira, O.; Oliveira, P. Proximal Point Algorithm on Riemannian Manifolds. *Optimization* **2002**, *51*, 257–270. [CrossRef]
42. Takahashi, W. *Introduction to Nonlinear and Convex Analysis*; Yokohama Publishers: Yokohama, Japan, 2009.
43. Saejung, S.; Yotkaew, P. Approximation of zeros of inverse strongly monotone operator in Banach spaces. *Nonlinear Anal.* **2012**, *75*, 742–750. [CrossRef]
44. Stampacchia, G. Formes Bilineaires Coercivites sur les Ensembles Convexes. *C. R. Acad. Paris* **1964**, *258*, 4413–4416.
45. Upadhyay, B.; Treanţă, S.; Mishra, P. On Minty Variational Principle for Nonsmooth Multiobjective Optimization Problems on Hadamard Manifolds. *Optimization* **2022**, *71*, 1–19. [CrossRef]
46. Cegielski, A. *Iterative Methods for Fixed Point Problems in Hilbert Spaces*; Lecture Notes in Mathematics; 2057; Springer: Berlin, Germany, 2012.
47. Facchinei, F.; Pang, J.S. *Finite-Dimensional Variational Inequalities and Complementarity Problems*; Springer Series in Operations Research; Springer: New York, NY, USA, 2003; Volume II.
48. Chen, J.; Liu, S. Extragradient-like method for pseudomonotone equilibrium problems on Hadamard manifolds. *J. Ineq. Appl.* **2020**, *2020*, 205. [CrossRef]
49. Shehu, Y.; Dong, Q.-L.; Jiang, D. Single projection method for pseudo-monotone variational inequality in Hilbert Spaces. *Optimization* **2019**, *68*, 385–409. [CrossRef]

Disclaimer/Publisher's Note: The statements, opinions and data contained in all publications are solely those of the individual author(s) and contributor(s) and not of MDPI and/or the editor(s). MDPI and/or the editor(s) disclaim responsibility for any injury to people or property resulting from any ideas, methods, instructions or products referred to in the content.

Article

Parameter Estimation Analysis in a Model of Honey Production

Atanas Z. Atanasov [1,†], Slavi G. Georgiev [2,3,*,‡] and Lubin G. Vulkov [3,‡]

- [1] Department of Agricultural Machinery, Agrarian Industrial Faculty, University of Ruse, 7004 Ruse, Bulgaria
- [2] Department of Informational Modeling, Institute of Mathematics and Informatics, Bulgarian Academy of Sciences, 1113 Sofia, Bulgaria
- [3] Department of Applied Mathematics and Statistics, Faculty of Natural Sciences and Education, University of Ruse, 7004 Ruse, Bulgaria
- * Correspondence: sggeorgiev@uni-ruse.bg or sggeorgiev@math.bas.bg; Tel.: +359-82-888-725
- [†] Current address: Department of Agricultural Machinery, University of Ruse, 8 Studentska Str., 7004 Ruse, Bulgaria.
- [‡] Current address: Department of Applied Mathematics and Statistics, University of Ruse, 8 Studentska Str., 7004 Ruse, Bulgaria.

Abstract: Honeybee losses are an extensive global problem. In this study, a new compartment model of honeybee population that mainly concerns honey production is developed. The model describes the interaction of the food stock with the brood (immature bees), adult bees and produced honey. In the present paper, the issue of an adequate model recovery is addressed and the parameter identification inverse problem is solved. An adjoint equation procedure to obtain the unknown parameter values by minimizing the functional error during a period of time is proposed. Numerical simulations with realistic data are discussed.

Keywords: honeybee population dynamics; existence of non-negative solutions; parameter identification analysis

MSC: 34A12; 34A55; 65L09; 92D25

Citation: Atanasov, A.Z.; Georgiev, S.G.; Vulkov, L.G. Parameter Estimation Analysis in a Model of Honey Production. *Axioms* **2023**, *12*, 214. https://doi.org/10.3390/axioms12020214

Academic Editor: Behzad Djafari-Rouhani

Received: 30 December 2022
Revised: 7 February 2023
Accepted: 8 February 2023
Published: 17 February 2023

Copyright: © 2023 by the authors. Licensee MDPI, Basel, Switzerland. This article is an open access article distributed under the terms and conditions of the Creative Commons Attribution (CC BY) license (https://creativecommons.org/licenses/by/4.0/).

1. Introduction

Honeybee colonies are important for agriculture and the environment. They help plant reproduction by pollination, while beekeeping redounds to the development of rural areas. Unfortunately, in recent decades, a ubiquitous decline in both managed and unmanaged colonies has been observed. This is a global problem, since the bees contribute to the ecological equilibrium. If the bee population shrinks or disappears, plants would not get pollinated and would die off. Then, herbivorous animals would not have food and would go extinct, and they would be followed by carnivorous animals, including humans. Thus, preventing bee colonies from losses is of a paramount importance for preserving live on Earth in general.

Of the many species of bees, only a small number of them are eusocial; *Apis mellifera* is an example of eusocial behavior [1]. This species form colonies thus the survival, reproduction and honey production are directly dependent on the size and the structure of the colonies [2].

Honey, produced by honeybees, is a sweet natural substance, derived greatly from the nectar of flowers and transformed by a group of enzymes, which are present in the saliva of the worker bees. The honey is also airy and evaporates by its filtering, and is eventually stored inside the hives. Honey from *Apis mellifera* is one of the most essential zoo-agricultural goods for commercial trade in the world [3]. Regarding the honey trade, the USA is the global leader in imports. Concerning production, China is the global leader, following by Turkey, Iran, Ukraine and the Russian Federation. Finally, with respect to quality, Bulgarian honey is the most pure and sweet [4].

Beekeepers produce a variety of agriculture products, in addition to honey, including royal jelly, propolis and beeswax. This paper aims to develop mathematical modeling of the honeybee population dynamics and, therefore, honey production.

The most fundamental honeybee population model is suggested by [5], where only two compartments are explored—the young hive bees and the matured forager bees. This model is extended in [6,7], where the brood, the age of the foragers and the food are also included in the studies, accounting for the delay of maturing. Such investigation is done in [8], where a different form of the recruitment rate is used. In the study [9], exogenous stress is assumed to impact the recruitment process, social inhibition and the queen laying rate, causing a potential colony decline.

There are models developed as an effort to understand the decrease in colony numbers in recent decades. A survey in the USA suggests that treating against disease and mite infestation in the right way lowers the chance of colony loss [10]. Extensive study of the transition from hive to forager bees is performed in [11]. A comparison between the losses in different parts of the world is performed in [12].

The mysterious disease, whose causal factors are not entirely agreed on, is called Colony Collapse Disorder (CCD). It is characterized by rapid loss of forager bees but absence of dead bodies near the hive, lack of pest and mite invasion of the hive, and bees' reluctance to consume food provided by the beekeeper. The first recorded massive colony loss is described as the 'Isle of Wight Disease' [13]. The effect of protein sources has been proposed as a potential cause for collapse [14]. A special CCD model is designed in [15], where the contagious adult bees are isolated from the others. A review of the suspected causal factors for the colony declines is summarized in [16].

Other models focus on particular parts of the surrounding environment such as food availability [17], age structure [18], seasonal effects [19], Varroa mites [20] and others [21,22], including the model memory property [23].

In [24], populations of adult and immature (brood) honeybees as well as their honeybee production are examined via mathematical and statistical modeling approaches. It is shown that, if a bee population is exposed to a stress factor (i.e., habitat destruction, Varroamites, climate variability, heavy metals, etc.), the number of individuals declines over time as well as the produced honey. The complex issue of the sustainability of honeybee colonies is important not only for the survival of the species but also for food security and the overall health of the environment. To ensure the sustainability of honeybee colonies, it is important to take measures such as providing adequate habitats, reducing pesticide exposure and promoting disease management practices. Aiming at the latter, the sophisticated processes of population dynamics have to be investigated via mathematical modeling.

In the present work we study the relationship between the population size of honeybees (*Apis mellifera*) and honey production if the bee colony is exposed to a number of stress factors that exogenously cause the death of individuals and therefore a possible reduction in honey production. Here lies the main originality of the study—suggesting a novel model for encountering the interaction between the bee castes and the amount of honey, stored in the hive.

Furthermore, in the investigation the inverse problem of identifying the food and honey consumption rates by the immature and adult bees is solved as well as the brood maturation rate. These quantities are of extreme importance for understanding the complex dynamics of the hive. It is done via the adjoint equations optimization approach. Such a study is performed in [25], where the contaminated bees are modeled as a separate compartment. Similar investigation is done in [26] but, for the coefficient identification, a trust-region reflexive algorithm is used.

This paper is organized as follows. In the next section, we extend the mathematical model, studied in [24], taking into account the food stock. What is more, we study the existence and non-negativity of the solutions. Section 3 is devoted to the parameter estimation analysis of the model. Section 4 is dedicated to numerical experiments regarding the direct and inverse problems. The paper is concluded in Section 5.

2. Mathematical Model

In this section, we introduce a mathematical model that explains the interaction between the food stock and the brood (immature bees), adult bees and the amount of produced honey.

Following the results in [24,27] we establish a mathematical model that presents the interactions among brood $B(t)$ at time t, adult bees $A(t)$ and the amount of honey production $M(t)$, taking into account the weight of food stock $F(t)$.

We assume that the brood grows at a rate β, proportionally to the number of adult bees. This is given by term $A/(A + \nu)$, where ν is the mean saturation rate (number of adult bees required for immature bees to achieve half of their maximal number). The number of bees surviving to the adult stage influences the number of immature bees.

The latter is modeled by the term ωB, where ω denotes the maturation rate to adult stage, and $1/\omega$ indicates the time spent before achieving the adult stage. The number of immature bees is decreased by natural death and it is modeled by the term $\mu_B B$, where μ_B denotes the natural mortality rate of the immature stage. Following this discussion and those in [24,27] we consider the following system of ODEs:

$$\frac{dF}{dt} = cA - \gamma B, \tag{1}$$

$$\frac{dB}{dt} = \beta \frac{A}{A+\nu} - \omega B - \mu_B B, \tag{2}$$

$$\frac{dA}{dt} = \omega B - \mu_A A - \sigma A. \tag{3}$$

$$\frac{dM}{dt} = \rho \frac{A}{A+u} - \alpha M - \delta A M. \tag{4}$$

The model (1)–(4) is illustrated in the diagram of Figure 1.

It is assumed in the derivation of Equation (3) that the number of adult bees diminish naturally and it is demonstrated by the term $\mu_A A$, where μ_A is the natural mortality rate of the adult stage. However, the bees can also die because of a stress factor. This is represented by the term σA, where σ is the death rate due to a stressor (climate change, loss of habitat, heavy metals or pesticides, poor beekeeper's management, etc.) acting on bees at the adult stage.

Equation (4) shows that the production of honey in hives increase at a rate ρ, which is influenced by the number of adult bees, given by the term $A/(A+u)$, where u is the mean saturation rate.

One important cause for decreasing of the honey is the feeding of immature bees, which is demonstrated by the term αM, where α is the honey loss rate.

The term $\delta A M$ represents the loss of honey production because of the consumption of adult bees, where δ is the adult bees' honey consumption rate.

For more details on the specifications of the parameters in the model we refer to Table 2 in [24].

We solve the system of ordinary differential Equations (1)–(4) with initial conditions

$$F(0) = F_0 \geq 0, \quad B(0) = B_0 \geq 0, \quad A(0) = A_0 \geq 0, \quad M(0) = M_0 \geq 0. \tag{5}$$

Using Theorem 7.1 in [28] one could easily prove that the subsystem (2)–(4) is positive (short for "non-negativity preserving") in the sense that, if

$$B(0) \geq 0, \quad A(0) \geq 0, \quad M(0) \geq 0,$$

then

$$B(t) \geq 0, \quad A(t) \geq 0, \quad M(t) \geq 0, \quad \forall\, t \geq 0.$$

This property is biologically relevant to the model.

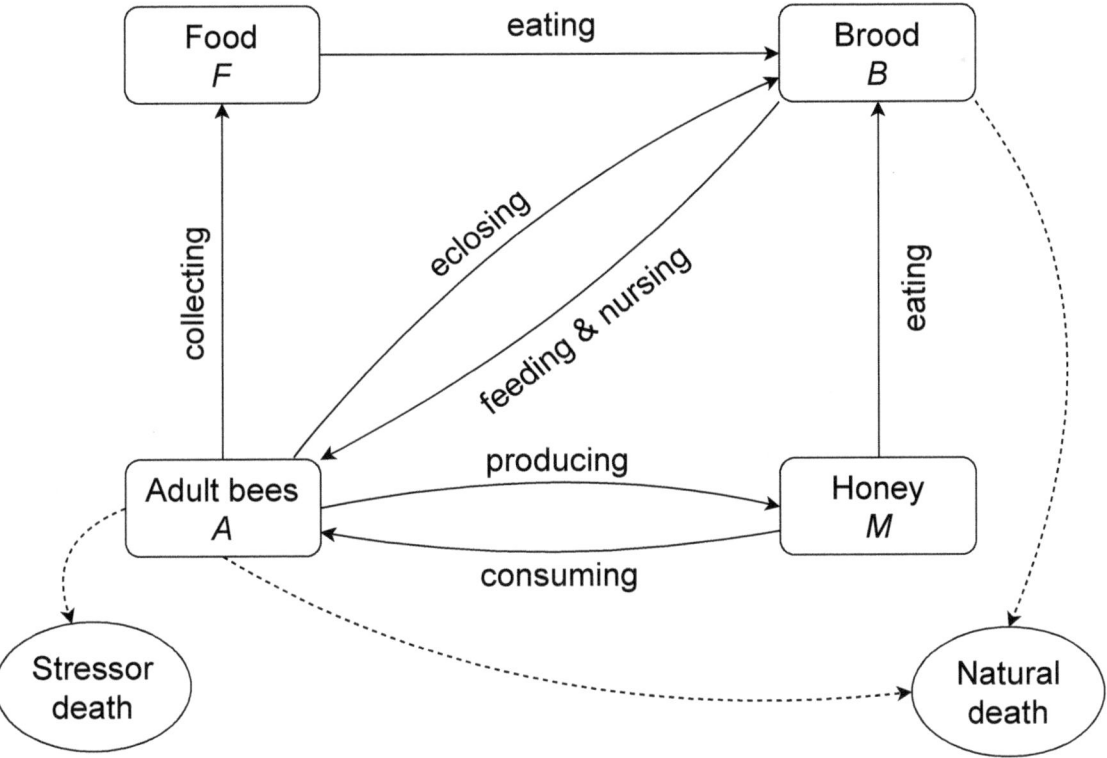

Figure 1. Schematic representation of model (1)–(4).

3. Parameter Identification

In this section, the parameter inverse problem is defined. Such problems appear very often in practice. The problem (1)–(5), where the values of the parameters are known, is well-posed and it is called a direct problem. However, in the real world, the values of some of the coefficients are not directly measurable but they are very important for professional honeybee management. Their reconstruction, provided that additional information is given, is referred to an inverse problem. Inverse problems are ill-posed and harder to solve. We employ the adjoint equation optimization approach [29,30].

The parameters to be reconstructed are $p = (p^1, p^2, p^3, p^4, p^5)$, $p^1 = \alpha$, $p^2 = \gamma$, $p^3 = \delta$, $p^4 = \sigma$, $p^5 = \omega$, and

$$p \in \mathbb{S}_{\text{adm}} = \left\{ p \in \mathbb{R}^5 : 0 < p^i < P^i, i = 1, \ldots, 5 \right\}. \quad (6)$$

The admissible set $\mathbb{S}_{\text{adm}}$ is defined by the biology of the honeybee [31]. To find the parameters p, though, some new information must be brought. In many cases it is possible to measure the model functions at some discrete times. In reality, counting the brood B is a difficult task, so we adopt measurements of the functions

$$\begin{aligned} F^{\text{obs}}(t_k) &= X_k, \\ A^{\text{obs}}(t_k) &= Y_k, \\ M^{\text{obs}}(t_k) &= Z_k \end{aligned} \quad (7)$$

for $k = 1, \ldots, K$. We assume all functions are measured at some predefined time instances. The observation times for every function may be different.

In practice, the observations are obtained from electronic devices equipping the hive. In a quasi-real setting, first the direct problem is solved and then the observations are extracted from the solution to the direct problem.

To solve the inverse problem, the least-square function

$$\Phi(p) = \Phi(\alpha,\gamma,\delta,\sigma,\omega) = \Phi_F(\alpha,\gamma,\delta,\sigma,\omega) + \Phi_A(\alpha,\gamma,\delta,\sigma,\omega) + \Phi_M(\alpha,\gamma,\delta,\sigma,\omega) =$$
$$\sum_{k=1}^{K}(F(t_k;p) - X_k)^2 + \sum_{k=1}^{K}(A(t_k;p) - Y_k)^2 + \sum_{k=1}^{K}(M(t_k;p) - Z_k)^2 \quad (8)$$

is minimized, e.g., by a gradient method [32], where $\Psi(t_k;p)$, $\Psi \in \{F,A,M\}$ are the theoretical quantities from the model and Ξ_k, $\Xi \in \{X,Y,Z\}$ are the observed values in practice.

Now we state an expression for the gradient of the function $\Phi_p := \Phi(p)$.

Theorem 1. *The gradient $\Phi'_p \equiv (\Phi'_\alpha, \Phi'_\gamma, \Phi'_\delta, \Phi'_\sigma, \Phi'_\omega)$ is given by*

$$\Phi'_\alpha = \int_0^T \varphi_M(t) M(t) dt, \quad (9)$$

$$\Phi'_\gamma = \int_0^T \varphi_F(t) B(t) dt, \quad (10)$$

$$\Phi'_\delta = \int_0^T \varphi_M(t) A(t) M(t) dt, \quad (11)$$

$$\Phi'_\sigma = \int_0^T \varphi_A(t) A(t) dt, \quad (12)$$

$$\Phi'_\omega = -\int_0^T \varphi_A(t) B(t) dt, \quad (13)$$

where the triple $\{\varphi_M, \varphi_F, \varphi_A\}$ is the unique solution of the adjoint system

$$\frac{d\varphi_F}{dt} = 2\sum_{k=1}^{K}(F - X)\delta(t - t_k), \quad (14)$$

$$\frac{d\varphi_A}{dt} = -c\varphi_F + (\mu_A + \sigma)\varphi_A + \left(\delta \cdot M - \rho\frac{u}{(A+u)^2}\right)\varphi_M + 2\sum_{k=1}^{K}(A - Y)\delta(t - t_k), \quad (15)$$

$$\frac{d\varphi_M}{dt} = (\alpha + \delta \cdot A)\varphi_M + 2\sum_{k=1}^{K}(M - Z)\delta(t - t_k), \quad (16)$$

$$\varphi_F(T) = \varphi_A(T) = \varphi_M(T) = 0. \quad (17)$$

Proof. We denote $\delta p = (\delta\alpha, \delta\gamma, \delta\delta, \delta\sigma, \delta\omega)$ and $\delta\alpha = \varepsilon h_1$, $\delta\gamma = \varepsilon h_2$, $\delta\delta = \varepsilon h_3$, $\delta\sigma = \varepsilon h_4$, $\delta\omega = \varepsilon h_5$.

If $\delta F(t;p) = F(t;p + \delta p) - F(t;p)$, $\delta A(t;p) = A(t;p + \delta p) - A(t;p)$ and $\delta M(t;p) = M(t;p + \delta p) - M(t;p)$, write the ODE system for $F(t;p + \delta p)$, $A(t;p + \delta p)$ and $M(t;p + \delta p)$ as (1), (3) and (4) with initial conditions F_0, A_0 and M_0 (5).

Then, calculate the differences of the corresponding equations to obtain an ODE system for $\delta F, \delta A$ and δM with zero initial conditions.

$$\frac{d}{dt}\delta F = c\delta A - \delta\gamma B, \quad (18)$$

$$\frac{d}{dt}\delta A = -(\mu_A + \sigma)\delta A - \delta\sigma A + \delta w B, \quad (19)$$

$$\frac{d}{dt}\delta M = \rho \frac{u\delta A}{(A+u)^2} - \delta \cdot M\delta A - (\alpha + \delta \cdot A)\delta M - \delta \alpha M - \delta \delta A M. \tag{20}$$

We find the increment of the functional $\Phi(\boldsymbol{p})$:

$$\Phi(\boldsymbol{p}+\delta\boldsymbol{p}) - \Phi(\boldsymbol{p}) = 2\sum_{k=1}^{K} \delta F(t_k;\boldsymbol{p})\big(F(t_k;\boldsymbol{p}) - X_k\big)$$

$$+ 2\sum_{k=1}^{K} \delta A(t_k;\boldsymbol{p})\big(A(t_k;\boldsymbol{p}) - Y_k\big) + 2\sum_{k=1}^{K} \delta M(t_k;\boldsymbol{p})\big(M(t_k;\boldsymbol{p}) - Z_k\big)$$

$$= 2\sum_{k=1}^{K} \int_0^T \delta F(t_k;\boldsymbol{p})\big(F(t_k;\boldsymbol{p}) - X_k\big)\delta(t-t_k)dt$$

$$+ 2\sum_{k=1}^{K} \int_0^T \delta A(t_k;\boldsymbol{p})\big(A(t_k;\boldsymbol{p}) - Y_k\big)\delta(t-t_k)dt$$

$$+ 2\sum_{k=1}^{K} \int_0^T \delta M(t_k;\boldsymbol{p})\big(M(t_k;\boldsymbol{p}) - Z_k\big)\delta(t-t_k)dt.$$

Let us multiply Equations (18)–(20) by smooth functions $\varphi_F(t)$, $\varphi_A(t)$ and $\varphi_M(t)$ s.t. $\varphi_F(T) = \varphi_A(T) = \varphi_M(T) = 0$ and integrate both sides of the results from 0 to T:

$$\int_0^T \left(\varphi_F \frac{d}{dt}\delta F + \varphi_A \frac{d}{dt}\delta A + \varphi_M \frac{d}{dt}\delta M\right) dt =$$
$$c \int_0^T \varphi_F \delta A dt - \delta \gamma \int_0^T \varphi_F B dt - (\mu_A + \sigma) \int_0^T \varphi_A \delta A dt$$
$$-\delta \sigma \int_0^T \varphi_A A dt + \delta w \int_0^T \varphi_A B dt + \rho u \int_0^T \varphi_M \frac{\delta A}{(A+u)^2} dt \tag{21}$$
$$-\delta \int_0^T \varphi_M M \delta A dt - (\alpha + \delta \cdot A) \int_0^T \varphi_M \delta M dt$$
$$-\delta \alpha \int_0^T \varphi_M M dt - \delta \delta \int_0^T \varphi_M A M dt.$$

On the other hand, integrating by parts and using the facts that $\varphi_F(T) = \varphi_A(T) = \varphi_M(T) = 0$ and $\delta F(0) = \delta A(0) = \delta M(0) = 0$, we obtain

$$\int_0^T \varphi_F \frac{d}{dt}\delta F dt + \int_0^T \varphi_A \frac{d}{dt}\delta A dt + \int_0^T \varphi_M \frac{d}{dt}\delta M dt =$$
$$-\int_0^T \delta F \frac{d\varphi_F}{dt} dt - \int_0^T \delta A \frac{d\varphi_A}{dt} dt - \int_0^T \delta M \frac{d\varphi_M}{dt} dt. \tag{22}$$

Let us place the expressions for $\frac{d\varphi_F}{dt}$, $\frac{d\varphi_A}{dt}$ and $\frac{d\varphi_M}{dt}$ from (14)–(16) in (22):

$$\int_0^T \left(\varphi_F \frac{d}{dt}\delta F + \varphi_A \frac{d}{dt}\delta A + \varphi_M \frac{d}{dt}\delta M\right) dt =$$
$$c \int_0^T \varphi_F \delta A dt - (\mu_A + \sigma) \int_0^T \varphi_A \delta A dt - \delta \int_0^T \varphi_M M \delta A dt$$
$$+ \rho u \int_0^T \varphi_M \frac{1}{(A+u)^2} \delta A dt - (\alpha + \delta \cdot A) \int_0^T \varphi_M \delta M dt$$
$$- 2\int_0^T \delta F \sum_{k=1}^K (F-X)\delta(t-t_k)dt - 2\int_0^T \delta A \sum_{k=1}^K (A-Y)\delta(t-t_k)dt$$
$$- 2\int_0^T \delta M \sum_{k=1}^K (M-Z)\delta(t-t_k)dt. \tag{23}$$

Equating (21) and (23) yields

$$2\int_0^T \delta F \sum_{k=1}^K (F-X)\delta(t-t_k)dt + 2\int_0^T \delta A \sum_{k=1}^K (A-Y)\delta(t-t_k)dt$$

$$+ 2\int_0^T \delta M \sum_{k=1}^K (M-Z)\delta(t-t_k)dt = \delta\alpha \int_0^T \varphi_M M dt$$

$$+ \delta\gamma \int_0^T \varphi_F B dt + \delta\delta \int_0^T \varphi_M A M dt$$

$$+ \delta\sigma \int_0^T \varphi_A A dt - \delta\omega \int_0^T \varphi_A B dt.$$

Rewriting the last expression give

$$\Phi(\alpha + \varepsilon h_1, \gamma + \varepsilon h_2, \delta + \varepsilon h_3, \sigma + \varepsilon h_4, w + \varepsilon h_5) - \Phi(\alpha, \gamma, \delta, \sigma, \omega) =$$

$$\left(h_1 \int_0^\tau \varphi_M M dt + h_2 \int_0^\tau \varphi_F B dt + h_3 \int_0^\tau \varphi_M A M dt + h_4 \int_0^\tau \varphi_A A dt - h_5 \int_0^\tau \varphi_A B dt \right)\varepsilon.$$

Now, taking $h_2 = h_3 = h_4 = h_5 = 0$, dividing both sides by εh_1 and taking the limit $\varepsilon \to 0$ we find the formula for Φ'_α in the theorem.

Analogously, we obtain the formulae for Φ'_γ, Φ'_δ, Φ'_σ and Φ'_ω (10)–(13). □

Employing the fundamental property of the Dirac-delta function $\int_0^T \mathfrak{f}(t)\delta(t-t_k)dt = \mathfrak{f}(t_k)$, $t_k \in (0, T)$, where $\mathfrak{f}(t)$ is a continuous function, (14)–(17) could be rewritten in its equivalent form:

$$\frac{d\varphi_F}{dt} = 0, \quad t \neq t_k, \; k = 1, \ldots, K,$$

$$\frac{d\varphi_A}{dt} = -c\varphi_F + (\mu_A + \sigma)\varphi_A + \left(\delta \cdot M - \rho \frac{u}{(A+u)^2}\right)\varphi_M, \quad t \neq t_k, \; k = 1, \ldots, K,$$

$$\frac{d\varphi_M}{dt} = (\alpha + \delta \cdot A)\varphi_M, \quad t \neq t_k, \; k = 1, \ldots, K,$$

$$[\varphi_F]_{t=t_k} = 2(F(t_k; \mathbf{p}) - X_k), \quad k = 1, \ldots, K,$$

$$[\varphi_A]_{t=t_k} = 2(A(t_k; \mathbf{p}) - Y_k), \quad k = 1, \ldots, K,$$

$$[\varphi_M]_{t=t_k} = 2(M(t_k; \mathbf{p}) - Z_k), \quad k = 1, \ldots, K,$$

$$\varphi_F(T) = \varphi_A(T) = \varphi_M(T) = 0.$$

Having obtained the gradient, we employ an iterative procedure as follows, where the new approximation $\mathbf{p}_{s+1}$ is defined by

$$\mathbf{p}_{s+1} = \mathbf{p}_s - \mathbf{r}\Phi'(\mathbf{p}_s), \tag{24}$$

where $\mathbf{r} \in \mathbb{R}_5^+$ are gradient multipliers. The iterations start at chosen $\mathbf{p}_0$ and end if $\|\triangle \mathbf{p}_s\| := \|\mathbf{p}_{s+1} - \mathbf{p}_s\| < \varepsilon_p$, where ε_p is a tolerance quantity, else increase $s := s+1$ and start a new iteration. The final approximation is denoted with $\check{\mathbf{p}}$ and it is called a nonlinear estimator.

4. Numerical Experiments

This section is devoted to presenting numerical tests which demonstrate the algorithm application. Firstly, the numerical algorithm is summarized. Then, the direct problem is solved and its solution is used to obtain measurements for the inverse problem.

4.1. Numerical Procedure

All the programming code is implemented in the MATLAB® environment. For solving the ODE systems (1)–(5) and (14)–(17), a Runge–Kutta-type method is used. The algorithm for solving the inverse problem could be described as follows:

1. Choose initial approximation p_0.
2. Set $s := 0$.
3. Until $\|\triangle p_s\| < \varepsilon_p$ do
    3.1. Solve system (1)–(5) with p_s to obtain F, B, A and M.
    3.2. Solve system (14)–(17) to obtain φ_F, φ_A and φ_M.
    3.3. Compute the gradient Φ'_p (9)–(13).
    3.4. Calculate p_{s+1} by (24) and set $s := s + 1$.
4. The estimator is set to $\check{p} := p_s$.

4.2. Direct Problem

Let us first solve the direct problem (1)–(5) with realistic data given in [24,27]. The adult food collection rate is assumed to be $c = 0.04$ g/bee/day. The larval consumption rate is $\gamma = 0.12$ g/bee/day. The brood reproduction rate is $\beta = 0.92$ bee/day. The adult maturation rate is $\omega = 0.95$ day^{-1}. The brood natural mortality rate is $\mu_B = 0.11$ day^{-1}. The adult bee natural mortality rate is $\mu_A = 0.29$ day^{-1}. The adult bee stressor mortality rate is $\sigma = 0.1$ day^{-1}. The honey production rate is $\rho = 0.23$ bees/day. The rate of natural honey loss is $\alpha = 0.018$ g/day. The honey consumption rate is $\delta = 0.571$ g/bee/day. The half saturation rates are $\nu = u = 1$ thousand bees.

We simulate the hive development for a typical foraging season, lasting $T = 100$ days. At the beginning of the season, there are $F_0 = 10$ kilograms of food stores, $B_0 = 2000$ larvae, $A_0 = 10{,}000$ adult bees and $M_0 = 1$ kilogram honey. The outcome is plotted in Figure 2.

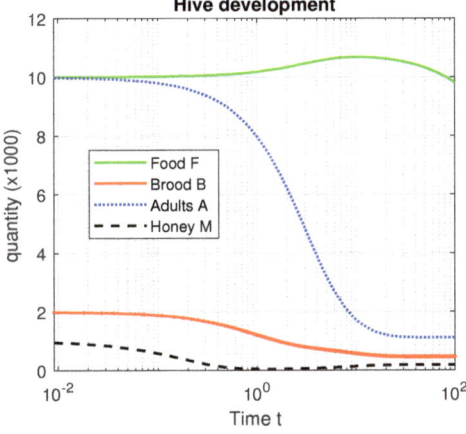

Figure 2. Solution to the direct problem (1)–(5).

It could be observed that the hive approaches its equilibrium state relatively fast. It is characterized by a small amount of honey as well as a small number of larvae and adult bees. This is approved by the phase space diagram for a fixed F_0 (Figure 3), which shows no dependence on the initial conditions. Only in case of $B_0 = A_0 = 0$, then the extinction equilibrium is approached.

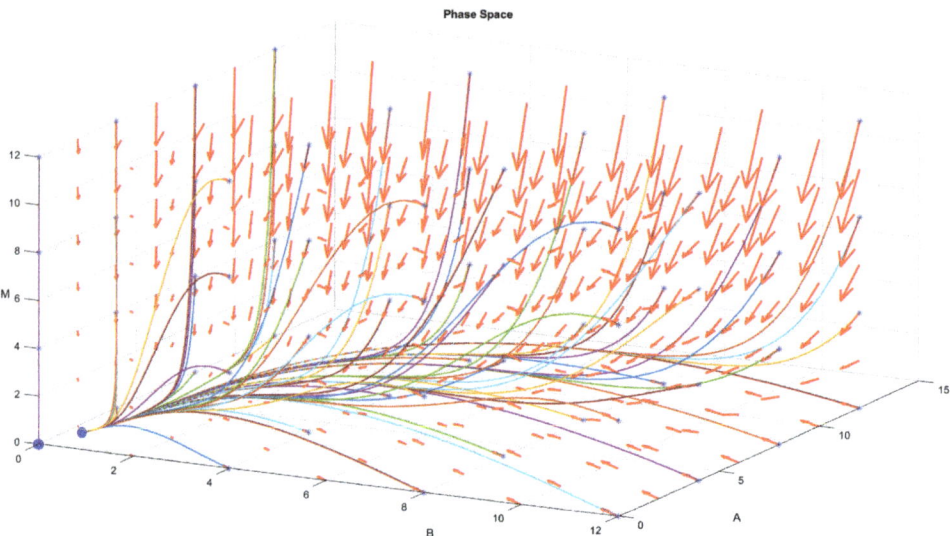

Figure 3. Phase space diagram: non-trivial equilibrium.

Of course, it is not always true. If there is a hazard present in the environment, i.e., the stress death rate is as high as $\sigma = 0.5$, then the extinction equilibrium is the only attractor, see Figure 4. This unarguably means that the hive would eventually collapse unless something is drastically changed.

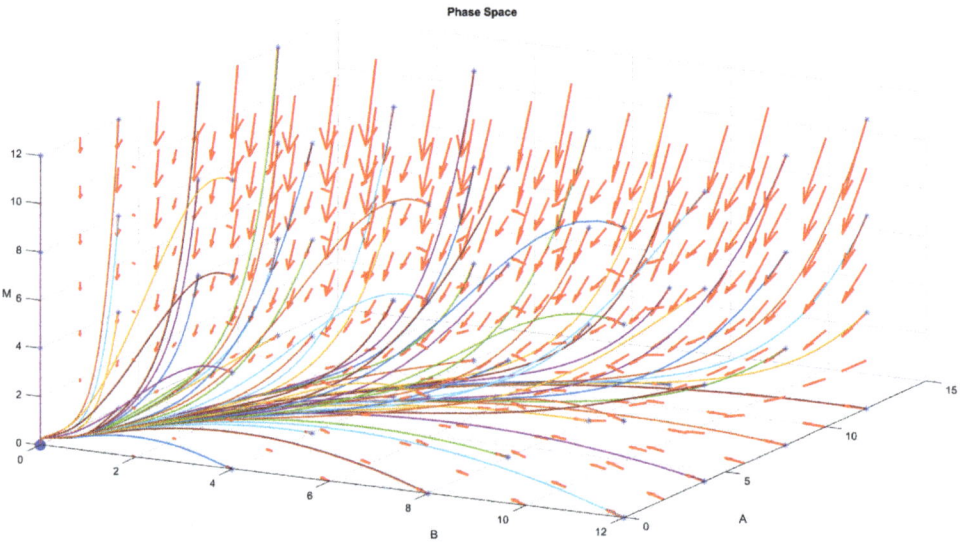

Figure 4. Phase space diagram: extinction equilibrium.

4.3. Inverse Problem

Let us solve the inverse problem of identifying the parameters (6) $p = (\alpha, \gamma, \delta, \sigma, \omega) = (0.018, 0.12, 0.571, 0.1, 0.95)$. The values of the other parameters and initial conditions remain the same as in the direct problem setting.

We define $K = 19$ equidistantly distributed observations of type (7), i.e., one observation in every 5 days. The admissible set is set to $\mathbb{S}_{adm} \equiv (0,1)^5$. The values r are tuned empirically and they are given in Table 1.

Table 1. Simulation with $\varepsilon_p = 8 \times 10^{-4}$.

Parameter	p^i	p_0^i	$\breve{p}^i$	$\lvert p^i - \breve{p}^i \rvert$	$\dfrac{\lvert p^i - \breve{p}^i \rvert}{p^i}$	r^i
α	0.018	0.02	0.0274	0.0094	0.5234	4×10^{-23}
γ	0.12	0.10	0.0991	0.0209	0.1746	7×10^{-5}
δ	0.571	0.50	0.3633	0.2077	0.3638	5×10^{-23}
σ	0.1	0.20	0.1886	0.0886	0.8862	1×10^{-25}
ω	0.95	1.00	0.8992	0.0508	0.0535	1×10^{-23}

The respective values (8) are $\Phi_F(\breve{p}) = 0.1815$, $\Phi_A(\breve{p}) = 3.7902$ and $\Phi_M(\breve{p}) = 0.3807$. The parameters are recovered with moderate precision, but the honeybee dynamics are reconstructed in an accurate manner. The root mean squared errors are small as $\mathrm{RMSE}_F = 0.0977$, $\mathrm{RMSE}_A = 0.4466$ and $\mathrm{RMSE}_M = 0.1416$.

Finally, we perform a test with perturbed measurements to explore the impact of the observation error on the parameter identification. Every electronic device has its instrumental error, so testing with noisy observation is meaningful. We add Gaussian noise to the observations (7), in particular the error in a single observation is not greater than 1% with 95% confidence. The results, following the same steps, are given in Table 2.

Table 2. Simulation with perturbed observations and $\varepsilon_p = 8 \times 10^{-4}$.

Parameter	p^i	p_0^i	$\breve{p}^i$	$\lvert p^i - \breve{p}^i \rvert$	$\dfrac{\lvert p^i - \breve{p}^i \rvert}{p^i}$	r^i
α	0.018	0.02	0.0269	0.0089	0.4942	4×10^{-23}
γ	0.12	0.10	0.0989	0.0211	0.1758	7×10^{-5}
δ	0.571	0.50	0.3731	0.1979	0.3465	5×10^{-23}
σ	0.1	0.20	0.1869	0.0869	0.8689	1×10^{-25}
ω	0.95	1.00	0.8927	0.0573	0.0603	1×10^{-23}

The outcomes are similar as the functional values are $\Phi_F(\breve{p}) = 0.2005$, $\Phi_A(\breve{p}) = 3.6929$ and $\Phi_M(\breve{p}) = 0.3403$. The root mean squared errors are again small as $\mathrm{RMSE}_F = 0.1027$, $\mathrm{RMSE}_A = 0.4409$ and $\mathrm{RMSE}_M = 0.1338$. All these demonstrate the robustness and the applicability of the suggested approach with realistic data.

5. Conclusions

Honeybees are one of the most important species on Earth. Their steady colony number decline is a major global problem. To fight this issue, professional honeybee management must take well-designed precautionary measures. The obtained results in this study help beekeepers to foresee the forward colony dynamics. It is crucial to have the ability to simulate the future development and it is here where mathematical modeling comes to the rescue. Then, adequate measures could be undertaken in order to prevent or to revert a colony collapse.

The novelty of the paper is twofold. To begin with, we proposed a new mathematical approach for modeling of honeybee colonies. We analyzed populations of immature and adult bees as well as their honey production. In the context of honeybee colony dynamics, we model the interaction between the different compartments, focusing on parameter recovery. Secondly, the defined ill-posed problem is solved by means of the adjoint equation optimization method. The reconstructed parameters are unobservable in reality but vital for the colony population dynamics. The computational examples with realistic data demonstrate how to apply the approach in practice.

There are many ways to further develop this research. The considered model could be extended to account for mites, viruses and other hazards. Temperature and seasonal effects also worth considering. What is more, activating the hereditary property via fractional-order derivatives almost always results in a better fit. A broader qualitative analysis to better understand the complex phenomena, processing in the hive, is on the agenda as well.

Author Contributions: Conceptualization, A.Z.A. and L.G.V.; methodology, S.G.G. and L.G.V.; software, S.G.G.; validation, S.G.G.; formal analysis, L.G.V.; investigation, S.G.G. and L.G.V.; resources, A.Z.A. and S.G.G.; data curation, A.Z.A. and S.G.G.; writing—original draft preparation, S.G.G.; writing—review and editing, S.G.G. and L.G.V.; visualization, S.G.G.; supervision, L.G.V.; project administration, A.Z.A.; funding acquisition, A.Z.A. All authors have read and agreed to the published version of the manuscript.

Funding: This research was funded by the Bulgarian National Science Fund under Project KP-06-PN 46-7 "Design and research of fundamental technologies and methods for precision apiculture".

Data Availability Statement: Not applicable.

Conflicts of Interest: The authors declare no conflict of interest.

References

1. Woodard, S.; Fischman, B.; Venkat, A.; Hudson, M.; Varala, K.; Cameron, S.; Clark, A.; Robinson, G. Genes involved in convergent evolution of eusociality in bees. *Proc. Natl. Acad. Sci. USA* **2011**, *108*, 7472–7477. [CrossRef] [PubMed]
2. Matilla, H.; Seeley, T. Genetic diversity in honey bee colonies enhances productivity and fitness. *Science* **2007**, *317*, 362–364. [CrossRef] [PubMed]
3. Farouk, K.; Palmera, K.; Sepúlveda, P. Abejas. In *InfoZoa Boletín de Zoología*; Universidad del Magdalena: Santa Marta, Colombia, 2014; Volume 6.
4. Bulgarian Honey. 2023. Available online: https://www.bulgarianhoney.com/quality.htm (accessed on 7 February 2023).
5. Khoury, D.S.; Myerscough, M.R.; Barron, A.B. A quantitative model of honey bee colony population dynamics. *PLoS ONE* **2011**, *6*, e18491. [CrossRef]
6. Khoury, D.S.; Barron, A.B.; Meyerscough, M.R. Modelling food and population dynamics honey bee colonies. *PLoS ONE* **2013**, *8*, e0059084. [CrossRef] [PubMed]
7. Meyerscough, M.R.; Khoury, D.S.; Ronzani, S.; Barron, A.B. Why do hives die? Using mathematics to solve the problem of honey bee colony collapse. In *The Role and Importance of Mathematics in Innovation: Proceedings of the Forum "Math-for-Industry"*; Anderssen, B., Ed.; Springer: Singapore, 2017; Volume 25, pp. 35–50.
8. Russel, S.; Barron, A.B.; Harris, D. Dynamics modelling of honeybee (*Apis mellifera*) colony growth and failure. *Ecol. Model.* **2013**, *265*, 138–169.
9. Booton, R.D.; Iwasa, Y.; Marshall, J.A.R.; Childs, D.Z. Stress-mediated Allee effects can cause the sudden collapse of honey bee colonies. *J. Theor. Biol.* **2017**, *420*, 213–219. [CrossRef]
10. Finley, J.; Camazine, S.; Frazier, M. The epidemic of honey bee colony losses during the 1995–1996 season. *Am. Bee J.* **1996**, *136*, 805–808.
11. Amdam, G.V.; Omholt, S.W. The hive bee to forager transition in honeybee colonies: The double repressor hypothesis. *J. Theor. Biol.* **2003**, *223*, 451–464. [CrossRef]
12. van der Zee, R.; Pisa, L.; Andronov, S.; Brodschneider, R.; Charriere, J.D.; Chlebo, R.; Coffey, M.F.; Cralisheim, K.; Dahle, B.; Gajda, A.; et al. Managed honey bee colony losses in Canada, China, Europe, Israel and Turkey for the winters of 2008–2009 and 2009–2010. *J. Apic. Res.* **2012**, *51*, 100–114. [CrossRef]
13. Bailey, L. The 'Isle of Wight Disease': The Origin and Significance of the Myth. *Bee World* **1964**, *45*, 32–37. [CrossRef]
14. Kulincevic, J.M.; Rothenbuhler, W.C.; Rinderer, T.E. Disappearing disease. Part 1—Effects of certain protein sources given to honey bee colonies in Florida. *Am. Bee J.* **1982**, *122*, 189–191.
15. Dornberger, L.; Mitchell, C.; Hull, B.; Ventura, W.; Shopp, H.; Kribs-Zaleta, C.; Kojouharov, H.; Grover, J. *Death of the Bees: A Mathematical Model of Colony Collapse Disorder*; Technical Report 2012-12, Mathematics Preprint Series; University of Texas at Arlington Mathematics Department: Arlington, TX, USA, 2012.
16. Hristov, P.; Shumkova, R.; Palova, N.; Neov, B. Factors associated with honey bee colony losses: A mini-review. *Vet. Sci.* **2020**, *7*, 166. [CrossRef] [PubMed]
17. Bagheri, S.; Mirzaie, M. A mathematical model of honey bee colony dynamics to predict the effect of pollen on colony failure. *PLoS ONE* **2019**, *14*, e0225632. [CrossRef] [PubMed]
18. Betti, M.I.; Wahl, L.M.; Zamir, M. Reproduction number and asymptotic stability for the dynamics of a honey bee colony with continuous age structure. *Bull. Math. Biol.* **2017**, *79*, 1586–1611. [CrossRef]
19. Switanek, M.; Crailsheim, K.; Truhetz, H.; Brodschneider, R. Modelling seasonal effects of temperature and precipitation on honey bee winter mortality in a temperate climate. *Sci. Total Environ.* **2017**, *579*, 1581–1587. [CrossRef]

20. Ratti, V.; Kevan, P.G.; Eberl, H.J. A mathematical model of forager loss in honeybee colonies infested with *Varroa destructor* and the acute bee paralysis virus. *Bull. Math. Biol.* **2017**, *79*, 1218–1253. [CrossRef]
21. Becher, M.A.; Osborne, J.L.; Thorbek, P.; Kennedy, P.J.; Grimm, V. Review: Towards a systems approach for understanding honeybee decline: A stocktaking and synthesis of existing models. *J. Appl. Ecol.* **2013**, *50*, 868–880. [CrossRef]
22. Torres, D.J.; Ricoy, V.M.; Roybal, S. Modelling honey bee populations. *PLoS ONE* **2015**, *10*, e0130966. [CrossRef]
23. Yıldız, T.A. A fractional dynamical model for honeybee colony population. *Int. J. Biomath.* **2018**, *11*, 1850063. [CrossRef]
24. Romero-Leiton, J.P.; Gutierrez, A.; Benavides, I.F.; Molina, O.E.; Pulgarín, A. An approach to the modeling of honey bee colonies. *Web Ecol.* **2013**, *22*, 7–19. [CrossRef]
25. Atanasov, A.Z.; Georgiev, S.G.; Vulkov, L.G. Reconstruction analysis of honeybee colony collapse disorder modeling. *Optim. Eng.* **2021**, *22*, 2481–2503. [CrossRef]
26. Atanasov, A.Z.; Georgiev, S.G.; Vulkov, L.G. Parameter identification of Colony Collapse Disorder in honeybees as a contagion. In *Modelling and Development of Intelligent Systems*; Simian, D., Stoica, L.F., Eds.; Springer: Dordrecht, The Netherlands, 2021; Volume 1341, pp. 363–377.
27. Hong, W.; Chen, B.; Lu, Y.; Lu, C.; Liu, S. Using system equalization principle to study the effects of multiple factors to the development of bee colony. *Ecol. Model.* **2022**, *470*, 110002. [CrossRef]
28. Hundsdorfer, W.; Vermer, J. *Numerical Solution of Time-Dependent Advection-Diffusion-Reaction Equations*; Springer: Berlin/Heidelberg, Germany, 2003.
29. Marchuk, G.I. *Adjoint Equations and Analysis of Complex Systems*; Kluwer: Dordrecht, The Netherlands, 1995.
30. Marchuk, G.I.; Agoshkov, V.I.; Shutyaev, V.P. *Adjoint Equations and Perturbation Algorithms in Nonlinear Problems*; CRC Press: Boca Raton, FL, USA, 1996.
31. Winston, W.L. *The Biology of the Honey Bee*; Harvard University Press: Cambridge, MA, USA, 1991.
32. Ma, C.; Jiang, L. Some research on Levenberg–Marquardt method for the nonlinear equations. *Appl. Math. Comp.* **2007**, *184*, 1032–1040. [CrossRef]

Disclaimer/Publisher's Note: The statements, opinions and data contained in all publications are solely those of the individual author(s) and contributor(s) and not of MDPI and/or the editor(s). MDPI and/or the editor(s) disclaim responsibility for any injury to people or property resulting from any ideas, methods, instructions or products referred to in the content.

Article

Two Convergence Results for Inexact Infinite Products of Non-Expansive Mappings

Alexander J. Zaslavski

Department of Mathematics, Technion-Israel Institute of Technology, Haifa 32000, Israel; ajzasl@technion.ac.il

Abstract: We analyze the asymptotic behavior of infinite products of non-linear operators which take a non-empty, closed subset of a complete metric space into the space, taking into account summable computational errors. Our results can be applied in methods for solving convex feasibility and optimization problems.

Keywords: complete metric space; convergence analysis; inexact iteration; infinite product; non-expansive mapping

MSC: 47H09; 47H10; 54E35

Citation: Zaslavski, A.J. Two Convergence Results for Inexact Infinite Products of Non-Expansive Mappings. *Axioms* **2023**, *12*, 88. https://doi.org/10.3390/axioms12010088

Academic Editor: Behzad Djafari-Rouhani

Received: 2 December 2022
Revised: 6 January 2023
Accepted: 12 January 2023
Published: 14 January 2023

Copyright: © 2023 by the author. Licensee MDPI, Basel, Switzerland. This article is an open access article distributed under the terms and conditions of the Creative Commons Attribution (CC BY) license (https://creativecommons.org/licenses/by/4.0/).

1. Introduction

The fixed-point theory of non-linear operators has been a rapidly growing area of research [1–19]. The starting point of this theory is Banach's classical result [20] on the existence of a unique fixed point for a strict contraction. Since that seminal paper, many developments have taken place in this field [18,19,21–30].

In our joint paper with D. Butnariu and S. Reich [3], it was established that if every sequence of iterates of a non-expansive operator converges, then this convergence property also takes place for every sequence of inexact iterates under the presence of summable errors. In our subsequent joint paper with D. Butnariu and S. Reich [31], this result was extended for inexact infinite products of non-expansive self-mappings of a complete metric space. Here, we analyze the convergence of inexact infinite products of non-expansive operators which take a non-empty, closed subset K of a complete metric space into the space, taking into account summable computational errors and obtaining a generalization of the result of [31] mentioned above. Namely, we show that for each pair of sequence of points $\{x_i\}_{i=0}^\infty$ and $\{y_i\}_{i=0}^\infty$ generated by our inexact infinite products which belong to the subset K, the distance between x_i and y_i tends to zero as $i \to \infty$.

2. Preliminaries

Suppose that (X, ρ) is a complete metric space equipped with a metric ρ. For an arbitrary element $\eta \in X$ and an arbitrary set $C \subset X$, put

$$\rho(\eta, C) = \inf\{\rho(\eta, \xi) : \xi \in C\}.$$

For any $\eta \in X$ and any $\gamma \in (0, \infty)$ put

$$B(\eta, \gamma) = \{\xi \in X : \rho(\eta, \xi) \leq \gamma\}.$$

For any operator $S : X \to X$, let $S^0 y = y$ for every point $y \in X$.

In our joint paper with D. Butnariu and S. Reich [3], we investigated the influence of computational errors on the asymptotic behavior of iterates of non-expansive operators in complete metric spaces and established the following theorem (see also Theorem 2.72 of [16]).

Theorem 1. *Assume that* $A : X \to X$ *satisfies*

$$\rho(A\xi, A\eta) \leq \rho(\xi, \eta) \text{ every pair of points } \xi, \eta \in X,$$

$F(A)$ *is the collection of all fixed points of the operator* A *and for every point* $\xi \in X$, *the sequence of iterates* $\{A^n \xi\}_{n=1}^{\infty}$ *converges* (X, ρ).
Assume that $\{r_n\}_{n=0}^{\infty} \subset (0, \infty)$ *satisfies*

$$\sum_{n=0}^{\infty} r_n < \infty$$

and that a sequence of inexact iterates $\{x_n\}_{n=0}^{\infty} \subset X$ *for every non-negative integer* n *satisfies*

$$\rho(x_{n+1}, A x_n) \leq r_n.$$

Then, the sequence $\{x_n\}_{n=1}^{\infty}$ *converges to a point of* $F(A)$.

Theorem 1 has important applications and is an essential ingredient in the superiorization and perturbation resilience of algorithms [21–23,25,26]. The superiorization methodology works by analyzing the perturbation resilience of an iterative algorithm, and then applying proactively such perturbations in order to make the perturbed algorithm perform something useful in an addition to its original task. This methodology is illustrated by the next discussion.

Assume that $(X, \|\cdot\|)$ is a Banach space equipped with the norm $\|\cdot\|$, $\rho(\xi, \eta) = \|\xi - \eta\|$ for all $\xi, \eta \in X$, an operator $A : X \to X$ satisfies

$$\|A(\xi) - A(\eta)\| \leq \|\xi - \eta\|, \ \xi, \eta \in X$$

and that for any point $\eta \in X$, the sequence $\{A^n \eta\}_{n=1}^{\infty}$ converges in the norm topology, $\xi_0 \in X$, $\{\alpha_t\}_{t=0}^{\infty} \subset (0, \infty)$ satisfies

$$\sum_{t=0}^{\infty} \alpha_t < \infty,$$

$\{u_t\}_{t=0}^{\infty} \subset X$ satisfies

$$\sup\{\|u_t\| : t = 0, 1, \dots\} < \infty$$

and that for every non-negative integer $t \geq 0$,

$$\xi_{t+1} = A(\xi_t + \alpha_t u_t).$$

Theorem 1 implies that $\{\xi_k\}_{k=0}^{\infty}$ converges and its limit ξ satisfies $A(\xi) = \xi$. In this case, the mapping A is called bounded perturbations resilient [22].

Now, assume that $\xi_0 \in X$ and the summable sequence of positive numbers $\{\alpha_t\}_{t=0}^{\infty}$ are given. We construct a sequence of iterates $\{\xi_t\}_{t=1}^{\infty}$ determined by the equation above. Under an appropriate choice of $\{u_t\}_{t=0}^{\infty}$, the sequence of inexact iterates $\{\xi_t\}_{t=1}^{\infty}$ has some useful properties. Namely, the sequence $\{f(\xi_t)\}_{t=1}^{\infty}$ can be decreasing, where f is a given objective function.

In our joint paper with D. Butnariu and S. Reich [31], we extended Theorem 1 for inexact infinite products of non-expansive self-mappings of a complete metric space. In the present paper, we investigate the convergence of inexact infinite products of non-expansive mappings which take a non-empty, closed subset K of a complete metric space into the space and obtain a generalization of the result of the work [31]. Namely, we show that for each pair of sequence of points $\{x_i\}_{i=0}^{\infty}$ and $\{y_i\}_{i=0}^{\infty}$ generated by our inexact infinite products which belong to the subset K, the distance between x_i and y_i tends to zero as $i \to \infty$.

The most important and well-known application of the results obtained in [3,31] and here is the convex feasibility problem: to find a common point of a family of convex, closed subsets C_i, $i = 1, \ldots, m$ of a Hilbert space. The convex feasibility problems arises in radiation planning and computer tomography. In order to solve this problem, one usually uses infinite products of projections on the sets C_i, $i = 1, \ldots, m$ or more advanced dynamic string-averaging projection methods [18,19,25]. Our results, as well as the results of [3,31], explain stability effects arising in numerical experiments under the presence of small computational errors [21].

3. A Convergence Result in a Metric Space

Assume that K is a non-empty, closed set in a complete metric space (X, ρ) equipped with the metric ρ. Denote by $\mathcal{A}$ the collection of all operators $S : K \to X$ for which

$$\rho(S(\eta), S(\xi)) \leq \rho(\eta, \xi),\ \eta, \xi \in K. \tag{1}$$

Assume that $\mathcal{R}$ is a collection of maps $T : \{1, 2, \ldots, \} \to \mathcal{A}$ which have the following two properties:

(a) For every map $T \in \mathcal{R}$ and every natural number s the map $\tilde{T}(t) = T(t+s)$, $t \in \{1, 2, \ldots\}$ belongs to $\mathcal{R}$;

(b) For any map $T \in \mathcal{R}$ and every pair $\{\xi_t\}_{t=0}^\infty$, $\{\eta_t\}_{t=0}^\infty \subset K$ for which

$$\xi_{t+1} = T(t+1)(\xi_t),\ \eta_{t+1} = T(t+1)(\eta_t),\ t = 0, 1, \ldots$$

the equation
$$\lim_{t \to \infty} \rho(\xi_t, \eta_t) = 0$$

is true.

We will prove the following result.

Theorem 2. *Assume that $T \in \mathcal{R}$, $\Delta > 0$, $\{\Delta_i\}_{i=1}^\infty \subset (0, \infty)$ satisfies*

$$\sum_{i=1}^\infty \Delta_i < \infty \tag{2}$$

and that $\{x_t\}_{t=0}^\infty$, $\{y_t\}_{t=0}^\infty \subset K$ satisfy for every non-negative integer t,

$$\rho(x_{t+1}, T(t+1)(x_t)) \leq \Delta_{t+1},\ \rho(y_{t+1}, T(t+1)(y_t)) \leq \Delta_{t+1}, \tag{3}$$

and
$$B(x_t, \Delta),\ B(y_t, \Delta) \subset K. \tag{4}$$

Then,
$$\lim_{t \to \infty} \rho(x_t, y_t) = 0.$$

4. Proof of Theorem 2

We may assume without loss of generality that
$$\Delta < 1.$$

Let
$$\epsilon \in (0, \Delta). \tag{5}$$

In view of Equation (2), there is an integer $n_0 \geq 1$ for which

$$\sum_{j=n_0}^\infty \Delta_j < \epsilon/9. \tag{6}$$

Set
$$\tilde{x}_{n_0} = x_{n_0} \tag{7}$$

and
$$\tilde{x}_{n_0+1} = T(n_0+1)(\tilde{x}_{n_0}). \tag{8}$$

By (3), (7) and (8),
$$\rho(\tilde{x}_{n_0+1}, x_{n_0+1}) = \rho(x_{n_0+1}, T(n_0+1)(x_{n_0})) \leq \Delta_{n_0+1}. \tag{9}$$

Equations (4), (6) and (9) imply that
$$\tilde{x}_{n_0+1} \in K.$$

Therefore, we can define
$$\tilde{x}_{n_0+2} = T(n_0+2)(\tilde{x}_{n_0+1}).$$

By induction, we define iterates $\tilde{x}_j$ for all natural numbers $j > n_0$. If $j > n_0$ is an integer and $\tilde{x}_j \in K$ was defined, then we set
$$\tilde{x}_{j+1} = T(j+1)(\tilde{x}_j). \tag{10}$$

Assume that $m > n_0$ is an integer and that $\tilde{x}_i \in K$, $i = n_0, \ldots, m$ are defined and that for each $i \in \{n_0+1, \ldots, m\}$,
$$\rho(\tilde{x}_i, x_i) \leq \sum_{j=n_0+1}^{i} \Delta_j. \tag{11}$$

(Clearly, by Equation (9), our assumption is true for $m = n_0 + 1$.) Equations (5), (6) and (11) imply that
$$\rho(x_m, \tilde{x}_m) \leq \sum_{j=n_0+1}^{\infty} \Delta_j < \epsilon/8 < \Delta/4. \tag{12}$$

By Equations (4) and (12), we have
$$\tilde{x}_m \in K$$

and then
$$\tilde{x}_{m+1} = T(m+1)\tilde{x}_m$$

is defined.

Equations (1), (3) and (11) imply that
$$\begin{aligned}\rho(\tilde{x}_{m+1}, x_{m+1}) &\leq \rho(T(m+1)(\tilde{x}_m), T(m+1)(x_m)) + \rho(T(m+1)(x_m), x_{m+1}) \\ &\leq \rho(\tilde{x}_m, x_m) + \Delta_{m+1} \\ &\leq \sum_{j=n_0+1}^{m} \Delta_j + \Delta_{m+1} = \sum_{j=n_0+1}^{m+1} \Delta_j.\end{aligned} \tag{13}$$

In view of (13), Equation (11) is true for $i = m+1$. By (4)–(6) and (13),
$$\rho(\tilde{x}_{m+1}, x_{m+1}) < \epsilon/8 < \Delta/8.$$

and
$$\tilde{x}_{m+1} \in K.$$

Thus, the assumption which was made for m is true for $m+1$ as well. By induction, we showed that $\tilde{x}_i \in K$ is defined for all integers $i \geq n_0$ and (11) is true for all integers $i \geq n_0 + 1$. Set
$$\tilde{y}_{n_0} = y_{n_0}$$

and if an integer $i \geq n_0$ and $\tilde{y}_i \in K$ is defined, then set
$$\tilde{y}_{i+1} = T(i+1)(\tilde{y}_i).$$

Arguing as before, we can show that for any natural number $i \geq n_0$, $\tilde{y}_i \in K$ is defined and that

$$\rho(\tilde{y}_i, y_i) \leq \sum_{j=n_0+1}^{i} \Delta_j. \tag{14}$$

Properties (a) and (b) imply that

$$\lim_{i \to \infty} \rho(\tilde{x}_i, \tilde{y}_i) = 0 \tag{15}$$

By Equation (15), there is a natural number $n_1 \geq n_0$ such that for any natural number $i \geq n_1$, we have

$$\rho(\tilde{x}_i, \tilde{y}_i) \leq \epsilon/4. \tag{16}$$

Equations (8), (11), (14) and (16) imply that for any natural number $i \geq n_1$,

$$\rho(x_i, y_i) \leq \rho(x_i, \tilde{x}_i) + \rho(\tilde{x}_i, \tilde{y}_i) + \rho(\tilde{y}_i, y_i)$$

$$\leq 2 \sum_{j=n_0+1}^{i} \Delta_j + \epsilon/4 \leq \epsilon/8 + \epsilon/8 + \epsilon/4.$$

Theorem 2 is proved.

5. A Weak Convergence Result

Assume that K is a non-empty, closed set in a Banach space $(E, \|\cdot\|)$ equipped with the norm $\|\cdot\|$ with a dual space $(E^*, \|\cdot\|_*)$. For each $\xi, \eta \in E$, put $\rho(\xi, \eta) = \|\xi - \eta\|$. Denote by $\mathcal{A}$ the collection of all maps $S : K \to E$, for which

$$\|S(\eta) - A(\xi)\| \leq \|\eta - \xi\|, \ \eta, \xi \in K. \tag{17}$$

Assume that $\mathcal{R}$ is a collection of maps $T : \{1, 2, \ldots, \infty\} \to \mathcal{A}$ which have the following two properties:

(a) For every map $T \in \mathcal{R}$ and every natural number s, the map $\tilde{T}(t) = T(t+s)$, $t \in \{1, 2, \ldots\}$ belongs to $\mathcal{R}$;

(b) For any map $T \in \mathcal{R}$ and each $\{x_t\}_{t=0}^{\infty}, \{y_t\}_{t=0}^{\infty} \subset K$ which satisfies

$$x_{t+1} = T(t+1)(x_t), \ y_{t+1} = T(t+1)(y_t), \ t = 0, 1, \ldots,$$

the sequence $\{x_t - y_t\}_{t=0}^{\infty}$ converges weakly in X to the zero.

We will prove the following result.

Theorem 3. *Assume that $T \in \mathcal{R}$, $\Delta > 0$, $\{\Delta_j\}_{j=1}^{\infty} \subset (0, \infty)$ satisfies*

$$\sum_{j=1}^{\infty} \Delta_j < \infty \tag{18}$$

and that $\{x_t\}_{t=0}^{\infty}, \{y_t\}_{t=0}^{\infty} \subset K$ satisfy for every non-negative integer t,

$$\|x_{t+1} - T(t+1)(x_t)\| \leq \Delta_{t+1}, \ \|y_{t+1} - T(t+1)(y_t)\| \leq \Delta_{t+1}, \tag{19}$$

and

$$B(x_t, \Delta), \ B(y_t, \Delta) \subset K. \tag{20}$$

Then the sequence $\{x_t - y_t\}_{t=0}^{\infty}$ converges weakly in X to the zero.

6. Proof of Theorem 3

We may assume without loss of generality that

$$\Delta < 1.$$

Let $f \in E^*$ satisfy

$$\|f\|_* \leq 1, \ \epsilon \in (0, \Delta). \tag{21}$$

In order to prove the theorem, it is sufficient to show that

$$\lim_{i \to \infty} f(y_i - x_i) = 0.$$

By (18), there is $n_0 \in \{1, 2, \ldots\}$, for which

$$\sum_{i=n_0}^{\infty} \Delta_i < \epsilon/8. \tag{22}$$

Set

$$\tilde{x}_{n_0} = x_{n_0} \tag{23}$$

and

$$\tilde{x}_{n_0+1} = T(n_0+1)(\tilde{x}_{n_0}). \tag{24}$$

By (19)–(24),

$$\|\tilde{x}_{n_0+1} - x_{n_0+1}\| \leq \Delta_{n_0+1}, \ \tilde{x}_{n_0+1} \in K. \tag{25}$$

By induction, we define $\tilde{x}_t \in K$ for every natural number $t > n_0$. If $i > n_0$ is an integer and $\tilde{x}_i \in K$ was defined, then we set

$$\tilde{x}_{i+1} = T(i+1)(\tilde{x}_i). \tag{26}$$

Assume that $m > n_0$ is an integer and that $\tilde{x}_i \in K$; $i = n_0, \ldots, m$ are defined using (26) and for each $i \in \{n_0+1, \ldots, m\}$,

$$\|\tilde{x}_i - x_i\| \leq \sum_{j=n_0+1}^{i} \Delta_j. \tag{27}$$

(It should be mentioned that by (25) our assumption is valid for $m = n_0 + 1$.) By (27), we have

$$\|x_m - \tilde{x}_m\| \leq \sum_{j=n_0+1}^{m} \Delta_j. \tag{28}$$

Set

$$\tilde{x}_{m+1} = T(m+1)(\tilde{x}_m).$$

Equations (17), (19), (28) and (29) imply that

$$\begin{aligned}
\|\tilde{x}_{m+1} - x_{m+1}\| &\leq \|T(m+1)(\tilde{x}_m) - T(m+1)(x_m)\| + \|T(m+1)(x_m) - x_{m+1}\| \\
&\leq \|\tilde{x}_m - x_m\| + \Delta_{m+1} \\
&\leq \sum_{j=n_0+1}^{m} \Delta_j + \Delta_{m+1} = \sum_{j=n_0+1}^{m+1} \Delta_j.
\end{aligned} \tag{29}$$

In view of (29), Equation (27) is true for $i = m + 1$. By (20)–(22) and (29),

$$\|\tilde{x}_{m+1} - x_{m+1}\| < \epsilon/8 < \Delta/8.$$

and

$$\tilde{x}_{m+1} \in K.$$

Thus, the assumption which was made for m is true for $m+1$ as well. By induction, we showed that $\tilde{x}_i \in K$ is defined for all integers $i \geq n_0$ by (26) and (27) holds for all integers $i \geq n_0 + 1$. Set

$$\tilde{y}_{n_0} = y_{n_0} \tag{30}$$

and if an integer $i \geq n_0$ and $\tilde{y}_i \in K$ is defined, then set

$$\tilde{y}_{i+1} = T(i+1)(\tilde{y}_i). \tag{31}$$

Arguing as before, we can show that for every integer $i \geq n_0 + 1$, $\tilde{y}_i \in K$ is defined and that

$$\|\tilde{y}_i - y_i\| \leq \sum_{j=n_0+1}^{i} \Delta_j. \tag{32}$$

Properties (a) and (b) and Equations (23), (26), (30) and (31) imply that

$$\tilde{x}_i - \tilde{y}_i \to 0 \text{ weakly in } E \text{ as } i \to \infty. \tag{33}$$

In order to complete the proof of our result, it is sufficient to show that the inequality

$$|f(x_i - y_i)| < \epsilon$$

is true for all sufficiently large natural numbers $i \geq 0$. By (33),

$$\lim_{i \to \infty} f(\tilde{y}_i - \tilde{x}_i) = 0.$$

Thus, there is a natural number $n_1 > n_0$ such that for every natural number $i \geq n_1$,

$$|f(\tilde{x}_i - \tilde{y}_i)| \leq \epsilon/8. \tag{34}$$

Following Equations (22), (27), (32) and (34), for every natural number $i \geq n_1$,

$$|f(x_i - y_i)| \leq |f(x_i - \tilde{x}_i)| + |f(\tilde{x}_i - \tilde{y}_i)| + |f(\tilde{y}_i - y_i)|$$

$$\leq \|f\|_* \|x_i - \tilde{x}_i\| + \epsilon/8 + \|f\|_* \|y_i - \tilde{y}_i\|$$

$$\leq 2 \sum_{j=n_0+1}^{\infty} \Delta_j + \epsilon/8 < \epsilon.$$

Theorem 3 is proved.

7. Conclusions

We analyze the asymptotic behavior of infinite products of non-linear operators which take a non-empty, closed subset K of a complete metric space into the space, taking into account summable computational errors and obtaining a generalization of the result of [31]. More precisely, we show that for each pair of sequence of points $\{x_i\}_{i=0}^{\infty}$ and $\{y_i\}_{i=0}^{\infty}$ generated by our inexact infinite products which belong to the subset K, the distance between x_i and y_i tends to zero as $i \to \infty$. The most important and well-known application of the results obtained in [3,31] and here is the convex feasibility problem: to find a common point of a family of convex, closed subsets C_i, $i = 1, \ldots, m$ of a Hilbert space. The convex feasibility problems arises in radiation planning and computer tomography. In order to solve this problem, one usually uses infinite products of projections on the sets C_i, $i = 1, \ldots, m$ or more advanced dynamic string-averaging projection methods [18,19,25]. Our results as well as the results of [3,31] explain stability effects arising in numerical experiments under the presence of small computational errors [21].

Funding: This research received no external funding.

Conflicts of Interest: The authors declare no conflict of interest.

References

1. Bejenaru, A.; Postolache, M. An unifying approach for some nonexpansiveness conditions on modular vector spaces. *Nonlinear Anal. Model. Control.* **2020**, *25*, 827–845. [CrossRef]
2. Betiuk-Pilarska, A.; Benavides, T.D. Fixed points for nonexpansive mappings and generalized nonexpansive mappings on Banach lattices. *Pure Appl. Func. Anal.* **2016**, *1*, 343–359.
3. Butnariu, D.; Reich, S.; Zaslavski, A.J.; Convergence to fixed points of inexact orbits of Bregman-monotone and of nonexpansive operators in Banach spaces. In *Proceedings of Fixed Point Theory and its Applications*; Yokahama Publishers: Yokahama, Mexico, 2006; pp. 11–32.
4. de Blasi, F.S.; Myjak, J. Sur la convergence des approximations successives pour les contractions non linéaires dans un espace de Banach. *C. R. Acad. Sci. Paris* **1976**, *283*, 185–187.
5. de Blasi, F.S.; Myjak, J. Sur la porosité de l'ensemble des contractions sans point fixe. *C. R. Acad. Sci. Paris* **1989**, *308*, 51–54.
6. Goebel, K.; Kirk, W.A. *Topics in Metric Fixed Point Theory*; Cambridge University Press: Cambridge, UK, 1990.
7. Goebel, K.; Reich, S. *Uniform Convexity, Hyperbolic Geometry, and Nonexpansive Mappings*; Marcel Dekker: New York, NY, USA; Basel, Switzerland, 1984.
8. Iyiola, O.S.; Shehu, Y. New convergence results for inertial Krasnoselskii–Mann iterations in Hilbert spaces with applications. *Results Math.* **2021**, *76*, 75. [CrossRef]
9. Jachymski, J. Extensions of the Dugundji-Granas and Nadler's theorems on the continuity of fixed points. *Pure Appl. Funct. Anal.* **2017**, *2*, 657–666.
10. Kanzow, C.; Shehu, Y. Generalized Krasnoselskii-Mann-type iterations for nonexpansive mappings in Hilbert spaces. *Comput Optim. Appl.* **2017**, *67*, 595–620. [CrossRef]
11. Kirk, W.A. Contraction Mappings and extensions. In *Handbook of Metric Fixed Point Theory*; Kluwer: Dordrecht, The Netherlands, 2001; pp. 1–34.
12. Kozlowski, W.M. *An Introduction to Fixed Point Theory in Modular Function Spaces*; Topics in fixed point theory; Springer: Cham, Switzerland, 2014; pp. 15–222.
13. Kubota, R.; Takahashi, W.; Takeuchi, Y. Extensions of Browder's demiclosedness principle and Reich's lemma and their applications. *Pure Appl. Func. Anal.* **2016**, *1*, 63–84.
14. Rakotch, E. A note on contractive mappings. *Proc. Am. Math. Soc.* **1962**, *13*, 459–465. [CrossRef]
15. Reich, S. Fixed points of contractive functions. *Boll. Unione Mat. Ital.* **1972**, *5*, 26–42.
16. Reich, S.; Zaslavski, A.J. *Genericity in Nonlinear Analysis (Developments in Mathematics, 34)*; Springer: New York, NY, USA, 2014.
17. Shehu, Y. Iterative approximations for zeros of sum of accretive operators in Banach spaces. *J. Funct. Spaces* **2016**, *2016*, 5973468. [CrossRef]
18. Zaslavski, A.J. *Approximate Solutions of Common Fixed Point Problems*; Springer Optimization and Its Applications; Springer: Cham, Switzerland, 2016.
19. Zaslavski, A.J. *Algorithms for Solving Common Fixed Point Problems*; Springer Optimization and Its Applications; Springer: Cham, Switzerland, 2018.
20. Banach, S. Sur les opérations dans les ensembles abstraits et leur application aux équations intégrales. *Fund. Math.* **1922**, *3*, 133–181. [CrossRef]
21. Butnariu, D.; Davidi, R.; Herman, G.T.; Kazantsev, I.G. Stable convergence behavior under summable perturbations of a class of projection methods for convex feasibility and optimization problems. *IEEE J. Sel. Top. Signal Process.* **2007**, *1*, 540–547. [CrossRef]
22. Censor, Y.; Davidi, R.; Herman, G.T. Perturbation resilience and superiorization of iterative algorithms. *Inverse Probl.* **2010**, *26*, 65008. [CrossRef] [PubMed]
23. Censor, Y.; Davidi, R.; Herman, G.T.; Schulte, R.W.; Tetruashvili, L. Projected subgradient minimization versus superiorization. *J. Optim. Theory Appl.* **2014**, *160*, 730–747. [CrossRef]
24. Censor, Y.; Reem, D. Zero-convex functions, perturbation resilience, and subgradient projections for feasibility-seeking methods. *Math. Program.* **2015**, *152*, 339–380. [CrossRef]
25. Censor, Y.; Zaknoon, M. Algorithms and convergence results of projection methods for inconsistent feasibility problems: A review. *Pure Appl. Func. Anal.* **2018**, *3*, 565–586.
26. Censor, Y.; Zur, Y. *Linear Superiorization for Infeasible Linear Programming*; Lecture Notes in Computer Science; Springer: Cham, Switzerland, 2016; Volume 9869, pp. 15–24.
27. Gibali, A. A new split inverse problem and an application to least intensity feasible solutions. *Pure Appl. Funct. Anal.* **2017**, *2*, 243–258.
28. Gibali, A.; Reich, S.; Zalas, R. Outer approximation methods for solving variational inequalities in Hilbert space. *Optimization* **2017**, *66*, 417–437. [CrossRef]
29. Takahashi, W. The split common fixed point problem and the shrinking projection method for new nonlinear mappings in two Banach spaces. *Pure Appl. Funct. Anal.* **2017**, *2*, 685–699.

30. Takahashi, W. A general iterative method for split common fixed point problems in Hilbert spaces and applications. *Pure Appl. Funct. Anal.* **2018**, *3*, 349–369.
31. Butnariu, D.; Reich, S.; Zaslavski, A.J. Stable convergence theorems for infinite products and powers of nonexpansive mappings. *Numer. Funct. Anal. Optim.* **2008**, *29*, 304–323. [CrossRef]

Disclaimer/Publisher's Note: The statements, opinions and data contained in all publications are solely those of the individual author(s) and contributor(s) and not of MDPI and/or the editor(s). MDPI and/or the editor(s) disclaim responsibility for any injury to people or property resulting from any ideas, methods, instructions or products referred to in the content.

Article

Fixed-Point Theorems for $\mathcal{L}_\gamma$ Contractions in Branciari Distance Spaces

Seong-Hoon Cho

Departments of Mathematics, Hanseo University, Seosan-si 356-706, Chungnam-do, Korea; shcho@hanseo.ac.kr

Abstract: In this paper, the concepts of Suzuki-type $\mathcal{L}_\gamma$ contractions and Suzuki–Berinde-type $\mathcal{L}_\gamma$ contractions are introduced, and new fixed-point theorems for these two contractions are established.

Keywords: fixed point; $\mathcal{L}$ contraction; $\mathcal{L}_\gamma$ contraction; Suzuki-type $\mathcal{L}_\gamma$ contraction; Suzuki–Berinde-type $\mathcal{L}_\gamma$ contraction; metric space; Branciari distance space

MSC: 47H10; 54H25

1. Introduction

In 2009, Suzuki [1] generalized the Banach contraction principle to compact metric space by introducing the notion of a contractive map $T : U \to U$, where (U, ϱ) is compact metric space, such that

$$\forall u, v \in U (u \neq v), \frac{1}{2}\varrho(u, Tu) < \varrho(u, v) \text{ implies } \varrho(Tu, Tv) < \varrho(u, v).$$

Berinde [2] introduced the notion of almost contractions:

A map $T : U \to U$, where (U, ϱ) is a metric space, is called almost contraction provided that it satisfies

$$\varrho(Tu, Tv) \leq q\varrho(u, v) + K\varrho(v, Tu),$$

where $q \in (0,1)$ and $K \geq 0$.

Berinde [2] generalized the Banach contraction principle by proving the existence of fixed points for almost contractions defined on complete metric spaces.

On the other hand, Branciari [3] gave a generalization of the notion of metric spaces, which is called Branciari distance spaces, by replacing triangle inequality with trapezoidal inequality, and he gave an extension of Banach contraction principle to Branciari distance spaces. He used the following to obtain the main results:

(1) each open ball is open set;
(2) each Branciari distance is continuous in each the coordinates;
(3) each topology induced by Branciari distance spaces is a Hausdorff topological space.

Sarma et al. showed that (1), (2), and (3) are false (see example 1.1 in [4]), and they extended the Banach contraction principle to a Branciari distance space under the assumption of Hausdorffness of the space (more specifically, the uniqueness of the limits of the converging sequences). Since then, some authors (for example, [5–7]) obtained fixed-point results in Branciari distance spaces under the assumption that the spaces are Hausdorff and/or the Branciari distances are continuous.

In particular, Kadelburg and Radenivić [8] investigated the existence of fixed points in Branciari distance spaces without the two conditions:

· Hausdorffness of Branciari distance spaces;
· Continuity of the Branciari distances.

After that, many authors ([4–6,9–26] and references therein) extended fixed-point results from metric spaces to Branciari distance spaces.

Given function ϑ from $(0,\infty)$ into $(1,\infty)$, we consider the following conditions:

(ϑ1) ϑ is non-decreasing;
(ϑ2) for any sequence $\{s_n\} \subset (0,\infty)$,
$$\lim_{n\to\infty} \vartheta(s_n) = 1 \Leftrightarrow \lim_{n\to\infty} s_n = 0;$$

(ϑ3) there are $q \in (0,1)$ and $k \in (0,\infty)$, such that
$$\lim_{s\to 0^+} \frac{\vartheta(s) - 1}{s^q} = k$$

(ϑ4) ϑ is continuous on $(0,\infty)$.

Jleli and Samet [22] obtained a generalization of the Banach contraction principle in Branciari distance spaces by introducing the concept of ϑ contractions, where $\vartheta : (0,\infty) \to (1,\infty)$ satisfies conditions (ϑ1), (ϑ2) and (ϑ3). Ahmad et al. [27] generalized the result of Jleli and Samet [22] to metric spaces by applying conditions (ϑ1), (ϑ2), and (ϑ4), and they introduced the notion of Suzuki–Berinde-type ϑ contractions and investigated the existence of fixed points for such contractions.

Very recently, Cho [24] introduced the concept of $\mathcal{L}$ contractions, which is a more generalized concept than some existing notions of contractions. He proved that every $\mathcal{L}$ contraction mapping defined on complete Branciari distance spaces possesses only one fixed point.

Afterward, the authors [23,28–33] gave generalizations of the result of [24].

In the paper, we introduce the new two concepts of Suzuki-type $\mathcal{L}_\gamma$ contractions and Suzuki–Berinde-type $\mathcal{L}_\gamma$ contractions, which are a generalization of the concept of $\mathcal{L}$ contractions, and we establish two new fixed point theorems for these two contractions in the setting of Branciari distance spaces. We give examples to support main theorem.

Let $\xi : [1,\infty) \times [1,\infty) \to (-\infty,\infty)$ be a function.
Consider the following conditions:

(ξ1) $\xi(1,1) = 1$;
(ξ2) $\xi(t,s) < \frac{s}{t}$ $\forall s, t > 1$;
(ξ3) $\xi(t,s) < \frac{\gamma(s)}{\gamma(t)}$ $\forall s, t > 1$, where γ is a non-decreasing self-mapping on $[1,\infty)$, satisfying $\gamma^{-1}(\{1\}) = 1$;
(ξ4) for any sequence $\{t_m\}, \{s_m\} \subset (1,\infty)$ with $t_m \leq s_m, m = 1,2,3,\cdots$,
$$\lim_{m\to\infty} t_m = \lim_{m\to\infty} s_m > 1 \Rightarrow \lim_{m\to\infty} \sup \xi(t_m, s_m) < 1.$$

A function $\xi : [1,\infty) \times [1,\infty) \to (-\infty,\infty)$ is said to be $\mathcal{L}$-simulation [24] whenever the conditions (ξ1), (ξ2), and (ξ4) are satisfied.

Note that $\xi(t,t) < 1$ $\forall t > 1$.

We say that $\xi : [1,\infty) \times [1,\infty) \to (-\infty,\infty)$ is an $\mathcal{L}_\gamma$-simulation provided that the condition (ξ1), (ξ3) and (ξ4) hold.

Remark 1. *If $\gamma(t) = t$ $\forall t \geq 1$, then $\mathcal{L}_\gamma$-simulation is $\mathcal{L}$-simulation.*

Denote $\mathcal{L}$ by the class of all $\mathcal{L}$-simulation functions $\xi : [1,\infty) \times [1,\infty) \to (-\infty,\infty)$, and $\mathcal{L}_\gamma$ by the collection of all $\mathcal{L}_\gamma$-simulation functions $\xi : [1,\infty) \times [1,\infty) \to (-\infty,\infty)$.

Example 1. *Let $\xi_b, \xi_w, \xi_c : [1,\infty) \times [1,\infty) \to (-\infty,\infty)$ be functions defined as follows, respectively:*

(i) $\xi_b(t,s) = \frac{[\gamma(s)]^r}{\gamma(t)}$ *for all $t, s \geq 1$, where $r \in (0,1)$;*

(ii) $\xi_w(t,s) = \frac{\gamma(s)}{\gamma(t)\phi(\gamma(s))}$ $\forall t, s \geq 1$, where ϕ is a non-decreasing and lower semi-continuous self-mapping on $[1, \infty)$, satisfying $\phi^{-1}(\{1\}) = 1$;

(iii) $\xi_c(t,s) = \begin{cases} 1 & \text{if } (s,t) = (1,1), \\ \frac{\gamma(s)}{2\gamma(t)} & \text{if } s < t, \\ \frac{[\gamma(s)]^\lambda}{\gamma(t)} & \text{otherwise}, \end{cases}$

$\forall s, t \geq 1$, where $\lambda \in (0,1)$.

Then, $\xi_b, \xi_w, \xi_c \in \mathcal{L}_\gamma$.

Note that if $\gamma(t) = t$ $\forall t \geq 1$, then $\xi_b, \xi_w, \xi_c \in \mathcal{L}$ (see [24]).

Example 2. Let $\xi_1, \xi_2, \xi_3 : [1, \infty) \times [1, \infty) \to (-\infty, \infty)$ be functions defined as follows:

(i) $\xi_1(t,s) = \frac{\gamma(\psi(s))}{\gamma(\varphi(t))}$, $\forall t, s \geq 1$, where ψ and φ are continuous self-mappings on $[1, \infty)$, satisfying $\psi(t) = \varphi(t) = 1 \Leftrightarrow t = 1$, $\psi(t) < t \leq \varphi(t)$, $\forall t > 1$ and φ is an increasing mapping;

(ii) $\xi_2(t,s) = \frac{\gamma(\eta(s))}{\gamma(t)}$, $\forall s, t \geq 1$, where η is a upper semi-continuous self-mapping on $[1, \infty)$, satisfying $\eta(t) < t$, $\forall t > 1$ and $\eta(t) = 1 \Leftrightarrow t = 1$;

(iii) $\xi_3(t,s) = \frac{\gamma(s)}{\gamma(\int_0^t \phi(u) du)}$, $\forall s, t \geq 1$, where ϕ is a self-mapping on $[0, \infty)$, satisfying $\forall t \geq 1$, $\int_0^t \phi(s) ds$ exists and $\int_0^t \phi(s) ds > t$, and $\int_0^1 \phi(s) ds = 1$.

Then, $\xi_1, \xi_2, \xi_3 \in \mathcal{L}_\gamma$.

Note that if $\gamma(t) = t$ $\forall t \geq 1$, then $\xi_1, \xi_2, \xi_3 \in \mathcal{L}$ (see [30]).

The following definitions are in [3].

A map $\varrho : U \times U \to [0, \infty)$, where U is a non-empty set, is said to be *Branciari distance* on U if the following conditions are satisfied:

for all $u, v \in U$ and for $z, w \in U - \{u, v\}$

(ϱ1) $\varrho(u,v) = 0 \Leftrightarrow u = v$;
(ϱ2) $\varrho(u,v) = \varrho(v,u)$;
(ϱ3) $\varrho(u,v) \leq \varrho(u,z) + \varrho(z,w) + \varrho(w,v)$ (trapezoidal inequality).

The pairs (U, ϱ) is said to be a *Branciari distance space*.

Note that Branciari distance space (U, ϱ) can not reduce the standard metric space and it does not have a topology which is compatible with ϱ (e.g., [34] and Remark 4 (3)). For such reasons, we call (U, ϱ) a Branciari distance space, not a rectangular metric space or a generalized metric space.

Remark 2. *If the triangle inequality is satisfied, the trapezoidal inequality is satisfied. However, the converse is not true. Thus, the class of Branciari distance spaces includes metric spaces.*

The notion of convergence in Branciari distance spaces is similar to that of metric spaces (e.g., [3]).

Let (U, ϱ) be a Branciari distance space and $\{u_n\} \subset U$ be a sequence and $u \in U$. Then, we say that

(·) $\{u_n\}$ converges to u, whenever $\lim_{n \to \infty} \varrho(u_n, u) = 0$;
(·) $\{u_n\}$ is a Cauchy sequence, when $\lim_{n,m \to \infty} \varrho(u_n, u_m) = 0$;
(·) (U, ϱ) is complete if every Cauchy sequence in U converges to some point in U.

Let (U, ϱ) be a Branciari distance space, and let τ_ϱ be the topology on U, such that

$$U - C \in \tau_\varrho \iff \forall \{u_n\} \subset C, \lim_{n \to \infty} \varrho(u_n, u) = 0 \text{ implies } u \in C. \tag{1}$$

The topology τ_ϱ induced by (1) is called a sequential topology.

A map $T : U \to U$ is said to be continuous at $u \in U$ if, and only if, $\forall V \in \tau_\varrho$ contains Tu, and there exists $W \in \tau_\varrho$ containing u, such that $TW \subset V$ (see [24]).

We say that T is continuous, whenever it is continuous at each point $u \in U$.

Remark 3. *A map $T : U \to U$, where (U, ϱ) is a Branciari distance space, is continuous if, and only if, the following condition holds:*

$$\lim_{n \to \infty} \varrho(Tu_n, Tu) = 0, \text{ whenever } \lim_{n \to \infty} \varrho(u_n, u) = 0 \text{ for any sequence } \{u_n\} \subset U.$$

Let us recall the following example in [4] where we can understand the characteristics of the branchiari distance spaces.

Example 3. *Let $U = \{0, 2\} \cup \{\frac{1}{n} : n \in \mathbb{N}\}$, and define a map $\varrho : U \times U \to [0, \infty)$ by*

$$\varrho(u, v) = \begin{cases} 0, (u = v), \\ 1, (u, v \in \{0, 2\}), \\ 1, (u, v \in \{\frac{1}{n} : n \in \mathbb{N}\}), \\ \frac{1}{n}, (u \in \{0, 2\} \text{ and } v \in \{\frac{1}{n} : n \in \mathbb{N}\}). \end{cases}$$

Then, (U, ϱ) is a Branciari distance space.

We have the following.

(i) Limit is not unique.
   We infer that

$$\lim_{n \to \infty} \varrho(\frac{1}{n}, 0) = \lim_{n \to \infty} \frac{1}{n} = 0 \text{ and } \lim_{n \to \infty} \varrho(\frac{1}{n}, 2) = \lim_{n \to \infty} \frac{1}{n} = 0. \qquad (2)$$

   Hence, the sequence $\{\frac{1}{n}\}$ is convergent to 0 and 2, and the limit is not unique.

(ii) The convergent sequence $\{\frac{1}{n}\}$ is not a Cauchy sequence.

$$\lim_{n, m \to \infty} \varrho(\frac{1}{n}, \frac{1}{m}) \neq 0, \text{ because } \varrho(\frac{1}{n}, \frac{1}{m}) = 1.$$

   Hence, $\{\frac{1}{n}\}$ is not a Cauchy sequence.

(iii) $\lim_{n \to \infty} \varrho(\frac{1}{n}, \frac{1}{2}) \neq \varrho(0, \frac{1}{2})$.

(iv) The open ball with center $\frac{1}{3}$ and radius $\frac{2}{3}$ is the set $B(\frac{1}{3}, \frac{2}{3}) = \{\frac{1}{3}, 0, 2\}$. There is no $r > 0$, such that

$$B(0, r) \subset B(\frac{1}{3}, \frac{2}{3}). \qquad (3)$$

Remark 4. (i) It folows from (2) that the sequential topology on U is not a Hausdorff space.

(ii) The Branciari distance ϱ is not continuous with respect to the sequential topology on U. In fact, let $y \in U$ be a fixed point, such that $y \neq 0$ and $y \neq 2$.
   We show that

$$\lim_{n \to \infty} \varrho(\frac{1}{n}, 2) = 0.$$

However,

$$\lim_{n \to \infty} \varrho(\frac{1}{n}, y) \neq \varrho(2, y).$$

Hence, $\varrho(\cdot, y)$ is not continuous with respect to the sequential topology on U.

(iii) From (3) the family $\{B(u, r) : u, r > 0\}$, where $B(u, r) = \{v : \varrho(u, v) < r\}$, is not a basis for any topology on (U, ϱ), and so there is no topology which is compatible with the Branciari distance ϱ.

(iv) It is known that the sequential topology is not compatible with the Branciari distance ϱ.

(v) There is no Cauchy sequence, so it is a complete Branciari distance space.

Note that Example 3 shows that the Branciari distance space is much weaker in mathematical structure than the metric space. As we have seen in the example above and Remark 4, there are some mathematical drawbacks to the Branciari distance. Nevertheless, it is attractive for researchers to study the existence of fixed points in this space without additional conditions such as the uniqueness of the limit of the converging sequence in Branciari distance spaces or/and continuity of a Branciari distance with respect to the sequential topology on a Branciari distance space.

Lemma 1 ([35]). *Let (U, ϱ) be a Branciari distance space, $\{u_n\} \subset U$ be a Cauchy sequence and $u, v \in U$. If there is a positive integer n_0, such that*

(i) $u_n \neq u_m \, \forall n, m > n_0$;
(ii) $u_n \neq u \, \forall n > n_0$;
(iii) $u_n \neq v \, \forall n > n_0$;
(iv) $\lim_{n \to \infty} \varrho(u_n, u) = \lim_{n \to \infty} \varrho(u_n, v)$,

then, $u = v$.

From now on, let φ be a function from $[0, \infty) \times [0, \infty)$ into $(-\infty, \infty)$, such that

$$\varphi(s, t) \leq \frac{1}{2}s - t, \; \forall s, t \in [0, \infty).$$

Note that if $\frac{1}{2}s < t \; \forall s, t \in [0, \infty)$, then the following conditions are satisfied.

(i) $\varphi(s, t) < 0$;
(ii) $\varphi(\min\{s, u\}, t) < 0$.

2. Fixed-Point Results

2.1. Fixed Points for Suzuki-Type $\mathcal{L}_\gamma$ Contractions

Let (U, ϱ) be a Branciari distance space.

A map T from U into itself is *Suzuk-type $\mathcal{L}_\gamma$ contraction* with respect to $\xi \in \mathcal{L}_\gamma$ provided that it satisfies the condition:

$\forall u, v \in U$ with $\varrho(Tu, Tv) > 0$

$$\varphi(\min\{\varrho(u, Tu), \varrho(v, Tu)\}, \varrho(u, v)) < 0$$
$$\Rightarrow \xi(\vartheta((Tu, Tv)), \vartheta(\varrho(u, v))) \geq 1 \quad (4)$$

where $\vartheta : (0, \infty) \to (1, \infty)$ is a function.

Lemma 2. *Let $l > 0$, and let $\{t_n\} \subset (l, \infty)$ be a sequence, such that*

$$t_n \leq t_{n-1} \, \forall n = 1, 2, 3, \cdots, \text{ and } \lim_{n \to \infty} t_n = l.$$

If $\vartheta : (0, \infty) \to (1, \infty)$ is non-decreasing, then we show that

$$\lim_{n \to \infty} \vartheta(t_n) = \lim_{n \to \infty} \vartheta(t_{n-1}) = \lim_{t \to l^+} \vartheta(t) > 1.$$

Proof. Since ϑ is non-decreasing and $\{t_n\}$ is non-increasing,

$$\lim_{t \to l^+} \vartheta(t) = \lim_{n \to \infty} \vartheta(t_n) \leq \lim_{n \to \infty} \vartheta(t_{n-1}) \leq \lim_{t \to l^+} \vartheta(t).$$

Thus, we established that $\lim_{n \to \infty} \vartheta(t_n) = \lim_{n \to \infty} \vartheta(t_{n-1}) = \lim_{t \to l^+} \vartheta(t) > \vartheta(l) > 1$. □

We now establish main theorem.

Theorem 1. Let (U, ϱ) be a complete Branciari distance space. Suppose that mapping T from U into itself is a Suzuki-type $\mathcal{L}_\gamma$ contraction with respect to $\xi \in \mathcal{L}_\gamma$. If ϑ is non-decreasing, then T possesses only one fixed point, and for every initial point $u_0 \in U$, the Picard sequence $\{T^n u_0\}$ is convergent to the fixed point.

Proof. Firstly, when a fixed point exists, let us show that it is unique.
Assume that $w = Tw$ and $u = Tu$, such that $u \neq w$.
Then, $\varrho(w, u) > 0$ and $\varphi(\min\{\varrho(w, Tw), \varrho(u, Tw)\}, \varrho(w, u))$
$= \varphi(\min\{0, \varrho(u, w)\}, \varrho(u, w)) \leq \frac{1}{2} \min\{0, \varrho(u, w)\} - \varrho(w, u) < 0$.
From (4), we have

$$1 \leq \xi(\vartheta(\varrho(Tw, Tu)), \vartheta(\varrho(w, u)))$$
$$= \xi(\vartheta(\varrho(w, u)), \vartheta(\varrho(w, u))) < 1$$

which is a contradiction.
Hence, $w = u$, and the fixed point of T is unique.
Secondly, let us show the existence of fixed points.
Let $u_0 \in U$, and let $\{u_n\} \subset U$ be a sequence defined by $u_n = Tu_{n-1} = T^n u_0$, $\forall n \in \mathbb{N}$.
If $u_{n_0} = u_{n_0+1}$ for some $n_0 \in \mathbb{N}$, then $u_{n_0} = Tu_{n_0}$, and the proof is completed.
Assume that

$$u_{n-1} \neq u_n \ \forall n \in \mathbb{N}. \tag{5}$$

We infer that

$$\varphi(\min\{\varrho(u_{n-1}, Tu_{n-1}), \varrho(u_n, Tu_{n-1})\}, \varrho(u_{n-1}, u_n))$$
$$= \varphi(\min\{\varrho(u_{n-1}, u_n), \varrho(u_n, u_n)\}, \varrho(u_{n-1}, u_n))$$
$$= \frac{1}{2} \min\{\varrho(u_{n-1}, u_n), 0\} - \varrho(u_{n-1}, u_n) < 0. \tag{6}$$

It follows from (4), (5), and (6) that for all $n \in \mathbb{N}$

$$1 \leq \xi(\vartheta(\varrho(Tu_{n-1}, Tu_n)), \vartheta(\varrho(u_{n-1}, u_n)))$$
$$= \xi(\vartheta(\varrho(u_n, u_{n+1})), \vartheta(\varrho(u_{n-1}, u_n)))$$
$$< \frac{\gamma(\vartheta(\varrho(u_{n-1}, u_n)))}{\gamma(\vartheta(\varrho(u_n, u_{n+1})))}. \tag{7}$$

Consequently, we show that

$$\gamma(\vartheta(\varrho(u_n, u_{n+1}))) < \gamma(\vartheta(\varrho(u_{n-1}, u_n))) \ \forall n \in \mathbb{N}$$

which yields

$$\vartheta(\varrho(u_n, u_{n+1})) < \vartheta(\varrho(u_{n-1}, u_n)) \ \forall n \in \mathbb{N}.$$

Thus,

$$\varrho(u_n, u_{n+1}) < \varrho(u_{n-1}, u_n) \ \forall n \in \mathbb{N}. \tag{8}$$

So, the sequence $\{\varrho(u_{n-1}, u_n)\}$ is decreasing, and hence there is an $l \geq 0$, such that

$$\lim_{n \to \infty} \varrho(u_{n-1}, u_n) = l.$$

We prove that $l = 0$.
Assume that $l > 0$.
Let $t_{n-1} = \vartheta(\varrho(u_{n-1}, u_n))$ and $t_n = \vartheta(\varrho(u_n, u_{n+1})) \ \forall n \in \mathbb{N}$.
Then, $t_n < t_{n-1} \ \forall n \in \mathbb{N}$.

By applying Lemma 2,
$$\lim_{n\to\infty} t_{n-1} = \lim_{n\to\infty} t_n = \lim_{t\to l^+} \theta(t) > 1.$$

By applying ($\zeta 3$), we have
$$1 \leq \lim_{n\to\infty} \sup \zeta(t_n, t_{n-1}) < 1.$$

This is a contradiction.
Thus,
$$\lim_{n\to\infty} \varrho(u_{n-1}, u_n) = 0. \tag{9}$$

Now, we show that $\{u_n\}$ is a Cauchy sequence.
On the contrary, assume that $\{u_n\}$ is not a Cauchy sequence.
Then, there is an $\epsilon > 0$ for which we can find subsequences $\{u_{m(j)}\}$ and $\{u_{n(j)}\}$ of $\{u_n\}$, such that $m(j)$ is the smallest index for which
$$m(j) > n(j) > j, \ \varrho(u_{m(j)}, u_{n(j)}) \geq \epsilon \text{ and } \varrho(u_{m(j)-1}, u_{n(j)}) < \epsilon. \tag{10}$$

From (10), we infer that
$$\begin{aligned}\epsilon &\leq \varrho(u_{m(j)}, u_{n(j)}) \\ &\leq \varrho(u_{n(j)}, u_{m(j)-2}) + \varrho(u_{m(j)-2}, u_{m(j)-1}) + \varrho(u_{m(j)-1}, u_{m(j)}) \\ &< \epsilon + \varrho(u_{m(j)-2}, u_{m(j)-1}) + \varrho(u_{m(j)-1}, x_{m(j)}).\end{aligned} \tag{11}$$

By letting $j \to \infty$ in (11), we have
$$\lim_{n\to\infty} \varrho(u_{m(j)}, u_{n(j)}) = \epsilon.$$

On the other hand, we obtain
$$\varrho(u_{m(j)}, u_{n(j)}) \leq \varrho(u_{n(j)}, u_{n(j)+1}) + \varrho(u_{n(j)+1}, u_{m(j)+1}) + \varrho(u_{m(j)+1}, u_{m(j)})$$
and
$$\varrho(u_{n(j)+1}, u_{m(j)+1}) \leq \varrho(u_{n(j)+1}, u_{n(j)}) + \varrho(u_{n(j)}, u_{m(j)}) + \varrho(u_{m(j)}, u_{m(j)+1}).$$
Thus,
$$\lim_{j\to\infty} \varrho(u_{n(j)+1}, u_{m(j)+1}) = \epsilon.$$

It follows from (9) that there exists $N_1 \in \mathbb{N}$, such that
$$\varrho(u_{n(j)}, u_{n(j)+1}) < \epsilon, \ \forall j > N_1.$$

Hence, we infer that $\forall k > N_1$
$$\begin{aligned}&\frac{1}{2}\min\{\varrho(u_{n(j)}, Tu_{n(j)}), \varrho(u_{m(j)}, Tu_{n(j)})\} \\ =&\frac{1}{2}\min\{\varrho(u_{n(j)}, u_{n(j)+1}), \varrho(u_{m(j)}, u_{n(j)+1})\} \\ <& \epsilon \\ \leq& d(u_{n(j)}, u_{m(j)})\end{aligned}$$

which implies
$$\varphi(\min\{\varrho(u_{n(j)}, Tu_{n(j)}), \varrho(u_{m(j)}, Tu_{n(j)+1})\}, \varrho(u_{n(j)}, u_{m(j)})) < 0, \ \forall j > N_1.$$

It follows from (4) that $\forall j > N_1$

$$1 \leq \xi(\vartheta(\varrho(Tu_{n(j)}, Tu_{m(j)})), \vartheta(\varrho(u_{n(j)}, u_{m(j)})))$$
$$= \xi(\vartheta(\varrho(u_{n(j)+1}, u_{m(j)+1})), \vartheta(\varrho(u_{n(j)}, u_{m(j)})))$$
$$< \frac{\gamma(\vartheta(\varrho(u_{n(j)}, u_{m(j)})))}{\gamma(\vartheta(\varrho(u_{n(j)+1}, u_{m(j)+1})))}$$

which implies
$$\gamma(\vartheta(\varrho(u_{n(j)+1}, u_{m(j)+1}))) < \gamma(\vartheta(\varrho(u_{n(j)}, u_{m(j)})))$$

and so
$$\vartheta(\varrho(u_{n(j)+1}, u_{m(j)+1})) < \vartheta(\varrho(u_{n(j)}, u_{m(j)})) \; \forall j > N_1.$$

Put
$$t_j = \vartheta(\varrho(u_{n(j)+1}, u_{m(j)+1})) \text{ and } t_{j-1} = \vartheta(\varrho(u_{n(j)}, u_{m(j)}))$$

Then, we have
$$t_j < t_{j-1} \; \forall j > N_1$$

and
$$\lim_{j \to \infty} \varrho(u_{n(j)+1}, u_{m(j)+1}) = \lim_{j \to \infty} \varrho(u_{n(j)}, u_{m(j)}) = \epsilon.$$

By Lemma 2,
$$\lim_{j \to \infty} t_j = \lim_{j \to \infty} t_{j-1} = \lim_{t \to \epsilon^+} \vartheta(t) > 1.$$

From (ξ3), we have
$$1 \leq \limsup_{j \to \infty} \xi(t_j, t_{j-1}) < 1$$

which leads to a contradiction.

Thus, $\{u_n\}$ is a Cauchy sequence.

It follows from completeness of U that there is $u \in U$, such that
$$\lim_{n \to \infty} \varrho(u_n, u) = 0. \tag{12}$$

We may assume that there is $m_0 \in \mathbb{N}$, such that
$$\varrho(u_{n+1}, u) < \varrho(u_n, u), \forall n > m_0.$$

We infer that $\forall n > m_0$
$$\varphi(\min\{\varrho(u_n, Tu_n), \varrho(u, Tu_n)\}, \varrho(u_n, u))$$
$$= \varphi(\min\{\varrho(u_n, u_{n+1}), \varrho(u, u_{n+1})\}, \varrho(u_n, u))$$
$$\leq \frac{1}{2} \min\{\varrho(u_n, u_{n+1}), \varrho(u, u_{n+1})\} - \varrho(u_n, u)$$
$$< 0.$$

Applying (4), we establish that
$$1 \leq \xi(\vartheta(\varrho(Tu_n, Tu)), \vartheta(\varrho(u_n, u))) < \frac{\gamma(\vartheta(\varrho(u_n, u)))}{\gamma(\vartheta(\varrho(Tu_n, Tu)))}, \forall n \geq m_0.$$

which implies
$$\gamma(\vartheta(\varrho(Tu_n, Tu))) < \gamma(\vartheta(\varrho(u_n, u))), \forall n \geq m_0.$$

Hence,
$$\varrho(Tu_n, Tu) < \varrho(u_n, u), \forall n \geq m_0$$

and hence,
$$\lim_{n \to \infty} \varrho(u_{n+1}, Tu) = 0. \tag{13}$$

Applying Lemma 1 with (12) and (13), we have $u = Tu$. □

The following example interprets Theorem 1.

Example 4. Let $U = \{1, 2, 3, 4\}$, and let us define $\varrho : U \times U \to [0, \infty)$ as follows:

$\varrho(1,2) = \varrho(2,1) = 3,$
$\varrho(2,3) = \varrho(3,2) = \varrho(1,3) = \varrho(3,1) = 1,$
$\varrho(1,4) = \varrho(4,1) = \varrho(2,4) = \varrho(4,2) = \varrho(3,4) = \varrho(4,3) = 4,$
$\varrho(u,u) = 0 \; \forall u \in U.$

Then, (U, ϱ) is a complete Branciari distance space, but not a metric space (see [6]). Define a map $T : U \to U$ by

$$Tu = \begin{cases} 2 & (u = 1, 2), \\ 4 & (u = 3), \\ 3 & (u = 4). \end{cases}$$

Let $\vartheta : (0, \infty) \to (1, \infty)$ be a function defined by

$$\vartheta(t) = \begin{cases} e^{\sqrt{t}} & (0 < t \leq 1), \\ 3 & (t > 1). \end{cases}$$

Then, ϑ is non-decreasing.

We prove that T is a $\mathcal{L}_\gamma$ contraction with respect to ξ_2, where $\xi_2(t,s) = \frac{\gamma(\eta(s))}{\gamma(t)}$, $\eta(s) = \frac{3}{2}s - \frac{1}{2} \; \forall s \geq 1, \gamma(t) = \frac{1}{2}t + \frac{1}{2} \; \forall t \geq 1$.
We have

$$\varrho(Tu, Tv) = \begin{cases} \varrho(2,2) = 0 & (u = 1, v = 2), \\ \varrho(2,4) = 4 & (u = 1, v = 3), \\ \varrho(2,3) = 1 & (u = 1, v = 4), \\ \varrho(2,4) = 4 & (u = 2, v = 3), \\ \varrho(2,3) = 1 & (u = 2, v = 4), \\ \varrho(3,4) = 4 & (u = 3, v = 4) \end{cases}$$

so

$\varrho(Tu, Tv) > 0 \Leftrightarrow (u = 1, v = 3), (u = 1, v = 4), (u = 2, v = 3), (u = 2, v = 4), (u = 3, v = 4).$

We establish that

$$\varrho(u,v) = \begin{cases} 1 & (u = 1, v = 3), \\ 4 & (u = 1, v = 4), \\ 1 & (u = 2, v = 3), \\ 4 & (u = 2, v = 4), \\ 4 & (u = 3, v = 4) \end{cases}$$

and

$$m(u,v) = \begin{cases} 1 & (u=1, v=3), \\ 3 & (u=1, v=4), \\ 0 & (u=2, v=3), \\ 0 & (u=2, v=4), \\ 1 & (u=3, v=4). \end{cases}$$

We infer that for all $u, v \in U$ with $\varrho(Tu, Tv) > 0$,

$$\varphi(m(u,v), \varrho(u,v)) \leq \frac{1}{2} m(u,v) - \varrho(u,v) < 0.$$

Thus, we have

$$\xi_2(\vartheta(d(Tu,Tv)), \vartheta(\varrho(u,v)))$$
$$= \frac{\gamma(\eta(\vartheta(\varrho(u,v))))}{\gamma(\vartheta(\varrho(Tu,Tv)))}$$
$$= \begin{cases} \frac{\gamma(\eta(\vartheta(1)))}{\gamma(\vartheta(4))} & (u=1, v=3), \\ \frac{\gamma(\eta(\vartheta(4)))}{\gamma(\vartheta(1))} & (u=1, v=4), \\ \frac{\gamma(\eta(\vartheta(1)))}{\gamma(\vartheta(4))} & (u=2, v=3), \\ \frac{\gamma(\eta(\vartheta(4)))}{\gamma(\vartheta(1))} & (u=2, v=4), \\ \frac{\gamma(\eta(\vartheta(4)))}{\gamma(\vartheta(4))} & (u=3, v=4) \end{cases}$$

which yields

$$\xi_2(\vartheta(\varrho(Tu,Tv)), \vartheta(\varrho(u,v)))$$
$$\geq \frac{\gamma(\eta(\vartheta(1)))}{\gamma(\vartheta(4))}$$
$$= \frac{\frac{1}{2}(\frac{3}{2}e - \frac{1}{2}) + \frac{1}{2}}{\frac{1}{2}3 + \frac{1}{2}} > 1, \text{ because } \frac{3}{2}e - \frac{1}{2} - 3 = \frac{3}{2}(e - \frac{7}{3}) > 0.$$

Hence, T is a $\mathcal{L}_\gamma$ contraction with respect to ξ_2. Thus, all hypotheses of Theorem 1 are satisfied, and T possesses a unique fixed point $u = 2$.

Note that T is not $\mathcal{L}$ contraction [24] with respect to $\xi_2(t,s) = \frac{\eta(s)}{t}$. In fact, for $u=3, v=4$, we establish that

$$\xi_2(\vartheta(\varrho(Tu,Tv)), \vartheta(\varrho(u,v))) = \frac{\eta(\vartheta(4))}{\vartheta(4)} < \frac{\vartheta(4)}{\vartheta(4)} = 1.$$

Note that Banach condition principle is not satisfied. In fact, if $u=3, v=1$, then

$$\varrho(T3, T2) \leq k\varrho(3,2), k \in (0,1)$$

which implies

$$k \geq 4.$$

Furthermore, the ϑ contraction condition [22] is not satisfied.
Note that ϑ satisfies conditions $(\vartheta 1), (\vartheta 2)$ and $(\vartheta 3)$.
If for $u=3, v=2$

$$\vartheta(\varrho(T3,T2)) \leq [\vartheta(\varrho(3,2))]^k, k \in (0,1)$$

then

$$\vartheta(4) \leq [\vartheta(1)]^k < \vartheta(1)$$

which is a contradiction.

Hence, T is not a ϑ contraction.

The following example shows that in Theorem 1, the condition that the function ϑ is non-decreasing cannot be dropped.

Example 5. *Let* $U = \{0, 2\} \cup \{\frac{1}{n} : n = 3, 4, 5, \cdots\}$, *and let* $\varrho : U \times U \to [0, \infty)$ *be a map defined by*

$$\varrho(u, v) = \begin{cases} 0 & (u = v), \\ 0 & (u, v \in \{0, 2\}), \\ 0 & (u, v \in \{\frac{1}{n} : n = 3, 4, 5, \cdots\}), \\ \frac{1}{n} & (u \in \{0, 2\} \text{ and } v \in \{\frac{1}{n} : n = 3, 4, 5, \cdots\}) \\ \frac{1}{n} & (u \in \{\frac{1}{n} : n = 3, 4, 5, \cdots\} \text{ and } v \in \{0, 2\}). \end{cases}$$

Then, (U, ϱ) *is a complete Branciari distance space.*
Define a mapping $T : U \to U$ *by*

$$Tu = \begin{cases} 2 & (u = 0), \\ 0 & (u = 2), \\ \frac{1}{n+1} & (u = \frac{1}{n}, n = 3, 4, 5, \cdots). \end{cases}$$

Let $\vartheta : (0, \infty) \to (1, \infty)$ *be a function defined by*

$$\vartheta(t) = \frac{1}{t} + 1$$

and let

$$\eta(s) = \frac{3}{2}s - \frac{1}{2} \ \forall s \geq 1, \gamma(t) = \frac{1}{2}t + \frac{1}{2} \ \forall t \geq 1.$$

We infer that

$$\varphi(\min\{\varrho(u, Tu), \varrho(v, Tu)\}, \varrho(u, v)) = \begin{cases} 0 & (u = 0, v = 2), \\ \frac{1}{2}\frac{1}{n+1} - \frac{1}{n} & (u = 0, v = \frac{1}{n}, n = 3, 4, 5, \cdots), \\ \frac{1}{2}\frac{1}{n+1} - \frac{1}{n} & (u = 2, v = \frac{1}{n}, n = 3, 4, 5, \cdots), \\ 0 & (u = \frac{1}{n}, v = \frac{1}{m}, m > n, n = 3, 4, 5, \cdots), \end{cases}$$

and we show that

$$\varrho(Tu, Tv) = \begin{cases} \frac{1}{n} & (u = 0, v = \frac{1}{n}, n = 3, 4, 5, \cdots), \\ \frac{1}{n} & (u = 2, v = \frac{1}{n}, n = 3, 4, 5, \cdots). \end{cases}$$

Thus, the following is satisfied:

$$\varrho(Tu, Tv) > 0 \text{ and } \varphi(\min\{\varrho(u, Tu), \varrho(v, Tu)\}, \varrho(u, v)) < 0 \Leftrightarrow (u = 0, v = \frac{1}{n}) \text{ and } (u = 2, v = \frac{1}{n})$$

where $n = 3, 4, 5, \cdots$.
Thus, we obtain that for $(u = 0, v = \frac{1}{n}), (u = 2, v = \frac{1}{n})$

$$\zeta_2(\vartheta(\varrho(Tu, Tv)), \vartheta(\varrho(u, v)))$$
$$= \frac{\gamma(\eta(\vartheta(\varrho(u, v))))}{\gamma(\vartheta(\varrho(Tu, Tv)))}$$
$$= \frac{\gamma(\eta(\vartheta(\frac{1}{n})))}{\gamma(\vartheta(\frac{1}{n+1}))}$$
$$= \frac{3n + 4}{2n + 6} > 1, \text{ where } n = 3, 4, 5, \cdots.$$

Thus, T is a $\mathcal{L}_\gamma$ contraction with respect to ξ_2. However, T has no fixed point. Note that $\vartheta(t) = \frac{1}{t} + 1$, $\forall t > 0$ is not a non-decreasing function.

The following Corollary 1 is obtained from Theorem 1.

Corollary 1. *Let (U, ϱ) be a complete Branciari distance space and $T : U \to U$ be a map. Suppose that there is $\xi \in \mathcal{L}_\gamma$, such that for all $u, v \in U$ with $\varrho(Tu, Tv) > 0$*

$$\xi(\vartheta(\varrho(Tu, Tv)), \vartheta(\varrho(u, v))) \geq 1.$$

If ϑ is non-decreasing, then T possesses only one fixed point.

Corollary 2. *Let (U, ϱ) be a complete Branciari distance space and $T : U \to U$ be a map. Suppose that there is $\xi \in \mathcal{L}$, such that for all $u, v \in U$ with $\varrho(Tu, Tv) > 0$*

$$\varphi(\varrho(u, Tu), \varrho(v, Tu)) < 0 \Rightarrow \xi(\vartheta(\varrho(Tu, Tv)), \vartheta(\varrho(u, v))) \geq 1.$$

If ϑ is non-decreasing, then T possesses only one fixed point.

Corollary 3. *Let (U, ϱ) be a complete Branciari distance space and $T : U \to U$ be a map. Suppose that there is $\xi \in \mathcal{L}$, such that for all $u, v \in U$ with $\varrho(Tu, Tv) > 0$*

$$\xi(\vartheta(\varrho(Tu, Tv)), \vartheta(\varrho(u, v))) \geq 1.$$

If ϑ is non-decreasing, then T possesses only one fixed point.

Remark 5. *(1) It does not take continuity of ϑ to obtain Corollary 3, and continuity of ϑ is not required to prove Theorem 2.1 of [24].*

(2) Corollary 2 is a generalization of Theorem 2.1 of [24].

2.2. Fixed Points for Suzuki–Berinde-Type $\mathcal{L}_\gamma$ Contractions

Let (U, ϱ) be a Branciari distance space.

A map $T : U \to U$ is a *Suzuk–Berinde-type $\mathcal{L}_\gamma$ contraction* with respect to $\xi \in \mathcal{L}_\gamma$, provided that the condition is satisfied:

$\forall u, v \in U$ with $\varrho(Tu, Tv) > 0$

$$\varphi(m(u, v), \varrho(u, v)) < 0$$

$$\Rightarrow \xi(\vartheta(\varrho(Tu, Tv)), \vartheta(\varrho(u, v) + Km(u, v))) \geq 1 \tag{14}$$

where $\theta : (0, \infty) \to (1, \infty)$, $K \in (0, \infty)$, and $m(u, v) = \min\{\varrho(u, Tu), \varrho(v, Tu)\}$.

Theorem 2. *Let (U, ϱ) be a complete Branciari distance space and $T : U \to U$ be a Suzuki–Berinde-type $\mathcal{L}_\gamma$ contraction with respect to $\xi \in \mathcal{L}_\gamma$. If ϑ is non-decreasing and continuous, then T possesses only one fixed point, and for every initial point $u_0 \in U$, the Picard sequence $\{T^n u_0\}$ is convergent to the fixed point.*

Proof. Let $u_0 \in U$ and let $\{u_n = T^n u_0\} \subset U$ be a sequence, such that

$$u_{n-1} \neq u_n \ \forall n = 1, 2, 3 \cdots. \tag{15}$$

We infer that

$$m(u_{n-1}, u_n) = \min\{\varrho(u_{n-1}, u_n), \varrho(u_n, u_n)\} = 0 \tag{16}$$

and

$$\varphi(m(u_{n-1}, u_n), \varrho(u_{n-1}, u_n)) \leq -\varrho(u_{n-1}, u_n) < 0. \tag{17}$$

It follows from (14), (15), (16) and (17) that $\forall n \in \mathbb{N}$

$$\begin{aligned}1 &\leq \xi(\vartheta(\varrho(Tu_{n-1},Tu_n)), \vartheta(\varrho(u_{n-1},u_n)+Km(u_{n-1},u_n)))\\ &= \xi(\vartheta(\varrho(u_n,u_{n+1})), \vartheta(\varrho(u_{n-1},u_n)))\\ &< \frac{\gamma(\vartheta(\varrho(u_{n-1},u_n)))}{\gamma(\vartheta(\varrho(u_n,u_{n+1})))},\end{aligned} \quad (18)$$

which shows that $\{\varrho(u_{n-1},u_n)\}$ is decreasing, because ϑ and γ are non-decreasing.
Hence,
$$\lim_{n\to\infty} \varrho(u_{n-1},u_n) = l$$
where $l \geq 0$.

We prove that $l = 0$.
Assume that $l > 0$.
Then, since ϑ is continuous, we have
$$\lim_{n\to\infty} \vartheta(\varrho(u_{n-1},u_n)) = \vartheta(l) > 1.$$

Let $t_{n-1} = \vartheta(\varrho(u_{n-1},u_n))$ and $t_n = \vartheta(\varrho(u_n,u_{n+1}))$ $\forall n \in \mathbb{N}$.
Then,
$$t_n < t_{n-1}\ \forall n \in \mathbb{N} \text{ and } \lim_{n\to\infty} t_{n-1} = \lim_{n\to\infty} t_n = \theta(l) > 1.$$

By applying ($\xi 3$), we show that
$$1 \leq \lim_{n\to\infty} \sup \xi(t_n, t_{n-1}) < 1,$$

which leads to a contradiction.
Thus,
$$\lim_{n\to\infty} \varrho(u_{n-1},u_n) = 0. \quad (19)$$

We shall show that $\{u_n\}$ is Cauchy.
On the contrary, assume that $\{u_n\}$ is not a Cauchy sequence.
Then, there is an $\epsilon > 0$ for which we can find subsequences $\{u_{m(j)}\}$ and $\{u_{n(j)}\}$ of $\{u_n\}$, such that $m(j)$ is the smallest index for which

$$m(j) > n(j) > j,\ \varrho(u_{m(j)}, u_{n(j)}) \geq \epsilon \text{ and } \varrho(u_{m(j)-1}, u_{n(j)}) < \epsilon. \quad (20)$$

As demonstrated in the proof of Theorem 1, we show that

$$\lim_{j\to\infty} \varrho(u_{m(j)}, u_{n(j)}) = \epsilon \text{ and } \lim_{j\to\infty} \varrho(u_{n(j)+1}, u_{m(j)+1}) = \epsilon. \quad (21)$$

From (19), there is an $N \in \mathbb{N}$, such that

$$\varrho(u_{n(j)}, u_{n(j)+1}) < \epsilon,\ \forall j > N.$$

Thus, we infer that $\forall j > N$

$$\varrho(u_{n(j)}, Tu_{n(j)}) = \varrho(u_{n(j)}, u_{n(j)+1}) < \epsilon \leq \varrho(u_{n(j)}, u_{m(j)}) \quad (22)$$

and
$$m(u_{n(j)}, u_{m(j)}) = \min\{\varrho(u_{n(j)}, u_{n(j)+1}), \varrho(u_{m(j)}, u_{n(j)+1})\}. \quad (23)$$

From (22) and (23), we obtain that

$$\varphi(m(u_{n(j)}, u_{m(j)}), \varrho(u_{n(j)}, u_{m(j)})) \leq \frac{1}{2} m(u_{n(j)}, u_{m(j)}) - \varrho(u_{n(j)}, u_{m(j)}) < 0.$$

By applying (14), we have

$$1 \leq \xi(\vartheta(\varrho(Tu_{n(j)}, Tu_{m(j)})), \vartheta(\varrho(u_{n(j)}, u_{m(j)}) + Km(u_{n(j)}, u_{m(j)})))$$
$$= \xi(\vartheta(\varrho(u_{n(j)+1}, u_{m(j)+1})), \vartheta(\varrho(u_{n(j)}, u_{m(j)}) + Km(u_{n(j)}, u_{m(j)})))$$
$$< \frac{\gamma(\vartheta(\varrho(u_{n(j)}, u_{m(j)}) + Km(u_{n(j)}, u_{m(j)})))}{\gamma(\vartheta(\varrho(u_{n(j)+1}, u_{m(j)+1})))}$$

which implies

$$\gamma(\vartheta(\varrho(u_{n(j)+1}, u_{m(j)+1}))) < \gamma(\vartheta(\varrho(u_{n(j)}, u_{m(j)}) + Km(u_{n(j)}, u_{m(j)})))$$

and so

$$\vartheta(\varrho(u_{n(j)+1}, u_{m(j)+1})) < \vartheta(\varrho(u_{n(j)}, u_{m(j)}) + Km(u_{n(j)}, u_{m(j)})).$$

Let

$$t_j = \vartheta(\varrho(u_{n(j)+1}, u_{m(j)+1})) \text{ and } s_j = \vartheta(\varrho(u_{n(j)}, u_{m(j)}) + Km(u_{n(j)}, u_{m(j)}))$$

Then,

$$t_j < s_j \; \forall j \in \mathbb{N}.$$

Applying (21) and (22), we obtain that

$$\lim_{j \to \infty} \varrho(u_{n(j)+1}, u_{m(j)+1}) = \epsilon$$

and

$$\lim_{j \to \infty} [\varrho(u_{n(j)}, u_{m(j)}) + Km(u_{n(j)}, u_{m(j)})] = \epsilon.$$

By continuity of ϑ, we have

$$\lim_{j \to \infty} t_j = \lim_{j \to \infty} s_j = \vartheta(\epsilon) > 1.$$

From (ξ3), we have

$$1 \leq \lim_{k \to \infty} \sup \xi(t_k, s_k) < 1$$

which leads to a contradiction.

Thus, $\{u_n\}$ is a Cauchy sequence.

It follows from the completeness of U that

$$\lim_{n \to \infty} \varrho(u_n, u) = 0 \text{ for some } u \in U. \tag{24}$$

We may assume that

$$\varrho(u_{n+1}, u) < \varrho(u_n, u) \; \forall n \in \mathbb{N}. \tag{25}$$

We infer that

$$m(u_n, u) = \min\{\varrho(u_n, u_{n+1}), \varrho(u, u_{n+1})\} \; \forall n \in \mathbb{N}. \tag{26}$$

From (25) and (26), we show that $\forall n \in \mathbb{N}$

$$\varphi(m(u_n, u), \varrho(u_n, u)) \leq \frac{1}{2} m(u_n, u) - \varrho(u_n, u) < 0.$$

It follows from (14) that $\forall n \in \mathbb{N}$,

$$1 \leq \xi(\vartheta(\varrho(Tu_n, Tu)), \vartheta(\varrho(u_n, u) + Km(u_n, u))) < \frac{\gamma(\vartheta((u_n, u) + Km(u_n, u)))}{\gamma(\vartheta(\varrho(Tu_n, Tu)))}$$

which implies

$$\gamma(\vartheta(\varrho(Tu_n, Tu))) < \gamma(\vartheta(\varrho(u_n, u) + Km(u_n, u))), \forall n \in \mathbb{N}.$$

Hence,

$$\varrho(Tu_n, Tu))) < \varrho(u_n, u) + Km(u_n, u) \; \forall n \in \mathbb{N},$$

and hence

$$\lim_{n \to \infty} \varrho(u_{n+1}, Tu) = 0. \tag{27}$$

By applying Lemma 1 with (24) and (27), we have $z = Tz$.

Now, we prove the uniqueness of the fixed points.

Let u and v be fixed points of T, such that

$$u \neq v.$$

Then, $\varrho(u, v) > 0$ and $m(w, u) = 0$. Hence, we have

$$\varphi(m(u, v), \varrho(u, v)) \leq -d(u, v) < 0.$$

Thus, from (14), we infer that

$$1 \leq \xi(\vartheta(\varrho(Tu, Tv)), \vartheta(\varrho(u, v) + Km(u, v)))$$
$$= \xi(\vartheta(\varrho(u, v)), \vartheta(\varrho(u, v))) < 1.$$

This is a contradiction. Thus, T possesses only one fixed point. □

The following example illustrates Theorem 2.

Example 6. *Let $U = \{0, 2\} \cup \{\frac{1}{n} : n \in \mathbb{N}\}$ and let $\varrho : U \times U \to [0, \infty)$ be a map defined as follows:*

$$\varrho(u, v) = \begin{cases} 0 & (u = v), \\ 1 & (u, v \in \{0, 2\}) \text{ or } (u, v \in \{\frac{1}{n} : n \in \mathbb{N}\}), \\ v & (u \in \{0, 2\} \text{ and } v \in \{\frac{1}{n} : n \in \mathbb{N}\}), \\ u & (u \in \{\frac{1}{n} : n = 1, 2, 3, \cdots\} \text{ and } v \in \{0, 2\}). \end{cases}$$

Then, (U, ϱ) is a complete Branciari distance space (see [4]).

Let $T : U \to U$ be a map defined by

$$Tu = \begin{cases} 0 & (u = 0 \text{ or } 2), \\ \frac{1}{n+1} & (u = \frac{1}{n}, n \in \mathbb{N}). \end{cases}$$

Let $\vartheta(t) = e^t \; \forall t \in (0, \infty)$ and $K = 3$.

We show that (14) is satisfied with the $\mathcal{L}_\gamma$ simulation ξ_b, where $\xi_b(t, s) = \frac{[\gamma(s)]^k}{\gamma(t)} \; \forall t, s \in (1, \infty)$, $k = \frac{1}{2}$ and $\gamma(t) = 1 + \ln t$, $\forall t \in (1, \infty)$.

We infer that

$$\varrho(Tu, Tv) > 0 \Leftrightarrow (u = \frac{1}{n}, v = 0), (u = \frac{1}{n}, v = 2), \text{ or } (u = \frac{1}{n}, v = \frac{1}{m}, n \neq m).$$

We consider the following two cases.

Case 1: Let $u = \frac{1}{n}$ and $v = 0$ (or $u = \frac{1}{n}$ and $v = 2$).

Then, we show that
$$m(u,v) = \frac{1}{n+1} \text{ and } d(u,v) = \frac{1}{n},$$
and
$$\varphi(m(u,v), \varrho(u,v)) = \varphi(\frac{1}{n+1}, \frac{1}{n}) < 0.$$

It follows from (14) that
$$\xi(\vartheta(\varrho(Tu,Tv)), \vartheta(\varrho(u,v) + Km(u,v)))$$
$$= \xi(\vartheta(\frac{1}{n+1}), \vartheta(\frac{1}{n} + \frac{3}{n+1}))$$
$$= \frac{[\gamma(\vartheta(\frac{1}{n} + \frac{3}{n+1}))]^{\frac{1}{2}}}{\gamma(\vartheta(\frac{1}{n+1}))}$$
$$\geq \frac{\sqrt{1 + \frac{4}{1+n}}}{1 + \frac{1}{1+n}} > 1$$

because that
$$\left(\sqrt{1 + \frac{4}{1+n}}\right)^2 - \left(1 + \frac{1}{1+n}\right)^2 = \frac{2n+1}{(1+n)^2} > 0.$$

Case 2: Let $u = \frac{1}{n}$ and $v = \frac{1}{m}, n \neq m$.
Then, we infer that
$$m(u,v) = 1 \text{ and } \varrho(u,v) = 1,$$
and so
$$\varphi(m(u,v), \varrho(u,v)) < 0.$$

Thus, we have
$$\xi(\vartheta(\varrho(Tu,Tv)), \vartheta(\varrho(u,v) + Lm(u,v)))$$
$$= \frac{[\gamma(\vartheta(\varrho(u,v) + Km(u,v)))]^{\frac{1}{2}}}{\vartheta(\varrho(Tu,Tv))}$$
$$= \frac{[1 + \ln e^4]^{\frac{1}{2}}}{1 + \ln e}$$
$$= \frac{\sqrt{5}}{2} > 1.$$

Hence, all assumptions of Theorem 2 hold, and T possesses only one fixed point $u = 0$. Notice that the almost contraction condition is not satisfied. In fact, let $u = \frac{1}{n}, v = \frac{1}{n+1}$. Then,
$$\varrho(T\frac{1}{n}, T\frac{1}{n+1}) \leq k\varrho(\frac{1}{n}, \frac{1}{n+1}) + K\varrho(\frac{1}{n+1}, T\frac{1}{n}), k \in (0,1), L \geq 0$$
so
$$\varrho(\frac{1}{n+1}, \frac{1}{n+2}) \leq k\varrho(\frac{1}{n}, \frac{1}{n+1}) + K\varrho(\frac{1}{n+1}, \frac{1}{n+1})$$
which yields
$$k \geq 1.$$

Furthermore, note that the Suzuki–Berinde-type ϑ contraction condition [27] is not satisfied. Let $\vartheta(t)$ satisfy conditions $(\vartheta 1), (\vartheta 2),$ and $(\vartheta 4)$.

For $u = \frac{1}{n}, v = \frac{1}{n+1}$, we infer that

$$\frac{1}{2}\varrho(\frac{1}{n}, T\frac{1}{n}) = \frac{1}{2} < \varrho(\frac{1}{n}, \frac{1}{n+1})$$

and

$$n(\frac{1}{n}, \frac{1}{n+1}) = \min\{\varrho(\frac{1}{n}, T\frac{1}{n}), \varrho(\frac{1}{n}, T\frac{1}{n+1}), \varrho(\frac{1}{n+1}, T\frac{1}{n})\} = 0.$$

If

$$\vartheta(\varrho(T\frac{1}{n}, T\frac{1}{n+1})) \leq [\vartheta(\varrho(\frac{1}{n}, \frac{1}{n+1}))]^k + Kn(\frac{1}{n}, \frac{1}{n+1}), \text{ where } k \in (0,1), K \geq 0$$

then

$$\vartheta(1) \leq [\vartheta(1)]^k < \vartheta(1)$$

which leads to a contradiction. Hence, T is not a Suzuki–Berinde-type ϑ contraction map.

The following Corollary 4 is obtained from the Theorem 2.

Corollary 4. *Let (U, ϱ) be a complete Branciari distance space and $T : U \to U$ be a map. Suppose that there are $\xi \in \mathcal{L}_\gamma$ and $K \geq 0$, such that for all $u, v \in U$ with $\varrho(Tu, Tv) > 0$*

$$\xi(\vartheta(\varrho(Tu, Tv)), \vartheta(\varrho(u,v) + Km(u,v))) \geq 1$$

If ϑ is non-decreasing and continuous, then T possesses only one fixed point.

By taking $\gamma(t) = t, \forall t \geq 1$ in Theorem 2 (resp. Corollary 4), we have the following Corollary 5 (resp. Corollary 6).

Corollary 5. *Let (U, ϱ) be a complete Branciari distance space and $T : U \to U$ be a map. Suppose that there are $\xi \in \mathcal{L}$ and $K \geq 0$, such that for all $u, v \in U$ with $\varrho(Tu, Tv) > 0$*

$$\varphi(m(u,v), \varrho(u,v)) < 0 \Rightarrow \xi(\vartheta(\varrho(Tu, Tv)), \vartheta(\varrho(u,v) + Km(u,v))) \geq 1$$

If ϑ is non-decreasing and continuous, then T possesses only one fixed point.

Corollary 6. *Let (U, ϱ) be a complete Branciari distance space and $T : U \to U$ be a map. Suppose that there are $\xi \in \mathcal{L}$ and $K \geq 0$, such that for all $u, v \in U$ with $\varrho(Tu, Tv) > 0$*

$$\xi(\vartheta(\varrho(Tu, Tv)), \vartheta(\varrho(u,v) + Km(u,v))) \geq 1$$

If ϑ is non-decreasing and continuous, then T possesses only one fixed point.

3. Consequence

By pplying simulation functions given in Examples 1 and 2, we have some fixed point results.

The following Corollary 7 is obtained by letting $\xi = \xi_b$ in Theorem 1.

Corollary 7. *Let (U, ϱ) be a complete Branciari distance space and $T : U \to U$ be a map. Suppose that there is $k \in (0,1)$, such that for all $u, v \in U$ with $\varrho(Tu, Tv) > 0$*

$$\varphi(m(u,v), \varrho(u,v)) < 0 \Rightarrow \gamma(\vartheta(\varrho(Tu, Tv))) \leq [\gamma(\vartheta(\varrho(u,v)))]^k.$$

If ϑ is non-decreasing and continuous, then T possesses only one fixed point.

Corollary 8. Let (U, ϱ) be a complete Branciari distance space and $T : U \to U$ be a map. Suppose that there is $k \in (0, 1)$, such that for all $u, v \in U$ with $\varrho(Tu, Tv) > 0$

$$\gamma(\vartheta(\varrho(Tu, Tv)) \leq [\gamma(\vartheta(\varrho(u, v)))]^k.$$

If ϑ is non-decreasing and continuous, then T possesses only one fixed point.

The following Corollary 9 is obtained by taking $\xi = \xi_b$ in Theorem 2.

Corollary 9. Let (U, ϱ) be a complete Branciari distance space and $T : U \to U$ be a map. Suppose that there are $k \in (0, 1)$ and $K \geq 0$, such that for all $u, v \in U$ with $\varrho(Tu, Tv) > 0$

$$\varphi(m(u, v), \varrho(u, v)) < 0 \Rightarrow \gamma(\vartheta(\varrho(Tu, Tv)) \leq [\gamma(\vartheta(\varrho(u, v) + Km(u, v)))]^k.$$

If ϑ is non-decreasing and continuous, then T possesses only one fixed point.

Corollary 10. Let (U, ϱ) be a complete Branciari distance space and $T : U \to U$ be a map. Suppose that there are $k \in (0, 1)$ and $K \geq 0$, such that for all $u, v \in U$ with $\varrho(Tu, Tv) > 0$

$$\gamma(\vartheta(\varrho(Tu, Tv))) \leq [\gamma(\vartheta(\varrho(u, v) + Km(u, v)))]^k.$$

If ϑ is non-decreasing and continuous, then T possesses only one fixed point.

Remark 6. (1) Corollary 8 is a generalization of Theorem 2.1 of [22] and Theorem 2.1 of [27], respectively. By taking $\gamma(t) = t, \forall t \geq 1$ in Corollary 8, Corollary 8 reduces Theorem 2.1 of [22] without condition ($\theta 2$) and ($\theta 3$) and reduces Theorem 2.1 of [27] without condition ($\theta 2$) and ($\theta 4$), respectively.
(2) Corollary 9 is a generalization of Theorem 3.2 of [27] to Branciari distance space without condition ($\theta 2$).

By taking $\xi = \xi_w$ in Theorem 1, the following result is obtained.

Corollary 11. Let (U, ϱ) be a complete Branciari distance space and $T : U \to U$ be a map. Suppose that for all $u, v \in U$ with $\varrho(Tu, Tv) > 0$

$$\varphi(m(u, v), \varrho(u, v)) < 0 \Rightarrow \gamma(\vartheta(\varrho(Tu, Tv))) \leq \frac{\gamma(\vartheta(\varrho(u, v)))}{\phi(\gamma(\vartheta(\varrho(u, v))))}.$$

where ϕ is a non-decreasing and lower semi-continuous self-mapping on $[1, \infty)$, satisfying $\phi^{-1}(\{1\}) = 1$. If ϑ is non-decreasing, then T possesses only one fixed point.

Corollary 12. Let (U, ϱ) be a complete Branciari distance space and $T : U \to U$ be a map. Suppose that for all $u, v \in U$ with $\varrho(Tu, Tv) > 0$

$$\gamma(\vartheta(\varrho(Tu, Tv))) \leq \frac{\gamma(\vartheta(\varrho(u, v)))}{\phi(\gamma(\vartheta(\varrho(u, v))))}.$$

where ϕ is a non-decreasing and lower semi-continuous self-mapping on $[1, \infty)$, satisfying $\phi^{-1}(\{1\}) = 1$. If ϑ is non-decreasing, then T possesses only one fixed point.

By taking $\xi = \xi_w$ in Theorem 2, the following Corollary 13 is obtained.

Corollary 13. Let (U, ϱ) be a complete Branciari distance space and $T : U \to U$ be a map. Suppose that there is $K \geq 0$, such that for all $u, v \in U$ with $\varrho(Tu, Tv) > 0$

$$\varphi(m(u, v), \varrho(u, v)) < 0 \Rightarrow \gamma(\vartheta(\varrho(Tu, Tv))) \leq \frac{\gamma(\vartheta(\varrho((u, v) + Lm(u, v))))}{\phi(\gamma(\vartheta(\varrho((u, v) + Km(u, v)))))}.$$

where ϕ is a non-decreasing and lower semi-continuous self-mapping on $[1,\infty)$, satisfying $\phi^{-1}(\{1\}) = 1$. If ϑ is non-decreasing and continuous, then T possesses only one fixed point.

Corollary 14. *Let (U, ϱ) be a complete Branciari distance space and $T : U \to U$ be a map. Suppose that there is $K \geq 0$, such that for all $u, v \in U$ with $\varrho(Tu, Tv) > 0$*

$$\gamma(\vartheta(\varrho(Tu,Tv))) \leq \frac{\gamma(\vartheta(\varrho((u,v) + Lm(u,v))))}{\phi(\gamma(\vartheta(\varrho((u,v) + Km(u,v)))))}$$

where ϕ is a non-decreasing and lower semi-continuous self-mapping on $[1,\infty)$, satisfying $\phi^{-1}(\{1\}) = 1$. If ϑ is non-decreasing and continuous, then T possesses only one fixed point.

Remark 7. *Corollary 12 is a generalization of Corollary 8 of [24]. In fact, if $\gamma(t) = t$, $\forall t \geq 1$ Corollary 12 reduces Corollary 8 of [24].*

Taking $\gamma(t) = t$ $\forall t \geq 1$ and $\theta(t) = 2 - \frac{2}{\pi} \arctan(\frac{1}{t^{\alpha}})$ $\forall t > 0$ in Corollary 14, the following result is obtained.

Corollary 15. *Let (U, ϱ) be a complete Branciari distance space and $T : U \to U$ be a map. Suppose that the condition holds:*
for all $u, v \in U$ with $\varrho(Tu, Tv) > 0$

$$\varphi(m(u,v), \varrho(u,v)) < 0$$

$$\Rightarrow 2 - \frac{2}{\pi} \arctan\left(\frac{1}{\varrho(Tu,Tv)^r}\right) \leq \frac{2 - \frac{2}{\pi}\arctan(\frac{1}{\varrho(u,v)^r})}{\phi(2 - \frac{2}{\pi}\arctan(\frac{1}{\varrho(u,v)^r}))}$$

where $r \in (0,1)$ and ϕ denote a non-decreasing and lower semi-continuous self-mapping on $[1,\infty)$, satisfying $\phi^{-1}(\{1\}) = 1$.
Then, T possesses only one fixed point.

4. Conclusions

One can use $\mathcal{L}_\gamma$ simulation functions to consolidate and merge some existing fixed-point results in Branciari distance spaces. By applying $\mathcal{L}_\gamma$ simulation functions to the main theorem, one can obtain some fixed-point results. Moreover, fixed-point theorems in the paper can be derived in the setting metric spaces, and by using $\mathcal{L}_\gamma$ simulation functions, the existing fixed-point theorem in the setting metric spaces can be interpreted.

Funding: This research received no external funding.

Institutional Review Board Statement: Not applicable.

Informed Consent Statement: Not applicable.

Data Availability Statement: Not applicable.

Conflicts of Interest: The author declares no conflict of interest.

References

1. Suzuki, T. A new type of fixed point theorem in metric spaces. *Nonlinear Anal.* **2009**, *71*, 5313–5317. [CrossRef]
2. Berinde, V. Approximating fixed points of weak contractions using the Picard iteration. *Nonlinear Anal. Forum* **2004**, *9*, 43–53.
3. Branciari, A. A fixed point theorem of Banach-Caccioppoli type on a class of generalized metric spaces. *Publ. Math. (Debr.)* **2000**, *5* 31–37.
4. Sarma, I.R.; Rao, J.M.; Rao, S.S. Contractions over generalized metric spaces. *J. Nonlinear Sci. Appl.* **2009**, *2*, 180–182. [CrossRef]
5. Aydi, H.; Karapinar, K.; Lakzian, H. Fixed point results on a class of generalized metric spaces. *Math. Sci.* **2012**, *6*, 46. [CrossRef]
6. Azam, A,; Arshad, M. Kannan fixed point theorem on generalized metric spaces. *J. Nonlinear Sci. Appl.* **2008**, *1*, 45–48. [CrossRef]
7. Chen, C.M. Common fixed-point theorems in complete generalized metric spaces. *J. Appl. Math.* **2012**, *2012*, 945915. [CrossRef]

8. Kadelburg, Z, Radenović, S. Fixed point results in generalized metric spaces without Hausdorff property. *Math. Sci.* **2014**, *8*, 125. [CrossRef]
9. Shatanawi, W.; Al-Rawashdeh, A.; Aydi, H.; Nashine, H.K. On a fixed point for generalized contractions in generalized metric spaces. *Abstr. Appl. Anal.* **2012**, *2012*, 246085. [CrossRef]
10. Kadelburg, Z, Radenović, S. On generalized metric spaces: A survey. *TWMS J. Pure Appl. Math.* **2014**, *5*, 3–13.
11. Arshad, M.; Ahmad, J.; Karapınar, E. Some common fixed point results in rectangular metric spaces. *Int. J. Anal.* **2013**, *2013*, 1–7. [CrossRef]
12. Arshad, M.; Ameer E.; Karapınar, E. Generalized contractions with triangular α-orbital admissible mapping on Branciari metric spaces. *J. Inequalities Appl.* **2016**, *2016*, 63. [CrossRef]
13. Aydi, H.; Karapinar, K.; Samet, B. Fixed points for generalized (α, ψ)-contractions on generalized metric spaces. *J. Inequalities Appl.* **2014**, *2014*, 229. [CrossRef]
14. Aydi, H.; Karapinar, K.; Zhang, D. On common fixed points in the context of Brianciari metric spaces. *Results Math.* **2017** *71*, 73–92. [CrossRef]
15. Bari, C.D.; Vetro, P. Common fixed points in generalized metric spaces. *Appl. Math. Commput.* **2012**, *218*, 7322–7325. [CrossRef]
16. Berzig, M.; Karapinar, E; Hierro, A. F. R.-L.-d. Some fixed point theorems in Branciari metric spaces. *Math. Slov.* **2017**, *67*, 1189–1202. [CrossRef]
17. Das, P. A fixed point theorem on a class of generalized metric spaces. *Korean J. Math. Sci.* **2002**, *9*, 29–33.
18. Karapinar, E. Some fixed points results on Branciari metric spaces via implicit functions. *Carpathian J. Math.* **2015**, *31*, 339–348. [CrossRef]
19. Karapinar, E.; Pitea ,A. On α-ψ-Geraghty contraction type mappings on quasi Branciari metric spaces. *J. Nonlinear Convex Anal.* **2016**, *17*, 1291–1301.
20. Kirk, W.A. Generlized metrics and Caristi's theorem. *Fixed Point Theory Appl.* **2013**, *2013*, 129. [CrossRef]
21. Samet, B. Discussion on "A fixed point theoremof Banach-Caccioppoli type on a class of generalized metric spaces" by A. Branciari. *Publ. Math. (Debr.)* **2010**, *76*, 493–494.
22. Jleli, M.; Samet, B. A new generalization of the Banach contraction principle. *J. Inequalities Appl.* **2014**, *2014*, 38. [CrossRef]
23. Saleh, H.N.; Imdad, M.; Abdeljawad, T.; Arif, M. New contractive mappings and their fixed points in Branciari metric spaces. *J. Funct. Spaces* **2020**, *2020*, 9491786. [CrossRef]
24. Cho, S.H. Fixed point theorems for $\mathcal{L}$-contractions in generalized metric spaces. *Abstr. Appl. Anal.* **2018**, *2018*, 1327691. [CrossRef]
25. Jleli, M.; Karapinar, E.; Samet, B. Further generalizations of the Banach contraction principle. *J. Inequalities And Appl.* **2014**, *2014*, 439. [CrossRef]
26. Erhan, I.M.; Karapınar, E.; Sekulic, T. Fixed points of (ψ, ϕ) contractions on rectangular metric spaces. *Fixed Point Theory Appl.* **2012**, *2012*, 138. [CrossRef]
27. Ahmad, J.; Al-Mazrooei, A.E.; Cho, Y.J.; Yang, Y.O. Fixed point results for generalized θ-contractions. *J. Nonlinear Sci. Appl.* **2017**, *10*, 2350–2358. [CrossRef]
28. Hasnuzzaman, M.D.; Imdad, M.; Saleh, H.N. On modified $\mathcal{L}$-contraction via binary relation with an application. *Fixed Point Theory* **2022**, *23*, 267–278. [CrossRef]
29. Moustafa, S.I.; Shehata, A. $\mathcal{L}$-simulation functions over b-metric -like spaces and fractional hybrid differetial equations. *J. Funct. Spaces* **2020**, *2020*, 4650761.
30. Cho, S.H. Fixed point theorems for set-valued $\mathcal{L}$-contractions in Braciari distance spaces. *Abstr. Appl. Anal.* **2021**, *2021*, 6384818. [CrossRef]
31. Cho, S.H. Generalized $\mathcal{L}$-contractive mapping theorems in partially ordered sets with b-metric spaces. *Adv. Math. Sci. J.* **2020**, *9*, 8525–8546. [CrossRef]
32. Barakat, M.A; Aydi, H.; Mukheimer, A.; Solima, A.A.; Hyder, A. On multivalued $\mathcal{L}$-contractions and an application. *Adv. Dfference Equations* **2020**, *2020*, 554. [CrossRef]
33. Barootkoob, S.; Lakzian, H. Fixed point results via $\mathcal{L}$-contractions on quasi w-distances. *J. Math. Ext.* **2021**, *15*, 1–22.
34. Suzuki, T. Generalized metric spaces Do not have the compatible topology. *Abstr. Appl. Anal.* **2014**, *2014*, 458098. [CrossRef]
35. Jleli, M.; Samet, B. The Kannan's fixed point theorem in a cone rectangular metric space. *J. Nonlinear Sci. Appl.* **2009**, *2*, 161–167. [CrossRef]

Article

Deterministic and Stochastic Prey–Predator Model for Three Predators and a Single Prey

Yousef Alnafisah [1,*] and Moustafa El-Shahed [2]

[1] Department of Mathematics, College of Sciences, Qassim University, P.O. Box 6644, Buraydah 51452, Saudi Arabia
[2] Department of Mathematics, Unaizah College of Sciences and Arts, Qassim University, P.O. Box 3771, Unaizah 51911, Saudi Arabia; elshahedm@yahoo.com
* Correspondence: nfiesh@qu.edu.sa

Abstract: In this paper, a deterministic prey–predator model is proposed and analyzed. The interaction between three predators and a single prey was investigated. The impact of harvesting on the three predators was studied, and we concluded that the dynamics of the population can be controlled by harvesting. Some sufficient conditions were obtained to ensure the local and global stability of equilibrium points. The transcritical bifurcation was investigated using Sotomayor's theorem. We performed a stochastic extension of the deterministic model to study the fluctuation environmental factors. The existence of a unique global positive solution for the stochastic model was investigated. The exponential–mean–squared stability of the resulting stochastic differential equation model was examined, and it was found to be dependent on the harvesting effort. Theoretical results are illustrated using numerical simulations.

Keywords: three predators; bifurcation; stochastic; stability; numerical simulations; Sotomayor's theorem

MSC: 37N25; 92D30; 93E03

Citation: Alnafisah, Y.; El-Shahed, M. Deterministic and Stochastic Prey–Predator Model for Three Predators and a Single Prey. *Axioms* **2022**, *11*, 156. https://doi.org/10.3390/axioms11040156

Academic Editor: Behzad Djafari-Rouhani

Received: 21 February 2022
Accepted: 22 March 2022
Published: 28 March 2022

Publisher's Note: MDPI stays neutral with regard to jurisdictional claims in published maps and institutional affiliations.

Copyright: © 2022 by the authors. Licensee MDPI, Basel, Switzerland. This article is an open access article distributed under the terms and conditions of the Creative Commons Attribution (CC BY) license (https://creativecommons.org/licenses/by/4.0/).

1. Introduction

Lotka and Volterra independently created two types of prey–predatory models known as the "Lotka–Volterra model" [1,2]. Since then, many scientists have modified and developed the Lotka–Volterra model to accurately describe the ecosystem. Numerous studies have examined the case of the presence of more than one predator [2–11]. Mukhopadhyay and Bhattacharyya [12] formulated a mathematical model of two predators living on a single biotic prey. They assumed that the predation function for the first predator follows the mass action kinetics, while the functional response for the second predator obeys the Holling type–II functional response. They also assumed that one of the predators is economically viable and undergoes harvesting at a rate proportional to its density. According to [13], in the northern Alaskan forest community, moose are the only large herbivores, constituting the primary prey for each of the three predators: black bears, gray wolves, and brown bears. Black bears have been known to attack and consume wolves if the opportunity presents itself. The main feature of this paper was to modify the interference of the predators in the system investigated in [12] by adding an extra predator $y(t)$ where the first predator (black bear) preys on the second predator (gray wolves) in addition to the prey. The focus was on the harvesting rates and carrying capacity parameters of the model. The paper is organized as follows: The mathematical model is given in Section 2. The existence, uniqueness, non-negativity, and boundedness of the system are all verified in Section 3. Section 4 investigates the local and global stability of the system's equilibrium points. The stochastic extension of the deterministic model is conducted in Section 5. The numerical simulations presented in Section 6 are used to verify the theoretical results. Finally, in Section 7, the conclusions are presented.

2. Mathematical Model

In this paper, we considered a four–species prey–predator model with one prey and three predators as follows:

$$\begin{aligned}
\frac{dx}{dt} &= rx(1 - \frac{x}{k}) - \beta_1 xy - \beta_2 xz - \frac{\beta_3 xw}{a+x}, \\
\frac{dy}{dt} &= m_1 xy + \delta yz - \mu_1 y - q_1 Ey, \\
\frac{dz}{dt} &= m_2 xz - \delta yz - \mu_2 z - q_2 Ez, \\
\frac{dw}{dt} &= \frac{m_3 xw}{a+x} - \mu_3 w - q_3 Ew,
\end{aligned} \quad (1)$$

where $x(t)$ is the population size of the single prey species. We assumed that $x(t)$ grows logistically in the absence of predators with intrinsic growth rate r and carrying capacity k. The first predator $y(t)$ has the ability to consume both the prey and second predator $z(t)$ with the Holling type I (linear) functional response. Let the interaction between the third predator $w(t)$ and prey follow the Holling type II functional response. Assume β_i ($i = 1, 2, 3$) denote the predation rates of the first, second, and third predators on the prey, respectively, and a is the half–saturation constant. Furthermore, let m_i ($i = 1, 2, 3$) denote the efficiency of the first, second, and third predators in the presence of the prey. Moreover, δ represents the predation rate of the first predator on the second predator. We assumed that the ecological efficiency of the second predator's biomass z in the first predator's biomass y is unity. We also assumed that the predators economically undergo harvesting at a rate proportional to their density. The constants q_i ($i = 1, 2, 3$) denote the catchability constants, while E represents the harvesting effort. The density of the first, second, and third predator populations decreases due to natural death at constant rates μ_1, μ_2, and μ_3, respectively.

3. Some Preliminary Results

3.1. Existence and Uniqueness

In this section, we investigate the existence and uniqueness of the solutions of the prey–predator system (1) in the region $\Theta_1 \times (0, T]$ where:

$$\Theta_1 = \left\{ (x, y, z, w) \in \mathbb{R}_+^4 : \max(|x|, |y|, |z|, |w|) \leq \varphi \right\},$$

for sufficiently large φ.

Theorem 1. *For each $X_0 = (x_0, y_0, z_0, w_0) \in \Theta_1$, there exists a unique solution $X(t) \in \Theta_1$ of the prey–predator system (1), which is defined for all $t \geq 0$.*

Proof. Define a mapping $F(X) = (F_1(X), F_2(X), F_3(X), F_4(X))$, in which:

$$\begin{aligned}
F_1(X) &= rx(1 - \frac{x}{k}) - \beta_1 xy - \beta_2 xz - \frac{\beta_3 xw}{a+x}, \\
F_2(X) &= m_1 xy + \delta yz - (\mu_1 + q_1 E)y, \\
F_3(X) &= m_2 xz - \delta yz - (\mu_2 + q_2 E)z, \\
F_4(X) &= \frac{m_3 xw}{a+x} - (\mu_3 + q_3 E)w.
\end{aligned} \quad (2)$$

For any $X, \bar{X} \in \Theta_1$, it follows from (1) that:

$$\begin{aligned}
\|F(X) - F(\bar{X})\| &= |F_1(X) - F_1(\bar{X})| + |F_2(X) - F_2(\bar{X})| + |F_3(X) - F_3(\bar{X})| + |F_4(X) - F_4(\bar{X})| \\
&= \left| rx(1 - \frac{x}{k}) - \beta_1 xy - \beta_2 xz - \frac{\beta_3 xw}{a+x} - r\bar{x}(1 - \frac{\bar{x}}{k}) + \beta_1 \bar{x}\bar{y} + \beta_2 \bar{x}\bar{z} + \frac{\beta_3 \bar{x}\bar{w}}{a+\bar{x}} \right|
\end{aligned}$$

$$+ |m_1 xy + \delta yz - (\mu_1 + q_1 E)y - m_1 \bar{x}\bar{y} - \delta \bar{y}\bar{z} + (\mu_1 + q_1 E)\bar{y}|$$
$$+ |m_2 xz - \delta yz - (\mu_2 + q_2 E)z - m_2 \bar{x}\bar{z} + \delta \bar{y}\bar{z} + (\mu_2 + q_2 E)\bar{z}|$$
$$+ \left| \frac{m_3 xw}{a+x} - (\mu_3 + q_3 E)w - \frac{m_3 \bar{x}\bar{w}}{a+\bar{x}} + (\mu_3 + q_3 E)\bar{w} \right|$$
$$\leq \left(r + \frac{2\varphi r}{k} + \frac{2\varphi}{a} + \rho_1 \varphi \right) |x - \bar{x}| + ((\mu_1 + q_1 E)(\varphi + 1) + (\beta_1 + 2\delta)\varphi)|y - \bar{y}|$$
$$+ (m_2 \varphi + \beta_2 \varphi + 2\delta \varphi + \mu_2 + q_2 E)|z - \bar{z}| + \left(\frac{2\varphi}{a} + \frac{2\varphi^2}{a^2} + \mu_3 + q_3 E \right) |w - \bar{w}|$$
$$\leq H_0 \|X - \bar{X}\|,$$

where:

$$H_0 = \max \left\{ r + \frac{2\varphi r}{k} + \frac{2\varphi}{a} + \rho_1 \varphi, \rho_2 \varphi + (\mu_1 + q_1 E), \rho_3 \varphi + (\mu_2 + q_2 E), \frac{2\varphi}{a} + \frac{2\varphi^2}{a^2} + (\mu_3 + q_3 E) \right\},$$

where $\rho_1 = (\beta_1 + \beta_2 + m_1 + m_2)$, $\rho_2 = (m_1 + q_1 E + \beta_1 + 2\delta)$, and $\rho_3 = (m_2 + \beta_2 + 2\delta)$. Hence, $F(X)$ satisfies the Lipschitz condition with respect to X. According to [14], as $F(X)$ is locally Lipschitz, then there exists a unique local solution to the three–predator-one-prey system (1). □

3.2. Non-Negativity and Boundedness

Considering the biological significance of the problem, we were only interested in non–negative and bounded solutions. The prey–predator system (1) can be written as follows:

$$\begin{aligned} x(t) &= x(0) e^{\int_0^t \frac{F_1(X(s))}{x} ds} \geq 0, \\ y(t) &= y(0) e^{\int_0^t \frac{F_2(X(s))}{y} ds} \geq 0, \\ z(t) &= z(0) e^{\int_0^t \frac{F_3(X(s))}{z} ds} \geq 0, \\ w(t) &= w(0) e^{\int_0^t \frac{F_4(X(s))}{w} ds} \geq 0, \end{aligned} \quad (3)$$

with initial values $x(0) = x_0 \geq 0$, $y(0) = y_0 \geq 0$, $z(0) = z_0 \geq 0$, $w(0) = w_0 \geq 0$. Thus, the solution of the model (1), with non–negative initial conditions remains non–negative. Furthermore, the solution satisfies the Lipschitz condition, as stated in Theorem 1. By Theorems 5 and 6 in [14], the solution of the prey–predator model (1) satisfies the non–negativity. The boundedness of the solutions of model (1) is given in the following theorem.

Theorem 2. *The solutions of the prey–predator model (1) starting in $\mathbb{R}_+^4$ are uniformly bounded.*

Proof. Let $(x(t), y(t), z(t), w(t))$ be any solution of the system (1) with non–negative initial conditions. Let $H_1(t) = x(t) + y(t) + z(t) + w(t)$, then:

$$\begin{aligned} \frac{dH_1}{dt} + \mu H_1 &\leq rx\left(1 - \frac{x}{k}\right) + \mu x \\ &\leq -\frac{r}{k}\left(x - \frac{k(r+\mu)}{2r}\right)^2 + \frac{k(r+\mu)^2}{4r}, \end{aligned}$$

where $\mu = \min\{\mu_1, \mu_2, \mu_3\}$, thus:

$$0 \leq H_1(t) \leq \frac{k(r+\mu)^2}{4\mu r}, \text{ as } t \to \infty.$$

As a result, all the solutions of the prey–predator model (1) that start in $\mathbb{R}_+^4$ are uniformly bounded in the region:

$$\Theta_2 = \left\{ (x, y, z, w) \in \mathbb{R}_+^4 : H_1(t) \leq \frac{k(r+\mu)^2}{4\mu r} + \zeta, \text{ for any } \zeta > 0 \right\}.$$

□

In the following, three critical parameters R_1, R_2, and R_3, can be used to classify the dynamics of the prey–predator model (1). The threshold parameter R_1 is defined by $R_1 = \frac{m_1 k}{(\mu_1 + q_1 E)}$, while the threshold parameter R_2 is defined by $R_2 = \frac{m_2 k}{(\mu_2 + q_2 E)}$. The threshold parameter R_3 is defined by $R_3 = \frac{m_3 k}{(\mu_3 + q_3 E)(a+k)}$. Using the next-generation method, one can obtain the basic reproduction number:

$$R_0 = \max \left\{ \frac{m_1 k}{(\mu_1 + q_1 E)}, \frac{m_2 k}{(\mu_2 + q_2 E)}, \frac{m_3 k}{(\mu_3 + q_3 E)(a+k)} \right\}.$$

One can note that the threshold parameter R_1 appears as a result of additional predator $y(t)$ in the system considered in [12].

4. Equilibria and Stability

The prey–predator model (1) has the following seven equilibrium points:

1. The trivial equilibrium point $E_0 = (0,0,0,0)$, which always exists;
2. The predator free equilibrium point $E_1 = (k, 0, 0, 0)$, which always exists;
3. The equilibrium point $E_2 = (\frac{(\mu_1+q_1 E)}{m_1}, \frac{r(\mu_1+q_1 E)(R_1-1)}{m_1 \beta_1 k}, 0, 0)$; E_2 exists if $R_1 > 1$;
4. The equilibrium point $E_3 = (\frac{(\mu_2+q_2 E)}{m_2}, 0, \frac{r(\mu_2+q_2 E)(R_2-1)}{m_2 \beta_2 k}, 0)$; E_3 exists if $R_2 > 1$;
5. The equilibrium point $E_4 = (\frac{a(\mu_3+q_3 E)}{m_3-(\mu_3+q_3 E)}, 0, 0, \frac{a r m_3(\mu_3+q_3 E)(a+k)(R_3-1)}{k \beta_3 (m_3-(\mu_3+q_3 E))^2})$; E_4 exists if $R_3 > 1$;
6. The equilibrium point $E_5 = (x_5, y_5, z_5, 0)$, where:

$$x_5 = \frac{k(\delta r + \beta_1(\mu_2 + q_2 E) - \beta_2(\mu_1 + q_1 E))}{\phi}, \quad y_5 = \frac{m_2 x_5 - (\mu_2 + q_2 E)}{\delta}, \quad z_5 = \frac{(\mu_1 + q_1 E) - m_1 x_5}{\delta},$$

where $\phi = \delta r + \beta_1 m_2 k - \beta_2 m_1 k$. E_5 exists if $\frac{(\mu_2+q_2 E)}{m_2} < x_5 < \frac{(\mu_1+q_1 E)}{m_1}$;

7. The coexistence equilibrium point $E_6 = (x_6, y_6, z_6, w_6)$, where:

$$x_6 = \frac{a(\mu_3 + q_3 E)}{m_3 - (\mu_3 + q_3 E)}, \quad y_6 = \frac{m_2 x_6 - (\mu_2 + q_2 E)}{\delta}, \quad z_6 = \frac{(\mu_1 + q_1 E) - m_1 x_6}{\delta},$$

$$w_6 = \frac{(a + x_6)}{k \beta_3} [r(k - x_6) - k \beta_1 y_6 - k \beta_2 z_6].$$

E_6 exists if $m_3 > \mu_3 + q_3 E$, $r x_6 + k \beta_1 y_6 + k \beta_2 z_6 < r k$ and $\frac{(\mu_2+q_2 E)}{m_2} < x_6 < \frac{(\mu_1+q_1 E)}{m_1}$.

One can note that the additional predator $y(t)$ causes two new equilibrium points E_2 and E_5 to be obtained, which were not present in [12]. Now, the local stability of the system (1) is investigated. The Jacobian matrix is given as follows:

$$J = \begin{pmatrix} r(1 - \frac{2x}{k}) - \beta_1 y - \beta_2 z - \frac{a \beta_3 w}{(a+x)^2} & -\beta_1 x & -\beta_2 x & -\frac{\beta_3 x}{a+x} \\ m_1 y & m_1 x + \delta z - (\mu_1 + q_1 E) & \delta y & 0 \\ m_2 z & -\delta z & m_2 x - \delta y - (\mu_2 + q_2 E) & 0 \\ \frac{a m_3 w}{(a+x)^2} & 0 & 0 & \frac{m_3 x}{a+x} - (\mu_3 + q_3 E) \end{pmatrix}.$$

The eigenvalues of J around the trivial point E_0 are r, $-(\mu_1 + q_1 E)$, $-(\mu_2 + q_2 E)$ and $-(\mu_3 + q_3 E)$; therefore, for all parameters, E_0 is a saddle with three–dimensional stable manifolds and a one–dimensional unstable manifold. The stability of the free predators' equilibrium point $E_1 = (k, 0, 0, 0)$ is studied as follows:

Theorem 3. *If $R_0 < 1$, then E_1 is locally asymptotically stable.*

Proof. The Jacobian matrix of the model (1) around $E_1(J(E_1))$ is as follows:

$$J(E_1) = \begin{pmatrix} -r & -\beta_1 k & -\beta_2 k & -\frac{\beta_3 k}{a+k} \\ 0 & m_1 k - (\mu_1 + q_1 E) & 0 & 0 \\ 0 & 0 & m_2 k - (\mu_2 + q_2 E) & 0 \\ 0 & 0 & 0 & \frac{m_3 k}{a+k} - (\mu_3 + q_3 E) \end{pmatrix}. \quad (4)$$

The eigenvalues of $J(E_1)$ are $-r$, $m_1 k - (\mu_1 + q_1 E)$, $m_2 k - (\mu_2 + q_2 E)$ and $\frac{m_3 k}{a+k} - (\mu_3 + q_3 E)$. Thus, E_1 is locally asymptotically stable if $R_0 < 1$. □

Theorem 4. *If $\frac{\beta_1 k}{(\mu_1 + q_1 E)} < 1$, $\frac{\beta_2 k}{(\mu_2 + q_2 E)} < 1$, and $\frac{m_3 k}{(\mu_3 + q_3 E)(a+k)} < 1$, then E_1 is globally stable.*

Proof. One can consider the positive–definite Lyapunov function as follows.

$$V_1 = \left(x - k - k \ln \frac{x}{k}\right) + y + z + w.$$

By calculating the time derivative of V_1, one obtains:

$$\frac{dV_1}{dt} \leq (x-k)\left(r(1-\frac{x}{k}) - \beta_1 y - \beta_2 z - \frac{\beta_3 w}{a+x}\right) + m_1 xy + \delta yz - (\mu_1 + q_1 E)y$$
$$+ m_2 xz - \delta yz - (\mu_2 + q_2 E)z + \frac{m_3 xw}{a+x} - (\mu_3 + q_3 E)w$$
$$\leq -\frac{r}{k}(x-k)^2 + (\beta_1 k - (\mu_1 + q_1 E))y + (\beta_2 k - (\mu_2 + q_2 E))z + \left(\frac{m_3 k}{a+k} - (\mu_3 + q_3 E)\right)w.$$

In accordance with Lyapunov–Sasalle's invariance principle, E_1 is globally stable when $\frac{\beta_1 k}{(\mu_1 + q_1 E)} < 1$, $\frac{\beta_2 k}{(\mu_2 + q_2 E)} < 1$, and $\frac{m_3 k}{(\mu_3 + q_3 E)(a+k)} < 1$. □

One can note that the global stability of E_1 depends on the parameters β_1, μ_1 and q_1 of additional predator $y(t)$, which were not present in [12]. The local bifurcation near the equilibrium point E_1 of the system (1) is now investigated using Sotomayor's theorem [15].

Theorem 5. *The prey–predator model (1) goes through a transcritical bifurcation regarding the bifurcation parameter q_1 around $E_1 = (k, 0, 0, 0)$ if $R_1 = 1$.*

Proof. The Jacobian matrix of the prey–predator model (1) at E_1 with $q_1 = q_1^* = \frac{\mu_1 k - \mu_1}{E}$ has a zero eigenvalue. The eigenvector corresponding to $J(E_1)Q_1 = 0$ is $Q_1 = (\nu_1, -\frac{r\nu_1}{\beta_1 k}, 0, 0)^T$, where ν_1 is any non-zero real number. Similarly, the eigenvector corresponding to $J(E_1)^T Q_2 = 0$ is given by $Q_2 = (0, \tau_2, 0, 0)^T$, where τ_2 is any non–zero number. Thus:

1. $Q_2^T F_{m_1}(E_1, m_1^*) = 0$;
2. $Q_2^T DF_{m_1}(E_1, m_1^*)Q_1 = \frac{-rE\nu_1 \tau_2}{\beta_1 k} \neq 0$;
3. $Q_2^T D^2 F(E_1, m_1^*)(Q_1, Q_1) = 2(m_1 \nu_1 + \delta \nu_3)\tau_2 \nu_2 \neq 0$.

In accordance with Sotomayor's theorem, the prey–predator model (1) has a transcritical bifurcation at q_1^*, which is equivalent to $R_1 = 1$. Therefore, the proof is complete. □

The stability around $E_2 = (x_2, y_2, 0, 0)$ is studied as follows:

Theorem 6. *If* $\frac{m_3 x_2}{(\mu_3+q_3 E)(a+x_2)} < 1$ *and* $\frac{m_2 x_2}{(\mu_2+q_2 E)+\delta y_2} < 1$, *then E_2 is locally stable.*

Proof. The eigenvalues of $J(E_2)$ are:

$$\lambda_1 = \frac{m_3 x_2}{a + x_2} - (\mu_3 + q_3 E),$$

$$\lambda_2 = m_2 x_2 - (\mu_2 + q_2 E) - \delta y_2,$$

$$\lambda_3 = \frac{-r x_2 - \sqrt{r^2 x_2^2 - 4 k m_1 \beta_1 x_2 y_2}}{2k},$$

$$\lambda_4 = \frac{-r x_2 + \sqrt{r^2 x_2^2 - 4 k m_1 \beta_1 x_2 y_2}}{2k}.$$

The eigenvalues λ_3 and λ_4 have negative real parts. Thus, if $\frac{m_3 x_2}{(\mu_3+q_3 E)(a+x_2)} < 1$ and $\frac{m_2 x_2}{(\mu_2+q_2 E)+\delta y_2} < 1$, then E_2 is locally stable. □

Theorem 7. *If* $\frac{m_3 x_2}{a(\mu_3+q_3 E)} < 1$ *and* $\frac{m_2 x_2}{(\mu_2+q_2 E)+\delta y_2} < 1$, *then E_2 is globally stable.*

Proof. One can consider the positive–definite Lyapunov function as follows:

$$V_2 = \left(x - x_2 - x_2 \ln \frac{x}{x_2}\right) + \frac{\beta_2}{m_2}\left(y - y_2 - y_2 \ln \frac{y}{y_2}\right) + \frac{\beta_2}{m_2} z + \frac{\beta_3}{m_3} w.$$

By taking the time derivative of V_2, one obtains,

$$\frac{dV_2}{dt} \leq (x - x_2)\left(r\left(1 - \frac{x}{k}\right) - \beta_1 y - \beta_2 z - \frac{\beta_3 w}{a+x}\right) + \frac{\beta_2}{m_2}(y - y_2)(m_1 x + \delta z - (\mu_1 + q_1 E))$$

$$+ \frac{\beta_2}{m_2}(m_2 x z - \delta y z - (\mu_2 + q_2 E) z) + \frac{\beta_3}{m_3}\left(\frac{m_3 x}{a+x} - (\mu_3 + q_3 E)\right) w$$

$$\leq -\frac{r}{k}(x - x_2)^2 + \beta_2\left(x_2 - \frac{\delta y_2}{m_2} - \frac{(\mu_2 + q_2 E)}{m_2}\right) z + \beta_3\left(\frac{x_2}{a+x} - \frac{(\mu_3 + q_3 E)}{m_3}\right) w.$$

Thus, E_2 is globally stable if $\frac{m_3 x_2}{a(\mu_3+q_3 E)} < 1$ and $\frac{m_2 x_2}{(\mu_2+q_2 E)+\delta y_2} < 1$. □

The stability of the equilibrium point $E_3 = (x_3, 0, z_3, 0)$ is investigated as follows:

Theorem 8. *If* $\frac{m_3 x_3}{(a+x_3)(\mu_3+q_3 E)} < 1$ *and* $\frac{m_1 x_3+\delta z_3}{(\mu_1+q_1 E)} < 1$, *then E_3 is locally stable.*

Proof. The eigenvalues of $J(E_3)$ are:

$$\lambda_1 = \frac{m_3 x_3}{a + x_3} - (\mu_3 + q_3 E),$$

$$\lambda_2 = m_1 x_3 - (\mu_1 + q_1 E) + \delta z_3,$$

$$\lambda_3 = \frac{-r x_3 - \sqrt{r^2 x_3^2 - 4 k m_3 \beta_2 x_3 z_3}}{2k},$$

$$\lambda_4 = \frac{-r x_3 + \sqrt{r^2 x_3^2 - 4 k m_3 \beta_2 x_3 z_3}}{2k}.$$

The eigenvalues λ_3 and λ_4 have negative real parts. Thus, if $\frac{m_3 x_3}{(a+x_3)(\mu_3+q_3 E)} < 1$ and $\frac{m_1 x_3+\delta z_3}{(\mu_1+q_1 E)} < 1$, then the equilibrium point E_3 is locally stable. □

Theorem 9. *If* $\frac{m_3 x_3}{a(\mu_3+q_3 E)} < 1$ *and* $\frac{m_1 x_3+\delta z_3}{(\mu_1+q_1 E)} < 1$, *then E_3 is globally stable.*

Proof. One can consider the positive–definite Lyapunov function as follows:

$$V_3 = \left(x - x_3 - x_3 \ln \frac{x}{x_3}\right) + \frac{\beta_1}{m_1} y + \frac{\beta_1}{m_1}\left(z - z_3 - z_3 \ln \frac{z}{z_3}\right) + \frac{\beta_3}{m_3} w.$$

By taking the time derivative of V_3, one obtains,

$$\frac{dV_3}{dt} \leq (x - x_3)\left(r(1 - \frac{x}{k}) - \beta_1 y - \beta_2 z - \frac{\beta_3 w}{a+x}\right) + \frac{\beta_1}{m_1}(m_1 xy + \delta yz - (\mu_1 + q_1 E)y)$$

$$+ \frac{\beta_1}{m_1}(z - z_3)(m_2 x - \delta y - (\mu_2 + q_2 E)) + \frac{\beta_3 w}{m_3}\left(\frac{m_3 x}{a+x} - (\mu_3 + q_3 E)\right)$$

$$\leq -\frac{r}{k}(x - x_3)^2 + \frac{\beta_1}{m_1}(m_1 x_3 + \delta z_3 - (\mu_1 + q_1 E))y + \beta_3\left(\frac{x_3}{a+x} - \frac{(\mu_3 + q_3 E)}{m_3}\right)w.$$

Thus, E_3 is globally stable if $\frac{m_3 x_3}{a(\mu_3 + q_3 E)} < 1$ and $\frac{m_1 x_3 + \delta z_3}{(\mu_1 + q_1 E)} < 1$. □

The stability of the equilibrium point $E_4 = (x_4, 0, 0, w_4)$ is studied as follows:

Theorem 10. *If $m_1 x_4 < \mu_1 + q_1 E$, $m_2 x_4 < \mu_2 + q_2 E$ and $1 < R_3 < 1 + \frac{am_3}{(\mu_3 + q_3 E)(a+k)}$, then E_4 is locally stable.*

Proof. The eigenvalues of $J(E_4)$ are:

$$\lambda_1 = m_1 x_4 - (\mu_1 + q_1 E),$$
$$\lambda_2 = m_2 x_4 - (\mu_2 + q_2 E),$$

The other eigenvalues are determined by:

$$\lambda^2 + x_4\left(\frac{r}{k} - \frac{\beta_3 w_4}{(a+x_4)^2}\right)\lambda + \frac{am_3 \beta_3 x_4 w_4}{(a+x_4)^3} = 0.$$

One can note that $\frac{r}{k} - \frac{\beta_3 w_4}{(a+x_4)^2} > 0$ is equivalent to $R_3 < 1 + \frac{am_3}{(\mu_3+q_3 E)(a+k)}$. Thus, if $m_1 x_4 < \mu_1 + q_1 E$, $m_2 x_4 < \mu_2 + q_2 E$, and $1 < R_3 < 1 + \frac{am_3}{(\mu_3+q_3 E)(a+k)}$, then E_4 is locally stable. □

The stability around $E_5 = (x_5, y_5, z_5, 0)$ is studied as follows:

Theorem 11. *If $\frac{m_3 x_5}{(\mu_3 + q_3 E)(a+x_5)} < 1$, then E_5 is locally stable.*

Proof. $J(E_5)$ is:

$$J(E_5) = \begin{pmatrix} -\frac{r x_5}{k} & -\beta_1 x_5 & -\beta_2 x_5 & -\frac{\beta_3 x_5}{a+x_5} \\ m_1 y_5 & 0 & \delta y_5 & 0 \\ m_2 z_5 & -\delta z_5 & 0 & 0 \\ 0 & 0 & 0 & \frac{m_3 x_5}{a+x_5} - (\mu_3 + q_3 E) \end{pmatrix}.$$

The first eigenvalue of $J(E_5)$ is $\lambda_1 = \frac{m_3 x_5}{a+x_5} - (\mu_3 + q_3 E)$. The other roots are determined by

$$\lambda^3 + c_1 \lambda^3 + c_2 \lambda + c_3 = 0,$$

where:

$$c_1 = \frac{rx_5}{k},$$
$$c_2 = m_1\beta_1 x_5 y_5 + m_2\beta_2 x_5 z_5 + \delta^2 y_5 z_5,$$
$$c_3 = \frac{\delta x_5 y_5 z_5 \phi}{k};$$

when $r\delta > \phi$, then $c_1 c_2 > c_3$. Hence, due to the Routh–Hurwitz criterion, all the eigenvalues of the Jacobian matrix $J(E_5)$ around E_5 have a negative real part. Thus, the proof is complete. □

The stability of the equilibrium point $E_6 = (x_6, y_6, z_6, w_6)$ is studied as follows:

Theorem 12. *If* $\frac{\beta_3 w_6}{(a+x_6)^2} < \frac{r}{k}$ *and* $\beta_2 m_1 < \beta_1 m_2$, *then* E_6 *is locally stable.*

Proof. The Jacobian matrix of the model (1) at E_6 is:

$$J(E_6) = \begin{pmatrix} -\frac{rx_6}{k} + \frac{\beta_3 x_6 w_6}{(a+x_6)^2} & -\beta_1 x_6 & -\beta_2 x_6 & -\frac{\beta_3 x_6}{a+x_6} \\ m_1 y_6 & 0 & \delta y_6 & 0 \\ m_2 z_6 & -\delta z_6 & 0 & 0 \\ \frac{am_3 x_6}{(a+x_6)^2} & 0 & 0 & 0 \end{pmatrix}.$$

The characteristic equation of the Jacobian matrix around E_6 is as follows:

$$\lambda^4 + B_1 \lambda^3 + B_2 \lambda^2 + B_3 \lambda + B_4 = 0, \tag{5}$$

where:

$$B_1 = x_6\left(\frac{r}{k} - \frac{\beta_3 w_6}{(a+x_6)^2}\right),$$
$$B_2 = x_6\left(\frac{a\beta_3 m_3 w_6}{(a+x_6)^3} + \beta_2 m_2 z_6\right) + y_6\left(\beta_1 m_1 x_6 + \delta^2 z_6\right),$$
$$B_3 = \delta y_6 z_6(B_1 \delta + x_6(\beta_1 m_2 - \beta_2 m_1)),$$
$$B_4 = \frac{a\beta_3 \delta^2 m_3 w_6 x_6 y_6 z_6}{(a+x_6)^3}.$$

The eigenvalues of the Jacobian matrix $J(E_6)$ have a negative real part if all coefficients of (5) are positive and $B_1 B_2 B_3 > B_3^2 + B_1^2 B_4$. □

Theorem 13. *If* $\frac{\beta_3 w_6}{a(a+x_6)} < \frac{r}{k}$ *and* $\beta_1 m_2 = \beta_2 m_1$, *then* E_6 *is globally stable.*

Proof. One can consider the positive–definite Lyapunov function as follows.

$$V_6 = \int_{x_6}^{x} \frac{x - x_6}{x} dx + \frac{\beta_1}{m_1} \int_{y_6}^{y} \frac{y - y_6}{y} dy + \frac{\beta_2}{m_2} \int_{z_6}^{z} \frac{z - z_6}{z} dz + \frac{\beta_3(a+x_6)}{a\, m_3} \int_{w_6}^{w} \frac{w - w_6}{w} dw.$$

By taking the time derivative of V_6, one obtains,

$$\frac{dV_6}{dt} \leq (x - x_6)\left(r(1 - \frac{x}{k}) - \beta_1 y - \beta_2 z - \frac{\beta_3 w}{a+x}\right) + \frac{\beta_1}{m_1}(y - y_6)(m_1 x + \delta z - (\mu_1 + q_1 E))$$
$$+ \frac{\beta_2}{m_2}(z - z_6)(m_2 x - \delta y - (\mu_2 + q_2 E)) + \frac{\beta_3(a+x_6)}{a\, m_3}(w - w_6)\left(\frac{m_3 x}{a+x} - (\mu_3 + q_3 E)\right)$$
$$\leq \left(\frac{\beta_3 w_6}{a(a+x_6)} - \frac{r}{k}\right)(x - x_6)^2.$$

In accordance with Lyapunov–Sasalle's invariance principle, E_6 is globally stable if $\frac{\beta_3 w_6}{a(a+x_6)} < \frac{r}{k}$ and $\beta_1 m_2 = \beta_2 m_1$. □

In this section, we show that at the positive equilibrium point E_6, a Hopf bifurcation arises, by taking the catchability constant q_3, as a bifurcation parameter. The following lemma is presented first.

Lemma 1. *The characteristic Equation (5) has a pair of purely imaginary roots, and the remaining roots have negative real parts if and only if $\frac{\beta_3 w_6}{a(a+x_6)} < \frac{r}{k}$ and $B_1 B_2 B_3 = B_3^2 + B_1^2 B_4$.*

Suppose (5) has two eigenvalues, which have negative real parts, and two complex conjugates eigenvalues (call them $\lambda = m(q_3) \pm i\, n(q_3)$ such that $m(q_3^*) = 0$, $n(q_3^*) > 0$, $\frac{dm}{dq_3}|_{q_3=q_3^*} \neq 0$. Substituting $\lambda = m(q_3) \pm i\, n(q_3)$ into (5) and separating the real and imaginary parts, one obtains:

$$m^4 + B_1 m^3 + B_2 m^3 + B_3 m + B_4 - (6m^2 + 3B_1 m + B_2)n^2 + n^4 = 0, \tag{6}$$

$$4m^3 + 3B_1 m^2 + 2B_2 m + B_3 - (4m + B_1)n^2 = 0. \tag{7}$$

Following [16,17], substituting (6) into (7), differentiating with respect to q_3, and utilizing $m(q_3^*) = 0$ and $n(q_3^*) \neq 0$, one obtains:

$$\frac{dm}{dq_3} = \left[\frac{\frac{d\Phi_1(q_3)}{dq_3}}{2B_1 \Phi_2(q_3)} \right]_{q_3=q_3^*} \neq 0,$$

where $\Phi_1(q_3) = B_1(q_3) B_2(q_3) B_3(q_3) - B_3^2(q_3) - B_1^2(q_3) B_4(q_3)$ and $\Phi_2(q_3) = 4B_4(q_3) - B_1(q_3) B_3(q_3) - B_2(q_3)^2$.

Theorem 14. *The system around the coexistence E_6 enters into Hopf bifurcation when q_3 passes q_3^* if the coefficients $B_j(q_3)$ ($j = 1,2,3,4$) at $q_3 = q_3^*$ satisfy the following conditions:*

1. $\Phi_1(q_3^*) = 0$;
2. $\Phi_2(q_3^*) \neq 0$;
3. $\frac{d\Phi_1(q_3)}{dq_3}|_{q_3=q_3^*} \neq 0$.

According to Theorem 14, there exists a Hopf bifurcation in the model (1), where the Hopf bifurcation is controlled by q_3.

5. Stochastic Models

In this section, we perform a stochastic extension of the deterministic model (1) in two ways. Firstly, a randomly fluctuating driving force can be directly added to the deterministic model. Secondly, the catchability constants are replace by random parameters.

5.1. Stochastic Perturbations

Considering the effect of environmental noise, one can introduce a stochastic perturbation into the system (1); the stochastic prey–predator model takes the form:

$$\begin{aligned}
dx &= rx(1 - \frac{x}{k}) - \beta_1 xy - \beta_2 xz - \frac{\beta_3 xw}{a+x} + \sigma_1 x\, dW_1, \\
dy &= m_1 xy + \delta yz - \mu_1 y - q_1 Ey + \sigma_2 y\, dW_2, \\
dz &= m_2 xz - \delta yz - \mu_2 z - q_2 Ez + \sigma_3 z\, dW_3, \\
dw &= \frac{m_3 xw}{a+x} - \mu_3 w - q_3 Ew + \sigma_4 w\, dW_4,
\end{aligned} \tag{8}$$

where $W_i(i = 1, 2, 3, 4)$ are independent standard Brownian motions with $W_i(0) = 0$ and $\sigma_i > 0$ denote the intensities of the white noise. In many applications, the solution of the Itô stochastic differential equation must preserve the positivity of the solutions [18–20]. According to Theorem 2.2 and Corollary 1 in [18], the solutions of (8) emanating from non–negative initial data (almost surely) remain non–negative if they exist. In the next theorem, another approach according to [17] to prove the existence and uniqueness of a positive global solution of model (8) is given.

Theorem 15. *For any given initial value $x_0, y_0, z_0, w_0 \in \mathbb{R}_+^4$, there exists a unique solution $x(t), y(t), z(t), w(t)$ of the system (8) on $t \geq 0$, and the global positive solution will remain in $\mathbb{R}_+^4$ with probability one.*

Proof. In accordance with Theorem 1, the coefficients of the system (8) satisfy the local Lipschitz conditions, then for $(x_0, y_0, z_0, w_0) \in \mathbb{R}_+^4$, there exists a unique local solution $(x(t), y(t), z(t), w(t))$ on $[0, \tau_e)$, where τ_e is the explosion time [21]. To ensure that this solution is global, one needs to prove that $\tau_e = \infty$ a.s. Let $s_0 > 0$ be sufficiently large for every coordinate x_0, y_0, z_0, w_0 in the interval $[\frac{1}{s_0}, s_0]$. For each integer $s > s_0$, we define the stopping time:

$$\tau_s = \inf\left\{t \in [0, \tau_e) : \min\{x(t), y(t), z(t), w(t)\} \notin \left(\frac{1}{s}, s\right) \text{ or } \max\{x(t), y(t), z(t), w(t)\} \notin \left(\frac{1}{s}, s\right)\right\}. \quad (9)$$

From (9), one can note that τ_s is increasing as $s \to \infty$. Assume $\tau_\infty = \lim_{s \to \infty} \tau_s$, then $\tau_\infty \leq \tau_e$ almost surely. Next, one needs to verify that $\tau_\infty = \infty$. If this is not true, then there exists a constant $T > 0$ and $\epsilon \in (0, 1)$ such that $P(\tau_\infty \leq T) \geq \epsilon$. As a result, there exists an integer $s_1 \geq s_0$ such that $P(\tau_s \leq T) \geq \epsilon$, $s \geq s_1$. Define the following C^2 positive–definite function $V_7(x, y, z, w)$ as:

$$V_7(x, y, z, w) = (x + 1 - \ln x) + (y + 1 - \ln y) + (z + 1 - \ln z) + (w + 1 - \ln w).$$

Using Itô's formula, one obtains:

$$dV_7 = \left[(x-1)\left(r(1-\frac{x}{k}) - \beta_1 y - \beta_2 z - \frac{\beta_3 w}{a+x}\right) + (y-1)(m_1 x + \delta z - (\mu_1 + q_1 E))\right.$$
$$+ (z-1)(m_2 x - \delta y - (\mu_2 + q_2 E)) + (w-1)(\frac{m_3 x}{a+x} - (\mu_3 + q_3 E)) + \frac{1}{2}\sum_{i=1}^{4}\sigma_i^2\Bigg]dt$$
$$+ \sigma_1(x-1)dW_1 + \sigma_2(y-1)dW_2 + \sigma_3(z-1)dW_3 + \sigma_4(w-1)dW_4$$
$$\leq \left[\mu_1 + \mu_2 + \mu_3 + \frac{1}{2}\sum_{i=1}^{4}\sigma_i^2 + \frac{r(k+1)}{k}x + (\beta_1 + \delta)y + \beta_2 z + \frac{\beta_3}{a}w\right]dt$$
$$+ \sigma_1(x-1)dW_1 + \sigma_2(y-1)dW_2 + \sigma_3(z-1)dW_3 + \sigma_4(w-1)dW_4$$
$$\leq \left[D_1 + \frac{2r(k+1)}{k}(x+1-\ln x) + 2(\beta_1 + \delta)(y+1-\ln y) + 2\beta_2(z+1-\ln z)\right.$$
$$\left.+ \frac{2\beta_3}{a}(w+1-\ln w)\right]dt + \sigma_1(x-1)dW_1 + \sigma_2(y-1)dW_2 + \sigma_3(z-1)dW_3 + \sigma_4(w-1)dW_4.$$

Using the following inequality $\Omega \leq 2(\Omega + 1 - \ln\Omega)$, where $\Omega > 0$, one obtains:

$$dV_7 \leq D_1 + D_2[(x+1-\ln x) + (y+1-\ln y) + (z+1-\ln z) + (w+1-\ln w)] + \sigma_1(x-1)dW_1$$
$$+ \sigma_1(x-1)dW_1 + \sigma_2(y-1)dW_2 + \sigma_3(z-1)dW_3 + \sigma_4(w-1)dW_4$$
$$\leq D_3(1+V_7)dt + \sigma_1(x-1)dW_1 + \sigma_2(y-1)dW_2 + \sigma_3(z-1)dW_3 + \sigma_4(w-1)dW_4,$$

where $D_1 = \mu_1 + \mu_2 + \mu_3 + \frac{1}{2}\sum_{i=1}^{4}\sigma_i^2$, $D_2 = \max\left\{\frac{2r(k+1)}{k}, 2(\beta_1+\delta), 2\beta_2, \frac{2\beta_3}{a}\right\}$, and $D_3 = \max\{D_1, D_2\}$. Following [21–25], integrating from 0 to $\tau_s \wedge T$ and taking the expectation by applying Gronwall's inequality, one obtains,

$$EV_7(x(\tau_s \wedge T), y(\tau_s \wedge T), z(\tau_s \wedge T), w(\tau_s \wedge T)) = V_7(x_0.y_0, z_0, w_0) + E\int_0^{\tau_s \wedge T} D_3(1+V_7)ds$$

$$\leq V_7(x_0.y_0, z_0, w_0) + D_3 T + D_3 \int_0^{\tau_s \wedge T} EV_7 ds$$

$$\leq \{V_7(x_0.y_0, z_0, w_0) + D_3 T\}e^{D_3 T}$$

$$= D_4,$$

Therefore, one obtains $V_7(x(\tau_s \wedge T), y(\tau_s \wedge T), z(\tau_s \wedge T), w(\tau_s \wedge T)) \geq (x+1-\ln x)$ Following [21–25], one can complete the remainder of the proof. □

Here, we allowed stochastic perturbations of x, y, z, w around the free predators' equilibrium point E_1. The linearized stochastic system can be written as:

$$dU(t) = f(U(t)dt + g(U(t))dW(t), \qquad (10)$$

where:

$$f(U) = \begin{pmatrix} -ru_1 - \beta_1 k u_2 - \beta_2 k u_3 - \frac{\beta_3 k u_4}{a+k} \\ (m_1 k - \mu_1 - q_1 E)u_2 \\ (m_2 k - \mu_2 - q_2 E)u_3 \\ \left(\frac{m_3 k}{(a+k)} - \mu_3 - q_3 E\right)u_4 \end{pmatrix}; g(U) = \begin{pmatrix} \sigma_1 u_1 & 0 & 0 & 0 \\ 0 & \sigma_2 u_2 & 0 & 0 \\ 0 & 0 & \sigma_3 u_3 & 0 \\ 0 & 0 & 0 & \sigma_4 u_4 \end{pmatrix},$$

$U(t) = (u_1(t), u_2(t), u_3(t), u_4(t))^T$. One can note that the free predators' equilibrium E_1 of the system (1) corresponds to the trivial solution of the system (10).

Following [17,20], let **B** be the set defined as $\mathbf{B} = [(t \geq t_0) \times R^n, t_0 \in R^+]$ and $V \in C_2^0(\mathbf{B})$ be a twice–differential function with respect to U and a continuous function with respect to t. Now, we require the following theorem to prove the asymptotically mean–squared stability of the trivial solution of (10).

Theorem 16. *Suppose that $V \in C_2^0(\mathbf{B})$ satisfies the following:*

$$K_1\|U\|^p \leq V(t, U) \leq K_2\|U\|^p \qquad (11)$$

$$LV(t, U) \leq -K_3\|U\|^p, \qquad (12)$$

where $p > 0$ and $K_i(i = 1, 2, 3)$ are positive constants. Then, the trivial solution of (10) is exponentially p–stable for $t \geq 0$.

Following [21,26,27], the Lyapunov operator $LV(t, U)$ associated with (12) is defined as:

$$LV(t, U) = \frac{\partial V(t, U)}{\partial t} + f^T(U)\frac{\partial V(t, U)}{\partial U} + \frac{1}{2}Tr\left[g^T(t, U)\frac{\partial^2 V(t, U)}{\partial U^2}g(t, U)\right]$$

Theorem 17. *The trivial solution of (10) is asymptotically mean–squared stable if:*

$$\sigma_1^2 < 2r, \; \sigma_2^2 < 2\mu_1(1-R_1), \; \sigma_3^2 < 2\mu_2(1-R_2), \; \sigma_4^2 < 2\mu_3(1-R_3).$$

Proof. Consider the following Lyapunov function:

$$V_7(t, U) = \frac{1}{2}\left(u_1^2 + u_2^2 + u_3^2 + u_4^2\right). \qquad (13)$$

The first condition of Theorem 16 holds for the Lyapunov function defined in (13) with $p = 2$. Now, Lyapunov operator $LV_7(t, U)$ becomes:

$$LV_7(t,U) = -(r - \frac{1}{2}\sigma_1^2)u_1^2 - (\mu_1 + q_1 E - m_1 k - \frac{1}{2}\sigma_2^2)u_2^2 - (\mu_2 + q_2 E - m_2 k - \frac{1}{2}\sigma_3^2)u_3^2$$
$$- (\mu_3 + q_3 E - \frac{m_3 k}{a+k} - \frac{1}{2}\sigma_4^2)u_4^2 - \beta_1 k u_1 u_2 - \beta_2 k u_1 u_3 - \frac{\beta_3 k}{a+k}u_1 u_4$$
$$\leq -(r - \frac{1}{2}\sigma_1^2)u_1^2 - \frac{\mu_1 + q_1 E}{2}(2(1 - R_1) - \sigma_2^2)u_2^2 - \frac{\mu_2 + q_2 E}{2}(2(1 - R_2) - \sigma_3^2)u_3^2$$
$$- \frac{\mu_3 + q_3 E}{2}(2(1 - R_3) - \sigma_4^2)u_4^2,$$

and this leads to $LV_7(t, U) \leq -K_3 \|U\|^2$, where:

$$K_3 = \min\left\{ (r - \frac{1}{2}\sigma_1^2), \frac{\mu_1 + q_1 E}{2}(2(1 - R_1) - \sigma_2^2), \frac{\mu_2 + q_2 E}{2}(2(1 - R_2) - \sigma_3^2), \frac{\mu_3 + q_3 E}{2}(2(1 - R_3) - \sigma_4^2) \right\}.$$

□

One can note that the conditions of Theorem 17 indicate that the exponential-mean-squared stability of the system (10) depends on the harvesting effort.

5.2. Random Harvesting

Here, we studied the effect of random harvesting on the three predators. The stochastic extension of (1) is as follows:

$$\begin{aligned}
\frac{dx}{dt} &= rx(1 - \frac{x}{k}) - \beta_1 xy - \beta_2 xz - \frac{\beta_3 xw}{a+x}, \\
\frac{dy}{dt} &= m_1 xy + \delta yz - \mu_1 y - (q_1 + \zeta_1) Ey, \\
\frac{dz}{dt} &= m_2 xz - \delta yz - \mu_2 z - (q_2 + \zeta_2) Ez, \\
\frac{dw}{dt} &= \frac{m_3 xw}{a+x} - \mu_3 w - (q_3 + \zeta_3) Ew.
\end{aligned} \quad (14)$$

The catchability parameters q_1, q_2, and q_3 were perturbed by independent Gaussian white noise terms ζ_1, ζ_2, and ζ_3 in the system (14) because, usually in the prey–predator system, harvesting is performed randomly, where $\zeta_i, i = 1, 2, 3$ are independent Gaussian white noises satisfying:

$$\langle \zeta_i(t) \rangle = 0, \text{ and } \langle \zeta_i(t_1)\zeta_i(t_2) \rangle = \delta_{ij}\delta(t_1 - t_2).$$

$\delta(t_1 - t_2)$ is the Dirac delta function; δ_{ij} is the Kronecker delta; $\langle . \rangle$ is the expectation.

Following [28], substituting $x(t) = e^{Z_1(t)}, y(t) = e^{Z_2(t)}, z(t) = e^{Z_3(t)}, w(t) = e^{Z_4(t)}$, into (14), one obtains:

$$\begin{aligned}
\frac{dZ_1}{dt} &= r(1 - \frac{e^{Z_1(t)}}{k}) - \beta_1 e^{Z_2(t)} - \beta_2 e^{Z_3(t)} - \frac{\beta_3 e^{Z_4(t)}}{a + e^{Z_1(t)}}, \\
\frac{dZ_2}{dt} &= m_1 e^{Z_1(t)} + \delta e^{Z_3(t)} - \mu_1 - (q_1 + \zeta_1)E, \\
\frac{dZ_3}{dt} &= m_2 e^{Z_1(t)} - \delta e^{Z_2(t)} - \mu_2 - (q_2 + \zeta_2)E, \\
\frac{dZ_4}{dt} &= \frac{m_3 e^{Z_1(t)}}{a + e^{Z_1(t)}} - \mu_3 - (q_3 + \zeta_3)E.
\end{aligned} \quad (15)$$

Using $Z_1 = x_6 + \xi_1$, $Z_2 = y_6 + \xi_2$, $Z_3 = z_6 + \xi_3$, $Z_4 = w_6 + \xi_4$, one obtains the following linearized system:

$$\begin{aligned}
\frac{d\xi_1}{dt} &= x_6\left(\frac{r}{k} - \frac{\beta_3 w_6}{(a+x_6)^2}\right)\xi_1 - \beta_1 y_6 \xi_2 - \beta_2 z_6 \xi_3 - \frac{\beta_3 w_6}{a+x_6}\xi_4, \\
\frac{d\xi_2}{dt} &= m_1 x_6 \xi_1 + \delta z_6 \xi_3 - \mu_1 - (q_1 + \zeta_1)E, \\
\frac{d\xi_3}{dt} &= m_2 x_6 - \delta y_6 \xi_2 - (q_2 + \zeta_2)E, \\
\frac{d\xi_4}{dt} &= \frac{am_3 x_6}{(a+x_6)^2}\xi_1 - (q_3 + \zeta_3)E,
\end{aligned} \quad (16)$$

where $\vec{\xi} = (\xi_1, \xi_2, \xi_3, \xi_4)$ are the stochastic perturbations around (x_6, y_6, z_6, w_6). The linearized system (16) can be written as:

$$d\vec{\xi}(t) = \mathbf{M}\vec{\xi}(t)dt + G(\vec{\xi}(t), t)d\mathbf{W}(t), \quad (17)$$

where:

$$\mathbf{M} = \begin{pmatrix} x_6\left(-\frac{rx_6}{k} + \frac{\beta_3 x_6 w_6}{(a+x_6)^2}\right) & -\beta_1 y_6 & -\beta_2 z_6 & -\frac{\beta_3 x_6}{a+x_6} \\ m_1 x_6 & 0 & \delta z_6 & 0 \\ m_2 x_6 & -\delta y_6 & 0 & 0 \\ \frac{am_3 x_6}{(a+x_6)^2} & 0 & 0 & 0 \end{pmatrix}; \quad G = \begin{pmatrix} 0 & 0 & 0 & 0 \\ 0 & -E & 0 & 0 \\ 0 & 0 & -E & 0 \\ 0 & 0 & 0 & -E \end{pmatrix}.$$

The solution of (17) can be written in the form:

$$\vec{\xi}(t) = e^{\mathbf{M}t}\vec{\xi}_0(t) + \int_0^t e^{\mathbf{M}(t-s)} G(s)d\mathbf{W}(s), \quad (18)$$

Following [12,29,30], one can assume that there exists a pair of positive constants θ_1 and γ_1 such that $\|e^{\mathbf{M}}\|^2 \leq \theta_1 e^{-\gamma_1 t}$. Furthermore, one can find another pair of positive constants θ_2 and γ_2 such that $|G|^2 \leq \theta_2 e^{-\gamma_2 t}$. Thus:

$$\begin{aligned}
E(|\vec{\xi}(t)|^2) &\leq 2|e^{\mathbf{M}t}\vec{\xi}_0|^2 + 2\int_0^t |e^{\mathbf{M}(t-s)}G(s)|^2 d(s) \\
&\leq 2\theta_1 e^{-\gamma_1 t}|\vec{\xi}_0|^2 + 2\theta_1 \theta_2 e^{-\min\{\gamma_1,\gamma_2\}t},
\end{aligned}$$

and as a result, the prey–predator system (14) will be exponentially mean–squared stable.

6. Numerical Simulations

In this part, the numerical simulations are compared with the previous theoretical analysis. The numerical simulation was conducted using the following parameters $r = 2$, $k = 0.1$, $\beta_1 = 0.1$, $\beta_2 = 0.5$, $\beta_3 = 0.1$, $m_1 = 0.1$, $m_2 = 0.2$, $m_3 = 0.1$, $\delta = 0.08$, $\mu_1 = 0.04$, $\mu_2 = 0.2$, $\mu_3 = 0.2$, $a = 0.6$, $q_1 = 0.1$, $q_2 = 0.1$, $q_3 = 0.1$, $E = 0.1$.

The effect of catchability constants can be shown by drawing the bifurcation diagram regarding q_1 as a bifurcation parameter. The transcritical bifurcation value is centered at $q_1^* = 0.2$ as indicated in Figure 1. Note that the bifurcations that are presented in Theorem 5 are illustrated because $q_1^* = 0.2$ is equivalent to $R_1 = \frac{m_1 k}{\mu_1 + q_1 E} = 1$.

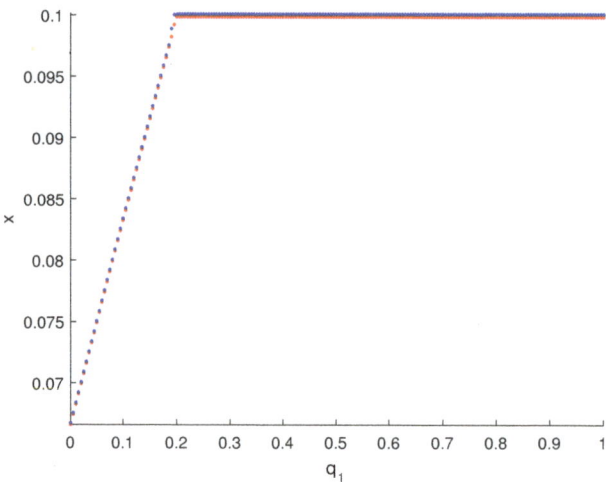

Figure 1. Bifurcation diagram of the model (1) with respect to q_1.

One can draw the bifurcation diagram regarding q_3 to indicate the effect of the harvesting. The supercritical Hopf bifurcation value is centered at $q_3^* = 0.254669$ as indicated in Figure 2. It can also be noted that for $q_3 > 0.254669$, the prey–predator model (1) is locally stable as indicated in Figure 3, while for $q_3 < 0.254669$, the system goes through the limit cycle behavior. One can find that all the conditions of Theorem 14 hold as $\Phi_1(0.254669) = 0$, $\Phi_2(0.254669) \neq 0$ and $\frac{d\Phi_1(q_3)}{dq_3}|_{q_3=0.254669} \neq 0$. This confirms the existence of a Hopf bifurcation at $q_3^* = 0.254669$. As a result, the harvesting parameter q_3 can break the oscillating behavior of the deterministic system (1) and drive it to the required state. In the same way, the bifurcation of the system can be studied using the parameter q_2, as shown in Figure 4.

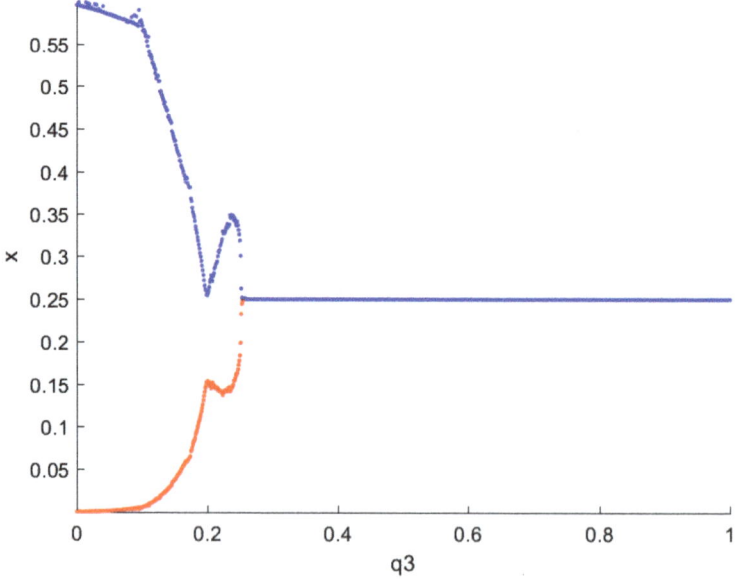

Figure 2. Bifurcation diagram of the model (1) with respect to q_3.

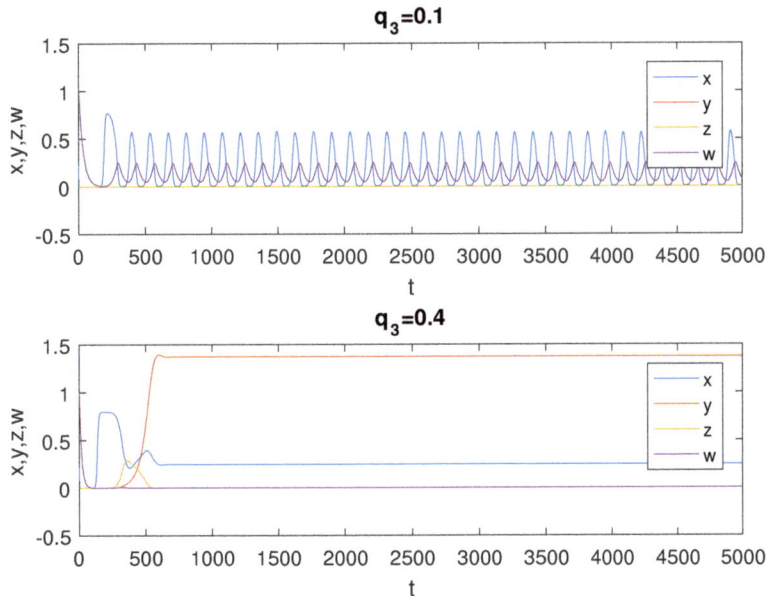

Figure 3. Time series of the model (1) with $q_3 = 0.1$ and $q_3 = 0.4$.

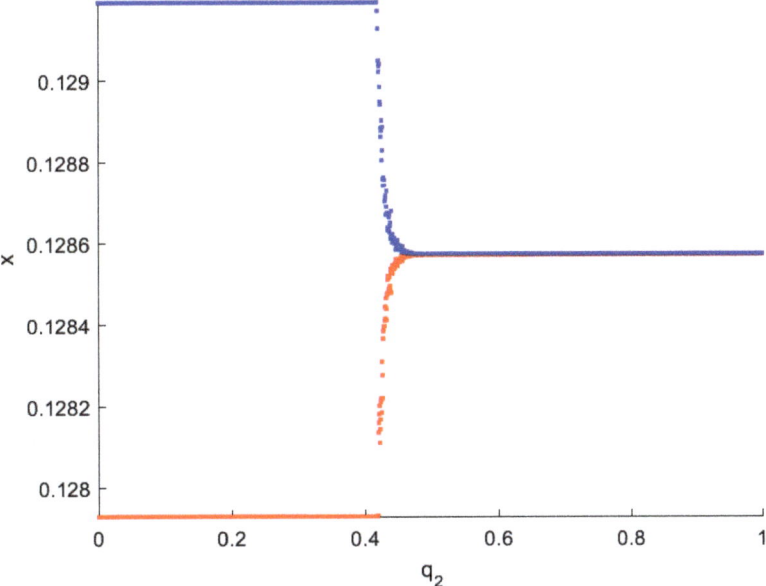

Figure 4. Bifurcation diagram of the model (1) with respect to q_2.

To better understand the effect of the caring capacity k, one can draw the bifurcation diagram with respect to k. It can be seen that the supercritical Hopf bifurcation value is localized at $k = 0.45$ as shown in Figure 5. The supercritical Hopf bifurcation value is centered at $k = 0.45$, as indicated in Figure 5. When $k > 0.45$, the prey–predator model (1) goes through limit cycle oscillation, as indicated in Figures 5 and 6. For $k < 0.45$, $E_4 = (0.075, 0, 0, 0.15 - 0.01125/k)$ is locally stable, as indicated in Figure 6. It can also be noted that the conditions of local stability that were established in Theorem 10 were verified because when $k = 0.4$, one has $R_3 = 2.8571 < 1 + \frac{(am_3)}{((\mu_3 + q_3 E)(a+k))} = 3.1429$.

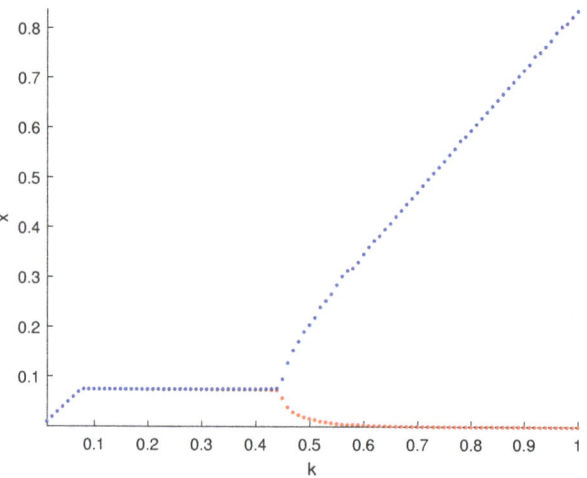

Figure 5. Bifurcation diagram of the model (1) with respect to k.

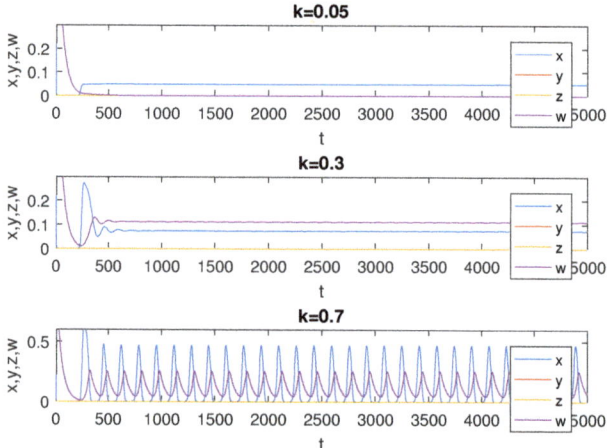

Figure 6. Time series of the model (1) with $k = 0.05$, $k = 0.3$, and $k = 0.7$.

To give some numerical findings for the prey predator system (8), one can use the Milstein method mentioned in [31,32]. The prey–predator system (8) reduces to the following discrete system.

$$\begin{aligned}
x_{j+1} &= x_j + hx_j\left(r(1-\frac{x_j}{k}) - \beta_1 y_j - \beta_2 z_j - \frac{\beta_3 w_j}{a+x_j}\right) + \sigma_1 x_j \sqrt{h}\epsilon_{1j} + \frac{\sigma_1^2}{2}x_j\left[\epsilon_{1j}^2 - 1\right]h, \\
y_{j+1} &= y_j + hy_j(m_1 x_j + \delta z_j - \mu_1 - q_1 E) + \sigma_2 y_j \sqrt{h}\epsilon_{2j} + \frac{\sigma_2^2}{2}y_j\left[\epsilon_{2j}^2 - 1\right]h, \\
z_{j+1} &= z_j + hz_j(m_2 x_j - \delta y_j - \mu_2 - q_2 E) + \sigma_3 z_j \sqrt{h}\epsilon_{3j} + \frac{\sigma_3^2}{2}z_j\left[\epsilon_{zj}^2 - 1\right]h, \\
w_{j+1} &= w_j + hw_j\left(\frac{m_3 x_j}{a+x_j} - \mu_3 - q_3 E\right) + \sigma_4 w_j \sqrt{h}\epsilon_{4j} + \frac{\sigma_4^2}{2}w_j\left[\epsilon_{4j}^2 - 1\right]h,
\end{aligned} \quad (19)$$

where h is a positive time increment and ϵ_{ij}, $(i = 1, 2, 3, 4)$ are independent random Gaussian variables $N(0, 1)$. Figure 7 represents the dynamical behavior of the model (8) when the noise strength is the law ($\sigma_i = 0.05$). One can note that for the given parameters, the strength of environmental noise is very close to zero, and the system behaves as a deterministic model. Following [33], one can note that in the deterministic case, if $R_0 < 1$, then the prey–predator system (1) has a predators' free equilibrium point $E_1 = (k, 0, 0, 0)$. In the stochastic model (14), if one gradually increases the intensities of fluctuation and keeps the remaining parameters unchanged, the fluctuations around E_1 become larger, as seen for the values of $\sigma_i = 0.2$ and 0.9 shown in Figure 7. The black line in Figure 7 represents the prey when ($\sigma_i = 0$). From Figure 8, it is seen that increasing the catchability constants has a stabilizing effect on the stochastic model (14).

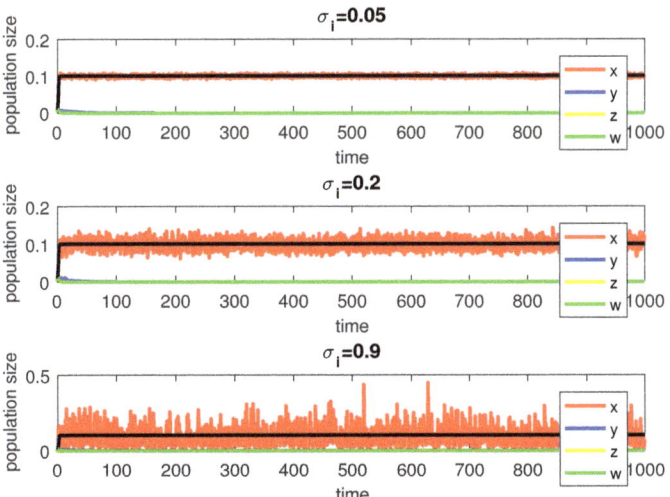

Figure 7. Fluctuation in the prey population with $\sigma_i = 0.05$, $\sigma_i = 0.2$, and $\sigma_i = 0.9$. The black line represents the prey when ($\sigma_i = 0$).

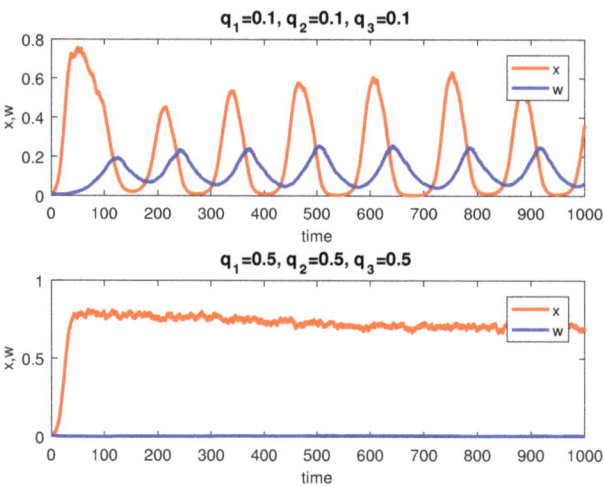

Figure 8. Numerical simulation of the system (14) with $(q_1 = q_2 = q_3 = 0.1)$ and $(q_1 = q_2 = q_3 = 0.5)$.

7. Conclusions

In this paper, a mathematical prey–predator model was proposed and analyzed. The interference of the predators in the system investigated in [12] was modified by adding an extra predator $y(t)$ where the first predator preys on the second predator in addition to the prey. The interaction between the three predators and single prey was studied. The impact of harvesting on the first and the second predator was investigated. Sufficient conditions were obtained to ensure local stability. It was concluded that the dynamics of the population can be controlled by harvesting. The harvesting rates of the three predator species played an important role in controlling the local and global dynamics of the prey–predator system. They can break the oscillating behavior of the deterministic system and drive it to the required state. To investigate the effect of environmental noise, we performed a stochastic extension of the deterministic model to study the fluctuation of the ecological factors. The existence of a unique global positive solution for the stochastic model was investigated. We used stochastic perturbation around the free predators' equilibrium point. Constructing an appropriate Lyapunov function and applying Itô's formula, we note that the deterministic model was robust with respect to stochastic perturbation. The criterion of stochastic stability depends on the intensities of noise $\sigma_i, i = 1, 2, 3, 4$. The exponential–mean–squared stability of the resulting stochastic differential equation model was examined, and it was found to be dependent on the harvesting effort.

Author Contributions: Methodology, Y.A.; software, M.E.-S.; validation, Y.A.; formal analysis, M.E.-S.; investigation, Y.A. and M.E.-S.; writing—original draft preparation,Y.A.; writing—review and editing, M.E.-S.; supervision, M.E.-S.; funding acquisition, Y.A. All authors have read and agreed to the published version of the manuscript.

Funding: The APC was funded by the Deanship of Scientific Research, Qassim University.

Data Availability Statement: Not applicable.

Acknowledgments: The researcher would like to thank the Deanship of Scientific Research, Qassim University, for funding the publication of this project.

Conflicts of Interest: The authors declare no conflict of interest.

References

1. Wikan, A.; Kristensen, Ø. Prey–predator interactions in two and three species population models. *Discret. Dyn. Nat. Soc.* **2019**, *2019*, 9543139. [CrossRef]
2. Sayekti, I.; Malik, M.; Aldila, D. One–prey two–predator model with prey harvesting in a food chain interaction. In Proceedings of the International Symposium on Current Progress in Mathematics and Sciences 2016 (ISCPMS 2016), AIP Conference Proceedings, Depok, Indonesia, 1–2 November 2016; AIP Publishing LLC: College Park, MD, USA, 2017; Volume 1862, p. 030124.
3. Ghosh, U.; Sarkar, S.; Mondal, B. Study of Stability and Bifurcation of Three Species Food Chain Model with Non–monotone Functional Response. *Int. J. Appl. Comput. Math.* **2021**, *7*, 63. [CrossRef]
4. Pal, D.; Kar, T.K.; Yamauchi, A.; Ghosh, B. Balancing maximum sustainable yield and ecological resilience in an exploited two–predator one–prey system. *Biosystems* **2020**, *187*, 104064. [CrossRef] [PubMed]
5. Kaviya, R.; Muthukumar, P. Dynamical analysis and optimal harvesting of conformable fractional prey–predator system with predator immigration. *Eur. Phys. J. Plus* **2021**, *136*, 136.
6. Fattahpour, H.; Zangeneh, H.R.; Nagata, W. Dynamics of Rodent Population with Two Predators. *Bull. Iran. Math. Soc.* **2019**, *45*, 965–996. [CrossRef]
7. Li, H.; Zhang, L.; Hu, C.; Jiang, Y.; Teng, Z. Dynamical analysis of a fractional-order predator-prey model incorporating a prey refuge. *J. Appl. Math. Comput.* **2016**, *54*, 435–449. [CrossRef]
8. Sambath, M.; Ramesh, P.; Balachandran, K. Asymptotic Behavior of the Fractional Order three Species Prey–Predator Model. *Int. J. Nonlinear Sci. Numer. Simul.* **2018**, *19*, 721–733. [CrossRef]
9. Das, D.K.; Das, K.; Kar, T. Dynamical Behaviour of Infected Predator–Prey Eco–epidemics with Harvesting Effort. *Int. J. Appl. Comput. Math.* **2021**, *7*, 66. [CrossRef]
10. Mondal, S.; Samanta, G. Impact of fear on a predator–prey system with prey-dependent search rate in deterministic and stochastic environment. *Nonlinear Dyn.* **2021**, *104*, 2931–2959. [CrossRef]
11. Zhang, Y.; Tian, B.; Chen, X.; Li, J. A stochastic diseased predator system with modified LG–Holling type II functional response. *Ecol. Complex.* **2021**, *45*, 100881. [CrossRef]
12. Mukhopadhyay, B.; Bhattacharyya, R. Effects of harvesting and predator interference in a model of two–predators competing for a single prey. *Appl. Math. Model.* **2016**, *40*, 3264–3274. [CrossRef]
13. Garneau, D.E.; Post, E.; Boudreau, T.; Keech, M.; Valkenburg, P. Spatio–temporal patterns of predation among three sympatric predators in a single–prey system. *Wildl. Biol.* **2007**, *13*, 186–194. [CrossRef]
14. Cresson, J.; Szafrańska, A. Discrete and continuous fractional persistence problems—The positivity property and applications. *Commun. Nonlinear Sci. Numer. Simul.* **2017**, *44*, 424–448. [CrossRef]
15. Perko, L. *Differential Equations and Dynamical Systems*; Springer Science & Business Media: New York, NY, USA, 2013; Volume 7.
16. Wiggins, S.; Golubitsky, M. *Introduction to Applied Nonlinear Dynamical Systems and Chaos*; Springer: New York, NY, USA, 2003; Volume 2.
17. Maji, C.; Mukherjee, D.; Kesh, D. Deterministic and stochastic analysis of an eco–epidemiological model. *J. Biol. Phys.* **2018**, *44*, 17–36. [CrossRef]
18. Cresson, J.; Puig, B.; Sonner, S. Stochastic models in biology and the invariance problem. *Discret. Contin. Dyn. Syst. B* **2016**, *21*, 2145. [CrossRef]
19. Cresson, J.; Sonner, S. A note on a derivation method for SDE models: Applications in biology and viability criteria. *Stoch. Anal. Appl.* **2018**, *36*, 224–239. [CrossRef]
20. Phan, T.A.; Tian, J.P.; Wang, B. Dynamics of cholera epidemic models in fluctuating environments. *Stoch. Dyn.* **2021**, *21*, 2150011. [CrossRef]
21. Mao, X. *Stochastic Differential Equations and Applications*; Woodhead Publishing: Cambridge, UK, 2007.
22. Cai, Y.; Mao, X. Stochastic prey–predator system with foraging arena scheme. *Appl. Math. Model.* **2018**, *64*, 357–371. [CrossRef]
23. Wei, C.; Liu, J.; Zhang, S. Analysis of a stochastic eco–epidemiological model with modified Leslie–Gower functional response. *Adv. Differ. Equ.* **2018**, *2018*, 119. [CrossRef]
24. Liu, Q.; Jiang, D.; Hayat, T.; Alsaedi, A.; Ahmad, B. A stochastic SIRS epidemic model with logistic growth and general nonlinear incidence rate. *Phys. A Stat. Mech. Appl.* **2020**, *551*, 124152. [CrossRef]
25. Li, Q.; Cong, F.; Liu, T.; Zhou, Y. Stationary distribution of a stochastic HIV model with two infective stages. *Phys. A Stat. Mech. Appl.* **2020**, *554*, 124686. [CrossRef]
26. Afanasiev, V.N.; Kolmanovskii, V.; Nosov, V. *Mathematical Theory of Control Systems Design*; Springer Science & Business Media: Dordrecht, The Netherlands, 2013; Volume 341.
27. Mukhopadhyay, B.; Bhattacharyya, R. A nonlinear mathematical model of virus–tumor–immune system interaction: Deterministic and stochastic analysis. *Stoch. Anal. Appl.* **2009**, *27*, 409–429. [CrossRef]
28. Mukhopadhyay, B.; Bhattacharyya, R. On a three–tier ecological food chain model with deterministic and random harvesting: A mathematical study. *Nonlinear Anal. Model. Control.* **2011**, *16*, 77–88. [CrossRef]
29. Mukhopadhyay, B.; Bhattacharyya, R. Effects of deterministic and random refuge in a prey–predator model with parasite infection. *Math. Biosci.* **2012**, *239*, 124–130. [CrossRef]
30. Ghosh, P.; Das, P.; Mukherjee, D. Persistence and stability of a seasonally perturbed three species stochastic model of salmonoid aquaculture. *Differ. Equ. Dyn. Syst.* **2019**, *27*, 449–465. [CrossRef]

31. Higham, D.J. An algorithmic introduction to numerical simulation of stochastic differential equations. *SIAM Rev.* **2001**, *43*, 525–546. [CrossRef]
32. Alnafisah, Y. The implementation of Milstein scheme in two–dimensional SDEs using the Fourier method. *Abstr. Appl. Anal.* **2018**, *2018*, 3805042. [CrossRef]
33. Cao, Y.; Denu, D. Analysis of stochastic vector–host epidemic model with direct transmission. *Discret. Contin. Dyn. Syst. B* **2016**, *21*, 2109–2127. [CrossRef]

MDPI
St. Alban-Anlage 66
4052 Basel
Switzerland
www.mdpi.com

Axioms Editorial Office
E-mail: axioms@mdpi.com
www.mdpi.com/journal/axioms

Disclaimer/Publisher's Note: The statements, opinions and data contained in all publications are solely those of the individual author(s) and contributor(s) and not of MDPI and/or the editor(s). MDPI and/or the editor(s) disclaim responsibility for any injury to people or property resulting from any ideas, methods, instructions or products referred to in the content.

www.ingramcontent.com/pod-product-compliance
Lightning Source LLC
LaVergne TN
LVHW070417100526
838202LV00014B/1477